THE MEDIEVAL INVENTION OF TRAVEL

THE MEDIEVAL INVENTION OF TRAVEL

SHAYNE AARON LEGASSIE

THE UNIVERSITY OF CHICAGO PRESS

CHICAGO AND LONDON

PUBLICATION OF THIS BOOK HAS BEEN AIDED BY A GRANT FROM THE
BEVINGTON FUND.

The University of Chicago Press, Chicago 60637
The University of Chicago Press, Ltd., London
© 2017 by The University of Chicago
Published 2017
Printed in the United States of America

26 25 24 23 22 21 20 19 18 17   1 2 3 4 5

ISBN-13: 978-0-226-44256-3 (cloth)
ISBN-13: 978-0-226-44662-2 (paper)
ISBN-13: 978-0-226-44273-0 (e-book)
DOI: 10.7208/chicago/9780226442730.001.0001

Library of Congress Cataloging-in-Publication Data

Names: Legassie, Shayne, 1979– author.
Title: The medieval invention of travel / Shayne Aaron Legassie.
Description: Chicago ; London : The University of Chicago Press, 2017. | Includes
    bibliographical references and index.
Identifiers: LCCN 2016040300 | ISBN 9780226442563 (cloth : alk. paper) | ISBN
    9780226446622 (pbk. : alk. paper) | ISBN 9780226442730 (e-book)
Subjects: LCSH: Travel writing—Europe, Western—History—To 1500. | Travel
    in literature. | Literature, Medieval—History and criticism. | Pilgrims and
    pilgrimages in literature.
Classification: LCC PN56.T7 L44 2017 | DDC 809/.93320902—dc23 LC record
    available at https://lccn.loc.gov/2016040300

♾ This paper meets the requirements of ANSI/NISO Z39.48-1992 (Permanence
of Paper).

CONTENTS

Phrased in very broad terms, the central contention of *The Medieval Invention of Travel* is that scholars have underestimated the significance of travel—as both material practice and philosophical abstraction—to the development of medieval travel writing. Though this book draws on earlier and later evidence, it focuses primarily on the years 1200–1500. During these three centuries, travel writing burgeoned and diversified to a degree that has no historical precedent. This remarkable literary flourishing shaped and was shaped by the period's evolving attitudes toward human mobility. This vital observation has been relegated to the background of previous scholarship, to the detriment of one of the most complex and consequential eras in the history of Western ideas about travel.

For three decades, medieval travel writing has been the focus of consistently path-breaking research. Concerned primarily with questions of geo-ethnographic representation, most broad-ranging treatments of the topic have compared how different travel writers represent a particular region of the world. Several major contributions have discussed "exotic" travel accounts written by European visitors to East Asia, including the well-known works of Marco Polo, William of Rubruck, and John Mandeville. A second group of studies has shed light on the richness and variety of texts written by medieval pilgrims to the Holy Land, a corpus once dismissed as an unremarkable monolith. More recently (and far less comprehensively), scholars have begun to turn their attention to individual accounts of late medieval travel within Europe and the Mediterranean. For the most part, these three lines of inquiry have developed independently of one another.

While there is much to commend this "area studies" approach to medieval travel writing, there is also cause to question its unexamined and near-total dominance. It is certainly true that, in many cases, medieval readers adopted a similar, geographically based logic in their classification of travel writing. Not surprisingly, the pilgrim who decided to write about his journey to Jerusalem was also likely to consult previous texts related to the Holy Land; the traveler who wished to write about a sojourn in India or China would likewise search out works about those regions of the world. That said, lines of authorial influence and habits of manuscript compilation suggest that, over the course of the long fourteenth century, the destination of the traveler became a less salient consideration in the way that travel writing was classified. Increasingly, accounts by "exotic" travel writers, Jerusalem pilgrims, and Mediterranean/European wayfarers are seen as sharing a common characteristic: they are the products of *travel* in the abstract. This emergent intuition marks a consequential turning point in the development of medieval ideas about human mobility and its relationship to literacy—one whose origins and implications cannot be apprehended without reading across modern scholarly canons.

Between 1200 and 1500, the authors and audiences of travel writing were engaged in what amounts to a prolonged cultural debate about the individual and collective benefits of voyages to various parts of the world. Out of this chaotic, multicentered, and open-ended discussion emerged a nebulous consensus with profound implications: a new, enduring view of *travel* as *literate labor*. In its guise as literate labor, travel was increasingly understood as an ennobling, taxing form of work, at once *physical and intellectual*, practicable in just about any place in the world, with intimate ties to the arts of literacy.

The medieval invention of travel-as-literate-labor was, at its core, a *reinvention* of classical ideals. In antiquity, heroism in travel was associated primarily with the exercise of self-mastery in the face of bodily temptation and travail. In the Middle Ages, the prestige-generating journey came to be understood as both a triumph over the flesh and—at the same time—as an intellectual enterprise, oriented toward the production of written knowledge. As travel writing became a more prominent feature of the medieval cultural landscape, the heroic traveler distinguished himself through regimes of self-discipline that incorporated, or modeled themselves after, practices of reading and writing.

By evoking the rhetorical concept of *inventio*—the process of discovering the contours of one's subject matter or the framework of one's argument—the title of this book hopes to underscore the open-ended nature of the medieval invention of travel, as well as the role that literacy of various kinds played in the formulation and rationalization of new, prestigious modes of mobility. The medieval invention of travel was a largely improvisational process that did not converge upon a single prescriptive model. Indeed, rather than resulting in a homogeneous approach to exploring and writing about the world, the reimagination of travel as literate labor ushered in an era of dazzling new possibilities. The story of late medieval travel writing is one in which destinations once deemed too familiar or unremarkable to comment on are subjected to the kinds of detailed analysis previously reserved for distant Asian kingdoms and sacred religious centers. It is, moreover, a story in which the clerical monopoly on intellectual authority is challenged by social actors once excluded from the production of official geoethnographic knowledge. Importantly, it is also the story of how a variety of literate dispositions and practices—academic, devotional, literary, and bureaucratic—were absorbed into the status-enhancing labor of travel, giving rise to novel methods of geoethnographic investigation and new opportunities for elite self-fashioning. Among the postmedieval practices heralded by medieval travel writers are: the antiquarian and ecological investigation of the Mediterranean; the French-Italian axis of the Grand Tour; and the value-laden distinction between *travel* and *tourism*.

In pursuing the central thread of its argument, then, *The Medieval Invention of Travel* necessarily calls for a reevaluation of the place currently assigned to the Middle Ages in historical surveys of travel writing. To many historiographers, medieval travelers are objects of envy and scorn. Dismissed as half-baked models of their modern counterparts, or as the impossibly lucky inhabitants of an age in which travel furnished an unthinkable sense of wholeness and satisfaction, "the medieval traveler" is seldom seen as relevant to our world.

A thoroughgoing rebuttal of these stereotypes must start by correcting a historiographical error native to medieval studies. A dubious piece of conventional wisdom holds that, in the history of travel writing, the period spanning 1350 to 1492 is—to quote Joan-Pau Rubiés—one of "relative stagnation."[1] This opinion is diametrically opposed to readily observable realities. Between 1350 and 1492, Latin Christians not only continued to write about their travels in Persia, India, and other parts of Asia, they also—and *not* insignificantly—documented journeys to places within Europe and the Mediterranean that they had never bothered to write about before. Moreover, the majority of extant copies of travel accounts written *before* 1350 were actually produced *after* 1350, during this so-called period of "stagnation." Many of these manuscripts altered the texts that they preserve in response to ongoing debates about travel and travel writing. The fifteenth century also yielded a historically unprecedented crop of travel accounts about the Holy Land. This varied and innovative corpus is almost always studied in strict isolation from other, potentially illuminating works of medieval and postmedieval travel writing. The crucial mediating role that pilgrims played between the high era of medieval travel writing about East Asia and the emergence of recognizably modern ways of writing about travel within Europe and the Mediterranean has, therefore, gone unremarked—and, as a result, so has a rich corner of intellectual and cultural history.

ACKNOWLEDGMENTS

It is humbling to reflect on the generosity that made this book possible.

Several entities within the University of North Carolina at Chapel Hill provided funding at crucial junctures of this enterprise. The College of Arts and Sciences awarded me the Junior Faculty Development Grant, which paid for books and manuscript reproductions. The Department of English and Comparative Literature supported several research trips to European libraries, as well as helpful research assistance from Adam Harris. Several other archival junkets were funded by UNC's Program in Medieval and Early Modern Studies. With resources allocated by the Andrew W. Mellon Foundation, MEMS also underwrote an entire semester of research leave, for which I am deeply grateful.

The staff of the following libraries provided invaluable support: Duke University, Columbia University, the British Library, the University of Cambridge, the Bibliothèque nationale de France, the Staatsbibliothek zu Berlin, the Biblioteca Nazionale Centrale di Firenze, and the Biblioteca Nacional de España.

Words fail when it comes to thanking the two anonymous readers who reviewed this manuscript for the University of Chicago Press. Both provided smart, thorough, and challenging feedback that greatly improved the book, and they did so in record-setting time. If mathematically possible, even greater thanks are owed to Randy Petilos, whose patience, candor, and good-humored counsel provided me with a revolutionary new outlook on professional life. Sue Cohan, who copyedited the manuscript, went above and beyond the call of duty.

Due to the sage advice of Margaret Aziza Pappano, Susan Crane, Paul Strohm, Jean Howard, and Patricia Grieve, the final incarnation of this book looks nothing at all like its archaic ancestor. Asifa Malik, Brenna Mead, Ellen Rentz, Scott Failla, Kamil Godula, Lisa Cooper, Derrick Higginbotham, Karl Steel, Brantley Lloyd Bryant, and Robert Hanning also furnished invaluable feedback in early phases. Meanwhile, invitations to speak at Syracuse University, Stanford University, the University of California at Los Angeles, and King's College London helped me refine and reframe my arguments.

Chapter 1 benefitted from the challenging insights of the Triangle Medieval Studies Seminar, which—along with the National Humanities Center—hosted the workshop where I aired the earliest version of my thoughts on William of Rubruck and Marco Polo. I would like to thank everyone who participated in that event, especially Brett Whalen, Patricia Claire Ingham, Anthony Bale, Marcia Kupfer, Fiona Somerset, and Jehangir Malegam. Chapter 3 came into its own when it was presented at the International Congress on Medieval Studies at Kalamazoo in 2015 as part of a panel organized by Suzanne Yeager and Anthony Bale. Additional thanks to Ellen Rentz for attending the panel and for sharing her knowledge of late medieval devotional writing. Chapter 6 is a better version of its original self, thanks to the input of Emily Beck, Chris Cannon, Michael Cornett, John J. Martin, and Albrecht Diem. A rather different version of the same chapter also appeared in the *Journal of Medieval and Early Modern Studies*.

Over the last six years, UNC has been an incomparable place to teach and to grow as an intellectual. Wonderful colleagues and brilliant students have proved to be the delightful norm. The Department of English and Comparative Literature has been a stimulating and collegial environment. Though I should, by rights, thank all eighty or so of my colleagues by name, I will have to settle for singling out a few whose mentorship and example have done the most to shape this book. As department chair, Beverly Taylor has provided material and moral support for this project from day one. My incomparable colleagues in Early Modern and Cinema Studies are among my most cherished interlocutors and professional role models: David Baker, Reid Barbour, Marsha Collins, Gregg Flaxman, Mary Floyd-Wilson, Megan Matchinske, Rick Warner, and Jessica Wolfe are all so amazing that I often forget that they are not medievalists. Similar honorary laurels must be extended to Florence Dore and Lanis Wilson, who are great friends and intellectual companions.

Glaire Anderson, E. Jane Burns, Marcus Bull, Tania String, and Brett Whalen are among the many warm and intelligent colleagues that I have gained through UNC's Program in Medieval and Early Modern Studies. I also owe a considerable debt to friends and collaborators from other institutions, among them Sarah Salih, Rory Critten, Chris Chism, and—especially—John Ganim.

Gavin Whitehead may be the only person in the world who has read every page of every version of this book. To say that I owe him everything is to say far too little.

Introduction: Travail and Travel Writing

In the Middle Ages, travel was nasty, brutish, and long. This forbidding reality—common to most preindustrial settings—was not lost on medieval travelers. In June of 1325, Moroccan jurist Ibn Battuta embarked on a heroic voyage that would span three decades and as many continents. The celebrated adventurer had scarcely departed his native Tangiers when he confronted what would be the first of many brushes with death. Stricken by a debilitating fever in the middle of the North African desert, Ibn Battuta struggled against time and delirium to secure the knot that would anchor him to his horse, fearful that he would otherwise tumble from his mount unconscious and perish alone in the sands.[1] The following year, Dominican missionary Jordanus of Sévérac dispatched a letter to his order from Thana (Thane), India, in which he detailed the city's recent public execution of several Franciscan missionaries. Jordanus did not neglect to mention his own, lesser martyrdoms:

> Who is able to tell all the hardships I have since endured? For I have been taken by pirates, cast into prison by Saracens, been accused, cursed, reviled, and left this long time past like a good-for-nothing vagabond, to go about in my shirt, without the habit of my order. . . . I suffer continually from bodily aliments. Tortured by pains, sometimes in the head, sometimes in the chest, in the stomach, or in all my limbs.[2]

Extreme adversity was not unique to the transcontinental itineraries of travelers such as Jordanus and Ibn Battuta. Though more modest in its geographical ambit, the 1395 Jerusalem pilgrimage of Nicola de Martoni—a diminutive notary from Carinola, Italy—was no less fraught with peril. Nicola's closest call occurred off the coast of Damascus, when the boat carrying him capsized. Plucked from the churning tides seconds before drowning, Nicola would soon discover that the terror of the incident had turned his hair and beard white.[3] Earlier in the fourteenth century, Franciscan Niccolò da Poggibonsi took up a crossbow to defend his pilgrim galley from Mediterranean pirates intent on selling the ship's passengers and crew into slavery. Though Niccolò lived to tell of his swashbuckling exploits, the Franciscans who accompanied him at different stages of his journey were not as fortunate; seven out of eight died abroad.[4] In 1433, Margery Kempe—an English widow in her fifties—braved filth, fleas, and threats of sexual violence to go on a relatively short-range pilgrimage across northern and central Europe. In the final leg of the journey, Kempe trekked overland through the Flemish wetlands to Calais (then, an English possession), during which time she "was so wery and so ovyrcomyn with labowr" that she often feared "hir spirit schulde a departyd fro hir body."[5] Rare is the medieval travel account that does not feature comparable—or even more dramatic— calamities.

The brutalizing conditions of medieval travel left their impress on the very languages used to immortalize the era's remarkable journeys for posterity. In both Middle English and romance vernaculars, the activities we associate with the modern English word *travel* are frequently subsumed under the term *travail* or some variant of *labor*.[6] *Travel* and *travail* have dark common origins in the Latin noun *trepalium*—a three-pronged metal device that ancient Romans used to torture prisoners. In the medieval languages that inherited the word, *travail* signified not only torture or affliction but also the physical and psychic energies expended—irretrievably and at great pains—in the process of *laboring over something*.[7] Today, travel is widely construed as a release from, or remedy for, work-related fatigue. Medieval travel was, by contrast, understood as an *intensification* of the pains and labors of everyday life rather than a restorative interval away from them. In the Middle Ages, there was no travel without travail.

The dangers and sacrifices inherent to medieval travel guaranteed that it would seldom be viewed as a value-neutral undertaking. For this reason, any attempt to comprehend late medieval travel writing is probably incomplete to the extent that it does not consider the cultural suspicion directed at its practitioners. During the later Middle Ages, the decision to travel was always potentially a questionable one; the decision to write about one's travels, perhaps even more so. The travails endured by the traveler were cited in arguments for, and against, individual journeys—and indeed, for, and against, entire modes of travel. Travel writers, meanwhile, resorted to the rhetoric of travail in order to justify their dubious literary activities, constitute their authority, and manage reader response. Perhaps most significant of all, the tools and habits of literacy were steadily assimilated to the ennobling travail of the heroic journey, a process that laid the groundwork for the Middle Ages' historically far-reaching reconception of travel.

THE MEDIEVAL RESISTANCE TO TRAVEL

Between 1100 and 1500, Eurasia enjoyed a degree of mobility and cross-cultural integration that had no obvious equivalent in antiquity. The geographical horizons of western Europe were dramatically expanded as a result—both physically and imaginatively. In the wake of the First Crusade (1095–99), the victorious Latin Christians suddenly found that they had political, economic, and spiritual interests in parts of the world that had, until that point, seemed far removed from their daily concerns. Along with the Crusades, the contemporaneous Norman conquests of England and southern Italy fueled the expansion of a French-speaking "aristocratic diaspora," which spread from the British Isles to central Europe, from Sicily to the Holy Land.[8] Scholarship continues to shed new light on the slightly later, but no less remarkable, expansion of Aragonese influence in the Mediterranean.[9] The same is true of the Castilian and Portuguese explorations of the Mediterranean and Atlantic during the later Middle Ages, which paved the way for Columbus's journey to the Americas and the circumnavigation of Africa.[10] While all of this was going on, Venice and Genoa were busy founding commercial colonies across the Mediterranean and Black Seas, at times triumphing over powerful military rivals, including the Byzantine Empire and the crowns of France and Aragon.[11] From these eastern Mediterranean outposts, Italian merchants and missionary friars followed land and maritime routes to Persia, India, China, and Southeast Asia. Janet Abu-Lughod rightfully cautioned against a triumphalist view of these developments, by emphasizing the belated, uneven nature of medieval Europe's reintegration into global circuits of economic and cultural exchange.[12] All the same, this ragtag assortment of dynastic landgrabs, colonial ventures, and emergent trade routes enabled the journeys of unprecedented numbers of missionaries, pilgrims, traders, crusaders, diplomats, and scholars. Even after the Black Death and the fragmentation of the Mongol Empire rendered overland travel through central Asia less feasible than before, maritime trade routes continued to connect India to the eastern Mediterranean and—by extension—to western Europe.

As travel of various kinds became a more familiar feature of the late medieval cultural landscape, so, too, did concerns about this reality. In many cases, the medieval resistance to travel was a prudent reaction to its uncertainty. The time, expense, and danger involved in even relatively short journeys demanded a careful reckoning of the potential consequences of a prolonged—or possibly permanent—absence from one's home. It was for this reason that pilgrims and crusaders settled outstanding debts, appointed powers of attorney, and wrote wills before departing for the Holy Land.[13] Even when travelers managed to return from their journeys relatively unscathed, their homecomings could be marred by tragic news of what had transpired in their absence. Having dwelled in India and China for twenty years, Ibn Battuta returned to Damascus to discover that the infant son he left there had died long ago, as had his father back in Morocco.[14] Shortly after, he returned to Tangiers, where he learned that his mother had also perished.[15] Away on pilgrimage less than a year, Nicola de Martoni was shattered to discover that his beloved wife, Constanza, had succumbed to illness while he was striving to survive the perilous journey back to her. Nicola ends the account of his pilgrimage with a moving Boethian reflection on her death and includes a transcription of the verse epitaph that he composed to honor her memory.[16]

Perhaps not surprisingly, questions about the ethics of travel animate some of the period's most influential works of fiction. The tension between the knight's domestic obligations and the allure of distant adventure is a defining theme of chivalric romance, from Chrétien de Troyes's *Erec and Enide* to Cervantes's *Don Quixote*. Canto 26 of Dante's *Inferno* explores the consequences of unchecked wanderlust through the figure of Ulysses. For no other reason than to see what lies beyond the Pillars of Hercules, Ulysses abandons his family a second time, on a voyage so perilous that Dante characterizes it as "mad."[17] In a soaring oratorical set piece, the Homeric hero convinces his men to disregard the risks involved in sailing through the Straits of Gibraltar, in the process sealing their collective doom. For this abuse of his rhetorical talents, Ulysses is confined for eternity to the circle of the false counselors.

Concerns about the maintenance of social order also fed the medieval resistance to travel. The movements of late medieval pilgrims were singled out for particular scrutiny, occasioning satire, moral panic, and—increasingly— institutionalized surveillance. In the early Middle Ages, monastic orders were the most vociferous opponents of pilgrimage, on the grounds that devotional travel exposed monks and nuns to the worldly enticements that they had renounced in taking their vows.[18] Throughout the high to late Middle Ages, malefactors of all stripes were accused of exploiting the pious façade of the pilgrim to indulge in vice and crime. Inquisitors routinely alleged the Cathars of Languedoc disguised themselves as pilgrims in order to disseminate their heterodox teachings undetected, a charge that seems to have had some basis in reality.[19] Female pilgrims had to contend with the suspicion that their devotional travels were simply a pretext for engaging in adultery, fornication, and/or heretical activity.[20] In late medieval England, the crackdown on "false pilgrims" was part of a larger postplague effort to curb the mobility of laborers and—by extension—their power to negotiate their wages; it was also a feature of renewed campaigns against heresy and sedition.[21] Valentin Groebner has documented parallel developments in German-speaking regions of fifteenth-century Europe.[22]

Literary works of the period do not merely *reflect* this circumspect stance toward the pilgrim; they stoke the flames of stereotype with unapologetic glee. Latin and vernacular texts alike teem with "false" pilgrims bent on infamy. A few examples will suffice to illustrate the longevity and pervasiveness of this phobic motif, which effortlessly transcended linguistic, geographical, and generic boundaries. The obscene twelfth-century poem "Farai un vers, pos mi sonelh" ("I will write a song since I am falling asleep") by Occitan troubadour William IX of Aquitaine relates the story of a sexual threesome involving the poet and two married women (with an unhappy—and enigmatic—assist from a ferocious red cat). En route to Auvergne, the poet is hailed by the two women, who address him as "Sir Pilgrim" (*don pelerin*). The crafty William pretends to be a deaf-mute in order to take advantage of his interlocutors, who presume that they will be able to take sexual advantage of *him* without anyone—including their husbands—finding out.[23] In Old French fiction, tricksters such as Reynard the Fox, Eustache the Monk, and Faus Semblant donned the pilgrim's mantle to see their devious schemes to completion.[24] In the thirteenth-century Latin exemplum collection of Caesarius of Heisterbach, the devil appears "in the form and apparel of a pilgrim" (*sub forma et habitu peregrini*) in an effort to lure a pious knight into damnation.[25] In Juan Ruiz's fourteenth-century *El libro de buen amor*, the cowardly Dame Lent attempts to slip out of her imminent battle with Don Carnival by appareling herself as a pilgrim and absconding to Jerusalem.[26] Reputed sodomite Álvar Rodríguez—a Christian squire ("*scudeiro*") with a penchant for Muslim youths—was a favorite target of satirical Galician-Portuguese poetry who supposedly "voyaged to the Holy Land and [after] used to say that he had lived as a Moor while he was over there (*andou aalen-mar e dizia que fora aló mouro*)."[27]

The figure of the nefarious pilgrim gave rise to another pejorative commonplace: the idea that the speech of pilgrims—even bona fide ones—was frivolous and unreliable. Chaucer's *House of Fame* embodies useless gossip in the form of "shipmen and pilgrimes, / With scrippes bret-ful of lesinges [bags filled to the rim with lies] / Entremedled [Mixed] with tydynges [news]."[28] It was thanks to Chaucer that, during the English Reformation, the term *Canterbury tale* became a synonym for *fable* or *lie*.[29] Several of the novellas in Giovanni Boccaccio's *Decameron* feature riotously spurious tales of travel, most notably the fraudulent pilgrimage account of Friar Cipolla in day 6, story 10. Given this context, it would seem that accused heretic William Thorpe was not at his most heretical when he dismissed pilgrims as "greete iangelers [janglers], tale tellers, and lyeris."[30]

The dim assessment of pilgrim discourse extended to the geoethnographic claims that devotional travelers made about the places that they visited. Antoine de La Sale wrote his travel account *Le Paradis de la Reine Sibylle* (1437) for no other reason than to debunk the supernatural yarns of pilgrims who descended into the subterranean caverns of Mount Vettore, located outside the Umbrian town of Norcia.[31] Jacques de Vitry maintained that pilgrims' "exaggerated reports of the East" were ultimately harmful because, even though they spurred others to journey to the Holy Land, they did so for the wrong reasons, thereby compromising the spiritual orientation of the pilgrimage from the start.[32] For similar reasons, fifteenth-century travel writer Santo Brasca lamented that many of his fellow pilgrims went to Jerusalem for the sole purpose of boasting about what they had seen to those not fortunate enough to travel there themselves.[33]

Given the widespread disparagement of the pilgrim's tale, it is little wonder that would-be travel writers—laymen and clerics, pilgrims and non-pilgrims—entered into their projects with apprehension. Clerical pilgrims to the Holy Land like Wilbrand of Oldenburg and Thietmar feared that they would be charged with vainglory for presuming to publish a travel account.[34] Franciscans John of Plano Carpini and Odoric of Pordenone anticipated that their incredible-but-true descriptions of East Asia would be dismissed as a pack of fables.[35] Around 1350, Petrarch repeatedly referred to his epistolary travel narratives as fripperies, reluctantly dashed off at the behest of friend and patron Giovanni Colonna.[36] In 1499, Arnold von Harff opened the German account of his globe-trotting adventures by deriding the vast number of "careless and troublesome chatterers (*Kläffer*)" who—not believing in anything they cannot see in their native lands—"maintain that every traveler's (*Pilger*) story is a lie."[37]

As von Harff's defiance suggests, whatever chilling effect moralists may have had on the practice of travel writing, their carping did not prove decisive. In fact, during the late Middle Ages, Latin Christians produced a staggering—and, indeed, unprecedented—number of travel accounts, written by a geographically widespread and socially diverse assortment of authors.[38] Travelers and travel writers alike sought to preempt objections to their undertakings by appealing to the inherent dignity of travail.

TRAVAIL AND AUTHORITY

In the Middle Ages, as in antiquity, the inevitable hazards of travel endowed it with a heroic aura. As Eric J. Leed has noted, the bodily signs of rigorous wayfaring are already treated as marks of distinction in *The Epic of Gilgamesh*.[39] The opening invocation of Homer's *Odyssey* celebrates its eponymous hero—"the man of ways" (*polutropos*)—for having successfully "wandered" land and sea. In Homer's Greek, the word *sea—pontos*—shares etymological origins with *panthah*, or "difficult passage." As Silvia Montiglio has noted, the two most common Greek words for "to wander" (*alaomai* and *planaomai*) are middle passive verbs; what this means is that, in classical Greek usage, when someone "wanders," that person is doing something, but at the same time, something is also *being done to him or her*.[40] Embedded in Homer's key terms, then, is the assumption that travel entails a heroic effort to overcome inertial forces and outflank death. These same beliefs inform the subterranean descent of Virgil's Aeneas, a journey that, following Homeric precedent, literalizes the notion of heroic travel as an improbable triumph over mortality.

In penitential pilgrimage, classical idealizations of travail found a distinctively medieval articulation. The obligatory pilgrimage of Christian penance apparently originated in sixth-century Ireland. By the thirteenth century, it had been appropriated by political authorities across Europe to punish violations of secular law.[41] Perhaps more significant, penitential journeys were increasingly undertaken on a voluntary basis. This development explains, for example, why Margery Kempe says that she suffered "gret thrist and gret penawns" en route to Calais, even though she (controversially) undertook her pilgrimage without the knowledge of her confessor.[42]

The penitential pilgrimage offered a legitimate, widely recognized, and adaptable set of propositions that Kempe and many others used to rationalize novel, or potentially circumspect, journeys.[43] Crusading was originally conceived as a kind of pilgrimage (*peregrinatio*). The crusader accrued spiritual blessings because he voluntarily subjected himself to the perils of both warfare *and* long-distance travel.[44] It was not long after the emergence of the Franciscan and Dominican Orders at the turn of the thirteenth century that friars started referring to their dangerous missionary campaigns as "pilgrimages."[45] The quest of Arthurian romance incorporated elements of both

pilgrimage and crusade. Underlying all of these reorientations of penitential pilgrimage is the ancient conception of the *peregrinus* as an exile or an
alien—a person within the Roman Empire who lacked the full legal protections of citizenship. When Augustine spoke of human life as a *peregrinatio*
oriented toward the heavenly Jerusalem, he was drawing on the ancient
political resonances of the term.[46] Augustine's metaphysical abstraction wa-
gers its intelligibility on a widely shared assumption that those displaced
from the familiar guarantees and privileges of home must, like Homer's
Odysseus, grapple heroically with exceptional levels of adversity.

The association of travel with asceticism proved a valuable rhetorical
resource to defenders and critics of various modes of medieval travel—
and of pilgrimage, in particular. The satirically drawn Palmer of William
Langland's fourteenth-century poem *Piers Plowman* solicits the admiration
of others by flaunting the labors of his travels. The Palmer festoons his
person with dozens of badges and ampules, which he has procured at far-
flung shrines such as Mount Sinai and Santiago de Compostela. These trinkets—or, as the Palmer calls them, "signs"—are meant to be "read" both as
forensic confirmation of his exceptional itinerary and as quantifications of
his travail: "Ye may se by my signes that sitten on myn hatte / That I have
walked [wel] wide in weet and in drye."[47] In his paean to Holy Land pilgrimage, fifteenth-century Dominican Felix Fabri also alludes to somatic "signs"
of the pilgrim's pious suffering, which include a "long beard growing from a
face which is serious and pale on account of his labors and danger." According to Fabri, the semiotic conventions that enable the pilgrim to manifest
his devoutness of purpose by refraining from shaving predate Christianity
itself, having been instituted by a pagan: the Egyptian "king" Osiris.[48]

In the fifteenth-century trial of alleged Lollard William Thorpe, travail
became a flash point in a public disputation about the legitimacy of pilgrimage as an institution. The defendant's examiner, Archbishop Arundel,
took issue with Thorpe's condemnation of pilgrimage by citing "the grete
trauaile" to which pilgrims subjected themselves. Thorpe scorned this argument, observing that racy singers and bagpipe players furnished the most
common soundtrack for these putatively austere journeys. Curiously, Arundel did not contest the accuracy of this generalization; instead, he defended
boisterous music on the grounds that it helped the barefoot pilgrim perse-
vere in his progress whenever he "smytith his too agens a stoon and hurtith
him soore and makith him blede."[49] For his part, Thorpe retorted that, insofar as most pilgrims "traueilen soore [their] bodies," they did so in pursuit
of fleshly—rather than spiritual—delights, thereby rendering their suffering
valueless.[50]

The travel of international merchants also sparked moral debates in which travail, or the alleged absence thereof, proved central. In his *De regimine principum*, Thomas Aquinas cited Aristotle's *Politics* to the effect that "commerce is more at odds with military prowess than are most other occupations. Merchants rest in the shade without toil, and while they enjoy delights their spirits grow soft and their bodies are rendered weak and unfitted for military exertions."[51] Popular preacher Bernardino of Siena (1380–1444) asserted that merchants' prolonged absences from their wives softened their libidinal resolve, encouraging them to engage in sodomy and other forbidden sex acts.[52] Petrarch criticized the empty, materialistic aspirations that prompted merchants to embrace the potentially lethal dangers of maritime travel.[53] A fourteenth-century manual written for Catalan merchants offers a contrasting perspective, extolling the mercantile profession as "the best and most profitable (*la millor e pus profitossa*) of the masculine arts," in part because long-distance trade requires young men "to withstand great travails and perils (*sostenir los grans traballs e perills*)."[54] This statement of occupational pride might be seen as a rebuttal of the arguments mounted by the likes of Bernardino, Petrarch, and Aquinas.

As several of the above-mentioned examples suggest, the concept of *travail* encompassed both the dangers and discomforts inherent in travel as well as the techniques used to manage and overcome them. The argument between Thorpe and Arundel, for instance, turns on the question of whether rowdy, profane song can be viewed as a legitimate component of the pilgrim's ascetic struggle, or whether, by its very nature, it should be considered the negation of pious travail. The assimilation of reading and writing to heroic ideals of travel proved a far less controversial affair. Over the course of the Middle Ages, an expanding array of literate practices and literary paradigms was absorbed into the regimes of self-discipline that conferred distinction on the experiences of the traveler.

TRAVEL AS LITERATE LABOR

Most experts in postmedieval travel writing acknowledge that *travel* is a loaded term and have felt obliged to confront this semantic fact. In modern English, the word *travel* assumed new class-based valences at the turn of the nineteenth century, when it began to align itself in opposition to *tourism*. The advent of the *travel-tourism* binary was a reaction to the rise of travel agencies and steam-powered transportation, which enabled the middle class to visit the cultural capitals that had formerly been the reserve of the Grand Tour. As James Buzard has shown, the "traveler" came to be identified with a refined sensibility deemed lacking in the "tourist." This allegedly superior sensibility was founded on the ideals of individualism, self-restraint, an informed appreciation of foreign surroundings, and a "proper" relationship to reading and writing—both during and after the journey.[55]

Mindful of these elitist connotations, some scholars of modern travel writing have rejected *travel* as their keyword of choice, opting instead for terms such as *displacement* or *mobility*. The aim of this rhetorical wager was to dislodge the voluntary, leisure-time experiences of white, upper-class European men as the normative model for knowing the world, thereby facilitating the study of the more constrained (and usually less prestigious) movements of women, slaves, refugees, domestic servants, and so on. James Clifford has proposed a different—and, to my mind, more useful—solution to the problematic origins of *travel*. Clifford maintains that *travel* is an ideal term for recovering lost histories of subaltern mobility *precisely because of* its exclusivist connotations, which can be harnessed to confer dignity on previously marginalized experiences, while at the same time inviting considerations of how disparities in wealth, status, and power affect any traveler's experience of the world.[56] What all of these critical discussions have in common is the acknowledgment that the activities that have been graced with the honorific *travel* presume the mastery of certain rhetorical postures and forms of cultural literacy that were, by design, historically accessible to few.

Even though medievalists have successfully adapted postcolonial critiques of modern ethnography in discussing the travel writing of the Middle Ages, they have not engaged the related scholarly debates about the concept of *travel*. However, it is important not to take *travel* for granted, since the Middle Ages were by no means innocent of the kinds of ideological distinctions found in postmedieval travel writing. In fact, a strong argument can be made that many of the elitist assumptions that are baked into modern idealizations of the traveler originate in the late medieval reinvention of travel as literate labor. As literacy of various kinds assumed a more prominent place in the heroic journey, the traveler's claim to prestige increasingly rested on the question of *which* literate dispositions and aptitudes had shaped his or her explorations of the world, and to what ends.

The tendentious contrast between the Latinity of clerical travel writers and the "illiteracy" of their lay counterparts was the earliest and most commonly invoked axis of differentiation. In his thirteenth-century *Narracio de mirabilibus urbis Romae*, the English cleric known simply as "Magister Gregorius" repeatedly derides his fellow travelers' assertions about the monuments of Rome. Gregorius reliably discredits the geographical investigations of the laity by equating them with orality and superstition. In the process of describing the tomb of Romulus, Gregorius pauses to gripe about pilgrims who "erroneously claim (*mentiuntur*) that [it] is the grain heap of the apostle Peter, which was transformed into a stone hill of the same size when Nero confiscated it." He adds: "It's an utterly worthless (*frivolum*) tale, typical of those told by pilgrims (*peregrini*)."[57] By contrast, Gregorius attributes his self-professedly superior insights into Rome to his mastery of Latin and, by extension, to his social access to the scholarly and ecclesiastical elite: "I shall give a wide berth to the worthless stories (*vanas fabulas*) of the pilgrims and the Romans . . . and shall record what I've been told by the elders, the cardinals, and the men of greatest learning (*viris doctissimis*)."[58]

As the *Narracio* also makes clear, the day-to-day self-discipline of the pilgrim is predicated on his or her relationship to reading and writing. Deficits in the traveler's learning express themselves externally, in the form of undignified interactions with Rome's monuments. According to Gregorius, the superstitions that surround the obelisk falsely identified as "St. Peter's Needle" encourage ignorant pilgrims to disseminate heretical beliefs—and to make a risible spectacle of themselves in the process: "They make great efforts to crawl underneath [the monument], where the stone rests on four bronze lions, claiming falsely that those who manage to do so are cleansed from their sins having made true penance."[59] Elsewhere, Gregorius strikes a more skeptical note about his own mastery of the art of travel, suggesting that the very Latinity that inoculates him against the contagious stupidity of the masses just might predispose him to other forms of waywardness. Gregorius's appreciation of classical aesthetics spurs him to explore Rome's ruined bathhouses and to admire a skillfully rendered statue of Venus, which, to his eyes, appeared "to blush in her nakedness." The problematic nature of Gregorius's reaction to the pagan statute is suggested by the fact that it occasions a lapse in his self-governance. This loss of control is registered spatially, as a kind of semivoluntary displacement: "Because of this wonderful image, and perhaps some magic spell that I am unaware of, I was drawn back three times to look at it despite the fact that it was two stades distant from my inn."[60]

Under the influence of many other intellectual traditions and cultural practices, late medieval travel writers from a variety of social backgrounds viewed the travel account as an opportunity to advance their own propositions about travel and its relationship to literacy. Though they come to a variety of conclusions on this question, travel writers tend to speak of travel as a method-governed mode of geoethnographic investigation that—when done correctly—confers benefits on the individual traveler and on readers of travel writing. By the end of the Middle Ages, travel is widely understood as an art of literate self-discipline, and its best practices equally relevant to pilgrims and adventurers, to those visiting Caracorum or Cologne.

OVERVIEW

The Medieval Invention of Travel is organized into three parts, each consisting of two chapters. This three-part structure mirrors the tripartite division that has shaped the study of medieval travel writing (i.e., texts written about journeys to East Asia, the Holy Land, and Europe / the Mediterranean). While these section divisions are an acknowledgment of the analytical advantages of this conventional schema, the arc of the book's argument is an attempt to highlight—and think beyond—its inherent limitations.

Part 1, "Subjectivity, Authority, and the 'Exotic,'" considers a body of travel writing about East Asia published between the mid-thirteenth and mid-fourteenth centuries. Interest in accounts of East Asian travel is responsible for galvanizing the study of medieval travel writing, in general. Animated by the rise of postcolonial theory and by the publication of Edward Said's *Orientalism* (1978), in particular, books such as Mary B. Campbell's *Witness and the Other World* (1988), Stephen Greenblatt's *Marvelous Possessions* (1991), as well as the more recent studies by Joan-Pau Rubiés (2000), Geraldine Heng (2003), Suzanne Akbari (2009), Kim M. Phillips (2014), and Shirin Khanmohamadi (2014) have focused predominantly on questions of ethnographic representation; they have been especially interested in exploring how the Middle Ages may have contributed to the ideas that justified modern European imperialism.[61] Phillips gives voice to an assumption that informs the majority of these studies when she remarks that most of the period's travel writing is so invested in geoethnographic description that its authors "pay little or no attention to the subjective experience of travel."[62] Together, chapters 1 and 2 challenge this assumption, by highlighting the indispensable part that the discourse of travail played in the conception and reception of works of exotic travel writing (even in the cases of works that lavish little narrative attention on the experiences of their authors).

Chapter 1, "Exoticism as the Appropriation of Travail," focuses on two accounts of travel into the Mongol Empire: the *Itinerarium* of Franciscan William of Rubruck (written ca. 1255) and the *Divisament dou monde* of Marco Polo and Rustichello da Pisa (ca. 1298). The *Divisament* is often compared dismissively to the *Itinerarium*, principally on aesthetic grounds. Modern readers have tended to prefer the "more subjective" narrative of William to the catalogue of grammatically impersonal descriptions dished up by Polo and Rustichello. However, the stylistic differences between the *Itinerarium* and the *Divisament* are not—as is widely held—a token of their authors' disparate literary aptitudes. On the contrary, each of these works renders subjective experience in a way that reinforces its ideological stance toward exoticism, a politically oriented mode of aestheticism that—in the Middle Ages—was founded on the symbolic appropriation of the traveler's travail. The prominence of William's "I" in the *Itinerarium* is a key component in the story of how he resisted Mongol rulers' attempts to exoticize his religious teachings and to spin his presence at their courts to their political advantage. By contrast, the deliberate marginalization of Polo's voice in the *Divisament* is foundational to the work's attempts to teach its European readers to emulate the exoticism of Khubilai Khan. This popularization of elite exoticism relied on the rise of luxury bookmaking at French-speaking courts. The illuminated courtly manuscript provided an ideal medium for reifying and redistributing the prestige that accrued to travelers like Polo by virtue of their travails.

Chapter 2, "Travail and Authority in the Forgotten Age of Discovery," examines the different ways that John of Plano Carpini's *Historia Mongalorum* (ca. 1247), Odoric of Pordenone's *Relatio* (1330), and *The Book of John Mandeville* (ca. 1350s–1371) leverage the mystique of travail to variously sidestep, supplement, and contest clerical notions of *auctoritas*. Emergent practices of bureaucratic writing were an essential resource to these authors and to their medieval readers, who imagine the relationship between authority and travail in strikingly diverse ways. The composition and reception history of these three works furnish a vital corrective to the truism that, in the Middle Ages, geographical knowledge was dominated by academic protocols of knowledge production. This misconception has occluded the complexity of medieval debates about the basis of the traveler's authority and about the disruptive implications of geographical discovery. It has, moreover, been routinely evoked in order to define the Middle Ages as the antithesis of "modernity" in historical surveys of travel, serving as an alibi not to think about the period at all.

Part 2, "Pilgrimage as Literate Labor," argues that pilgrims to Jerusalem were at the vanguard of the reinvention of travel as literate labor. Drawing on long traditions of devotional and scholarly activity in the Holy Land, the authors of pilgrimage accounts viewed reading, writing, and their associated aptitudes as an essential part of self-discipline that distinguished the heroic traveler from his frivolous counterparts. In the process, they reimagined travel as an artful regulation of mind, soul, *and* body, oriented toward self-examination and the creation of useful geoethnographic knowledge. The full import of this contribution to the history of ideas about travel has, however, gone unnoticed. This oversight is largely the result of the fact that the most illuminating studies of the medieval pilgrimage account have tended to treat their subject in overstrict isolation from related medieval and post-medieval approaches to travel writing.

Chapter 3, "Memory Work and the Labor of Writing," argues that pilgrims to Jerusalem influentially identified heroic travel with regimes of self-discipline organized around the activities of reading and writing. Around the turn of the thirteenth century, clerical pilgrims to the Holy Land consolidate what I call the "synthetic tradition" of travel writing about the region. Influenced by monastic theories about the role played by memory in written composition, the synthetic tradition placed a premium on the traveler's ability to render a vivid, coherent verbal map of the places he had visited during his pilgrimage. Synthetic travel writers portrayed deliberate self-regulation during the journey as a prerequisite for success in the post-pilgrimage labor of composing the written account. In the fourteenth century, an alternative to the synthetic tradition emerged: the travel diary. The diary made the habit of writing part of the pilgrim's daily regime and ultimately raised the bar in terms of what counted as success in the recollection of one's travels. Originating in bureaucratic writing practices, the travel diary took root in Italy among lay and clerical pilgrims, and was quickly picked up by travelers from other parts of Europe. The astonishing popularity of the diary prompted latter-day practitioners of the synthetic tradition to champion disciplined note-taking in the field as an essential part of Holy Land pilgrimage. By the close of the Middle Ages, taking notes during any journey was an unambiguous mark of authority and trustworthiness on the part of the would-be travel writer.

Chapter 4, "The Pilgrim as Investigator," argues against the repeatedly discredited—yet seemingly indestructible—stereotype that depicts the medieval pilgrim to the Holy Land as an uncritical tourist who does little more than recycle hoary observations about well-worn routes. In reality, pilgrimage to the region entailed active, skeptical, and often painstaking investigations into past and present realities. Mindful of the limitations of authoritative sources and faced with a continually changing landscape, medieval travel writers developed a number of approaches to unearthing evidence and evaluating competing claims about the Holy Land. At the turn of the twelfth century, the labor of investigation assumed a particularly prominent place in the ideal pilgrimage. As a consequence, travel writers began to engage and debate the investigative methods, interests, and emphases of their predecessors and contemporaries. At the end of the thirteenth century, a handful of particularly influential Dominican authors drew on the precedent provided by exotic travel writing in order to extend their investigations into the less familiar world beyond the Holy Land. The advent of the travel diary in the fourteenth century fostered the opposite impulse, encouraging pilgrims to bring the techniques previously used to investigate Jerusalem and East Asia to the European and Mediterranean locales that they visited en route to the Holy Land. This inward geographical turn contributed to an increased self-consciousness about different approaches to knowing the Holy Land and conferred legitimacy on writing about shorter-range journeys.

Part 3, "Discovering the Proximate," takes an in-depth look at Petrarch and Pero Tafur, two travel writers who draw on and reorient the impulses of both exotic travel writing and the pilgrimage account. Petrarch and Tafur conceive of travel as an art of geoethnographic investigation and as an occasion for acute self-examination. For both travel writers, the elite journey is governed by techniques that can—in theory—be abstracted from any particular itinerary. Prior to the fourteenth century, a journey was normally deemed worthy of a written account if it yielded useful knowledge about sacred centers and/or remote, unknown places. With Petrarch and Tafur, the cultivation of new perspectives on familiar destinations, or even on the activity of travel itself, is justification enough.

Chapter 5, "Becoming Petrarch," focuses on a group of letters written by Petrarch during three different journeys, undertaken over the course of ten years (1333–43). Petrarch collected these letters in his epistolary anthology *Letters on Familiar Matters* (1350s). Through the editorial manipulation of his correspondence, Petrarch traces an autobiographical arc, in which his youthful enthusiasm for travel and vernacular poetry transitions to a more mature period of civic-minded engagement with Latin philology and classicizing poetics. The final batch of letters, written from Naples in 1343, announces Petrarch's world-weary realization that literature is unlikely to effect political change, and signals his doubts about the benefits of subjecting himself to the rigors of future travel. Ultimately, Petrarch distinguishes himself from most of his contemporaries by resisting the tendency to assimilate literate labor to the art of travel. In the years following 1343, Petrarch will increasingly speak of travel as a toilsome, and often unprofitable, distraction from the daily reading and writing undertaken in his library, a routine of self-discipline rooted in the home and focused principally on moral—rather than political—reform.

Chapter 6, "The Chivalric Mediterranean of Pero Tafur," considers the fifteenth-century Castilian knight's account of his travels, now com-

monly known as the *Andanças*. Like Petrarch, Tafur writes about places
with which his readers are almost certainly familiar, many of them Mediterranean ports of call. In contrast to Petrarch, chivalric romance provides
Tafur with the literary lens through which he idealizes his travels. Tafur
speaks of his journey as an elite mode of education, one that relies on his
intimacy with Muslim and Greek Orthodox hosts. At numerous junctures
in Tafur's narrative, these sentimental ideals come into conflict with his
conception of knightly travel as a sequence of dangerous, prowess-honing
travails, undertaken in defense of the cultural and territorial integrity of
Latin Christendom. Tafur's account never entirely reconciles the competing impulses to view religious others as peers and role models on the one
hand, and as mortal enemies on the other. It does, however, take a decisive
stance on another question, championing the educational value of travel
within Europe and the Mediterranean while rejecting more perilous and exotic itineraries in East Asia. This position allies the otherwise adventurous
Tafur to Petrarch, and more generally to the gentlemen-humanists of the
Renaissance, the Enlightenment, and the age of the Grand Tour.

The coda, "Beyond 1500; or, Travel's Labors Lost," explores the implications of this book's arguments about the Middle Ages by entertaining a
thought experiment: what if the nineteenth century were seen as the end
point of the phenomena discussed in this book rather than 1500? The perfection of the steam engine was a technological achievement that transformed humanity's experience of time and space. Many of the people who
witnessed the triumph of steam power were forced to ponder what would
be left of *travel* once the certainty of travail had been rendered a thing of
the past. Their expressions of uncertainty arguably signal a historical rupture far more significant than the arbitrary, field-defining fence erected between the Middle Ages and the Renaissance.

A FINAL NOTE ON KEY TERMS

Developing a working definition for *travel writing* is a rite of passage for all
studies on the subject.[63] The apparent timelessness and ubiquity of stories
about travel encourages a broad, inclusive approach to defining the term.
Walter Benjamin imagined the tales of the overseas voyager as one half of
a primordial dialectic that gave rise to all storytelling (the other being the
local yarns of the stay-at-home peasant).[64] Meanwhile, Michel de Certeau
famously pronounced: "Every story is a travel story."[65] For obvious reasons,
few studies of travel writing adopt such generous definitions. They therefore face the task of explaining which titles have been included and which

excluded, whether fictional or pseudohistorical works should be considered alongside letters and diaries, which texts should be grouped together and on what grounds, and so forth.

The quandary is perhaps even more pronounced in the case of the Middle Ages. As Fredric Jameson has observed, the advent of print capitalism furnishes publishers with a profit-oriented incentive to ensure the transparency and stability of literary genres.[66] The literary cultures of the Middle Ages wield generic terms in ways that sometimes seem chaotic and contradictory.[67] With a few notable exceptions (i.e., legal documents and lyric poetry), medieval writing was seldom organized into coherent and stable generic systems.[68] Faced with the exceptionally complex terrain that nourished medieval travel writing, scholars have developed a number of resourceful approaches to classifying works.[69]

The following formal/generic terms underpin the central arguments of this book: *travel writing*, *travel account*, *travel narrative*, and *travel book*. *Travel writing* is the most general of the four concepts and resembles Joan-Pau Rubiés's notion of "travel literature," which he defines as "a varied body of writing" that "takes travel as an essential element for its production" but in which travel is "not necessarily a theme, nor even a structuring element."[70] My use of *travel writing* encompasses first-person travel accounts as well as works of descriptive topography, whether or not the knowledge conveyed in them is the result of the author's own travels. I use *travel account* to refer to works that contain a significant amount of geo-ethnographic description that purportedly derives from the travels of the text's author or of someone close to him or her. The *travel account* may be dominated by the first- or third-person voice, and may or may not focus primarily on the experience of the voyage that underpins its claims.

The term *travel narrative* is deployed in an even more specific way. Drawing on the familiar formulation of Jan Borm, I define *travel narrative* as:

> any narrative characterized by a non-fiction dominant that relates (almost always) in the first person a journey that the reader supposes to have taken place in reality while assuming or presupposing that the author, narrator, and principal character are but one or identical.[71]

Also relevant is Mary B. Campbell's more straightforward assertion that travel narrative is "fully inhabited by its narrator" and tends to "be fully narrative"—meaning that geoethnographic description is embedded within, and subordinated to, the relatively continuous story of the journey.[72]

There is a common misconception that travel narrative as I define it above is rare, or virtually nonexistent, in the Middle Ages. This alleged dearth supposedly reflects the Middle Ages' aversion to empiricism, its disinterest in individual experience, and its dogmatic fixation on theological authority. It is true that some of the most successful works of medieval travel writing—including the accounts of John of Plano Carpini, Burchard of Mount Sion, John Mandeville, and Marco Polo / Rustichello da Pisa—privilege geoethnographic description over the narration of experience. However, as my analyses of these works suggest, each of them appears to do so with different aims in mind, and not because they all subscribe to the same benighted set of epistemological beliefs. In any event, the truism that travel narrative is rare in the Middle Ages does not withstand scrutiny for long once one focuses on texts written after 1350, many of which were composed by pilgrims to the Holy Land.

Finally, *travel book* refers to the work of travel writing in its dimension as a material object, usually a manuscript codex. This term is particularly useful in situations in which the form and content of a given text are somehow illuminated by a consideration of the material practices and social networks that sustained its production and circulation. Though this nested set of terms was not used by medieval authors and readers, it will hopefully furnish basic coordinates that will facilitate synchronic and diachronic comparisons of various works of travel writing without fetishizing or overlooking their formal differences.

PART I

Subjectivity, Authority, and the "Exotic"

According to Giovanni Boccaccio's biography of Dante, some early audiences of the *Divine Comedy* believed that its author had been—quite literally—to hell and back. While strolling one day through the streets of Ravenna, Dante reportedly overheard a group of townswomen marveling at him in hushed tones:

> "Ladies, do you see that man who goes back and forth to Hell as he pleases, and returns with news about those who are there?" To which another of them naively (*semplicemente*) responded: "Truly, you are right: Do you not see how his beard is crisped and his complexion darkened (*la barba crespa e il color bruno*) by the heat and smoke of that place?" Hearing these words spoken behind him, and realizing that they were due to the women's credulity, he was pleased by the high opinion they had of him, and—smiling a little—he moved onward.[1]

On the one hand a cautionary tale about the importance of leaving literary interpretation to the professionals, this anecdote also highlights the evidentiary limitations of one of the medieval travel writer's most cherished bids for authority: an appeal to the physical travails of travel.[2]

Dante and Boccaccio were born into a world of expanding geographical and literary horizons—factors that inform the above-mentioned anecdote and that spawned novel forms of travel writing. Starting in the 1240s, European travel writers began following the Mongol Empire's secure overland routes into central and East Asia. They returned with astonishing, improbable accounts of regions that had been but dimly known even to the Roman Empire. Prior to this point, travel writers tended to be monks or cathedral clergy, who wrote about places (such as the Holy Land or Rome) that had also been described in the works of ancient authorities. Most of them envisioned concrete and relatively unproblematic readerships—usually a royal patron or the religious community to which they belonged.

None of this was true for those who wrote about their travels to East Asia between 1240 and 1370. These authors were members of emergent and increasingly self-assertive groups: merchants, friars, and the nobility. Faced with the advent of new reading communities, most anticipated broad, socially mixed audiences who—like the women from Boccaccio's vignette—might interpret their efforts in ways that they had not intended. The most common fears that travel writers voiced were that their accounts would be dismissed as untruthful or that they would fall into hands ill equipped to derive the benefits that they sought to impart to their readers.

References to travail were central to how exotic travel writers negotiated their amorphous and potentially fractious audiences. Previous scholarship on exotic travel writing during the Middle Ages has focused primarily on the analysis of ethnographic discourses and has underestimated the conceptual importance of travel to these works. However, even accounts that invest little rhetorical energy in detailing the experiences of their authors ask that their readers view the text's geoethnographic descriptions through the lens of the pains and labors that produced them.

The rhetoric of travail was also leveraged by medieval readers of travel writing. Particularly successful accounts—like those of Marco Polo, Odoric of Pordenone, and John Mandeville—passed back and forth between clerical, courtly, and bourgeois readerships. As they did so, they were not only translated from one language to another, but often also revised to conform to the expectations of different audiences. Radical revisions of the text's content and/or form were common. Many of these changes were ideologically motivated rewritings of the author's statements about how and why he embraced the labors of travel and travel writing. What this means is that the manuscript tradition of any given account is also potentially a document of ongoing cultural debates about the nature of the benefits gained through travel—and about the role that travel writing plays in transmitting those benefits to others.

While monographs on individual travel writers such as Marco Polo and John Mandeville have examined manuscript traditions in order to identify broad areas of consensus and disagreement among medieval readers, surveys of exotic travel writing have made limited use of the evidence provided by manuscript variants. However, as the following two chapters will show, the medieval invention of travel was a project in which both authors and readers played essential parts (albeit to the occasional consternation of the former group).

CHAPTER ONE

Exoticism as the Appropriation of Travail

The Greek-derived word *exotic* entered into written English (via French) in 1600, in Ben Jonson's *Every Man out of His Humor*. The turn of phrase that marked its debut was fittingly sensationalist: "Magique, Witch-craft, or other such Exoticke Artes."[1] In 1633, Thomas Johnson's revision of John Gerard's *The herball; or, Generall historie of plantes* classified the fruit of the clove tree as "Exoticke," in part because of the strange sensations that its English investigator experienced upon putting it inside his mouth.[2] By 1650, *exotic* was both an adjective and a noun, applied not only to spe-cies and customs imported into England from "outside" but also to the resi-dent aliens that were one's neighbors and to foreign authors—both ancient and modern—whose works paved the way for one's own scholarship. As these examples suggest, many early uses of *exotic* describe phenomena that, in *après coup* fashion, give rise to the very boundaries that supposedly pre-exist them and that they allegedly breach.

The rise of postcolonial studies prompted scholars of travel writing to consider how their objects of study participate in such ideologically moti-vated constructions of "the outside."[3] In *Culture and Imperialism*, Edward Said remarked:

If you were British or French in the 1860s you saw, and you felt, India and North Africa with a combination of familiarity and distance, but never with a sense of their separate sovereignty. In your narratives, his-tories, travel tales, and explorations your consciousness was represented as the principal authority, an active point of energy that made sense not just of colonizing activities but of exotic geographies and peoples.[4]

According to Said, exoticism is an aesthetic mode that reifies cultural dif-ference in ways that alternately naturalize and dissemble the violent foundations of imperial hegemony: "The exotic replaces the impress of power with the blandishments of curiosity."[5] While Said focused on highbrow exoticism, Anne McClintock subsequently argued that the Victorian marketing of soap, fruit salts, and tea relied on exoticizing tableaux to sell not only household commodities but also nationalist and imperialist ideologies to masses who were not necessarily clamoring to read Flaubert or attend the latest production of Verdi's *Aida*.[6] Meanwhile, Gayatri Spivak and Graham Huggan have suggested that the literary works of authors from postcolonial countries are commodified by the Anglo-American academy in ways that perpetuate the exoticisms of the nineteenth century.[7]

Like the term *exotic* itself, postcolonial critiques of exoticism emerge from realities that postdate the Middle Ages. Nevertheless, there *was* a medieval analogue for the aesthetic mode that modern scholars call *exoticism*. This chapter focuses on one of medieval exoticism's characteristic expressions: *the prestige economy of long-distance knowledge*. This term refers to a constellation of symbolic conventions, material practices, and structures of feeling that enabled medieval people to accrue social, political, and economic advantage through their association with the foreign. The travails of the traveler, and the symbolic appropriation thereof, were the foundation of this economy.

Anthropologist Mary W. Helms has shown that, in nearly all preindustrial societies, the field of inquiry that we call *geography* overlaps significantly with *cosmology*.[8] For this reason, the act of overcoming geographical distance is charged with the powers of the sacred. Because knowledge of faraway lands attains this mystical character, it proves fundamental to cults of royal and priestly charisma. In some cultures, monarchs and high priests bolster their authority by traveling to distant places in person, returning as what Helms calls "long-distance specialists."[9] In others, elite persons appropriate the mystique of long-distance specialists without ever leaving their native lands, through ensuring their privileged access to foreign visitors and the exotic commodities that accompany them. Among medieval rulers, this second approach tended to prevail over the first (which might partially explain the ambivalence of medieval attitudes toward the heroic travels of Ulysses and Alexander the Great). Long-distance specialists also stand to profit by making their labors available for appropriation, economically (through financial awards and social promotion) and symbolically (through their prestigious proximity to the powerful).

Just as the critical interrogation of nineteenth-century exoticism cast the era's attitudes toward travel and travel writing in a new light, an appreciation of the prestige economy of long-distance knowledge is indispensable to analyses of the same phenomena in the Middle Ages. This is certainly the case with two frequently compared works of travel writing: the *Itinerarium* of William of Rubruck (1253) and the *Divisament dou monde* of Marco Polo and Rustichello da Pisa (1298). Scholars have often treated the *Itinerarium* and the *Divisament* as a contrasting diptych. The account of William of Rubruck is generally lauded for its skepticism, its dialogic approach to ethnographic description, and its vivid, personal rendering of its author's experiences.[10] Featuring "a plot and a character," the *Itinerarium* balances narrative and exoticizing description in a way that conforms to modern expectations of how travel writing should be done.[11] By contrast, the *Divisament* is faulted for confining its discussion of the Polo family's experiences to a slim preface. The rest of the bulky work is given over to impersonal geoethnographic descriptions of Asia, with occasional anecdotes about Marco's travels scattered throughout. Even Polo's nineteenth-century champion Henry Yule conceded that, in the *Divisament*, "impersonality is carried to excess."[12] Making matters worse for the *Divisament* is its allegedly crude style, particularly its penchant for oral-formulaic refrains and its inconsistent use of the first-person narrative voice.[13]

Recent scholarship has softened the tone of such negative comparisons, observing that Polo and Rustichello did not set out to write a first-person travel narrative. However, there is still no consensus about what they actually *did* intend to write.[14] The unanswered question of *why* these texts might have adopted the formal and stylistic tendencies that have shaped their critical fortunes is a compelling one. After all, it was not inevitable that William of Rubruck—even though he was writing a letter—would situate his description of the Mongol Empire within the framework of a relatively continuous first-person narrative. Likewise, nothing prevented the makers of the *Divisament*—a work that drew heavily on the conventions of Arthurian fiction—from embedding geoethnographic description within the framework of a highly subjectivized series of episodes based on Polo's real-life adventures.

In following pages, I argue that the formal tendencies that distinguish the *Itinerarium* from the *Divisament* are more meaningfully contextualized as traits that allow the two works to express their divergent attitudes toward the role played by the prestige economy of long-distance knowledge in cross-cultural exchanges with the Mongol Empire. The notorious instability of the "I" in the *Divisament* and the work's apparent suppression of Marco's experience are deliberate choices that allow the work to rationalize its transformation of Polo's travails into a novel kind of exotic commodity: a travel book designed for lay readers within—and outside—courtly settings. The displacement of Polo allows the *Divisament* to bring the figures of Khubilai Khan and Rustichello to the fore, a rhetorical maneuver that is key to the work's self-rationalization. By contrast, the prominence of the first-person voice in William's account asserts his alienation from the materialism and cultural relativism of the Mongol court. Among its other narrative effects, the "I" of the *Itinerarium* registers its author's resistance to the manner in which he is exoticized by his foreign hosts. William ultimately concludes that the relativistic impulses of courtly exoticism are structurally incompatible with the universalizing claims of his faith, a conviction that prompts the Franciscan—whom modern readers have admired for his urbanity—to call for a crusade against the Mongol people.

EXOTICISM AND ITS DISCONTENTS:
WILLIAM OF RUBRUCK

In 1253, Friar William of Rubruck subjected himself to a harrowing trek from the Crimea to Caracorum, where he stayed at the court of Mongol ruler Möngke Khan (ruled 1251–59). At some point prior to this journey, William had been sent by his order to the Palestinian port town of Acre, at the time still under Latin Christian control. It was there, or perhaps in Cyprus, that William crossed paths with king and future saint Louis IX of France, who was about to lead his followers into the disastrous Seventh Crusade. Taking advantage of William's plans to visit the western edge of the Mongol Empire, Louis asked the Franciscan to carry a royal "letter of friendship" to the Mongol baron Sartach, who had reportedly converted to Christianity.[15] The French king also donated lavish books, liturgical instruments, and probably traveling money, all intended to support William's ministry. Upon his return to Acre in 1255, William of Rubruck discovered that his royal patron, having suffered crushing defeat and captivity at the hands of the Egyptian sultan, had been ransomed and returned to Paris. Unable to get permission to leave Acre for France, William dispatched a book-length letter to Louis IX—the richly observed first-person travel narrative now known as the *Itinerarium*.

The disconnect between the appealing stylistic qualities of the *Itinerarium* and the murderous agenda that they serve has no doubt contributed to the scholarly tendency to pass over its conclusion with scant comment. The traits for which the *Itinerarium* is praised—its dialogism, careful observation, and immediate rendering of experience—are not ends in themselves; they are marshaled to paint William's journey as a failure. The Franciscan's plot-driven narrative makes the pain, hunger, humiliation, and fear of its author the center of attention. The final, bloodthirsty pages of the account clarify what is at stake in this persistent emphasis on William's wasted pains. Taking leave of Louis, William advises the crusade-happy monarch to wage a holy war against the Great Khan. According to William, "It would be a very easy thing to subjugate" the lands between Constantinople and the Mongol Empire. He adds:

> Of old, brave men made their way through these regions [i.e., Hungary, Armenia, Anatolia] and all went well with them, although they had very brave men resisting them, whom God has now wiped off the face of the earth. . . . I say to you with confidence, if your peasants, I will not say kings or knights, were willing to [travel overland] as do the Kings of the Tartars and to be content with the same kind of food, they could take possession of the whole world.[16]

In contrast to fellow Franciscan Roger Bacon—a medieval admirer of the *Itinerarium*—William is pessimistic about the prospect of bringing the Mongol Empire into the Christian fold through peaceable means and eager to embrace violence as an alternative.[17]

William's famous first impressions of the Mongol Empire would seem to foreshadow this grim perspective: "It seemed indeed to me as if I were stepping into some other world (*aliud seculum*)."[18] Nevertheless, the *Itinerarium* does not, in fact, attribute the futility of its author's mission to Mongol alterity. Instead, it implicates an area of cultural common ground shared by Christendom and the Mongol Empire: the prestige economy of long-distance knowledge. The *Itinerarium* points to the travails endured by William as evidence of the futility of engaging the Great Khan through conventional diplomatic appeals to exoticism. William suggests that such efforts have not only failed to contain the threat of Mongol expansion but have also created an environment in which preaching has been rendered all but useless as a tool for negotiating cultural and confessional difference.

As a Franciscan, William of Rubruck had taken a vow of poverty that barred him from full participation in the prestige economy of long-distance knowledge, which, throughout the medieval world, was inextricably bound to the exercise of temporal power and the traffic in luxury goods. Farfetched animals, rare gems, and foreign handicrafts were among the commodities most commonly exchanged within courtly and diplomatic settings. Like many politically symbolic gifts, these objects were "luxuries" valued for their scarcity, craftsmanship, beauty, utility, or ownership history; however, they can also be considered "exotic" luxuries because a significant part of their value derived from their distant origins—and, more specifically, from the effort expended in conveying them to the places where they changed hands.[19] Spices were one of the more widely diffused exotic luxuries in medieval Europe. In the Middle Ages, the high prices commanded for pepper, cinnamon, and aloe wood were propped up by fanciful accounts of the perils involved in harvesting them in the East and transporting them to their point of consumption in the West.[20] In contrast to their Marxian counterparts, then, the commodities that circulate within the prestige economy of long-distance knowledge do anything *but* conceal the truth of structural inequality; on the contrary, their exchange makes a spectacle of the alienation of labor.[21]

This is one reason why the ceremonial presentation of distantly fetched gifts became a standard gesture of political submission in "tributary economies" throughout the premodern world.[22] The exotic aesthetics that were so carefully cultivated at the courts of medieval rulers were grounded in the logic of microcosm. The ruler constitutes a cosmic center, an "unmoved mover," whose majesty pulls the world's diversity into his or her orbit. The distance traveled by an exotic object to that center is an index of the ruler's wealth and power. The greater the number of distant places represented by such objects, the better.

In fact, in the cosmopolitan courts of medieval Europe, Asia, and Africa, even *people* entered into the prestige economy of long-distance knowledge as so many reifications of the labor involved in overcoming the geographical distance between the sovereign center and points outside. A few examples will suffice to illustrate the prevalence of this cultural logic in different medieval settings. Take, for instance, Murasaki Shikibu's description of fictional festivities at the court of the Japanese emperor, from her eleventh-century epic *The Tale of Genji*: "The entire court accompanied His Majesty on the progress itself, as did the Heir Apparent. The musicians' barges rowed around the lake, as always, and there were all sorts of dances from Koma [Korea] and Cathay [northern China]."[23] Iberian traveler Benjamin of Tudela, writing in Hebrew roughly a century later, describes a procession orchestrated by the caliph of Baghdad in this way: "He is accompanied by all the nobles of Islam dressed in fine garments and riding on horses, the princes of Arabia, the princes of Togarma and Daylam (Gilan), and the princes of Persia, Media and Ghuzz, and the princes of the land of Tibet, which is three months' journey distant."[24] "The Story of Jullanar and the Sea"—included in the oldest extant manuscript of the *1001 Nights* (early fourteenth century)—opens with the description of a former king of Persia whose vast wealth and power is measured by his ability to collect con-

cubines from every known corner of the world.[25] Petrarch lauded his patron Robert I of Anjou, the king of Naples, as a ruler whose magnificence
was shown by the fact that, much like a Roman emperor, he ruled over
"multi-lingual and multi-customed people (*dissonantes lingua et moribus
populi*)."[26]

These economic and political frameworks help explain why the prestige economy of long-distance knowledge was at once an opportunity and
an obstacle for William of Rubruck. In agreeing to deliver Louis's letter of
friendship to Sartach, William unwittingly guaranteed that his words and
actions would be evaluated according to the protocols of international diplomacy. Despite his repeated protestations to the contrary, William is treated
as though he were the king's official representative. As a consequence of
this misconception, William had to renounce what appears to have been
his original plan—to minister to Christian captives at the western edge of
the Mongol Empire—in favor of a much more physically demanding itinerary. Sartach—perceiving the potentially treasonous odor of arrogating to
himself the sovereign's prerogative to receive the representative of a foreign
ruler—sends William higher up the Mongol hierarchy, to his father, Batu.
The same logic impels Batu to pack William off to Caracorum, in order to
confer with *his* superior, Möngke Khan.[27]

In addition to being rerouted roughly two thousand miles eastward in
the blistering cold of winter, William was perpetually inconvenienced by
the expectation that he came bearing exotic valuables. Having heard reports
of previous friars' journeys to the Mongol Empire, William knew enough
to try to manage his hosts' expectations regarding gifts.[28] In 1246, John of
Plano Carpini stated that "so many gifts were bestowed by the envoys" to
the Mongol ruler "that it was marvelous to behold." These gifts included
"silk, samite, velvet . . . girdles of silk threaded with gold . . . [and] camels
decked with brocade and with saddles on them having some kind of contriv-
ance on which men could sit."[29] Though armed with such foreknowledge,
William probably did not anticipate the prospect of offering the Great Khan
a basket of fruit after diplomats from India had presented the Mongol ruler
with "eight leopards and ten greyhounds trained to sit on the back of a leopard like a horse."[30] In an effort to extricate himself from the materialistic
expectations of international diplomacy, William continually insists that,
even though he carries letters written by Louis, he cannot give rich gifts because has not been vested with the wealth and authority of a royal representative: "I took care never to say I was your ambassador (*nuncium*)."[31] This
legalistic distinction recalls the kinds of arguments that were waged during
the contemporaneous *Usus pauper* controversy, in which the Franciscan

Order sought to define the acceptable parameters for "using" property that the friars were prohibited from "owning"—such as land, clothing, money, and books.[32]

Unfortunately, most of the Mongol officials William encounters have no time for such scholastic subtleties. From the moment the travelers cross over into Mongol territory, they are importuned for gifts (and for their unofficial counterpart: bribes). Border guards demand the "knives, gloves, purses, and belts" of William's servants and decry him as a fraud (*baratator*) when he declines their request.[33] The Franciscan vow of poverty also prevents William from *receiving* luxury gifts from his hosts, which also proves problematic. As he prepares for his departure from Möngke's court, William feels obliged to make a parting concession to the Great Khan's magnanimity:

> The scribes were holding three garments or tunics and they said to us: "You do not wish to receive gold or silver and you have been here a long time praying for the Khan; he begs you at least to accept each one of you, a simple tunic, so that you may not leave him empty-handed." We then had to accept them out of respect to him, for they take it ill when their gifts are disdained.[34]

(The *Itinerarium* hastens to add that William ordered his servant to sell these gifts and distribute the proceeds to the poor.)

On account of their poverty, William, his Franciscan traveling companion, and their servant suffer the derision and neglect of their hosts. The guide who conveys them across the frozen steppes to Caracorum "had the greatest disdain for us, and felt disgusted at having to conduct such insignificant men."[35] At one point, William's guides defecate in his presence without distancing themselves "so far as one can toss a bean" (and without even ceasing to converse with one another while heeding the call of nature).[36] The food rations were so meager during the trek across central Asia that William's companion repeatedly became "so hungry that he would say . . . almost in tears 'It seems to me as if I have never had anything to eat.'"[37] A lack of basic provisions continued to plague the travelers, even after they arrived in Caracorum, where they had to weather arctic temperatures without sufficient food, fuel, or blankets. At one point, Möngke supplies William's company of three with "one thin little ram," meant to sustain them for six days. Out of compassion, the travelers share this meager repast with "many starving people." Of this experience, William states: "There I experienced how great a martyrdom it is to bestow bounty in one's poverty."[38]

The distance that William of Rubruck strikes from the materialism of courtly culture has an obvious precedent in Francis of Assisi's visit to Sultan Al-Kamil of Egypt (1180–1238). In the account found in Bonaventure's *Legenda maior* (ca. 1260), Francis and his companion Illuminatus cross crusading battle lines in order to speak with Al-Kamil about matters of faith.[39] The sultan, impressed by what he hears, invites Francis to dwell permanently at his court. Francis consents, on the condition that Al-Kamil and his subjects renounce Islam. Naturally, this proposal is met with less than enthusiastic support from the court's Muslim scholars. Undaunted, Francis challenges the Islamic clerics to an ordeal by fire, in order to settle the question of whose religion is the authentic one. The sultan—fearing civil unrest—squelches the incendiary challenge. As a consolation prize, the ruler offers Francis generous alms to be used for charity work and church building. Francis, however, declines "because he was accustomed to flee the burden of money and did not see a root of true piety in the Sultan's soul."[40]

This episode suggests that the Franciscan mandate to reform and universalize Christianity is structurally incompatible with the prestige economy of long-distance knowledge. In his fresco *The Trial by Fire* (also known as *Proof of Fire before the Sultan*), Giotto put a finer point on the crux of this impasse. The painting depicts the sultan ensconced above and behind a fire that separates the austerely clad Francis (who, it should be recalled, was the son of a silk merchant) from an extravagantly frocked group of multiethnic Muslim clerics (fig. 1). Giotto suggests a causal relationship between the overvaluation of courtly luxury on the one hand and stubborn adherence to doctrinal "error" on the other. This link is embodied in the bearded figure on the left, who—stalking away from the confrontation—uses the luxuriant folds of his robe to stop his ears against Francis's discourse. Giotto's painting and the vignette on which it is based associate courtly exoticism with the sovereign's self-serving cultivation of ethnic and religious pluralism. These same positions animate the *Itinerarium*'s fine-grained depiction of William's travails, which are treated as the outcome of his steadfast rejection of the norms that lubricate cross-cultural exchange throughout the medieval world.

That said, the precedent furnished by Francis of Assisi's exchange with Al-Kamil was not entirely restrictive. In fact, it authorized William of Rubruck and other Franciscan visitors to foreign courts to engage in acts of tactical self-exoticization. On the occasion of their first audience with Möngke Khan, William and his companion enter the imperial court chanting a hymn in celebration of the Nativity. Though liturgical chant was a standard expression of piety for William and other Franciscan travelers to Asia, the unfamiliar beauty of polyphony was also something that could potentially

Figure 1. Giotto (di Bondone), *Proof of Fire before the Sultan* (1325). Fresco.
Cappella Bardi, Santa Croce, Firenze. (Photograph: Scala / Art Resource, New York.)

elevate the stature of the friar and his religion in the wonder-struck eyes of
foreign hosts. In letters dispatched from Khanbaliq in 1305–6, Franciscan
missionary John of Montecorvino reports having purchased forty boy slaves,
whom he has converted to Christianity and trained as a choir. According
to John, the boys' vocal performances outside the palace of the Great Khan
caused great "wonder" (*mirabile*) among the citizens of Khanbaliq and gar-
nered imperial sponsorship for the church that the Franciscan had recently
founded in the city.[41]

The *Itinerarium* suggests that William and his companion knowingly
played up the exoticism of their liturgical performance by manipulating
their appearance. Just before their first audience with Möngke, the two
Franciscans shave their beards "according to the fashion of our native land."
This last-minute grooming is intended to call attention to their strangeness,
and—by extension—to the travail that they have endured in traversing the
distance that separates their homes from the Great Khan's court. Appearing
to flatter Möngke while actually praising God, William emphasizes the laborious nature of the journey that has brought him into the ruler's presence:
"We have come a long way (*de longe*); first, if it please you, we will sing

praises to God, who has brought us safely from such a long distance away as far as here (*de tam longinquo usque huc perduxit*)."[42]

Unfortunately, these self-exoticizing gestures do not produce their desired effect. The Franciscans' clean shave initially leads Möngke's guards to mistake them for a far more common sight: *tuins*, or Buddhist monks. This episode and others like it illustrate that William cannot necessarily control the spirit in which his tactical exoticism is received. In fact, the bellicose conclusion of the *Itinerarium* is best understood as the outcome of several frustrated attempts on the part of William to turn the prestige economy of long-distance knowledge to his pastoral advantage. The surprising call to arms that concludes his travel narrative grows out of a sustained analysis of the cultural logic of exoticism.

TACTICAL EXOTICISM AND THE PROBLEM OF THE SACRED

As one of the growing number of Franciscans who were also ordained priests, William of Rubruck's views on the psychology and sociology of courtly exoticism were influenced by theological discussions of wonder. The objects that fed the premodern appetite for the wondrous were various: the eclectic collections of cathedral treasuries and Renaissance *Wunderkammern*, monstrous births and meteorological omens, and the ornate costumes and special effects of courtly spectacle, to name just a few examples.[43] One of the most common medieval Latin words for *wonder* is *admiratio*, a concept that encompassed an equally diverse range of affective responses, including stupefaction, terror, puzzlement, titillation, disbelief, reverence, and morbid curiosity.[44] As Caroline Bynum has shown, theologians developed a concept of sacred *admiratio*, which introduced a principle of nonappropriation into medieval economies of wonder. Bynum argues that the dictum that the lives of martyrs should be "admired but not imitated" was born of the same impulse that viewed the miracle of transubstantiation as a marvel whose terrifying sublimity made it qualitatively distinct from other object-causes of wonder. In both cases, it would be reckless and prideful to attempt to domesticate the sacred or to appropriate it to oneself.[45]

The theological delineation of sacred *admiratio* was closely related to the development of a theoretical distinction between two object-causes of wonder: the *marvel* and the *miracle*.[46] The wonder experienced in the presence of the marvel was widely depicted as subjective in origin, usually the product of the viewer's ignorance about the existence, origins, or underlying

causes of the marvelous object. Marvels included natural phenomena—such
as the magnetic properties of the lodestone—as well as man-made artifacts
such as automata. In many cases, the ignorance of the wondering subject
was a function of the geographical distance that separated the beholder from
the places where the marvel was found with greater frequency. The spatially
determined nature of many marvelous phenomena was apparent to medieval travel writers, who self-consciously recorded their astonishment when
they discovered variations on otherwise banal sights. Marco Polo rhapso-
dized about the variety and beauty of China's chickens.[47] In Damascus,
Thietmar was wonder-struck to find ordinary violets blooming in winter.[48]
By contrast, the wonder experienced in an encounter with the miraculous
was not the product of geographical accident or some other trick of perspective. The miracle was a divinely authored suspension of nature's laws—a
testament to God's omnipotence. It engendered wonder by virtue of the
majesty of its origins, and it did so regardless of where in the world it happened to occur (and was, perhaps, more marveled at the *closer* it occurred
to the viewer's home).

Repeatedly, William of Rubruck strives to stir his hosts to sacred *admiratio*, only to discover—time and again—that he and his teachings are
received with what appears to be an undignified mixture of cultural relativism and politico-economic calculation. The liturgical books and instruments that William uses in his missionary activities are the catalyst for
many of these disappointments. These problems start early on, when William stages a liturgical procession at Sartach's court. The *Itinerarium* takes
palpable delight in the theatricality of the occasion, lavishing uncharacter-
istic attention on the richness of the objects that surround William and his
companion:

> Wearing the most precious vestments, I held before my breast a very
> lovely cushion, the Bible that you gave me, and the most beautiful psal-
> ter presented to me by Her Majesty the Queen, in which there were
> some fine illuminations. . . . Then, we went in singing the "Salve Re-
> gina." There was a bench standing near the entrance with cosmos and
> some cups on it, and all his wives had assembled, and the Mongols com-
> ing in with us thronged about us. Coiac took Sartach the thurible with
> some incense and this he examined carefully, holding it in his hand.
> Next he handed him the psalter, which he had a good look at, as did the
> wife who was sitting next to him; then he took the Bible. Sartach en-
> quired if the Gospel were included. I replied, "Yes indeed, the whole of
> Holy Scripture."[49]

The emphasis on the splendor of William's "props" is, on the one hand, an acknowledgment of the generosity of his royal donors. On the other hand, the pride taken in the material and craftsmanship of the objects is justified by the assumption that their splendor will dazzle William's non-Christian spectators, making them more receptive to the truth claims of the Roman church.

As this exchange makes clear, the danger of using "exotic" objects to promote the universalizing truths of Christianity is that William cannot prevent his interlocutors from valuing them solely on account of their novelty, beauty, and exchange value. Sartach appears to inspect the thurible and gilded manuscripts with a disappointing mixture of aestheticism and anthropological detachment. In asking if William's Bible contains the Gospels, Sartach seeks to classify his visitors: to which of the many sects known to the Mongols do these strange newcomers belong? William answers the relativistic spirit of this question with the universalizing assertion that his version of the Bible is the *only* true version, containing not just the Gospels but also *every other* text that has any right to be considered sacred.

The disappointing denouement of this liturgical performance alerted William to the potential pitfalls of ecclesiastical exoticism, an issue that preoccupied many medieval writers. Throughout the Middle Ages, mummified crocodiles, nautilus shells, ostrich eggs, and "dragon" bones (usually whales' ribs) sat in monastic and cathedral treasuries alongside consecrated liturgical instruments and the relics of saints.[50] The didactic use of such objects was widespread, but even proponents of such pedagogical methods felt the need to rationalize them. In his *Moral Treatise on the Eye* (ca. 1274–89), Peter of Limoges defended those who hung ostrich eggs in their churches, on the grounds that these decorative objects would remind prelates to serve their congregations well and not to "imitate the ostrich in its neglect of its young."[51] Durandus of Mende offered a completely different rationale for the same practice, claiming that, because ostrich eggs are "seldom seen," they "will cause admiration" and "attract the people to the church to touch them."[52] Hugh of Saint-Victor, meanwhile, found no redeeming justification for clerics who kept pet apes in order to inspire awe in the laity.[53] Though a knight, Arnold von Harff also had strong opinions about clerical appeals to the exotic, which he felt were too often used to cheat gullible pilgrims. Von Harff arrived at this conviction through experience; his eastern travels taught him what a crocodile looked like, and—by extension—that the "dragon" he had been shown in a Roman church was actually one of them.[54]

The aftermath of William's audience with Sartach suggests that the problems inherent in ecclesiastical exoticism are greatly magnified in multiconfessional contexts. The illuminated manuscripts and liturgical instruments that William brandished during his procession attract the unwelcome attention of a Nestorian official named Coiac:

> We . . . [had loaded] one cart with the books and the things for Mass (*capella*) and another [cart] with bread, wine, and fruit. Then [Coiac] had all the books and vestments spread out, and a crowd of Tartars, Christians, and Saracens on horseback surrounded us. Coiac examined these things, then asked if I would not give them all to his lord. On hearing this I was terrified (*expavi*). I did not like his words; but, putting a good face on it, I replied: "Sir, we beg that your master will be so good as to receive this bread, wine, and fruit, not indeed as a gift, for it is little enough, but as a blessing, so that we may not come into his presence empty-handed. . . . The vestments, however, are blessed (*sacrate*) and it is not lawful (*non licet*) for any but priests to touch them." He then bade us to put them on to appear before his master, which we did.[55]

Though William prevails on this occasion, he is unpleasantly surprised later on, when Coiac's brother refuses to send the books and vestments along with him to the *orda* (i.e., mobile encampment) of Batu: "You brought these to Sartach, now you want to take them to Batu. . . . Don't talk so much and be off with you!" Disappointed, William recalls: "I had one consolation and that was when I became aware of their covetousness I removed from among the books the Bible and the Sentences and the other books I was particularly fond of. Her Majesty the Queen's psalter I did not dare to take, as it had attracted too much notice on account of the gold illuminations in it."[56]

The standoff between William and the servants of Sartach is a clash between two competing regimes of value. When Coiac looks at the tokens of benediction that William intends to give to Sartach, he sees groceries. To Coiac, the glittering manuscripts and liturgical instruments are a more fitting tribute to his master. William, meanwhile, is scandalized by this suggestion. The Franciscan attempts to reframe his presentation of the "bread, wine, and fruit" by clarifying what he means to communicate in giving them to the Mongol baron. The trick is to get Coiac to view these common household items through an unfamiliar interpretive framework, so that they are no longer deemed insulting trifles. Moreover, William tries to bring his interlocutor around to the view that, even though his books and ritual instruments look like the kind of rich, exotic gifts normally given to

Mongol rulers by foreign guests, they are actually a special class of object whose economic exchange is categorically prohibited everywhere in the world. That this prohibition extends even to touching the objects suggests that the panic experienced by William on this occasion is rooted in the most particular and least negotiable of cultural phenomena: taboo.

Within a given cultural field, sacred objects are distinguished from the generality of things by the norms that restrict the manner in which they can be accessed, displayed, and transferred from one party to another.[57] As a priest (sacerdos), William of Rubruck represents a class of social actors charged with policing the boundary between sacred objects and ordinary commodities. (By contrast, Marco Polo, like merchants in many other historical societies, represents the impulse to set an ever-greater number of objects into economic circulation, including forbidden ones.)[58] In sorting his effects into two different carts, William literalizes the distinction between the nonsacred and the sacred (sacrate). As etymology would suggest, things that are sacrate are, by force of interdict, "set apart" as untouchable and/or unappropriatable.[59]

The objects that comprise what William calls his capella—which include the chalice, paten, and possibly a portable altar—are the ones he is most anxious to shield from grasping hands. Before they could be used in the consecration of the host, such instruments themselves had to be sanctified through the ritual of consecration.[60] In theory, consecration removes objects from the commercial and gift economies in which they are normally manufactured and exchanged—and in which objects that look just like them continue to be produced and traded on a routine basis. The taboo that forbade the laity's access to consecrated objects was an extension of the prohibition against their commodification. Aquinas conveys something of the force of this prohibition when, citing the Council of Nicea, he writes that "the beams of a dedicated church" ought to be burned, rather than reused, once they are replaced with new ones. He adds:

> On no account are [the old beams] to be discarded for the works of the laity. We read there, too, that "the altar covering, chair, candlesticks, and veil are to be burned when worn out; and their ashes are to be placed in the baptistry, or in the walls, or else beneath the flag-stones, *so as not to be defiled by the feet of those that enter.*"[61]

Due to their physical proximity to the altar where the flesh and blood of Christ are consumed, liturgical vessels, the cloths that they touch, and sometimes even the timber that shields them all from the elements mark the boundary between the divine and the human, the priesthood and the laity, the sacred and the profane. For William of Rubruck, to surrender the *capella* up to the prestige economy of long-distance knowledge is to approach the undoing of his world—and even his fundamental sense of self.

The gilded manuscripts, vestments, and *capella* are the first of several metallurgical artifacts that occasion anxious ruminations on the part of the *Itinerarium*. Such episodes highlight the structural tension between the avidity, eclecticism, and aestheticism of the prestige economy of long-distance knowledge on the one hand and—on the other—the missionary's insistence on the exclusive truth of his teachings. Though popular imagination reductively associates the Mongol Empire with conquest, plunder, and smashing stuff, its rulers were enthusiastic patrons of the arts.[62] Mongol elites displayed a particular fondness for skilled metalwork, and—in the thirteenth century—began relocating artisans from conquered territories to Caracorum.[63] The *Itinerarium* speaks at length about William's interactions with one such figure, the Parisian-born goldsmith Guillaume Boucher, who enjoyed a favorable position at the court of Möngke.[64] The Mongol mania for metallurgy impressed itself on William the closer he came to the court of the Great Khan, as did his sense of the pointlessness of his attempts to capitalize on that enthusiasm as a missionary.

During his stay in Caracorum, William of Rubruck gains access to members of the imperial family by latching on to the more established Nestorian and Armenian clerics who routinely visit them. The influence of the eastern Christians is bolstered by their possession of a miracle-working silver cross, brought to Caracorum from the distant, sacred center of Jerusalem. The *Itinerarium*'s circumspect description of the object reflects the uneasy character of William's alliance with these members of competing Christian sects. As described by William, the design of the cross embodies heterodox eastern beliefs about the Incarnation:

> This cross had been brought by a certain Armenian who had come with the monk, so he said, from Jerusalem and it was of silver weighing some four marks, and had four precious stones in the angles and one in the middle but it had no figure of the Savior, for the Armenians and Nestorians are ashamed to see Christ nailed to the cross. [65]

William is further scandalized by the arrogance of a particular Nestorian monk, who exploits the mystique of the silver cross to cement his status as a favorite at court. William accompanies the suspect monk on a visit to Möngke's second wife, Cota, who has been stricken with a life-threatening disease. The Nestorian monk has vowed to heal her with the help of the miraculous cross:

> The monk made her get up from the couch and adore the cross, kneeling down three times and touching her forehead to the ground, and he stood with the cross on the west side of the dwelling and she was on the east. This done they changed places and the monk went with the cross to the east side, she to the west; then, although she was so weak she could hardly stand on her feet, he insolently ordered her to prostrate again and adore the cross three times toward the east according to the Christian custom, and she did so. [66]

When Cota's illness worsens, the Great Khan threatens the monk with decapitation. William, sensing an opportunity, offers to assist the harried Nestorian. Upon entering Cota's chamber a second time, however, William is horrified to discover metal objects arrayed about the room in ways that suggest necromancy. The *Itinerarium* places the blame for this shocking spectacle on his Nestorian and Armenian counterparts, who—in their pursuit of influence and financial gain—have

> never instructed [Cota] in the faith nor advised her to be baptized. I, for my part, sat there speechless, unable to say a word, though she did go on teaching me the language. Nor do the priests rebuke [the Mongols] for any kind of sorcery, for there I saw four swords drawn halfway out of their sheaths, one at the head of the lady's couch, and another at the foot, and the other two on each side of the doorway. I also saw a silver chalice such as we use, which had perhaps been taken or stolen from a church in Hungary, and it was hung up on the wall full of ashes and on top of the ashes was a black stone, and the priests never teach them that such things are evil. [67]

Although William and Cota cannot understand each other, the Franciscan nevertheless consents to read the Latin account of the crucifixion from the gospel of John over the sickbed of the ailing woman. And there William finds himself: intoning unintelligible words about the death of Christ—an event deliberately not represented on the Nestorian cross—just one more medicine man among so many other brandishers of magic swords, purloined chalices, and exotic nostrums.

Such weary realizations suffuse the *Itinerarium*. William is palpably disappointed by his participation in a public disputation, in which he and the Nestorians enter into debate with Muslims and Buddhists. The event—staged as a courtly entertainment—proves frustratingly inconclusive.[68] More disturbing still are the legions of long-distance flatterers who flock annually from all corners of the world to pay ceremonial homage to the Great Khan's drinking chalice, during celebrations of his birthday and the New Year. While studying such festivities, William realizes that—from the perspective of Möngke—a Franciscan visitor is interchangeable with any of the other farfetched figures who travel from afar to pay tribute to the ruler:

> On that day [i.e., the Latin Christian Feast of the Epiphany], [Möngke] Khan had made a great feast; and it is his custom to hold court on such days as his soothsayers tell him are feast days or that the Nestorian priests say are for some reason sacred. Christian priests come first with their paraphernalia, and they pray for him and bless his cup; when they retire the Saracen priests come and do likewise; they are followed by pagan priests who do the same. [One] monk told me that the Khan only believes in the Christians; however, he wishes them all to come and pray for him. But he was lying, for he does not believe in any of them as you will hear later; yet they all follow his court like flies honey; and he gives to them all and they all think they enjoy his special favor and they all prophesy good fortune for him.[69]

The "I" that anchors William's narrative is one that speaks from a position of defiant marginality vis-à-vis the marvel-loving Mongol court, one that registers a resistance to the exoticizing appropriation of his person, his religion, and the travail of his travels. The *Itinerarium*'s call to crusade is founded on the conviction that the efforts of the missionary will inevitably be co-opted by the political and epicurean orientation of the prestige economy of long-distance knowledge. Readers of Marco Polo and Rustichello da Pisa's *Divisament dou monde* would, meanwhile, search in vain for anything resembling the pearl-clutching polemic of the *Itinerarium*. Whereas William of Rubruck monitors the exchange of commodities and ideas in order to assess their doctrinal orthodoxy, Polo and Rustichello shrug off such concerns and celebrate the prestige economy of long-distance knowledge as an object of wonder in its own right.

THE WONDER OF IMPERIAL WONDER

The *Divisament dou monde* of Marco Polo and Rustichello da Pisa dates from around 1298, and was probably first composed in a dialect of French known as Franco-Italian.[70] Polo and Rustichello—an author otherwise known for his Arthurian prose epics—collaborated on the *Divisament* while both were being held as prisoners of war in Genoa. The *Divisament* claims that its observations about the realm of Khubilai Khan (ruled 1260–94) originate in the firsthand experience of Polo and his two traveling companions: Marco's father, Nicolò, and his uncle Maffeo. In the 1260s, the elder Polos traveled eastward from Crimea to the court of Khubilai, in order to trade in precious stones. They returned to the Great Khan's lands in the early 1270s, this time with young Marco in tow. Traveling via Jerusalem—where, at the request of Khubilai, they obtained oil from the lamps that lit the Holy Sepulcher—the Polo family reached the Great Khan's vacation capital of Shangdu in 1274. The Venetian merchants lived in East Asia for approximately seventeen years. According to the *Divisament*, the Polos were a regular fixture at Khubilai's court, with young Marco becoming the ruler's most trusted foreign ambassador, and purportedly—though less likely—a provincial governor. The Polo family undertook the return voyage to Venice in the early 1290s, arriving around 1295.[71]

The *Divisament* achieved instant popularity among courtly, clerical, and bourgeois readers and became one of the most widely read works of travel writing in the Middle Ages. It survives in approximately 135 manuscripts. Within a couple of decades of its publication, the work was translated into Venetian, Tuscan, Continental French, and Latin. Many translators and copyists made radical revisions to the text. In Italian, the work circulated under the title *Il milione*, and in French it was known by names such as *The Book of the Great Khan* and *The Romance of the Great Khan*.[72] If the number of extant copies is any indication, the most popular medieval version of the work was a Latin translation rendered from the Venetian by Dominican friar Francesco Pipino. It was Pipino's moralizing version of Polo's travels that Christopher Columbus studied in preparation for his westward journey to Asia; the conquistador's personally annotated copy of the printed text is held in the library of Seville's Institución Colombina.[73]

By any measure, the *Divisament* was a novel work for its time. Its descriptions of East Asia and the reign of Khubilai Khan were, in themselves, marvelous and unprecedented. Moreover, the *Divisament* sought a socially mixed, geographically wide-ranging reading public, which it addressed in

the vernacular. Circa 1300, Latin, Arabic, and Hebrew were still the preferred languages for travel and geographical writing throughout Latin Christian Europe, a fact that reflects the predominantly scholarly and clerical
audiences for which such works were destined. Even geographies and travel
accounts designed for lay readers—such as Al-Idrisi's *Kitab Rujar* (Roger's
book), Gervase of Tilbury's *Otia imperialia*, and William of Rubruck's
Itinerarium—were far more likely to be written in Latin (or even Arabic)
than in the vernacular. A work like Brunetto Latini's thirteenth-century
Livres dou Trésor translated geographical knowledge and other learned topics for the benefit of a Francophone public, but did so in a way that fore-
grounded its basis in Latinate learning. Occasional references to biblical
history and the romances of Alexander the Great aside, the *Divisament*
strikes a conspicuous distance from classical texts and anything resembling
scholarly or theological authority.

This circumvention of Latinity is consistent with its authors' efforts to
extend the prestige economy of long-distance knowledge beyond its customary enclaves. This gambit relied on two unconventional propositions:
the *popularization* of long-distance knowledge in the form of a vernacular
travel book and the *maximal transferability* of the prestige of the long-
distance specialist, achieved through the technology of the manuscript codex. This agenda is hinted at in the famous opening of the *Divisament*,
which repurposed turns of phrase from Rustichello's Arthurian fiction:

> Lord emperors and kings, dukes and marquises, counts, knights, and bur-
> gesses, and all people who want to know about the diverse races (*jenera-
> sions*) of men and the diverse wonders (*deversités*) of diverse regions of
> the world, take this book and have it read. And here you will find all of
> the greatest marvels and the great wonders of Great Armenia and of Per-
> sia and of the Tartars and of India, and many other regions, as recounted
> by Master Marco Polo, wise and noble citizen of Venice.[74]

In order to succeed in their project, Polo and Rustichello had to educate—
and thereby *constitute*—their readership in the act of addressing it.

The indoctrination of the *Divisament*'s audience was effected through
the very rhetorical and stylistic tendencies that many modern readers of
the work have found off-putting. Collectively, the work's inconsistent use
of pronouns, its repetition of oral-formulaic refrains, and its privileging of
impersonal description over experientially centered narrative work to dis-
place the figure of Marco Polo as the cynosure of the travel account. Polo is,
in fact, doubly decentered in the text that preserves the memory of his jour-

ney: eclipsed both by his literary collaborator and—more important—by his Mongol patron.

The authority—and perhaps even the cultural intelligibility—of the *Divisament* hinges on its treatment of Khubilai Khan. Presiding over the richest, most sprawling empire the world had ever known, Khubilai is also an unrivaled connoisseur of exotic knowledge. In choosing Marco Polo as his preferred long-distance specialist, the figure of the Great Khan underwrites the prestige value of Polo and Rustichello's book. At the same time, the Mongol ruler serves an important didactic function, as a normative model for the *Divisament*'s ideal readership, which had to be taught how to take pleasure in travel writing, in a manner befitting a king.

It is clear that, in contrast to William's *Itinerarium*, the *Divisament* happily conflates political and cultural authority in the figure of the Mongol emperor. Khubilai is presented as an unrivaled connoisseur of the exotic, whose discerning tastes are, moreover, the consequence of his unrivaled wealth and power. If one line sums up the *Divisament*'s view on this issue, it is: "There never was, nor do I think there is, any man capable of taking such great pleasure (*si grant seulas*) nor such great delight (*si grant delit*) in all of the world as this man does, nor any who has the power to do it."[75] The imperial household in Khanbaliq bears out this point. A treasure-house of exotica, Khubilai's palace gathers into itself a kaleidoscopic collection of fish, birds, and beasts. It even boasts a man-made mountain covered in lapis lazuli, a structure that is used to display the most grandiose—and most nakedly symbolic—of the Great Khan's collections:

> And I tell you that the great lord, whenever anyone tells him about the existence of a beautiful tree, has it taken with all of its roots and much of earth and he has it carried to that mountain by elephants . . . no matter how large the tree is . . . and in this manner he obtains the most beautiful trees in the world.[76]

Once deeply rooted in Khubilai's subject territories, the trees in his garden form a microcosm of his dominion and testify to the triumph of imperial will over geographical distance. By underscoring the incalculable wealth and labor-power that underpins Khubilai's acquisition of these and other wonders, the *Divisament* presents Marco's ability to sate imperial appetite for the exotic as a marvel in itself.

Indeed, the superlative nature of traveler and emperor reflect and reinforce each other, serving as twin bases for the *Divisament*'s bid for credibility and cultural capital. This seems, in any event, to be the point that the opening chapters of the *Divisament* set out to prove. These chapters, which provide the work's most sustained account of the Polo family's experiences, culminate in the courtly, sentimental tale of Marco's coming-of-age. Having left the familiar realities of Venice behind, young Marco applies himself to the study of Asian languages while helping his elders with the family business. One day, Khubilai Khan summons the Venetian youth to his court and entrusts him with a diplomatic errand. Like an enterprising merchant, Marco embarks on this assignment having already identified an unmet demand. As it turns out, Khubilai is bored to tears by the postembassy debriefings delivered by his most experienced ambassadors:

> They were not able to describe to him (*no li savoient dir*) the wonders (*noveles*) of the countries where they had been, and Khubilai called them fools and unlearned (*foux et non saiçhan[ç]*), and added that he would rather have heard about the wonders and customs and the usages of that strange land than to hear a report about the matter for which he had sent them. And whenever he went on a messenger's errand abroad, Marco, who knew this well, would always fix his concentration (*met[t]toit son entent*) on all of the wonders (*nuvités*) and all of the strange things he would see in order to recount them to the Great Khan.[77]

Marco thus makes certain to return from his first assignment with an abundant stock of thrilling anecdotes. The *Divisament* trumpets his success as a rite of passage: "After this journey, the youth was referred to as Master Marco Polo, and so this book will refer to him from now on." As a result of his skill as a long-distance specialist, Polo is sent on numerous other diplomatic errands, and thereby comes to visit "more of those strange zones than any other man ever born."[78]

The account of Polo's rise to prominence at the Mongol court signals the *Divisament*'s unique conceptions of travel and long-distance specialism. While the accounts of exotic travel writers such as John of Plano Carpini, William of Rubruck, and Odoric of Pordenone tend to equate heroism in travel with overcoming physical travail, the *Divisament* depicts travel as an art involving intellectual self-discipline. There is an oblique suggestion of somatic self-regulation in the discussion of Polo's diplomatic errands; this implied bodily discipline serves the needs of the intellectual labor that distinguishes Marco from his competitors. Only by regulating the tempo and quotidian habits of his journeys can Marco investigate and commit to memory the exotic marvels with which he will later delight his master.

The phrase used to talk about the mental effort that Polo exerts during his marvel-hunting campaigns—*met[t]toit son entent*—may originate in the mnemonic theory of the language arts classroom, and suggests the *Divisament*'s possible debt to clerical traditions of travel writing on the Holy Land (see chapter 3).

Equally striking, unlike the works of most Franciscan travelers, the *Divisament* does not justify long-distance specialism in terms of its practical applications. When the chronically underwhelmed Khubilai Khan derides his ambassadorial corps for their dry, business-oriented accounts, he champions the same vision of nonutilitarian exoticism advanced by Polo and Rustichello's book. Khubilai's role as defender of this position is the primary reason why the *Divisament* treats him as "both the subject and the object of wonder"—to borrow Sharon Kinoshita's turn of phrase.[79] If, as the *object* of readers' wonder, Khubilai is the foundation of the work's claims to authority, as the *subject* of wonder, he serves as a model for aspirational readers. Polo and Rustichello encourage their audience to view their engagement with the *Divisament* as an opportunity to emulate the delight that the Great Khan once took in the singular talents of his preferred long-distance specialist.

The deliberate decentering of the Polo family's perspectives on Asia facilitates readerly identification with Khubilai. In a rather flamboyant fashion, the *Divisament*'s account of Nicolò and Maffeo's first journey alludes to the fact that they witnessed many astonishing things, only to then defer the task of describing them: "They discovered great marvels and wonders (*diverses coses*) that we will not tell you about here, because Master Marco, the son of Master Nicolò, also saw these things and he will tell you all about them later on in this book."[80] This deferral is immediately followed by an account of the elder Polos' first contact with the Great Khan. This arrival scene extends over two chapters. One is struck by the deliberateness with which the episode reserves the experience of wonder for the figure of Khubilai Khan:

VI. How the Two Brothers Came to the Great Khan
And when Masters Nicolò and Maffeo were come to the great lord, he received them honorably and met them with great joy and great celebration (*grant joie et gran feste*): he took great pleasure in their coming. He asks them about many things: first, about emperors, especially how they administered justice in their realms and their territories, and about how they went to battle, and about all of their deeds. And after he asked about kings and princes and the other barons.

VII. How the Great Khan Inquired of the Two Brothers about the
Condition of the Christians
And then he asked about the Pope (*meser l'apostoille*) and about the condition of the Roman Church and about the customs of the Latin Christian peoples. And Masters Nicolò and Maffeo told him the truth about
each topic, so well and orderly and wisely (*ordreemant et sajemant*), like
wise men, for they knew very well the Tartar tongue, which is called
"Tartaresce."[81]

The impressions of the brothers Polo—which one imagines were no less
wonder-struck—are decidedly passed over in these chapters. Instead, the
emphasis of this narrative is on how the merchants awed Khubilai with
their rhetorically light-footed deeds of long-distance specialism.

The same thing happens in the *Divisament*'s subsequent account of the
Polos' second journey. Here, the narrative seems disinterested *even in* young
Marco's first impressions of the dazzlingly unfamiliar world of the Mongol
Empire. In fact, readers gain no insight into how this momentous journey
might have affected the young Venetian; instead, they are promised that the
wonders witnessed by Marco Polo will be catalogued "later on in our book."[82]
When the *Divisament* finally makes good on this promise, it embeds its
descriptions of distant wonders within a series of abstract itineraries, and
only rarely does it focalize the marvels of Asia through Marco's perspective.
As a result of these decisions, Khubilai emerges as the figure that most frequently shares the experience of wonder with the audience of the *Divisament*. It is the Mongol emperor—rather than the European traveler—who
serves as the most consistent point of identification for readers of the work.

The *Divisament*'s centering of Khubilai's perspective at the expense of
Polo's also allows it to disregard the very dimensions of courtly exoticism
that unsettled William of Rubruck. This rhetorical advantage is particularly
apparent in two episodes, which both involve the Great Khan's efforts to
acquire sacred relics. According to the *Divisament*, in 1284, a group of Muslim pilgrims returning from the remote island kingdom of Seilan (Sri Lanka)
informed Khubilai about a mysterious mountaintop shrine located on top of
the "Peak of Adam" (Sri Pada). The pilgrims climbed this mountain in order
to venerate a footprint miraculously pressed into a slab of marble, one of
many relics supposedly left there by Adam following his exile from Eden.[83]
Intrigued by these reports, Khubilai dispatches an embassy to the king of
Seilan, to request some of the shrine's relics.

At this point, the story breaks off, giving way to a discussion of competing claims about the significance of the mountain shrine that has captured

Khubilai's imagination. According to the *Divisament*, "idolaters" also go on pilgrimage to the mountain, to honor not Adam but rather "Sagamoni Burcan"—a prince who once renounced royal luxury in favor of a life of solitude and meditation. The account of this prince-turned-ascetic is a garbled version of the life of Siddhārtha Gautama, who was, in Polo's day, already revered as a Christian saint thanks to the legend of Barlaam and Josaphat.[84] At first, the *Divisament* seems to contradict the Muslims' account, since—according to "Christian" doctrine—Adam was not laid to rest in Seilan but rather in "another part of the world."[85] However, Polo and Rustichello do not actually refute the Muslim position; they simply "do not maintain" that it is true. The waters are muddied further by Khubilai's apparent endorsement of the Muslim traditions surrounding the shrine. The emperor wants to obtain the shrine's relics because he believes they belong to "the world's first man."[86] Returning to its account of embassy to Seilan, the *Divisament* drops the unresolved question of the origins of the relics, in a way that suggests the ultimate insignificance of the controversy.

The anecdote of the embassy resumes with the king of Seilan declining Khubilai's request for the relics. The ambassadors of the Great Khan eventually succeed in overcoming the monarch's initial resistance with the promise of a massive financial payment. When news of this success reaches Khubilai in Khanbaliq, he mandates that members of all religious-ethnic groups participate in the ceremonial reception of the relics. And they do:

> Then the Great Khan commands all of the people / confessional groups (*jens*)—clerics and the laity—to go out and greet those relics, for they were given to understand that they once belonged to Adam. And why make a long tale of it? Know that all of the people / confessional groups of Khanbaliq go out to meet these relics; and the clergy received them and carried them to the Great Khan, who received them with great joy and great festivity and great reverence (*con grant joie e con grant feste e con grant reveren[c]e*).[87]

In the end, Khubilai Khan "resolves"—or, rather, *dissolves*—the theological disagreement surrounding the relics in an aestheticized display of sovereign power.

Many readers have judged the *Divisament*'s use of stock phrases such as "with great joy and great festivity and great reverence" as a stylistic vice. Translators—medieval and modern—have often purged these upwellings of chivalric exuberance from their renderings of the work.[88] However, here, and at other junctures in the *Divisament*, the work's apparently crude oral-formulaic machinery performs a sophisticated ideological function. In his Arthurian works, Rustichello uses the tag line "con grant joie e con grant feste" when recounting the reception of knights-errant into the homes of royal or noble hosts.[89] The *Divisament* deploys this same formula in the scenes in which the Great Khan extends his welcome to the Polos; its recurrence suggests a set of xenophilic structures of feeling so organic that they express themselves in the manner of a physiological reflex. By introducing this same stock phrase into its account of the disputed relics of Seilan, the *Divisament* scuttles the potentially troubling specter of interconfessional dispute, displacing the mutually exclusive claims of theology with a chivalric or courtly relativism that not only overcomes, but even relishes, religious division.

In another narrative sequence that would surely set William of Rubruck's teeth on edge, the *Divisament* extends this relativistic logic to a relic associated with Christ. When the elder Polos take leave of Khubilai at the end of their initial journey, the ruler asks them to return with a phial of the miraculous, self-igniting oil used to illuminate the Holy Sepulcher of Jerusalem.[90] Upon rearrival, the Polos—this time accompanied by Marco—present the Great Khan with the desired object: "Then, they give him the holy oil, about which he feels great joy and which he holds very dear (*il fist grant joie et le tient mout chier*)."[91] One can easily imagine the uneasy question that William would ask if he had read these pages from the *Divisament*: has this gift swayed the Mongol emperor toward accepting the truth claims of Christianity, or does he view the relic as just another curio in his self-aggrandizing collection? Polo and Rustichello never raise this question; in fact, they seem to foreclose it deliberately. The chivalric literary formula ensures that the emphasis of the entire episode is on the courtly spirit in which the ruler receives the farfetched token from his foreign visitors rather than the motives that prompted him to request it in the first place. This is typical of the way that the *Divisament* sidesteps thorny theological thickets by foregrounding elite, secular expressions of cosmopolitanism.

As has often been noted, many early translations of the *Divisament*—especially those executed within ecclesiastical and bourgeois circles—downplayed the work's orientation toward courtly culture. The degree of ideological coherence that the *Divisament* gains through its chivalric "trappings" is evidenced by the fact that translators who eradicated them had to find alternative ways to construct the authority of Marco Polo and his book. In 1320, Dominican friar Francesco Pipino translated a Venetian-language version of the *Divisament* into Latin. Pipino reduced the Venetian text's already attenuated descriptions of the Mongol court, downplayed the relationship between Polo and Khubilai, and eliminated any mention of Rustichello. In the absence of the aegis provided by Khubilai Khan, Pipino is moved to acknowledge that some of his readers might doubt Polo's claims because they contain "many things that are, to us, unheard of and unusual." Such uncertainties can nevertheless be laid aside, he argues, because Polo has a sterling reputation among his fellow Venetians. Pipino adds that Marco's claims were verified by the deathbed confession of his uncle, also a man of repute in Venice.[92] These authenticating gambits draw on legal-bureaucratic standards of proof used in the travel accounts of Franciscans John of Plano Carpini and Odoric of Pordenone (see chapter 2). In Pipino's translation, they serve as a substitute for the *Divisament*'s original bid for credibility, which was founded on its depiction of the cultural and political authority of Khubilai Khan.

"TAKE THIS BOOK": REIMAGINING LONG-DISTANCE SPECIALISM

Polo and Rustichello discerned in the medium of the book new possibilities for producing and disseminating the knowledge—and the prestige—of the long-distance specialist. *Take this book and have it read*. There is a popularizing, even evangelizing, tenor to this opening address. However, as the *Divisament*'s hierarchically ordered catalogue of ideal readers suggests, there was no room for lèse majesté in this democratizing agenda. Indeed, emperors and kings are accorded pride of place within the audience imagined by Polo and Rustichello, as the agency that confers value on the commodities that circulate within the prestige economy of long-distance knowledge—including the *Divisament*. Once validated by the embrace of imperial and royal power, the *Divisament* can then be copied and exchanged within less exalted circles, by those who—in circulating the book—appropriate to themselves a share of the mystique that surrounds Khubilai Khan and the long-distance specialist who once served him with distinction.

Through the medium of the book, Rustichello also carved out a novel niche for himself within the prestige economy of long-distance knowledge. If Polo's mystique as a long-distance specialist derives from his intimacy with the Mongol ruler, Rustichello forges yet another link in this chain of borrowed glamour. In a passage that recalls the description of the historically unprecedented wealth and power of Khubilai Khan, Rustichello extols Polo as the greatest traveler ever to have lived:

> I would have you know that, from the time that our Lord God fashioned
> with his hands Adam, our first father, until this point in time there has
> been neither Christian nor pagan nor Tartar nor Indian nor any man of
> any race that has known or explored so many of diverse parts of the
> world and its great marvels as has this Master Marco.[93]

The conviction that Marco Polo has learned more about the world's diversity than any other human being allows Rustichello to construe the composition of the *Divisament* as an ethical imperative:

> [Marco] told himself that it would be a great harm if he did not have all
> of the great marvels he had seen put into writing . . . so that other people
> who had not seen or did not know about them could hear of them and
> know of them through this book.[94]

These claims about the scale and significance of the *Divisament*'s contribution to posterity elevate Rustichello far above the humble station of scribe
and imbue his labors with the force of a moral imperative. It was, after
all, Rustichello's literary know-how that would preserve the long-distance
knowledge gathered during the travels of Marco Polo and transform it so
that it would be intelligible to a heterogeneous reading public.

Rustichello's insistence on the importance of his efforts is reinforced
by the *Divisament*'s inconsistent use of the first-person voice. Much of the
time, this "I" refers to Rustichello and at other junctures to Polo. Occasionally, the referent of the "I" is indeterminate. Likewise, "we" and "our"
sometimes refer to Marco and Rustichello, and in other contexts, to the
Polo family. Michel Zink has observed that the consistent, fully psycholo-
gized use of the narrative "I" was not a common feature of Old French
prose prior to Jean de Joinville's *Life of Saint Louis* (ca. 1305).[95] It is not
particularly remarkable, then, that the first-person voice of the *Divisament*
emerges sporadically, and that, when it does, its referent varies from case
to case. However, what we might be tempted to classify as an "inchoate"
or "naive" use of the first-person voice might just as well be characterized
as "tactical," insofar as it is consistently leveraged to Rustichello's benefit.

The protean quality of the *Divisament*'s first-person voice disarms
value-laden distinctions between the travail of the traveler and the literate
labors of his collaborator. Many of the same sequences that foreground Khubilai Khan as the subject/object of wonder also call attention to the part that
Rustichello played in shaping the *Divisament*. In such passages, Rustichello
insists that the pain and effort involved in "their travels" is just one of the

ingredients that gave rise to "our book." A similarly self-interested manipulation of narrative voice is evident in one of the *Divisament*'s rare moments of suspense. The anecdote recounts Polo's narrow escape from a band
of murderous nomads, who disorient wayfarers by using sorcery to darken
the sun. At the climax of this perilous adventure, Rustichello chimes in to
reassert his function as mediator between Polo's experience and the book's
audience:

> And now I have told you of this plain and this race of people that conjure
> darkness in order to rob. And I tell you that the same Master Marco was
> nearly taken by those people in that darkness, but he escaped to a castle
> called Caonalmi, and his companions were captured and were sold and
> some were killed. Now I will tell you about other things.[96]

The jarring transition between the indeterminate "I" of the first sentence
and the "I" of Rustichello in the second effectively displaces the traveler
from the scene of his travails, and—by extension—from his privileged position within the prestige economy of long-distance knowledge.

The way that Rustichello imagined himself as a middleman in the business of long-distance specialism depended not only on the growth of vernacular reading publics but also on new attitudes toward book ownership
among royal and aristocratic readers. Between the thirteenth and fifteenth
centuries, the patronage and presentation of illuminated manuscripts was
an increasingly common feature of elite gift giving, especially in French-
speaking courts. The first surviving example of a French-language manuscript with a presentation miniature was given to King Philip III of France
in 1274.[97] Some presentation miniatures depict the author or translator presenting a copy of his or her work to the manuscript's intended recipient;
others depict a scene in which the party who commissioned the manuscript
presents the book as a gift. The scenes rendered in presentation miniatures
did not necessarily commemorate the gift exchange "as it happened," but
rather in an idealized form meant to flatter the manuscript's recipient.[98]
In fact, copies of manuscripts originally given to royal patrons often reproduced not just the text of the exemplar but also its presentation miniature, even when the new copy was destined for an entirely different patron.
Joyce Coleman has observed that through such visual genealogies of the
manuscript-object, "prestige would pass on to later exemplars . . . and to
those copies' owners."[99]

It is within this context that we should consider the fact that, in 1307,
Marco supposedly gave "the first copy" of the *Divisament* to Thibaud de

Chepoix, the vicar-general of Charles de Valois, the son of Philip III. Three court French manuscripts of the *Divisament* include colophons that state that they have been copied from the very manuscript that Polo gave to Thibaud.[100] It would seem that, for some early readers of the *Divisament*, a given copy of the work was more valuable the closer it could be linked to Polo and/or an illustrious patronage context. It was through inserting himself into such imagined chains of transmission that Rustichello attempted to lay claim to his share of the long-distance specialist's prestige. While obviously not exclusive to travel writing, the practice of linking a manuscript copy to a prestigious "original" was one of many conventions of courtly book production that proved amenable to the *Divisament*'s efforts to leverage the authority of courtly culture in order to expand the prestige economy of long-distance knowledge beyond royal and clerical milieus.

The success of this gambit is proved by the fact that the *Divisament* found an even wider and more diverse audience than its creators had anticipated (including clerics, a group not mentioned in the work's opening address). Rustichello was the most obvious victim of this success. Several of the *Divisament*'s medieval translators found its shifting first-person voice gratuitous or puzzling. The court French translation regularized the work's use of pronouns.[101] The earliest Venetian version overwrote Rustichello's expository interventions. Here, for instance, is how it renders the tale of Marco's escape from the nomad-sorcerers:

> Now I have told you about that plain and that race of people that make darkness come in order to rob. . . . And I tell you that I, Marco, once found myself in great danger of being captured by that people in that darkness, but I fled to a nearby castle that was called Chalosebini, but things went worse for my companions, who were captured. And some died and others were sold into slavery.[102]

As mentioned above, Pipino's popular Latin version completely effaced Rustichello. Such departures from the Franco-Italian *Divisament* are representative of the work's complex, open-ended reception, about which it is difficult to make totalizing statements.

This caveat issued, it must also be said that the conception of travel and long-distance specialism advanced by Marco Polo and Rustichello da Pisa exerted a considerable influence in court circles. The *Divisament* rendered the travel book intelligible as a commodity that could be exchanged in much the same spirit as an exotic animal, luxury textile, or mechanical wonder. In so doing, the work pioneered subject positions that proved indispensable to subsequent long-distance middlemen and to travel writers of various stripes, including pilgrims to Rome and the Holy Land.

THE TRAVEL BOOK AS EXOTIC COMMODITY

The royal court furnished travel writers like Polo and Rustichello with a layman's alternative to the authorizing stamp of Latinity. In return, the travel book offered sovereigns and their imitators—eager to equate cultural patronage with political authority—a unique new way to appropriate the travail of the long-distance specialist. This symbiotic relationship helped travel writing become a known commodity within the prestige economy of long-distance knowledge and the broader literary landscape of the later Middle Ages.

To illustrate how this worked in practice, let us consider the example of King Charles V of France (ruled 1364–80), whose bibliophilia earned him the moniker "the Wise." During Charles's reign, the presentation miniatures of courtly manuscripts assumed a more markedly political character—probably in reaction to the English dynastic claims that sparked the Hundred Years' War.[103] The library of Charles V boasted five copies of the *Divisament*, the earliest extant version of *The Book of John Mandeville*, and a luxury map now identified as the *Catalan Atlas* (see figs. 8 and 9, in chapter 6), which drew on both of these works of travel writing.[104]

The *Catalan Atlas* dates from around 1375 and is attributed to the Mallorcan workshop of Jewish cartographers Abraham and Jehuda Cresques. Although it is not known who commissioned the work, the *Atlas* may owe its existence to a series of reciprocal gift exchanges between the crowns of France and Aragon. The *Atlas* was first inventoried in the library of Charles V in 1380. That same year, Charles received a letter from his niece's husband, the future King Joan I of Aragon. It read, in part:

> Most dear uncle, it pleases us very much to read in French as in our own language, which is why we ask you to send us three books written in the French tongue, namely: the Chronicles of France, Titus Livius, and Mandeville.[105]

In another letter dispatched in 1380, Joan requested copies of Mandeville and Machaut from his mother-in-law, the Duchess of Bar, sister to the French king.[106] The deaths of Charles V and Joan I did not end the exchange of gifts of long-distance knowledge between the royal houses. Charles VI asked for an up-to-date world map from Joan's eventual successor, Pedro IV of Aragon, in 1381.[107]

The hybrid form and content of the *Catalan Atlas* suggest why the monarchs of France and Aragon found luxury maps and travel books congenial to their political and cultural self-presentation. The *Atlas* crystallizes (and makes available for appropriation) the travail and long-distance knowledge of a dazzling cross section of medieval society. The work draws on scholarly, devotional, chivalric, and mercantile approaches to mapping the world. The *Atlas* reproduces the rhumb lines and detailed coastal contours of the portolan chart, a genre of map based on the painstaking observations of Mediterranean merchants and mariners, who crafted and kept such charts aboard their ships as navigational aids as early as the twelfth century.[108] Some of the *Atlas*'s other formal elements—its copious drawings of exotic figures, its explanatory glosses, and its Jerusalem-centered conception of the world—harken back to far older clerical efforts at cartography. As mentioned above, the chivalric travel accounts of Polo and Mandeville furnished a third source of information.[109] The *Atlas* also features several depictions of merchants traveling along the trade routes that supplied late medieval sovereigns with the exotic luxuries that they prized so highly, allowing the royal owner of the map collection to relish the expenditures of labor that brought such products into his own surroundings. As Jerry Brotton has observed, the *Atlas* even represents the efforts involved in extracting and transporting the very raw materials—such as gold and precious stones—used to manufacture the costly pigments that adorn its surfaces.[110] In sum, as the owner of this jewel-like object, Charles held in his hands the labor, pain, and knowledge of countless travelers.

The royal interest in luxury maps and travel books furnished more humble social actors with opportunities to work the prestige economy of long-distance knowledge to their own advantage. Baldassare degli Ubriachi—a Florentine merchant who traded in diamonds and ivory—wrote to his trading partner in Mallorca in 1399, asking him to commission *Atlas*-style maps from the Cresques workshop. Baldassare planned to present the maps as gifts to the rulers of the kingdoms where he sold his wares, in the hope that his liberality would secure him a tax exemption or two.[111] The earliest surviving manuscript of *The Book of John Mandeville*, produced in 1371, was commissioned as a gift for King Charles V by his royal physician, Gervais Chrétien.[112] The previous year, Charles had founded a medical college at the University of Paris, which would eventually be named after Gervais.

The French version of the *Divisament* found in the sumptuous *Livre de merveilles* (Paris: BNF Fr. 2810) suggests the influence that the work of Polo and Rustichello had on raising the profile of the travel book as an exotic commodity. The *Livre des merveilles* was produced, at least in part, by the workshop of the Boucicaut Master (active 1400–1430) for John the Fearless, Duke of Burgundy. John initially intended to keep the luxe manuscript for himself; however, in 1413, he ended up presenting the volume to his estranged uncle, the famous bibliophile (and brother of Charles V) John, Duke de Berry.[113] The *Divisament* is the first item in this manuscript, which also includes *The Book of John Mandeville* and French renditions of the works of Odoric of Pordenone, Hetoum of Armenia, William of Boldensele, and Riccoldo of Montecroce. Most of the translated works were rendered from Latin into French in the previous century (around 1351) by Benedictine monk John le Long (Jan le Lange) of Saint-Bertin at Saint-Omer, near Calais.[114] The *Livre de merveilles* brings together types of travel writing that, prior to the fourteenth century, tended to be treated as discrete subgenres. It includes works that speak at length about pilgrimage to the Holy Land (Riccoldo, Boldensele, and Mandeville) with exoticizing accounts of the East and South Asia (Polo, Odoric, Hetoum, and—once again—Mandeville). Translations of works originally written in Latin by clerics (Riccoldo, Boldensele, Odoric, Hetoum) are included alongside French works written by laymen (Mandeville and Polo). The politically resonant iconography of the *Livre*'s frontispieces lends a sense of unity to these disparate texts. The frontispieces alternate between two archetypal scenes: one in which the traveler is parting from home with the blessing of a king or pope (Odoric, Mandeville, Polo, Riccoldo) or one in which the travel writer is presenting his finished travel book to a powerful patron (Boldensele, Hetoum).

The cultural authority of the court—whether secular or ecclesiastical—is so essential to the way that the illuminators of the *Livre* view travel and travel writing that many of the scenarios depicted in the frontispieces have no basis in the texts themselves.[115] The image that introduces Hetoum of Armenia's *Fleur des estoires de la terre d'Orient* is particularly interesting in this regard (fig. 2). The painting depicts Hetoum genuflecting before John the Fearless and presenting the duke with his account of Mongol civilization. This is, of course, a historical impossibility. Hetoum had returned to his native Armenia before John's birth and died long before the duke reached adulthood.

Despite the fictive nature of the scene it presents, the Hetoum frontispiece nevertheless conveys an anthropological "truth." With breathtaking economy, the illuminator captures the cultural logic that endows the tech-

Figure 2. Hetoum of Armenia presents his book to John the Fearless, with courtiers later examining the same volume by the window. From *Le livre des merveilles* (ca. 1400–1420). Bibliothèque nationale de France, ms. fr. 2810, f. 226r. (Photograph: BNF, Paris.)

nology of the book with its unique capacity to reify and put into circulation the cultural capital of the long-distance specialist. On the left-hand edge of the image, an enthroned John the Fearless is depicted in Roman-imperial profile, draped in robes of state. With curious members of John's court looking on, a kneeling Hetoum proffers a bound copy of his account. To the extreme right of the scene, two men—seemingly indifferent to Hetoum's gesture—peruse what appears to be a different book. Recent technical research on the *Livre des merveilles* has rendered a far more interesting perspective on these marginal figures. Visual enhancing technologies reveal that the book being examined by the rapt courtiers is open to a page that contains a miniature version of the Hetoum frontispiece in which they themselves are depicted.[116] This playful *mise en abyme* exploits the narrative conventions of medieval painting—in which sequential events unfold from left to right within a continuous spatial field—to dramatize the network of political and social relations that sustain, and are sustained by, the circulation of the travel book.

This idealized image of courtly consumption echoes many of the *Divisament*'s attitudes and propositions. Like the *Divisament*, it depicts the relationship between the long-distance specialist and his patron as a mutually aggrandizing one. This relationship presumes the existence of a spectating public. Like any other exotic commodity designed for courtly ostentation, ownership of the travel book reaffirms the exalted status of its owner, who—in embracing the book—affirms its value as a commodity and its authority as a text. Finally, in inscribing his own labor within this fictive scene, the painter of the Hetoum frontispiece follows the example of Rustichello da Pisa, who presented his role in crafting the *Divisament* as an indispensable contribution the production of the long-distance knowledge found in its pages.

John the Fearless's decision to give this particular manuscript to his uncle as a New Year's gift also hints at the *Divisament*'s influence on the courtly practices on which it had wagered its success. Among the Duke de Berry's inventoried possessions was a cycle of tapestries depicting the majesty of the Great Khan.[117] The inventories of the Duke de Berry suggest that, as Polo and Rustichello intended, courtly readers of the *Divisament* identified with the figure of Khubilai Khan as consumers of exotic knowledge. The duke's lavish, Khan-like expenditures on precious gems, exotic animals, and foreign art objects became the topic of mutinous grumbling on the part of his political adversaries.[118] Brigitte Buettner has observed that the occasion in which the *Livre des merveilles* was offered to the older duke recalls Polo and Rustichello's description of the massive celebration of New Year's Day in the Mongol Empire, which culminated in the ceremonial presentation of tributary gifts to Khubilai Khan.[119] The fourteenth-century revival of New Year's gift giving in French-speaking courts has long been a puzzle to social historians. A convincing argument has been mounted that early humanist interest in ancient Roman customs might account for its sudden reanimation in the late Middle Ages.[120] An equally plausible impetus for this "rediscovery" of New Year's gift giving is the popularity of the *Divisament dou monde* in the same French-speaking courts that revived the ritual.

The *Divisament* influentially defined the subjectivity of the long-distance specialist in terms of his subjectivation within structures of political power. In a literary culture that associated travel writing with pompous self-importance and mendacity, the patron-servant relationship furnished the would-be travel writer with a humble rhetorical posture while endowing his account with an aura of legitimacy, derived from the political authority of the patron. Intriguingly, this subject position appealed to authors who wrote about journeys far less exotic than Polo's.

John Capgrave's *The Solace of Pilgrims* is a decidedly conventional topographical description of Rome, written in the wake of the author's 1450 pilgrimage to the Eternal City. Capgrave addressed the work to the financial sponsor of his journey, Sir Thomas Tuddenham (1401–62).[121] Given the scholarly pretensions of the *Solace*, it is no surprise that Capgrave situates his work within the tradition of learned topographical writing on the Holy Land, especially the "book of seynt jerom whech is called *de distanciis locorum*."[122] But then, the *Solace* proceeds to name less intuitive precedents:

> Also ther was a man of uenys [Venice] which thei called marcus paulus he laboured all the soudanes londe and descryued on to us . . . the stately array of the grete cane houshold. Eke jon maundeuyle knyth [knight] of yngland aftir his labour made a book ful solacious on to his nacyoun. Aftyr all these grete cryeris of many wonderfull thingis I wyl folow with a smal pypying of swech straunge sitis [sights] as I haue seyn and swech straunge thingis as I haue herd.[123]

In casting his "smal pypying" as a minor-key version of the books written by Polo and Mandeville, Capgrave gives his bookish account a glamorous makeover. Similarly, the analogy that the *Solace* makes between its content and the tidings of the town crier lends Capgrave's account an air of novelty that its contents belie while grounding its authority in the world of secular patronage and public affairs.

Then there is the case of Anselmo Adorno, who dedicated his *Itinerarium*—a humanist travel account based on his pilgrimage to the Holy Land—to King James III of Scotland. In his prologue, Adorno situates himself within a learned tradition of Greco-Roman travel, associated with figures such as Plato and Pythagoras. The sole medieval precedent mentioned by Adorno is Marco Polo, who is extolled as the man who "among all travelers merits the highest glory and crown of triumph."[124]

The frontispiece of the presentation copy of Bertrandon de la Broquière's

Figure 3. Bertrandon de la Broquière, in Ottoman drag, presenting his book to Philip the Good. Bibliothèque nationale de France, ms. fr. 9087, f. 153r. (Photograph: BNF, Paris.)

unconventional pilgrimage account (fig. 3) offers yet another example. The painting depicts the adventurous Bertrandon in Ottoman garb, genuflecting before his patron Philip the Good, Duke of Burgundy. Like the Hetoum frontispiece commissioned by Philip's father, John the Fearless, this later presentation miniature manipulates history. The image condenses the scene of Bertrandon's homecoming with the subsequent event of the publication of his travel account, a work that he undertook later, and only then at the prompting of Philip the Good. This narrative condensation emphasizes that the book offered up to the duke is the outgrowth of the toil of Bertrandon's perilous overland journey from the Holy Land to Burgundy, via Ottoman territory. The exportation of the *Divisament*'s notion of long-distance specialism to the accounts of pilgrims reflects—and contributes to—the flattening of distinctions between pilgrimage and exotic exploration (a topic explored in chapter 4).

CONCLUSION

When scholars speak about subjectivity and travel writing, they generally refer to a small subset of grammatical and narratological considerations. The political orientation of medieval exoticism encouraged works like the *Itinerarium* and the *Divisament* to render the subjectivity of the traveler in relation to the political, social, and economic networks that converged upon the majestic figure of the Great Khan. For this reason, the rhetorical techniques that each work uses to render the subjectivity of the traveler are inflected by its ideological stances toward temporal power, courtly materialism, and religious pluralism and—in the case of the *Divisament*—by the kind of reader that the text hopes to bring into being.

The success of the *Divisament* illustrates another point that deserves to be underscored: the evolution of medieval travel writing was influenced by many *nonliterary* developments in the history of literacy. While scholars are accustomed to asking how the rise of vernacular literature or the generic conventions of chivalric fiction inflect works like the *Divisament*, it is far less common to pose the same question with regard to the material practices of book production. As the following chapter shows, the advent of travel writing about East Asia was sustained by the legal and bureaucratic forms of writing that were becoming an increasingly important part of public life across late medieval Europe. This development provided travel writers with the rhetorical resources they needed to convert travail into a source of moral and intellectual authority in an unpredictable and potentially contentious cultural environment.

CHAPTER TWO

Travail and Authority in the Forgotten Age of Discovery

In the fields of European travel writing and geographical exploration, the year 1492 is widely identified as the starting point of "modernity." The first voyage of Columbus is said not only to have discovered an unknown continent but also to have inaugurated an epistemological revolution. In theory, this epochal rupture enabled the values of empiricism and curiosity to supplant the episteme of the Middle Ages, defined by its putative obeisance to classical and theological authority. Anthony Grafton typifies this position when he writes, "In 1500, European thinkers saw their world as a narrow, orderly place . . . in which few surprises could await the explorer of the past or the present."[1] In Grafton's account, the placid attitude that supposedly prevailed prior to Columbus was founded on the unquestioning acceptance of the claims of ancient and medieval *auctores*. Grafton maintains that the eventual realization that Columbus had discovered an uncharted landmass about which the ancients knew nothing led to the gradual increase in the value accorded to empirical observation in matters of geography (and to the trait of novelty in knowledge production, more generally). Grafton develops a nuanced analysis of the debates and contradictions that shaped early modern geographical writing, yet positions this illuminating tableau—gratuitously—against the backdrop of a Middle Ages that never actually existed.

For the authors and readers of late medieval travel writing, the world was anything but a place where "few surprises could await the explorer." When travelers began writing accounts of their voyages to the Mongol Empire in the 1240s, they made astonishing claims that surpassed anything found in ancient texts. These travel writers addressed broad readerships of clerics and laypeople, some of whom were unfamiliar with, or indifferent to, the protocols of scholarly reading that normally conferred authority on ancient, rather than modern, writings. At the same time, as a praxis, academic reading did not offer viable procedures for authenticating the number of unprecedented—and potentially vital—geoethnographic discoveries that proliferated throughout the later Middle Ages. In the absence of any single, institutionalized set of standards for authenticating new geographical claims, the travails of travel were a potent source of authority for those who returned from distant lands with novel tidings. For travel writers, the challenge was to translate this embodied mode of authority into textual form, so that audiences who would never have the opportunity to examine the traveler in person would credit his account and read it in the spirit in which he intended.

This chapter discusses three works published between 1247 and sometime slightly after 1350, the period widely considered the high-water mark of medieval travel writing: John of Plano Carpini's *Historia Mongalorum*, Odoric of Pordenone's *Relatio*, and *The Book of John Mandeville*. In different ways and to different ends, these works appeal to the adversities of travel in order to bolster their credibility and to assert different degrees of authorial control over the text. The examples of Odoric and Mandeville show that copyists and translators frequently altered the texts that they transmitted in ways that qualified or overwrote the original bases of the travel writer's claims to authority. Some of these revisions were undertaken by readers eager to bring the text into line with the protocols of academic reading, but many others were not. By highlighting the multiplicity of medieval conceptions of authority, this chapter challenges the rationale that equates modernity in travel writing with the triumph of "empiricism" (nebulously defined) over "authority" (narrowly identified with the reading practices of the medieval university). As a first step toward that goal, it seems necessary to dislodge the baseless belief that the contours of the medieval world map were fixed and unilaterally dictated by *auctoritas*-revering theologians.

AUTHORITY IN AN AGE OF DISCOVERY

Sometime around 1332, the Dominican friar Menentillus of Spoleto intercepted a letter written by John of Montecorvino, the Franciscan missionary responsible for building the first Latin Christian church in China. John's efforts were officially recognized in 1313, when Pope Clement V appointed him bishop of Khanbaliq (Beijing).[2] The letter that Menentillus chanced upon contained the bishop's descriptions of South and East Asia. Menentillus copied the epistle—which included astronomical measurements taken in various parts of India—and dispatched it with all possible haste to fellow Dominican Bartholomew of Santo Concordio, with the affectionate statement: "I know of the great curiosity (*chura*) you have about all branches of learning . . . especially things that are unknown to you."[3]

Menentillus and Bartholomew typify the late medieval enthusiasm for cutting-edge geographical knowledge, a cultural appetite that flies in the face of received wisdom. Stereotype depicts the Middle Ages as an epoch that adhered dogmatically to the assertions of ancient *auctores* such as Aristotle, Cicero, and Augustine while greeting the claims of "modern" writers with a mixture of indifference and twitching aggression. In the realm of medieval higher learning, the *auctor* was not just any other writer, but one whose time-tested works were seen as repositories of truth and wisdom.[4] The academic conception of *auctoritas* instituted a hierarchy among texts, which had the undeniable effect of privileging ancient works over modern ones. In the twelfth century, Walter Map reflected on the disadvantages that this value system visited upon modern authors. Map remarked that the chief defect that had denied his own works the respect they deserved was the fact that their author was alive, adding (with characteristic wit): "I have no intention of correcting this fault by my death."[5]

Though conservative in character, methods of scholarly reading did not render those who practiced them impervious to the usefulness and the pleasures of intellectual discovery. Moreover, schools and universities were not the sole arbiters of authority. In fact, when it came to the production of geographical knowledge, the claims of "modern" travelers—many "illiterate" by Latinate standards—were often more timely, useful, and accurate than anything found in the works of ancient *auctores*.

The sudden expansion of the Mongol Empire into the eastern regions of Europe in the thirteenth century alarmed Latin Christian intellectuals, who were confronted with the potentially dangerous consequences of their ignorance about the world outside Europe. Roger Bacon argued that Christian diplomats, merchants, and missionaries needlessly imperiled their international projects—and their lives—out of "their ignorance of the nature of the world's places."[6] For Robert Grosseteste, the general lack of knowledge of contemporary Asia illustrated the dire straits into which Christianity had fallen. The apostles had spread the gospel to every quarter of the world, Grosseteste maintained, but now Christians had become "compressed, as if confined within an acute angle."[7]

In contrast to Grosseteste, many other late medieval voices lauded their age as one marked by unprecedented advances in geographical knowledge. As mentioned in chapter 1, the *Divisament dou monde* boasted that Marco

Polo had traveled more widely than any man "since Adam." This included Alexander the Great, one of the few figures from antiquity that the *Divisament* mentions by name. Alexander's quasi-historical conquests of Persia, India, and the Far East were the subject of a fantastical body of literature that, for centuries, had served as a principal source of European information about Asia.[8] In the 1350s, John Marignolli, a Franciscan missionary from Florence, boasted that he had seen the monument that Alexander erected to mark the farthest extent of his travels in India. Friar John is quick to add that he not only journeyed beyond this limit but also erected his own monument to the east of Alexander's. Bearing inscriptions in Latin and "Indian," this memorial was "intended to last until the world's end."[9] Nearly a century later, humanist and Papal Secretary Poggio Bracciolini declared that Venetian merchant and traveler Nicolò di Conti had gone "farther than any other traveler has penetrated," including Alexander the Great.[10] Poggio recorded Nicolò's recollections about Asia in writing, augmenting them with the testimony of other travelers. He eagerly quizzed an ecclesiastical dignitary visiting Rome from Ethiopia about the source of the Nile, animated by what he called "a great desire to learn those things which appear to be have been unknown to ancient writers and philosophers, and also to Ptolemy, who was the first [*sic*] that wrote upon this subject."[11] Even Petrarch grudgingly conceded that his own era had surpassed the cultural achievements of antiquity in at least one pursuit: navigation. In a 1363 letter written from Venice, Petrarch describes the departure of a cargo ship, and imagines the itinerary of its crew members as they "cross the Ganges and the Caucasus . . . [and] arrive in India, farthest China, and the Eastern Ocean."[12] Petrarch contends that if Jason and Hercules could have seen the same vessel, they would "not call it a ship but an image of a mountain floating on the sea." He adds that, if Tiphys—the helmsman of the Argonauts—were confronted with the astonishing reach of medieval Italian commerce, he would "blush at having gotten so great a reputation" for the paltry pond-hop that yielded the Golden Fleece.[13] As the above comments suggest, medieval people were acutely aware that they could not rely on classical *auctores* for a full and accurate picture of the world.

The travel writing of the late Middle Ages abounds in acknowledgments of this reality. When the *Relatio* of Franciscan traveler Benedict the Pole—who accompanied John of Plano Carpini into the heart of the Mongol Empire—mentions the Black Sea, it glosses the topographical reference with a citation from Ovid's poetry of exile: "This land has a lot of wormwood, as Ovid remarks in his epistles: 'The bitter wormwood shivers in the endless plains.'"[14] Like one last backward glance toward the cusp of the familiar, this poetic allusion initiates an itinerary that outstrips the geographical scope of the classical literary tradition. Medieval travelers were routinely struck by the geoethnographic inaccuracies of not only pagan texts but also Christian *auctores*. En route to Caracorum, William of Rubruck paused to measure the circumference of the Caspian Sea. He discovered that, on foot, the body of water "can be gone round in four months." This finding contradicted Isidore of Seville, who asserted that the Caspian emptied out into the ocean.[15] William's efforts to confirm what Isidore and Solinus wrote about the monstrous races that supposedly inhabited East Asia yielded similar results.[16] John of Montecorvino likewise failed to unearth corroborating evidence for the existence of monsters in India and China; he was, moreover, met with blank stares when he made inquiries into earthly paradise, which several theological authorities located in East Asia.[17] In a similar vein, John Marignolli—perhaps referring to the body of legends surrounding Alexander the Great—criticized "histories and romances" for perpetuating the belief in monstrous humans.[18]

Somewhat more surprisingly, John cited the experience of his travels to argue that the Vulgate Bible erred in stating that, after their exile from Eden, Adam and Eve wore clothing made of animal skins (*pelliceas*). John suggested that a scribal error had converted the word *filiceas*—or vegetable fiber—into *pelliceas*. This paleographic conjecture was based on John's experiences in India, where he acquired and wore a vegetable-fiber tunic. He brought the garment back with him to his native Florence, where it was deposited in the sacristy of the Franciscan Church of Santa Croce, perhaps because he succeeded in convincing his brothers of the object's relevance to scripture.[19] John's boldly declared doubts about the textual fidelity of the official Bible of the Roman church illustrate just how much the experience of travel could contest modes of authority based on scholarly tradition.

Indeed, the dearth of reliable information about Asia and Africa imparted by ancient and patristic *auctores* prompted some scholars to accord surprising weight to relatively recent works of travel writing. Vincent of Beauvais cited extensively from the accounts of John of Plano Carpini in his *Speculum historiale*; likewise, Roger Bacon drew extensively on William of Rubruck for his *Opus majus*. Pietro d'Abano's *Conciliator differentiarum philosophorum* (1310) relied on cosmographical information gleaned from Marco Polo.[20] Francesco Pipino, who produced a widely read Latin translation of Polo's account, also cited the Venetian traveler as an authoritative source in his universal chronicle.[21]

As the examples of Polo and Nicolò di Conti suggest, geography was a rare area of knowledge in which merchants and shipmen enjoyed status as academic authorities. In 1403, cartographer Francesco Beccari explained that he had decided to alter the way that he had been depicting Sardinia and the Atlantic coastline based on the objections of mariners, who contradicted the then-dominant practices of master mapmakers.[22] In his fourteenth-century German translation of *The Book of John Mandeville*, Otto von Diemeringen, a canon of Metz Cathedral, suspected that his readers might doubt the veracity of the work because it was "new" and some of its subject matter difficult to credit. To shore up the credibility of the *Book*, Otto glossed his translation with citations drawn from works "of natural history written in Latin."[23] Leaving nothing to chance, Otto also made a less scholarly appeal to the authority of groups of "merchants from twenty-eight different countries, who come [regularly] to Bruges, and happily hear this book read."[24]

Shipmen and traders more than earned their reputation as geoethnographic experts. Late medieval missionaries and diplomats bound for Asia and Africa followed trails blazed by Genoese and Venetian merchants.[25] Commercial pursuit yielded dramatic geographical discoveries closer to home, as well. Sometime around 1320, Genoese shipman Lanceloto Malocello became the first known resident of mainland Europe to set foot on the shores of the Canary Islands since antiquity. Malocello's discovery caused a considerable intellectual stir, since prior to his excursion medieval knowledge of the archipelago had been limited to hazy ancient references to the "Fortunate Islands."[26] His achievement was commemorated on a portolan chart produced in 1339 by Genoese-Catalan cartographer Angelino Dulcert. The so-called Dulcert Map (Paris: BNF, GE B-696) is the first extant document to name one of the Canary Islands after Malocello. Today, that same island is known as Lanzarote, a Castilian translation of Malocello's chivalric first name. In 1487, Venetian ambassador Josafa Barbaro looked back on the geographical triumphs of the previous two centuries, which he attributed to the "merchandise and marinership" of his native Venice.[27]

Of course, not everyone reflexively credited the assertions of merchants and sailors. The very qualities that made new geographical knowledge desirable—its utility, its novelty, and its basis in experience—did, in fact, make it hard to assimilate within scholarly regimes of knowledge production. However, this is *not* to say that medieval intellectuals dismissed experience and empirical observation out of hand. Case in point: Around 1400, Florentine humanist Domenico Silvestri compiled a geographic gazetteer of the world's islands, which he titled *De insulis et earum proprietatibus* (On islands and their properties). Silvestri reflected on the peculiar methodological difficulties that faced would-be geographers, noting that the names and relative locations of islands differed from one ancient author to the next.

Adding to the confusion, geographical reality was itself mutable, vulnerable to sudden, dramatic transformation by accidents of climate and geology.[28] In the case of Asia, the situation was more challenging still, since ancient Roman authors disagreed about matters as basic as the number of islands found in the Indian Ocean. Notwithstanding his keen awareness of the deficiencies of classical texts, Silvestri still could not bring himself to abandon them wholesale in favor of the claims made by the *Relatio* of Odoric of Pordenone, which he ultimately did not include in his treatise:

> I would have set down some of these islands were it not for the fact that mixing the histories (*historias*) of ancient authorities with the lies (*fabulas*) of new ones (*novorum*) that have not been decisively tested/proved (*probatorum*) in our time would accomplish nothing more than to diminish faith in the truth with lies (*mendaciis*); even if what Odoric writes is true, it is still prudent to take as our guide and to follow those whose antiquity and authority inspire more confidence or those confirmed through live testimony (*testimonnio vive vocis comperio*).[29]

Here, Silvestri might sound like a caricature of the *auctoritas*-worshiping medieval scholar. However, he is neither as dogmatic about the status of ancient writings nor as dismissive of novel information as this lone passage might suggest. In the same prologue, Silvestri admits that he *has* drawn on Marco Polo, despite his initial disinclination to do so. Silvestri changed his mind when he and his friend Giovanni Nigro solicited the testimony of one "Fantinum, a Venetian soldier, and a valiant man," who had recently returned from India and who confirmed Polo's claims about it.[30] Though Silvestri is admittedly cautious, his skepticism toward Odoric does not grow out of an unqualified deference to ancient opinion but is instead the product of a methodological impasse. The problem with the "new" travel writers of the early fourteenth century is not simply that they are not ancient enough to be taken seriously, but also—one might say—that they are not *new* enough, either. For Silvestri, the relatively recent works of Polo and Odoric had not been tested by time, nor could their authors—who had died earlier in the century—be examined in a face-to-face exchange. Silvestri's interview with Fantinum gave him the cover he needed to draw on Polo's insights, which he ultimately deemed superior to those of classical authors.

Like many medieval authors and readers of travel writing, Silvestri supplements, and even supplants, academic notions of *auctoritas* with conceptions of authority that originate in law. As the verb *comperio* suggests, Fantinum and Polo are both imagined as legal witnesses, each one lending weight to the claims of the other. The "testimony" that vindicates Polo is considered authoritative because it is delivered viva voce by a man respected by his fellow citizens. This conceit recalls the procedural standard of canon law that required at least two witnesses to avow the same truth before it could be entered into evidence. Like Silvestri, the first Latin Christian travelers to write about East Asia took advantage of the increasing prevalence of official written documents in the everyday lives of their audiences. These travel writers drew on documentary convention in order to ground their authority in the travails of their journeys and to guide the behavior of their socially mixed readerships.

TRAVAIL, TESTIMONY, AND AUTHORIAL CONTROL: JOHN OF PLANO CARPINI

Mary B. Campbell has called the premodern travel writer "a kind of witness . . . to an alienated experience."[31] The analogy that Campbell draws between geoethnographic knowledge and legal testimony would have been perfectly intuitive to medieval readers of travel writing. John of Plano Carpini, for one, counted on it.

John's *Historia Mongalorum* (ca. 1247) is the oldest surviving book-length account of Latin Christian travel to East Asia. While John did not pretend to the *auctoritas* enjoyed by the likes of Augustine or Aristotle, he did want his *Historia* to possess the qualities associated with authoritative texts: "intrinsic worth and authenticity" (to borrow the formulation of Alastair Minnis).[32] John feared that some readers would doubt that he had traveled to the Mongol Empire at all. He also worried that the material realities of manuscript production would alter the text of the *Historia* in ways that would produce compromising and/or contradictory versions of the work. In an effort to bolster his credibility and to discourage unwelcome manipulations of his text, John appealed to two sources of authority: (1) the extreme suffering he endured as a traveler and (2) the evidentiary weight of official documentation, and of written testimony, in particular.

In the winter of 1246, John—at the time in his sixties—left Poland for Kiev in the company of fellow Franciscan Benedict the Pole. The pair rode on horseback from the Caspian Sea region to Caracorum, a punishing overland trek more than three thousand miles long. Thanks to the Mongol Empire's efficient network of equestrian relay stations, the Franciscans completed the journey in just two and a half months (though the brutalizing tempo of their progress forced them to bandage their limbs in order to minimize stress injuries).[33] Upon arriving in Caracorum, John delivered two papal bulls addressed to Mongol emperor Güyük Khan (ruled 1246–48) from Pope Innocent IV. In these documents, Innocent reproved Güyük for recent Mongol conquests in eastern Europe and urged him to convert to Christianity. The Great Khan responded with the unsettling command that the pope come to Caracorum in person and submit himself before the Mongol emperor . . . or else. Having dwelt nearly a year among the Mongols, John and Benedict carried this less than auspicious riposte back to Innocent, who, at the time, was staying in Lyon, France.

During their return journey, the two friars marshaled their recollections of what they had seen and heard. The result was the first recension of the work now known as the *Historia Mongalorum*. This text was copied by several eager parties as John and Benedict made their way to Lyon, against John's better judgment. John later completed a revised, amplified version of the *Historia* meant to make the account more creditworthy.[34] Vincent of Beauvais was evidently convinced; the encyclopedist incorporated extracts from the second recension into his *Speculum historiale*.[35] The testimony of Benedict the Pole would furnish material for two additional, unrelated descriptions of the Mongol Empire: the *Relatio* of Benedict the Pole and *The Tartar Relation*, compiled by someone named C. de Bridia.[36]

When John published the expanded version of the *Historia* in 1247, he knew that he was attempting to describe an alien, seminomadic world that well exceeded the confines of mainstream geographical knowledge. John addressed his potentially dubious account to a broadly conceived readership: "all the faithful of Christ to whom this present writing may come."[37] This imaginary audience was one that transcended the institutions that normally conferred authority on written works: monasteries, cathedrals, universities, and—increasingly—royal and aristocratic courts.

With these unconventional circumstances in mind, John stressed the sense of urgency that prompted him to compose his account, and the great pains that he and Benedict endured to do so. The *Historia* sought to prepare Christendom for the almost certain eventuality of armed conflict with the Mongol Empire, asking, in turn, that its readers resist the impulse to deride and dismiss its incredible claims:

> But if for the attention of our readers we write anything which is not known in your parts, you ought not on that account to call us liars (*mendaces*), for we are reporting for you things we ourselves have seen or have heard from others whom we believe to be worthy of credence (*fide dignos*). Indeed it is a very cruel thing that a man should be brought into ill-repute by others on account of the good that he has done.[38]

This plea is supported by an emotional appeal to the trials that John and Benedict endured:

> And although we feared we might be killed by the Tartars, or other people, or imprisoned for life, or afflicted with cold, heat, injuries, and exceeding great trials (*laboribis*) almost beyond our powers of endurance— all of which, with the exception of death and imprisonment for life, fell to our lot in various ways in a much greater degree than we had conceived beforehand—nevertheless we did not spare ourselves in order to carry out the will of God as laid down in the Lord Pope's mandate, and be of some service to Christians that, at all events, having learned the truth about the desire and intention of the Tartars, we could make this known to the Christians; then if by chance they made a sudden attack they would not find the Christian people unprepared (as happened on another occasion on account of the sins of men) and inflict a great defeat on them.[39]

Thanks to the reminiscences of Franciscan chronicler Salimbene of Adam, we know that John also emphasized his travails in face-to-face encounters with his readers. Salimbene met John in a Franciscan house in France. During his stay in the friary, John would read from the *Historia* during communal meals. Salimbene notes that the book's strange content caused doubt and confusion among audience members. He depicts John as a patient, humble commentator on his own work, one whose authority was reinforced by the exceptional hardships he had overcome during his journey:

> Brother John told us of the many tribulations he had gone through to get to the high lord of the Tartars: the fatigue of the long journey, the great difficulties, the hunger, the cold, the heat. . . . And whenever the Brothers marveled over the work or did not understand some part that was being read, he himself explained the matter and expounded at large on the details.[40]

Such live readings afford persuasive opportunities that written publication does not: the capacity to allay doubt and to persuade through personality. The broad audience that John imagined would not necessarily have the chance to size him up in person or benefit from his clarifications. In disseminating his claims via the medium of the book, John sought to neutralize audience disbelief while also preventing uninformed readers from "elucidating" (or otherwise embroidering) the *Historia* on his behalf.

By way of compensating for the limitations of the book as a medium, John leaned on his readers' familiarity with and respect for the authority of official writing. In the second recension of the *Historia*, John added a ninth chapter, which contains a brief account of his and Benedict's journey. (Apparently, out of modesty, he said little about their experiences in the first recension.)[41] This supplemental chapter provided a spatiotemporal context that made the text's references to the mortifications of the journey more concrete and meaningful. It also provided a framework for organizing the names of witnesses that the two Franciscans met during their travels, which were added to the second recension in order to "avoid any doubt in the minds of anyone as to our having been to the Tartars."[42] This roster—which extends for more than two print pages—follows depositional practice, identifying witnesses by name, rank, profession, and native land. Among the named parties are Italian merchants, Russian princes, Nestorian Christian captives, and even the citizenry of entire towns. The order of the witness list is governed by the sequence of places that John and Benedict visited during their journey, which have themselves been previously outlined in the condensed travel narrative of the ninth chapter.

As both a northern Italian and a Franciscan, John of Plano Carpini inhabited a milieu in which official writing commanded considerable authority. Thanks to the increasingly complex economies of mercantile city-states and the relative continuity of Roman legal tradition, northern Italy was an early center for the production of notarial documents. One testament to the broad cultural authority granted to Italian notaries is the fact that they were among the first authors of civic chronicles.[43] Official documentation was also an important source for the historiographical and hagiographical writings that helped legitimate and define the values of the young Franciscan Order. As an active participant in the order's early expansion, John played an important bureaucratic role in founding new Franciscan houses in Scandinavia, Germany, and eastern Europe, and may even have served as provincial of Spain.[44] John also knew many prominent Franciscan historians—including Thomas of Celano, Jordan of Giano, and Salimbene of Adam—whose writings likewise relied on official testimonial conventions. John was certainly aware that the sanctity of Francis and other early Franciscan luminaries was established through the compilation of testimonial dossiers, in keeping with the papacy's relatively recent efforts to centralize the canonization process and bring it into line with the evidentiary procedures of inquisition.[45]

This cultural background helps explain why, in the *Historia*, literary and scholarly commonplaces are so often mediated by the procedural orthodoxies of bureaucratic writing. John's prologue echoes the topos—already ancient in the Middle Ages—that historical and geographical writing should, when possible, be based on autopsy; when forced to resort to second-hand report, the historian or geographer should rely only on the testimony of trustworthy witnesses. John avows his strict adherence to these standards:

> Therefore whatever, with your welfare in mind, we shall write to put you on your guard, you ought to believe all the more confidently inasmuch as we have either seen everything with our own eyes, for during a year and four months and more we traveled about both through the midst of [the Tartars] and in company with them and we were among them, or we have heard it from Christians who are with them as captives and are, so we believe, to be relied upon.[46]

Far less conventional is John's suggestion that the *Historia*'s audience should view his approach to gathering testimony as a model for how *they* should participate in the book's dissemination:

> We beg all those who read the foregoing account not to cut out or add anything, for, with truth as guide, we have written everything we have seen or heard from others who we believe are to be trusted and, as God is witness, we have not knowingly added anything.[47]

John of Plano Carpini found in documentary writing an attractive alternative to common bookmaking practices, particularly the loose habits of copyists, who—as a matter of routine—reduced, reordered, and interpolated nonauthorial material into the texts they reproduced. For John, the problem with such scribal interventions is that they create multiple—and potentially contradictory—versions of the text and thereby undermine the *Historia*'s already precarious claims to authority. John addresses this concern explicitly, in a passage that explains why readers might potentially encounter two different versions of his account—and why they should not discount his claims if they do:

> People . . . we came across on our journey to Poland, Bohemia, Germany, Liège and Champagne wanted to have [the draft version of this book] so they copied it before it was complete and in a very abbreviated form, for we had not then had a quiet time [in which] we could finish it. . . . Therefore let no one be surprised that in the present account there are

more facts and they are more correct than in the former, for having some leisure we corrected this copy so that it is complete and perfect, at least more perfect than the unfinished one.[48]

John's assertions of authorial control recall a comparably curious passage from Gervase of Tilbury's *Otia imperialia* (ca. 1215). In a lengthy digression, Gervase criticizes the painters of maps for embroidering geographical fact with fancies of their own devising. In explaining his objections to this practice, Gervase—a canon lawyer—directs readers to Gratian's *Decretum*. The cited passage has nothing to do with painters or maps; instead, it warns would-be legal professionals about the tendency of witnesses to filter the raw testimony of what they have seen or heard through the distorting lens of their prejudices and speculations. Gervase writes:

> The very variety of painters has resulted in the production of pictures which depart from the truth of the places themselves—those pictures which are commonly called *mappae mundi*—since very often the painter (*pictor*), like any kind of witness (*testis*), mars by the falsity (*mendacio*) of a part the whole formulation of his evidence (*testimonii*), when he adds material of his own (*de suo adicit*), as it says in the *Decretum*, C.3 q.9, "Pura et simplex."[49]

In the absence of a set of best cartographic practices, Gervase looks to his own field of expertise—canon law—in order to articulate a normative approach to mapmaking. John does something similar when he presents the *Historia* as a testimonial record of what he has seen and heard, one whose content should not be compromised by the revision or amplification of copyists.

In effect, John of Plano Carpini relies on readers' familiarity with the conventions of legal documentation to hedge the *Historia* with the kind of textual protections that institutions of learning extended to ancient *auctores*. Just as commentators, compilers, and scribes were not supposed to pass their own assertions off as Aristotle's, readers of the *Historia* are asked to show their respect for the travails of John of Plano Carpini by refraining from comparable acts of textual adulteration. Nearly a hundred years later, another Italian Franciscan, Odoric of Pordenone, ventured even farther into Asia than John. Like John's *Historia*, Odoric's *Relatio* presented itself as the testimony of one who had suffered too greatly to be doubted reflexively by stay-at-home readers.

TRAVAIL, REVELATION, AND THE AUTHORITY
OF COMMUNITY: ODORIC OF PORDENONE

Sometime around 1318, Franciscan friar Odoric of Pordenone (d. 1331) departed Venice for Pera (today, the district of Beyoğlu, Istanbul)—a Genoese
colony on the Bosporus, opposite Constantinople. This was the first leg
of an approximately fourteen-year missionary journey through Asia, which
Odoric undertook with a Franciscan companion (perhaps James of Ireland)
and a servant whose name is lost to history.[50] Though the exact itinerary
of Odoric and company is unclear, they seem to have visited Persia, India,
China, and various island kingdoms in Southeast Asia. In the Indian city of
Thana (modern-day Thane), Odoric took possession of the bodily remains of
four Franciscan missionaries martyred there just prior to his arrival. Odoric
translated these relics to Zayton (Quanzhou), where they were reinterred
under the supervision of Andrew of Perugia, a Franciscan bishop and missionary stationed in China. Odoric also paid a visit to fellow Franciscan
John of Montecorvino. He returned to Venice in 1329.

In 1330, in the Franciscan house of Padua, Odoric dictated an account
of his travels to fellow brother William of Solagna. The resulting book—
known by many titles in the Middle Ages but now commonly referred to
as the *Relatio*—was put into writing at the request of Guidotto of Bassano,
the Franciscan provincial minister. Odoric died shortly after, in 1331, and
therefore never knew about the success of the *Relatio*, which survives in
an estimated 117 manuscripts, both in Latin and in vernacular languages,
including French, German, Italian, and Castilian. It was also the main (unacknowledged) source for the description of East Asia found in *The Book of
John Mandeville*.

Early in the *Relatio*, it is clear that Odoric of Pordenone will be a different kind of geoethnographic authority than John of Plano Carpini. Unlike
John, Odoric does not stake his reputation on the utility of the *Relatio*. Indeed, the work's preface promises the pleasures of exoticism while extolling
the novelty of its contents as its principal asset:

> Albeit many other stories of sundry kinds concerning the customs and
> peculiarities of different parts of this world have been related by a variety
> of persons, yet would I have you to know that I also, Friar Odoric of
> Friuli, can truly rehearse many great marvels (*mirabilia*) which I did hear
> and see when, according to my wish, I crossed the sea and visited the
> countries of the unbelievers in order to win some harvest of souls.[51]

Though the *Relatio* does not mention any works of travel writing by name, its borrowings from Polo and Rustichello's *Divisament dou monde* are well known. Notwithstanding its areas of overlap with previous travel accounts, one fourteenth-century reader, the Franciscan chronicler John of Winterthur, found the *Relatio* decidedly groundbreaking, declaring its content "strange and almost unheard of in our age."[52]

The *Relatio* dealt with the challenge posed by its novelty by programmatically conflating travail, mystical experience, and the production of geo-ethnographic knowledge. As a result, there is a strong sense that the source of the text's authority is the product of divine dispensation rather than human endeavor. From the start, the authority of the *Relatio* was inextricably linked to public assertions that Odoric had died a saint. Responding to rumors of supernatural happenings at Odoric's tomb, Bishop Pagano della Torre ordered a mixed group of clerics and citizens from Udine to gather testimony in 1331. The committee deposed more than seventy witnesses, whose statements were certified and recorded by a notary public named Guecello. The resulting dossier, which incorporated a revised version of the *Relatio*, was forwarded to the papal Curia in Avignon, to support Odoric's canonization. Although Odoric would have to wait until 1755 for his official beatification, the 1331 effort to canonize him ensured the broad geographic diffusion of the *Relatio*. It was in Avignon that Franciscan Henry of Glatz first heard about Odoric and his account. Henry created yet another Latin recension of the *Relatio*, which circulated widely in Germany and Bohemia. Meanwhile, Guecello's version found its way to England, where it attracted the interest of scholarly readers.[53] John le Long's vernacular translation of Odoric's account also ensured it an early readership in Francophone courts.

The *Relatio* rarely remarks on the day-to-day realities of Odoric's journey, and seldom explains when, how, or why he traveled from one place to the next. A notable exception to this rule is the prolonged narrative sequence that details the martyrdom and posthumous miracles of the four Franciscan missionaries put to death in Thana in 1321. The sequence stands out from the rest of the *Relatio* for its length, its spatiotemporal specificity, and its attention to a historical episode that predates Odoric's presence in India. Indeed, the unique qualities of this portion of the work have led at least one scholar to suggest that it is a later interpolation.[54]

The tale of the Franciscans' martyrdom serves as the background to the story of the role that Odoric played in translating their remains from India to China. This heroic *translatio* required Odoric to withstand pains and perils that, in themselves, border on martyrdom. While staying in

"Upper India" (southern China), Odoric was delivered from certain death by the miracle-working remains of the missionaries. According to the *Relatio*, Odoric fell asleep with the relics under his head, when a group of "Saracens," hoping to exterminate him, set fire to the house where he was lodged. The entire dwelling is instantly engulfed in flames, except for the corner of the house where Odoric has taken refuge with the relics.[55] When Odoric finally escapes the fire, it comes crashing down on the nook where he had been crouching.

This miracle is followed by another. This time, Odoric is sailing toward Columbum with the relics when the wind suddenly dies, bringing his ship to a standstill. After a while, the crew grows restless and suspects that their stasis is caused by the presence of dead bodies aboard the ship. Under pressure, the captain tells Odoric in Armenian that he will have to cast the relics into the sea if the wind does not return. Odoric and his companions respond by praying to the Virgin Mary for a favorable wind, to no avail. Then, Odoric orders his servant to cast one of the martyr's bones into the sea. To the relief of all, an advantageous wind arises, delivering the rest of the relics from the same fate as the miracle-working bone. The sequence ends with Odoric successfully reinterring the remains of the missionaries in the Franciscan church at Zayton, where they continue to work miracles and command the reverence of not only Christians but also "pagans and Saracens."[56]

There is one other episode in the *Relatio* that foregrounds the perils confronted by Odoric; it, too, entails a brush with the otherworldly. The sequence in question relates Odoric's well-known adventure in a valley possessed by demons.[57] For reasons unknown, Odoric undertakes a solo exploration of the notorious vale. Upon entering the valley, he hears alarming, disembodied strains of music and sees corpses scattered across the landscape. More unsettling still, looming over the canyon is a menacing stone outcrop shaped like a human head. Suddenly, Odoric pauses his march through the valley when he espies a trove of silver coins spread out in such abundance that they resemble the scales of a fish. The Franciscan—in obvious violation of his vow of poverty—begins to fill the folds of his garments with treasure. A cacophony of drums and cymbals then startles Odoric and puts an end to this greedy enterprise. Jettisoning his gains, the Franciscan devoutly processes through the remainder of the valley, repeatedly intoning the prayer *Verbum caro factum est*. When he at last emerges on the other side of the infamous canyon, he is hailed as a hero by a group of wonder-struck Muslims.

There is an individualistic—and even autohagiographic—tone to Odoric's tales of peril.[58] Indeed, these sequences provided a template for subsequent legends about Odoric and his travels. Hagiographies of Odoric depict his perilous voyage to Asia as one phase in a longer ascetic career. According to the *Chronica XXIV Generalium Ordinis Fratrum Minorum*—a semi-official Franciscan history compiled in the second half of the fourteenth century—as a young friar, Odoric was known for devotional fervor and extreme self-abnegation.[59] Early in his spiritual career, Odoric prayed in a church for three consecutive nights, during which time the devil appeared before him in the guise of an Italian townsman and subsequently attempted to strangle him. The *Chronica* rounds out its portrait of Odoric by drawing on and adding to the *Relatio*'s account of his sojourn in Asia. In an episode not recounted in the *Relatio*, Odoric is stricken with a crippling ailment that prevents him from traveling. Unfortunately, this malady afflicts him while he is passing through a country that is persecuting Christians. Unable to find anyone who dares to host him, Odoric convalesces for a year under a giant tree, subsisting on nothing more than its fruit and the water that seeps out of its bark. In another episode that seems to originate with the *Chronica*, Odoric has a vision of the Virgin Mary, who directs him toward a dying Indian woman in need of the Eucharist. Perhaps not surprisingly, the *Chronica* also incorporates the demonic valley episode from the *Relatio* as well as its account of the miracles associated with the martyrs of Thana.

The spiritual authority accorded to Odoric by members of his order accounts for the confidence with which the *Relatio*, in contrast to John of Plano Carpini's *Historia*, dismisses would-be skeptics. This defiant attitude expresses itself in what might be called "the motif of authorial withholding." The *Relatio* repeatedly calls attention to the fascinating things that it has been forced to omit due to the imaginative limitations of the reading public. Statements of the following kind recur throughout the work:

> Of all I purpose not to speak, though I shall be the first to tell of many which seem to a number of people past belief. Nor, indeed, could I myself have believed these things, had I not heard them with my own ears or seen them myself.[60]

The motif of authorial withholding does not so much imbue Odoric with an aura of authority as it does reduce authority to the phenomenon of aura—in this case, understood as the mysterious, unfathomable distance that separates the knowledge of the mystical traveler from the mundane experience of his audience.[61] This distance is conferred in large part by the way the work conflates geoethnographic observation, divine revelation, and travail. Bridging the auratic gap between Odoric and readers of the *Relatio* is the

authorizing institution of the Franciscan house of Padua, which vouches
for the truth value of the text. The earliest Latin manuscripts of the *Relatio*
contain the following oath:

> I, Friar Odoric of Friuli, of the Order of the Friars Minor, [avow and bear
> witness] (*testificor et testimonium perhibeo*) before my reverend father,
> Friar Guidotto, Minister of the province of Saint Anthony, that every-
> thing that is written above I either saw with my own eyes or heard from
> trustworthy men (*hominibus fide dignis*).[62]

It has been suggested that this oath is a sign that Odoric's superiors doubted
his story.[63] However, the inclusion of this depositional formula is, if anything, an official endorsement on the part of the Franciscans of Saint Anthony's, analogous to the seal of approval offered by modern institutions
such as the Royal Geographical Society.

The authenticating function of the *Relatio*'s documentary framework
essentially creates a split audience for the *Relatio*. There is, on the one
hand, the audience that solicits, evaluates, and records the traveler's testimony. In effect, it is the rhetorical "job" of the Franciscans of Padua to believe Odoric on behalf of the secondary audience: the future readers of the
Relatio. Confident that his claims are accepted by his primary audience,
"Odoric" is free to dismiss skeptics among his secondary one.

The reason why Odoric's name appears in scare quotes in the previous
sentence—and why, perhaps, it should always be implicitly surrounded by
them when discussing his narration of his experiences—is that Odoric exerted far less control over the *Relatio* than John of Plano Carpini did the
Historia. The *Relatio* presents itself as a deposition, a documentary genre
that is, by nature, collaborative—the product of interrogation, dialogue, and
selective preservation. The depositional framing of the *Relatio* calls attention to its official and communal character; this characterization of the text
is echoed by the colophon added by William of Solagna, who recorded Odoric's recollections in writing:

> The [aforementioned things] I, Friar William of Solgna, have put in writ-
> ing (*in scriptis redegi*) exactly as the aforementioned Friar Odoric de-
> scribed them, in the year of our Lord 1330, in the month of May, in
> Padua, in the place of Saint Anthony. Nor did I strive for a difficult or
> ornate style of Latin, but rather wrote things as he narrated them, so that
> it would be easy for everyone to understand what is written here.[64]

In lending the weight of his signature to the *Relatio*, William guarantees the truth value of Odoric's claims and the fidelity with which they have been textualized. It is common scholarly practice to refer to William as Odoric's "scribe," which suggests a more passive role than the one that William seems to claim for himself—one that seems more akin to that of a notary. James Brundage has observed that the documents produced by notaries were considered "public instruments whose authority did not depend on witnesses, seals, or other authenticating devices." Brundage adds, "A formal declaration by a public notary (*manum publicam*) that he had prepared them, authenticated by his personal sign, guaranteed their reliability."[65] William vows that he has not engaged in the types of textual embellishment that Gervase of Tilbury laid at the feet of cartographers. Yet, as the colophon also makes clear, this does not mean that the *Relatio* is a word-for-word transcript. Indeed, William suggests that a faithful account of Odoric's testimony could have been rendered in sophisticated Latin rather than the simple, Italianate Latin style for which he opted. William presents this colloquial style as a kind of translation: an accommodation to a community of readers with discrepant degrees of familiarity with Latin.

Recent research into the manuscript tradition of the *Relatio* has revealed dramatic regional variations in terms of how readers responded to its authorizing and authenticating gestures. Marianne O'Doherty has observed that all surviving manuscripts of the *Relatio* produced in England were written in Latin. English copies of the *Relatio* were collected with learned texts such as Sacrobosco's *De sphaera*, and some were subjected to rigorous notation and commentary.[66] The full title given to the *Relatio* in one English manuscript (Oxford: Bodleian Digby 11) suggests that, for scholarly readers, the documentary origins of the work were accepted as a guarantee of its authenticity, if not authority: "Itinerarium Odorici de Ordine Minor, approbatum sub manu notarii publici de mirabilibus Indie [Itinerary of Odoric of the minorite order about the marvels of India, authenticated by the hand of a public notary]."[67] An entirely different reality characterizes the reception of the *Relatio* in medieval Italy. Within Tuscany and the Veneto, the *Relatio* was quickly translated into the vernacular and circulated within mercantile and bureaucratic reading circles. Alvise Andreose has observed that Italian copyists and translators of the *Relatio* radically revised the text, according to the tastes of its various audiences.[68] These translations tended to downplay the hagiographical accounts of Odoric's travails and to add to the *Relatio*'s observations about foreign commerce and exotic marvels.

The radical nature of Italian refashionings of the *Relatio* has prompted

Giulio Cesare Testa to suggest that the work was "of uncertain status, and—in a certain sense—lacking in authority" (*"statuto incerto e privo, in certo senso, di autorità"*).[69] There are, however, grounds for qualifying this statement. As Alison Cornish has shown, the translation of Latin works into Italian dialects focused on writers such as Virgil, Livy, Cicero, and Ovid, precisely *because* they enjoyed cultural capital as *auctores*. Translations into *volgare* routinely transformed the contours of the Latin text as an accommodation to those untrained in university reading practices.[70] It is possible that Domenico Silvestri's skeptical reaction to the *Relatio* was based, at least in part, on his familiarity with one or more *volgarizzamenti* of the work, which tended to marginalize the very rhetorical trappings designed to secure the authority of the Latin text, in the interest adjusting it to a bourgeois audience.

This was precisely the fate that John of Plano Carpini feared for the *Historia*. John was cognizant of the fact that the authority of the traveler and the authority of the book were related to each other in ways that were not necessarily settled, or even predictable.[71] His foresight is borne out by the textual tradition of the *Relatio*, and even more so by that of *The Book of John Mandeville*, the Middle Ages' most popular—and enigmatic—work of travel writing.

DISAVOWING EXCEPTIONALISM, UNIVERSALIZING TRAVAIL: JOHN MANDEVILLE

The authority claimed by Odoric of Pordenone and John of Plano Carpini is based in large part on the exceptional nature of their travails. By contrast, *The Book of John Mandeville* seeks authority in the universal character of its author's afflictions. Which is odd, since it is not entirely clear who Mandeville actually was, or whether he traveled to any of the places he describes. Mandeville identifies himself as a knight from the English town of Saint Albans. He alleges that he embarked on a thirty-four-year globe-trot in 1324, and composed his *Book* after his homecoming in 1358.

Notwithstanding heroic efforts by modern scholars, the true circumstances surrounding the *Book*'s composition are shrouded in enigma. The work's date of composition can be narrowed to sometime between the 1350s and 1371. However, there is still no scholarly consensus regarding which of the two earliest renditions of the *Book* is the original: the Insular French or the Continental French version.[72] A third French version, known as the Liège (or sometimes the "Interpolated Continental"), began to circulate widely before the end of the fourteenth century. Doubts about the date, authorship, and evolution of the *Book* are the result of Mandeville's dependence on earlier texts. The first half of the *Book* consists of an adaptation and amplification of the pilgrimage account of Dominican William of Boldensele. The *Book*'s second half is based primarily on the *Relatio* of Odoric of Pordenone. Mandeville fleshed out his two primary sources with more than two dozen others—among them the version of John of Plano Carpini's *Historia*, which he found in Vincent of Beauvais.[73] The *Book* survives in approximately three hundred copies in ten languages. It enjoyed a robust afterlife in print, and its influence can be seen in various spheres of late medieval and early modern culture: as a source for cartographers and explorers, as material for the London stage, as the only travel account owned by Leonardo da Vinci, and as evidence in the 1599 heresy trial of Italian miller Domenico Scandella, to mention just a few better-known examples.[74]

The distinctiveness of the *Book*'s appeal to travail is crystallized in its striking revision of the demonic valley episode from Odoric's *Relatio*. As others have noted, the *Book* multiplies and exaggerates the dangers and the temptations that Mandeville faced in what it calls "The Perilous Valley."[75] The crag that, in the *Relatio*, is shaped like a human head is converted by the *Book* into a sentient, fire-breathing demon that has "shifting and . . . flashing eyes" and emits a stench so foul "that one can hardly stand it."[76] The scattered corpses that unnerve Odoric are stacked in ubiquitous heaps in the *Book*. The coins that tempt Odoric undergo similar rhetorical inflation; according to Mandeville, the valley conceals hoards of gold and silver trinkets, as well as "precious stones and jewels in abundance on every side."[77]

Yet, for all of these narrative enhancements, Mandeville actually undercuts the heroic individualism of his source. In the allegorizing hands of Mandeville, the dangerous excursion into the Perilous Valley becomes a miniaturized image of his larger journey, of the cultural practice of travel more generally, and—by tropological extension—of the pilgrimage of human life. According to the *Book*, Mandeville explores the Perilous Valley in the company of fourteen fellow travelers. Eleven companions are Christian laymen and—in an oblique nod to Odoric—two are described as "Friars Minor . . . from Lombardy."[78] Under the spiritual guidance of the friars, the fellowship solemnly mark themselves with the sign of the cross (a ritual associated with pilgrimage and crusade).[79] The laymen confess themselves to the friars and take communion before assaying the valley. Far more explicitly than its source, the *Book* universalizes the dangerous passage as a spiritual and moral test:

> People say that [the valley] is one of the entrances to Hell. In this valley
> there is much gold and much silver, and that is why many pagans, and
> many Christians too, often go into it to seek the treasure that is there.
> But few of them return—especially the pagans, and also the Christians
> who go because they are greedy to have things—for they are soon stran-
> gled by the Devil.[80]

According to Mandeville, even Christians who resist temptation suffer "as-
saults . . . and threats both in air and on the ground, and blows, and thun-
ders, and storms; and people always fear that God might take vengeance for
misdeeds done against his will."[81] Surviving a foray into Mandeville's Perilous Valley is not, as was the case with Odoric, an intimation of one's unique
proximity to the divine but rather the reward for exercising a self-discipline
that could theoretically be replicated by anyone.

The manner in which the *Book* reframes Odoric's adventure reflects its
penchant to speak of travel in universalizing, ethical terms. The *Book* treats
travel as a discretionary activity that entails irrecoverable sacrifices of time,
money, energy, and sometimes even life. While potentially ennobling, these
costs need to be weighed against the traveler's particular motivations and
constraints. In sympathetic tones, Mandeville enumerates the various considerations that prompt pilgrims to Jerusalem to forego the further pilgrimage to Egypt and Mount Sinai:

> because of poverty they lack the means, or because they do not have
> [a sufficient number of traveling companions], or because they cannot
> endure the hardships (*endurer la peine*), or because they are too afraid
> to cross the desert, or because they are in a great hurry to return to
> their wives and children, or for other good reasons (*ascuns causes reso-
> nables*).[82]

The *Book*'s peculiar preoccupation with the ethics of travel conspicuously
colors its treatment of the legendary voyages of Alexander the Great. In
contrast to travel writers such as Marco Polo and John Marignolli, Mandeville depicts Alexander in much the same way that Dante does Ulysses—as
a rash traveler who imperils his life and the lives of his companions in the
reckless, vain pursuit of forbidden knowledge.[83] In a similar spirit, Mandeville's *Book* derides the folly of "many very willful Lords" ("meintz grantz
seignurs et de grant volunté") who have set out to visit earthly paradise.
Knowing that the journey entails the navigation of unthinkably perilous
waters and confrontations with hordes of voracious beasts, these reckless

explorers forfeit their lives in a futile attempt to obtain knowledge that God has placed off-limits to humans.[84] The *Book* does not, however, issue a blanket condemnation of geographical curiosity but rather stresses the importance of thinking about which motivations justify particularly perilous journeys—and which do not.

The *Book*'s advocacy of self-restraint in travel extends to the manner in which Mandeville takes up the mantle of long-distance specialist. In a radical reorientation of Odoric's motif of authorial withholding, Mandeville refrains from talking about everything he has witnessed, out of respect for future travelers and not as expression of contempt for skeptical members of his audience:

> If I described (*devisoie*) as many things as there are over there, someone else who took the trouble and labored bodily (*qe se peneroit et travailleroit le corps*) to go into those far places and find out about the country would be hindered (*empeschez*) by my words from reporting on anything foreign, for he would have nothing new (*de novel*) to say in which the listeners could take pleasure (*prendre solacz*), and it is always said that new things (*choses novelles*) give pleasure. Thus I shall keep quiet now without recounting any more diversities that exist over there, so that whoever wishes to go to those parts might find there enough to say.[85]

Mandeville implies that the suffering inherent in travel entitles all travelers to the pleasure of entertaining others with tales of previously undocumented wonders. The use of the verb *empescher* (the ancestor of *impeach* and *impede* in modern English) even suggests that the discovery and diffusion of new knowledge about the outside world is the telos of travel. *Empescher* comes from the Latin *impedicare*, "to fetter or ensnare." In Insular French usage, the term maintained a close connection to its etymological origins, especially in legal contexts, where it signified both lawful arrest and the unlawful waylaying or imprisonment of travelers.[86] In the context of the above-cited passage, the appearance of the term suggests that denying the traveler the opportunity to report previously undiscovered phenomena is tantamount to impeding the completion of his or her journey. For this reason, Mandeville disavows the individualism of the long-distance specialist. Rather than asserting his authority by shaming, taunting, or dismissing circumspect readers, Mandeville attempts to interpellate them into a league of investigator-ascetics, who might one day join him in subjecting themselves to the ardors of travel, in the ongoing, collective effort to unearth—and bear witness to—the diverse marvels of the world.

The *Book* calls upon its readers in yet another way that distinguishes it from previous works of travel writing. Unlike John of Plano Carpini (who relies on a roster of eyewitnesses) and Odoric of Pordenone (whose claims are underwritten by the Franciscans of Saint Anthony's in Padua), Mandeville does not impose an authorizing middleman between himself and his audience. Instead, the *Book* stakes its authority on a species of crowdsourcing *avant la lettre*, beckoning qualified readers to correct any inaccuracies that they might find in its pages. Mandeville's explanation of why he wrote in French rather than Latin suggests that this proto-crowdsourcing model is intended as a corrective to academic conceptions of *auctoritas*:

> Know that I should have put this writing into Latin so as to explain things more briefly (*pur plus brifment deviser*), but because more [people] understand French (*romancz*) better than Latin, I have put it into French (*en romancz*) so that everyone (*chescun*) can understand it, and the knights (*luy chivaler*) and the lords (*ly seignurs*) and the other noble men (*autre noble hommes*) who know no Latin or a little, and who have been beyond the sea know and understand if I tell the truth (*voir*) or not. And if I err in describing through not remembering or otherwise, they can amend and correct it, for things long passed out of view get forgotten and human memory cannot retain or contain everything.[87]

Iain Higgins has convincingly argued that this passage asserts that the subject matter of the *Book* merits, but has forgone, the prestige of Latinity.[88] While this is certainly true, Mandeville seems to be making an even more assertive claim for French, presenting it not as a humble alternative to Latin but as a *rival* to it. Had he composed his *Book* in the language of academic and theological authority, the readers best qualified to evaluate its claims would have been prevented from doing so. Those readers are not clerics but rather members of the landowning political elite, who have themselves traveled overseas. In locating the ultimate authority of the *Book* in the collective experience of travelers like himself, Mandeville champions the superiority of geographical knowledge gained through travail in foreign lands over that gleaned at home through bookish pursuits.

The *Book of John Mandeville* makes one final, intriguing gesture toward the travails of its author. In a farewell to his readers, Mandeville relates the difficult circumstances that surrounded the writing of the *Book*. As Higgins notes, this passage is couched in "quasi-juridical" rhetoric, which superficially resembles the formulaic phrases used to authorize Odoric's *Relatio*:

Et jeo Johan Maundeville dessusdit, qe m'en party de noz pays et et pas-
say la mer l'an de grace M^{il} CCC XXII, qy mointe terre et moint passage
et mointe pays ay puis cerchez, et qy ay esté en mointe bone compaignie
et en mointe beal fait come bien qe jeo ne feissse unques ne beal fait ne
beal emprise, et meintenant suy venuz a repos maugré mien pur goutes
artetikes qe moy destreignent. En prignant solaz en moun cheitif repos,
en recordant le temps passé, ay cestes choses compilez et mises en escrit,
si come il me poet souvenir, l'an de grace M^{il} CCC L VIme a XXXIIII^{te} an
qe jeo m'en party de noz pays.

And I John Mandeville abovesaid,—who left our countries and crossed
the sea in the year of our grace 1322, who has since sought out, many
lands and many journeys and many countries, and who has been in
much good company and in many a fine undertaking (although I never
did any fair deed nor fine adventure), and now have come to rest despite
myself because of the arthritic gouts, which constrain me—while taking pleasure in my miserable rest, in [recording/recollecting] time past,
have compiled these things and put them into writing, such as I can remember, in the year of grace 1356, in the thirty-fourth year since I left
our countries.[89]

In contrast to the juridical formulas found in the *Relatio*, the conclusion of
the *Book* lacks the essential details that imbue Odoric's account with the
weight of official, public memory. There is no notarial signature guaran-
teeing the truth value of the text. Moreover, even though Mandeville tells
readers that he is a native of Saint Albans, he does not specify that he wrote
his *Book* there, and does not say that anyone in his hometown vouches for
the work or even knows about its existence. The possibility that "Mandeville" is not who he claims to be probably explains this lack of specificity. The *Book* wields the place-bound language of communal memory and
institutional authority from an undisclosed location, a rhetorical flourish
that—whatever its ultimate motivations—is consistent with the iconoclas-
tic, universalizing logic that informs its ruminations on travel and travel
writing.

It is almost as though the *Book*'s quasi-juridical features are meant to
dramatize a renunciation of legal and documentary authority, in favor of
an appeal to the sanctity of the traveler's suffering. The *Book*'s reference
to Mandeville's gout is, as others have noted, a transparent ploy for sympa-
thy.[90] At the same time, it functions as what Roland Barthes called a "reality

effect" (*effet de réel*).[91] The implications of this particular "reality effect" come into focus only when one considers medieval assumptions about the causes, symptoms, and treatment of gout.

In essence, Mandeville presents his gout as a continuation of the travails of his journey, one that racks his body long after his travels have theoretically come to an end. While medieval texts apply the word *gout* to various disorders, Mandeville seems to have the most common sense of the term in mind: a painful, immobilizing inflammation in one or more joints of the foot—usually at the base of the big toe. Also known—then as now—by the Latin name *podagra*, gout is caused by the accumulation of barbed urate crystals in the soft tissue around the bone. In the Middle Ages, extensive travel was implicated in the onset of gout. Andrew and Nicholas became patron saints for sufferers of *podagra* because they were associated, respectively, with fishermen and shipmen—vocational groups whose prolonged exposure to cold, damp air supposedly predisposed them to the arthritic malady.[92] Arnaut Daniel's twelfth-century Occitan lyric "Ans q·el cim" presumes the link between gout and the rigors of travel. In the poem, Arnaut construes his absence from his lady as a punishingly long pilgrimage; fortunately, the love that he feels for her insulates him from the physical hardships of the road, so that, in his words "no·m frezis freitz ni gels ni buerna, / ni·m fai dolor mals ni gota ni febres" ("cold, frost, and fog do not chill me / and neither gout nor fever can cause me pain").[93]

If Mandeville's painful ailment is the direct consequence of the asceticism of his travels, then the composition of his *Book* provides an occasion to reflect on the inevitable end of the journey that is life. Somewhat perplexingly, Rosemary Tzanaki has argued that Mandeville's gout is an attempt at irony, since the affliction would have been seen by medieval readers as ill suited to the dignity of knightly estate.[94] However, due to the enduring influence of Galen and Hippocrates, medieval people associated gout with older men (which, following his thirty-four-year journey, fairly characterizes Mandeville), and with *wealthy* older men, in particular.[95] Gout's associations with overindulgence and old age encouraged Petrarch—Mandeville's contemporary—to view the malady as an opportunity for introspection and self-reform. Across his letters and treatises, Petrarch depicts the endurance of gout as an ethical challenge, one that should be met with a stoic defiance of pain and a withdrawal from the worldly pursuits of youth—including travel.[96] Mandeville suggests that the composition of his *Book* is part of a similar program of pain management and self-examination—undertaken in an effort to die better than he has lived. This grave voice, which addresses readers from the threshold of death, is not one that has the time or the appe-

tite for frivolity and deception. Its credibility is grounded in the aging Mandeville's heroic confrontation with the painful biological consequences of
devoting his life to the physically exacting enterprise of knowing the world.

Higgins has shown that the passages discussed in this section were among
the ones most frequently, and radically, altered by readers of the *Book*.[97] I
would argue that Mandeville scholars have yet to appreciate the full implications of this fact. The nature and number of these revisions suggest a
broad, decisive repudiation of the grounds on which Mandeville attempted
to stake the authority of the *Book*. These changes to the text—some done
silently, others explicitly—reflect the seemingly widespread sense that the
assertions of the *Book* should not be allowed to rest on an abstract philosophical celebration of the traveler's travail.

FANTASIES OF AUTHORITY: REWRITING MANDEVILLE'S TRAVAILS

Four fifteenth-century versions of the *Book* produced in England—three
written in Middle English and one in Latin—include a curious addition,
made in Mandeville's voice. Known as the "papal interpolation," the passage "corrects" Mandeville's validation of lay experience and his reliance
on the moral authority of his travails.[98] In all four versions, Mandeville's
geoethnographic claims are subjected to the scrutiny of the clerical estate. Though varying from one another in many details, the renditions of
the papal interpolation all maintain that Mandeville has traveled to Rome
to have his *Book* examined and authorized. In two of the Middle English
texts—the Egerton and the Defective versions—the pope checks the *Book*
against an unnamed Latin work after which "the *Mappa Mundi* is made."
The nameless text is said to contain everything described in Mandeville's
account "and mykill mare" ("and much more").[99] The Cotton version likewise has Mandeville claim that he has "remytted my boke to ben examyned
+ preued [proved/tested]" by the pope. In words that resemble the other two
Middle English versions, Cotton declares that such measures are necessary
because readers generally refuse to believe anything that they cannot see
with their own eyes, "ne be the Auctour ne the persone neuer so trewe."[100]
The sole Latin version of the papal interpolation survives in the unique
Cosin manuscript (Durham, UK: Durham University MS. Cosin V. iii.7).
Unlike its Middle English counterparts, Cosin supplies a specific title for
the volume used to "test" Mandeville's *Book*: the *Polychronicon* of English
cleric Ranulf Higden.

The papal interpolation is not just a repudiation of Mandeville's propositions about travel writing; it is also a reflection of the ideological fantasies and utopian yearnings of an age racked by larger crises of authority. As Higgins observes, the mere identification of the pope with the city of Rome is a "partisan gesture," since it implicitly rejects the legitimacy of the rival papacy based in Avignon between 1309 and 1378.[101] The papal interpolation idealizes the Roman Curia in ways that recall Michel Foucault's notion of "heterotopia": an actually existing utopia in which all of a culture's other sites "are simultaneously represented, contested, and inverted."[102] The Cotton version emphasizes the devotional aspects of Mandeville's voyage to Rome, especially the English knight's eagerness to confess his sins to the pope. This confession is treated as an official rite of passage back into the Christian fold following Mandeville's long and problematic residence among "so many dyuerse folk of dyuerse secte."[103] In the Defective/ Egerton versions, Rome is a good place to verify the *Book* because it is a cosmopolitan center of learning: "ther beth in Rome evermore men dwellynge of diverse nacions of the worlde."[104] More precisely, then, the papal interpolation treats the Roman Curia as what Foucault called a heterotopia of "compensation"—one that is "as perfect, as meticulous, and as well arranged" as the rest of the world is "messy, ill constructed, and jumbled."[105] Yet, the earliest versions of the papal interpolation (dating from the turn of the fifteenth century) send Mandeville to a Rome that had ceased to exist in reality: a formerly significant world capital that had also ceded its place as Europe's unrivaled center of spiritual, intellectual, and cultural authority.

Dated sometime after 1485, Cosin is the latest of these versions, and it reflects a different reality.[106] By the time the Cosin manuscript was written down, the papacy had been reestablished in Rome for nearly seventy years. Cosin projects back onto the fourteenth century an anachronistic image of the Roman Curia as it probably appeared during the papacy of Sixtus IV (1471–84), who—in addition to commissioning the Sistine Chapel— oversaw large-scale architectural improvements to Rome and the dramatic augmentation of the Palatine (now Vatican) Library. The pope of the Cosin version is surrounded by a cosmopolitan court. This Holy Father examines the *Book* not only against the specific work of a well-known *auctor* but also against a cutting-edge technological invention:

> And he had a cardinal demonstrate to me a certain round instrument— crafted in a painstaking (*curiose*) and marvelous fashion—in which were contained figures or paintings of nearly every kingdom and race of people, a little marvel that is called *The Sphere of the World* . . . . And there I encountered every type of man and animal contained within my

aforementioned little book, and so taking leave of my lord the Pope, I obtained his blessing, he having verified and confirmed that which is described within my book.[107]

The wondrous gadget described in this passage may reflect the Cosin translator's familiarity with the first globes produced in Europe. The earliest surviving example of such an object is the *Erdapfel* ("Earth-Apple") of Bavarian Renaissance man Martin Behaim, produced in 1492 for the city of Nuremburg. (Behaim's globe, it should be noted, cited Mandeville as an authority.)[108] The presence of such an object at the Roman Curia is representative of Cosin's confident enhancement of the powers attributed to the pope in earlier versions of the papal interpolation.

The widely disseminated Liège version of the *Book* opts to found Mandeville's authority on the kinds of legal/documentary devices used in the accounts of John of Plano Carpini and Odoric of Pordenone. The Liège redactor radically alters Mandeville's claims about the circumstances surrounding the composition of his account, so as to cloak the *Book* in civic and juridical authority. The Liège version gets its name from its decision to situate Mandeville's arthritic convalescence—as well as the writing of the *Book*—in the town of Liège. Overwriting the vague domestic coordinates of Mandeville's retirement, the Liège version ensconces the world traveler in a decidedly local habitation and even furnishes the names of corroborating witnesses:

> in the year of grace abovesaid 1357, upon the thirty-fifth year since I left my homeland, in the noble city of Liège in Basse-Sauvenière in the inn of Hannekin known as "Le Volt," at the request and entreaty of the honorable and discreet master Jean de Bourgoigne commonly called [Jean] "of the Beard," a physician who attended/examined (*vizitoit*) me during my illness, and while attending/examining me recognized me and remembered that he had seen me in the court of the Sultan of Egypt with whom he was living when I went there.[109]

Intriguingly, medieval documents record the existence of an inn called "Le Volt" owned by one Hannekin. Jean de Bourgoigne, meanwhile, was not only a physician who resided close to this inn but also the author of a well-known treatise on the plague.[110] These two prominent citizens are called upon to bear witness to the long illness of Mandeville. Jean also verifies Mandeville's presence at the sultan's court in Cairo. A slightly later tradition, probably instigated by fourteenth-century civic chronicler Jean de

Outremeuse, claimed that Jean de Bourgoigne and Mandeville were actually the same person. This belief won enough support to be inscribed on the tomb that allegedly contained the body of Mandeville, located in Liège's Church of the Guillelmins.[111]

The Liège version and its satellite myths accord the medical profession a conspicuous degree of authority in geoethnographic matters. Outremeuse's spurious identification of Mandeville as the renowned author of medical treatises provided an impetus for the lapidary that would eventually circulate under Mandeville's name. The Chantilly manuscript of the *Book* (Chantilly: Musée Condé MS. 699) is bound with this lapidary and with other scientific works, also attributed to Mandeville.[112]

The seeds of this reinvention of Mandeville as a medical expert may have been planted by the *Book*'s discussion of his gout. The phrase *goutes artetikes* puzzled many of Mandeville's medieval readers. Michel Velser— who translated the Continental French version of the *Book* into German at the turn of the fifteenth century—confessed that he did not know how to render *goutes artetikes* into his native tongue, but correctly surmised that it was called *podagra* in Latin. Velser left a small space for readers with greater medical knowledge to insert the right word if they happened to know it.[113] This would suggest that, for a German-speaking reader like Velser, the Latin term was more "vernacular" than the French phrase deployed by Mandeville (notwithstanding the Germanic roots of the word *goutes*). This conjecture finds support in the fact that *podagra* is the word used to identify the bodily affliction of the Fisher King in Wolfram von Eschenbach's Middle High German romance *Parzival*.[114] Velser's candid admission of ignorance suggests the unspoken motives that may have prompted Middle English translators to omit the phrase *goutes artetikes* and attribute Mandeville's suffering to old age, fatigue, or generalized malaise.[115] One possible explanation for the puzzlement of the *Book*'s translators is that, as an English-born speaker of French, Mandeville overestimated his audience's familiarity with medical jargon. It is highly likely (though not decisively proved) that the *Book* was originally composed in Insular French, a language in which there was a uniquely long and "precocious" tradition of translating Latin medical texts into the vernacular.[116] It is also possible that the confusing phrase was chosen archly, for its potentially disarming mixture of familiarity and obscurity. A cursory examination of any dictionary of Middle English—or of Old or Middle French—reveals that *goutes* and its variants were not especially obscure, nor were forms of the Greek-derived *artetikes*. The uncertainty of Mandeville's readers may have been caused by the union of the two terms, which—on their own—were familiar enough for perceptive readers to hazard a guess about the nature of the knight's suffering, yet, when combined, were technical-sounding enough to make them doubt themselves. In other words, it is possible that, embedded in the quasi-recondite term *goutes artetikes* is an implicit appeal to the authority of the medical expert, who has—as readers are permitted to infer—inspected and diagnosed the travel-worn body of Mandeville. It was just such an inference that opened the door to the Liège version's introduction of Jean de Bourgoigne onto the scene of the *Book*'s genesis.

Even before the Liège interpolation, the bodily symptoms of Mandeville's travails had been invoked as a mode of proof. One of the few truly marked differences between the Insular and Continental versions of the *Book* is that the latter includes a longer, more open-ended, rendition of the Perilous Valley episode. In the Continental, Mandeville and his companions undergo a barrage of physical punishments not mentioned in the Insular. They are buffeted by winds and knocked to the ground by demons in the shape of wild beasts. During a thunderstorm, the travelers fall into a swoon and experience supernatural visions. Those who are lucky enough to emerge from the valley alive bear "a black scar as large as a hand" ("*vne noire tache du large dune main*"), left by their invisible assailant. In the case of Mandeville, the mark is located on the neck:

> I bore the mark (*l'enseingne*), black as coal, for more than 18 years. Many people saw it. But having later repented of my sins and having tried to serve God as best as my shortcomings would allow, this mark (*tache*) has completely vanished and the skin is whiter in that place than in any other. But the blow (*coup*) is still quite visible there, and will be as long as my flesh lasts.[117]

In referring to his wound/scar as an *enseingne*, this vignette suggests that Mandeville's travel-worn body is a text that can be—and has been—scrutinized and decoded. In Old and Middle French, *enseingne* signified a number of objects used to confirm the identity of people or the authenticity of objects. Its range of meanings included: birthmark, pilgrimage badge, heraldic device, stigmata, a mark left by penal branding, as well as a personal or official seal (used to "sign" letters, documents, or counterfeitable goods).[118]

The significance of Mandeville's *enseingne* is overdetermined in a way that recalls the mystifying tactics that underpin the authority of Odoric of Pordenone. To the end, it remains unclear what the enigmatic mark on Mandeville's neck actually signifies. Is the *enseingne* a punitive mark or a badge of honor? Does it betoken the knight's completion of his penitential pilgrimage through the valley, or is it a warning addressed to excessively curious travelers? On the one hand, the knight's scar recalls the stigmata imprinted into the flesh of saints like Francis of Assisi. On the other hand, the blow (*coup*) to the neck recalls the ceremonial dubbing of knights, also known as the *accolade*, a word that derives from the Latin phrase "to the neck" (*ad-collum*). The ceremony of dubbing has come to conjure images of the kneeling knight receiving a decorous sword tap on each shoulder, but during the Middle Ages, the ritual could also involve a bare-handed blow to the side of the neck.[119] If the passage through the Perilous Valley evokes this chivalric rite of passage, whose *enseingne* is imprinted on Mandeville's neck, and who delivered the *coup* that put it there? These doubts are left deliberately unresolved by the text, allegedly in response to a prohibition issued by the Tuscan friars who accompanied Mandeville's fellowship into the valley and who forbade them from disclosing the secrets of God. In this way, the Continental version manages to preserve the auratic distance ensured by the motif of authorial withholding while attributing this individualistic gesture to the dictates of members of Odoric's order.

When Michel Velser tried to make sense of the Continental version of the Perilous Valley episode, he initially found himself at a loss: "Item, before I go any further, I, Michel Velser, who translated this book into German, want to say something, and let it displease no man. It is true—all that I have read in this book, although, in my opinion, I have never read anything as unbelievable as this material."[120] This qualification is followed by a lengthy autobiographical anecdote, the ultimate purpose of which is to legitimize the story of Mandeville's brush with the supernatural in the mysterious valley.

Velser, a native of Bavaria, relates a story drawn from his own business-related travel to the Italian Piedmont.[121] Velser lived for some time in the northern Italian jurisdiction of Castello di Bardassano, where he had been appointed to an administrative position. It was during this period of his life that he began to study French—and when he first encountered *The Book of John Mandeville*. One day during Lent, Velser sent for a Franciscan confessor from the neighboring town of Chieri. When the friar arrived, he found Velser poring over Mandeville's account:

> He asked me what the book talked about. I told him. Then, he said,
> "Come to the city of Chieri and I will show you in our library a book
> that our Guardian made on his death bed. Then see the wonders and ask
> what he saw, for he traveled to many lands beyond the sea." And shortly

I saw this book, and it was chained down in the Franciscan Cloister in the city of Chieri. The monk in question was from Chieri from a family named Raschier. Then, I saw in this book that he went with Sir John (*Hans*) Mandeville through the valley, although he did not name him, but he did speak of an English knight, and that they were thirteen people, and when they came out from there, there were only nine of them; and he sustained a mark on his body as did Sir John. And only then did I believe it was true, because the one confirmed the other, and the [first] monk thought that he [the dead guardian] was a blessed man.[122]

The mysterious chained book is probably a distorted reference to the *Relatio* of Odoric of Pordenone. If this is the case, Velser is describing a version of the *Relatio* that has not survived or that perhaps never existed. As we have seen, Odoric's adventure in the demonic valley contradicts Mandeville's in matters large and small. In terms of Velser's story, the most significant discrepancy is that the *Relatio* treats Odoric's adventure as a solo trek and certainly does not allude to the presence of an English knight.

It is ultimately impossible to know for certain what book Velser was shown or whether he or someone else—for whatever reason—mischaracterized its contents. For the sake of argument, let us presume that Velser has not confected the entire anecdote. Velser may have been shown a version of the *Relatio* in which a copyist or commentator had added a reference to a travel account written by an English knight, perhaps in the form of a marginal gloss. It could also be the case that Velser's Franciscan hosts, not wanting to disappoint their guest, were not painstakingly accurate in their précis of the chained book's contents. Or maybe Velser, succumbing to confirmation bias, examined the friary's volume and either overlooked or ignored elements of it that were discordant with Mandeville's account.

We are on more certain ground in unpacking the assumptions that underlie Velser's conceptions of proof and authority. The fact that the book detailing the travels of the Italian friar is chained in the library of a specific Franciscan house shows that it is highly valued by the community, which knew its author intimately. This communal endorsement is based on the saintly reputation and noble lineage of the Franciscan travel writer. Ultimately, Velser ties the authority of Mandeville's *Book* to the book written by this friar; the authority of both accounts hinges on the judgment of the Franciscan community of Chieri regarding the man who once lived among them. Of course, this entire logical edifice rests on the fact that Mandeville—whoever he might have been—inscribed two nameless Tuscan friars into the Perilous Valley anecdote, allowing readers like Velser to link his *Book* to the one that he plagiarized. Similar tautologies suffuse the reception history of *The Book of John Mandeville*. The accounts of Odoric and Mandeville were frequently bound in the same medieval manuscripts and cross-referenced against each other (ironically, sometimes to the detriment of Odoric's reputation).[123]

Impostures like *The Book of John Mandeville* are colorful test cases, highlighting the limitations of a given society's procedures for determining official truths. Mandeville and the medieval authors of lesser known travel-writing hoaxes—such as Johannes Witte de Hese's *Itinerarius* and the anonymous *Libro del conoscimiento de todos los reinos* (Book of the knowledge of all of the kingdoms)—took advantage of an intellectual and cultural terrain in which new geographical discovery was not unusual and in which appeals to the travails of travel were easy to manufacture and carried considerable evidentiary weight.[124] The success of such literary pranks should be viewed in conjunction with the efforts of Mandeville's readers to reorient his claims to authority. They are all the product of their makers' savvy navigation of the loosely integrated spheres of medieval cultural production, and they shine light on a widespread, self-conscious exploitation of the gaps and fissures that resulted from the existence of competing centers of intellectual authority.

While the *Book*'s author and some of its readers seem to have delighted in the liberty afforded by this polycentric terrain, others—like the parties that introduced and augmented the papal interpolation—did so while fantasizing about the existence of a unipolar intellectual world, in which there was a single uncontested head of the Latin Christian church, who also served as the arbiter of, and ultimate authority on, matters of geoethnographic controversy. This heterotopic vision of the Roman Curia is, essentially, an avatar of modern scholarship's cartoonish rendition of the intellectual landscape of the Middle Ages: a closed, complacent, and hierarchical system, in which theological and academic authority readily scuttled the subversive implications of new geographical discovery. It is important to remember that the fantasies expressed in the papal interpolation of Mandeville's *Book* were just that: fantasies. The existence and the reception history of *The Book of John Mandeville* paints a more chaotic, and more truthful, portrait of an era at once thrilled and troubled by its discoveries, which outstripped the knowledge that it had inherited from the predecessors it so revered.

CONCLUSION

A long scholarly tradition treats empiricism and authority in matters of geographical knowledge as timeless entities locked in a protracted, epoch-defining battle for dominance. Among the manifest errors of this account, one of the most glaring is its one-dimensional understanding of medieval notions of authority, which, in reality, evolved in response to the expansion of official record keeping, the rise of vernacular reading publics, and—yes—the hunger for new geographical knowledge. Though less centralized than it would be in some subsequent historical settings, the production of geoethnographic knowledge in the Middle Ages was no less plagued by doubt and internal dissension. Like their modern counterparts, medieval readers were—to borrow from the subtitle of Anthony Grafton's book—by no means inured to "the shock of discovery."

PART II

Pilgrimage as Literate Labor

The assumption that geographical thought in the Middle Ages was dominated by theological authority has had a particularly unfortunate effect
on the reception of medieval pilgrimage accounts. The stereotype of the
docile, uninquisitive pilgrim has given book-length surveys of travel writing license to dispense with the Middle Ages in just a few paragraphs, on
the grounds that there just isn't much to say on the topic. Let the following
passage stand in for dozens of others in the annals of modern scholarship:

> Since the pilgrims' experience of travel was thus heavily influenced by
> the texts handed down to them, it is not surprising that pilgrim accounts
> frequently take their descriptions of Holy Places from other texts—the
> predestined nature of the pilgrim's experience makes a fresh description
> unnecessary, and perhaps even impossible. Thus pilgrims' accounts are
> particularly uniform and, curiously for the modern reader, many of them
> hardly record the experience of a foreign, and "other" world at all.[1]

There is a more melancholic variation on this stereotype, which romanti-
cizes the medieval pilgrim as a happy soul unburdened by the existential
doubts that plague the modern traveler.[2] While less overtly dismissive, this
nostalgic view likewise presumes that medieval pilgrimage was less searching and self-aware than latter-day modes of mobility. The historiographical
plot arc that shapes the story of western attitudes toward travel is, in sum,
dogmatically committed to the myth of pilgrim alterity. This myth is ultimately a trite and reflexive assertion of the absolute epochal difference of
the Middle Ages.

An article of faith among medievalists has done much to reinforce this
misconception—namely, that the travel writing of pilgrims to the Holy

Land is so qualitatively different from travel writing about East Asia that each constitutes its own self-enclosed corpus. One (quite excellent) study of twentieth-century travel narrative makes the consequences of this position clear when it treats the pilgrim as a foil for both Marco Polo and the dashing explorers of the "Age of Discovery":

> Narratives of pilgrimage faded in importance as narratives of encounter and conquest proliferated on the bookshelves of the fifteenth, sixteenth, and seventeenth centuries. Adventurers, those sailors and soldiers who set out from European ports to traverse the globe, understood themselves as dauntless men unbound by insular tradition, men unwilling to be contained by the world as it was contemporaneously mapped, men willing to defy the superstitions and fixed itineraries of earlier travelers. Marco Polo, Christopher Columbus, Captain Cook—they sailed off, jumped onto unknown shores, named the land and its inhabitants, conquered and pacified those who resisted, pushed further into interiors, and crossed frontiers.[3]

This argument is typical in placing Polo on the side of modernity while relegating pilgrimage to the medieval past, dismissing it as a mode of travel forever abandoned in favor of the "modern" project of mapping and plundering the New World. Indeed, until recent scholarship by early modernists proved otherwise, it was widely held that pilgrimage—particularly to the Holy Land—withered on the vine in 1492, in dutiful acknowledgment of its utter irrelevance to the postmedieval world. It turns out that pilgrims not only continued to voyage overseas to Jerusalem long after Columbus's bungled search for Asia, they also continued to write about their journeys in significant (if diminished) numbers.

Chapters 3 and 4 explore how pilgrim-authors shifted the grounds on which the traveler claimed the authority to write about his or her experiences. The account of Holy Land pilgrimage increasingly supplemented the quantitative rhetoric of travail endured with a qualitative rhetoric, which emphasized the techniques of self-governance and methods of geo-ethnographic investigation adopted during the journey. In effect, Jerusalem pilgrims diminished the stature of physical travail, by focusing on the behavioral regimes that empowered them to overcome it; many of these self-disciplinary activities incorporated, or were modeled after, practices of reading and writing. In reorienting heroic travel away from travail and toward literate labor, pilgrims developed a constellation of precepts and practices that were adopted by travelers to destinations other than the Holy Land.

While pilgrims to Rome, Santiago de Compostela, and Saint Patrick's Purgatory produced a notable number of travel accounts during the Middle Ages, they did not do so in the staggering numbers that Jerusalem pilgrims did. This quantitative difference contributed to a qualitative one, as the seeming ubiquity of accounts of pilgrimage to the Holy Land fostered the most complex, socially diverse, and self-reflexive tradition of travel writing to emerge during the Middle Ages.

CHAPTER THREE

Memory Work and the Labor of Writing

The traveler has long been burdened by the obligation not to forget. In Homer's *Odyssey*, figures such as Circe and the Lotus Eaters raise the menacing possibility that the traveler might fail to remember his way back home. This was a special kind of forgetting, a terrifying—and perversely alluring—surrender of the self to the dehumanizing appetites of a foreign world. With such a prospect in mind, Plato argued that Athenian citizens ought to be barred from traveling until the age of forty, since younger men were more apt to "unlearn what they are taught" when exposed to foreign customs.[1] For Homer and Plato, the psychic and sensual intensities of travel have the power to disrupt the regimes of self-discipline that unite the traveler's native community and define his privileged position within it.

The Middle Ages developed a unique, and historically significant, variation on the theme of memory and travel. A number of medieval travel writers—most of them pilgrims to the Holy Land—feared that, having achieved the day of their homecoming, they would fail to remember the journey. The dilemma faced by Felix Fabri offers a window onto this characteristically medieval concern. For much of 1480, Fabri—a Dominican from the town of Ulm—toiled away at his desk. He did so in vain. Try as he might, Fabri could not conjure "a clear description" of his recent nine-day sojourn in the Holy Land.[2] He was particularly troubled by his inability to answer basic questions about the layout and relative orientations of the places he had visited, which appeared to his mind's eye "shrouded in a dark mist as though I had beheld them in a dream."[3] Discomfited by these failures, Fabri judged his pilgrimage "imperfect, superficial, distracted, and confused."[4] He blamed his muddled impressions on his Franciscan tour guides, who had whisked him and his companions from one site to the next so that they were forced "to run around the holy places without understanding and feeling what they were."[5]

Fabri was so dissatisfied with the experience that he risked the censure of his order by requesting permission to embark on a second—more leisurely—pilgrimage, a journey that he would eventually undertake in 1483–84. Following this second voyage, Fabri produced no fewer than four books based on his travels, in both Latin and German. Today, the most famous of these is his *Evagatorium*, a massive Latin account that is the product of careful observation and painstaking research into the works of previous travel writers.[6] The exhaustive reading that fortified Fabri for his second pilgrimage also positioned him to become the most sophisticated synthesizer of the conventions and debates that had shaped the development of travel writing on the Holy Land over the course of the previous ten centuries. For this reason, the story of Fabri's two pilgrimages will serve as a recurring point of reference for the present chapter, which argues that Jerusalem pilgrims developed a set of ideas about the relationship between memory, literacy, and travel, the influence of which has yet to be recognized. Drawing on devotional and scholarly traditions (many of them centuries old), these pilgrim-authors present their books as the culmination of the ennobling spiritual and intellectual labor of their journey—and as a triumph over travel's temptations and travails.

The first two sections of this chapter sketch the intellectual and devotional contexts that help explain why memory—and, in particular, the memory *of and for place*—loomed so large in pilgrims' conceptions of successful travel. The first section explores how the metaphors of "the book of memory" and "the book of the world" influenced medieval views of geography and travel—and even the design of medieval travel books. The second section examines the ritual practices that comprised *the memory work of pilgrimage*. The commemorative rituals in which pilgrims to the Holy Land participated were not ends in themselves but rather the first step in a lifelong exercise of the intellect, which involved the meditative reconstruction of the places in which he or she had worshiped. This memory work was conditioned by the mnemonic theories of the liberal arts classroom, and— like formal education in the trivium—aimed to effect permanent change in those who engaged in it.

The subsequent three sections of the chapter consider how late medieval conventions of learned and bureaucratic writing informed the theory and practice of devotional travel. The third section discusses a predominately clerical approach to travel writing about the Holy Land, which I call the *synthetic tradition*. Drawing on common medieval ideas about the roles played by memory in written composition, synthetic travel writers present their texts as manifestations of the devout self-discipline of pilgrimage. Today, the writers of the synthetic tradition have a reputation for subordinating subjective experience to abstract topographical description. This misleading judgment is based on critics' lack of familiarity with medieval mnemonic theory, which led synthetic travel writers to view the process of writing topographical description after the conclusion of the pilgrimage as part of "the subjective experience of travel"—and not as an activity exterior or antithetical to it.

The fourth section considers the work of Fabri and another contributor to the synthetic tradition, fourteenth-century Franciscan Niccolò da Poggibonsi. Niccolò and Fabri repeatedly discuss the note-taking practices they adopted during their journeys, with a specificity that makes them unique within the synthetic tradition. Their emphasis on writing in transit registers their debt to, and rivalry with, the travel diary, the topic of the fifth and final section. The diary illustrates how the late medieval expansion of literacy—facilitated by the availability of paper and the rise of urban professional classes—made the habits of writing that the traveler adopted *during* the journey a topic of debate and self-reflection among travel writers. Throughout the chapter, I will also pause to consider how the ideas and practices pioneered by Holy Land pilgrims influenced the reception history of Marco Polo, John Mandeville, and other "exotic" travel writers of the Middle Ages.

THE BOOK OF MEMORY AND THE BOOK OF THE WORLD

The very education that empowered medieval travel writers to leave behind memorials of their journeys shaped their perceptions of the world as they traveled through it. Searching for the language to explain the qualitative difference between his two pilgrimages, Felix Fabri drew on the familiar experiences of the language arts classroom:

> I regarded this [first] pilgrimage as merely the preamble (*praeambulum*) to that which I intended to make. As a student who means to commit some passage to memory (*aliquam memoriae commendare*) first reads it over carelessly (*perfunctorie lectionem praevidet*), and then reads it again slowly and leisurely, taking sufficient time to impress (*imprimendi*) it on his mind, so I did with regard to my determination; and I was far from being satisfied with the things I saw, nor did I commit them to memory (*memoriae commendaveram*), but kept them for a future pilgrimage.[7]

Two learned conceits intersect in this passage: the book of memory and
the book of the world. Fabri likens his initial exposure to the Holy Land to the
preliminary phases of *lectio*, in which the pilgrim/student skims over the
landscape/text in order to acquaint himself with its overall contours. His
second journey is implicitly compared to *meditatio*, a slower and more ab-
sorbing practice, in which the student internalizes the text through sustained and focused reflection.[8] It is only through great discipline and effort
that the pilgrim succeeds in imprinting the Holy Land (both chapter and
verse) onto the pages of memory's tome. In the Middle Ages, both of these
book-related metaphors were commonplace and already ancient. For this
reason, it is perhaps too easy to take them for granted—and, in the process,
to fail to observe the extent to which they informed the behavior of travelers
like Fabri.

The conceptual vocabulary of ancient and medieval rhetoricians abounds
in analogies that equate the movements of mind, body, and signifier. The
venerable Isidore of Seville was peddling long-venerable ideas when he
linked travel, memory, and the language arts in his etymology of the word
littera ("letters"):

> The use of letters was invented for the sake of remembering things,
> which are bound by letters lest they slip away into oblivion. With so
> great a variety of information, not everything could be learned by hear-
> ing, nor retained in the memory. Letters (littera) are so called as if the
> term were *legitera*, because they provide a road (iter) for those who are
> reading (legere), or because they are repeated (iterare) in reading.[9]

Few scholars of travel writing can resist pointing out that *metaphor* is itself
a metaphor, one whose kinetic origins are disclosed in modern Greek, a
language in which the word *metaphor* means "bus." *Apostrophe* describes
a diversion or "turning away" from the through-line of an argument or narrative, while the Latin *ductus* refers to the manner in which the structure
of a written work "guides" readers through its subject matter.[10] These and
dozens of other terms show how central travel is to premodern conceptions
of reading, writing, and cognition.

Conversely, the metaphors of the "book of the world" and "the book of
memory" suggested that travel was a kind of reading.[11] Learned convention
textualized the material world in a number of ways. In the Middle Ages,
Asia, Europe, and Africa were not called "continents" but rather "parts"
(*partes*)—the same term used to describe the textual units (books, chapters, verses, lines, and so on) that resulted from the scholarly division (*di-*

visio) of academic texts, for the purposes of memorization and formal analysis.[12] Medieval travel writing routinely subjects cities, monuments, and
landscapes to the procedures of textual commentary and exegesis—layering
moral, historical, and even eschatological inferences atop physical reality.

The bookish stances that many medieval travel writers adopt toward
topographical description reflect geography's place in the teaching of the
trivium. Jerome characterized geographical knowledge as an indispensable
tool for interpreting the Bible and pagan texts like the *Aeneid*.[13] Augustine's *On Christian Doctrine* seconded this opinion by including a familiarity with biblical places and place-names as part of the basic knowledge of
"things" necessary for the correct interpretation of scriptural "signs."[14] The
research of Patrick Gautier Dalché suggests the influence of these ideas on
early medieval grammarians, who seem to have used maps in teaching students to read the Bible and other schoolroom texts.[15] Throughout the Middle
Ages and Renaissance, maps continued to serve pedagogical and mnemonic
functions in classrooms and libraries.[16]

Meanwhile, the spatialized models of memory that medieval travel writers inherited from antiquity reinforced the importance of keeping places and
their names distinct from one another. Pedagogy viewed the well-trained
memory as one that could essentially be mapped, its contents anchored in
unique "places" (*loci*) within larger imaginary structures.[17] The goal of such
memory techniques was to increase the ease and flexibility of retrieval,
which in turn facilitated activities such as cross-referencing, written composition, and extemporaneous speaking.[18] Alphabetized coffers and architectural monuments—including palaces, cathedrals, and amphitheaters—were
all recommended as decent imaginary filing systems.[19] Of obvious importance to travel writing, cities and roads were also among the artificial mnemonic devices endorsed by rhetoricians.[20]

In a context in which geography was central to textual analysis and in
which the formal training of memory was the foundation of intellectual
life, sound toponymic recall was a hallmark of scholarly authority. This
is why Gervase of Tilbury implored readers not to charge him with "ignorance or mendacity" for using ancient toponyms at certain junctures of his
Otia imperialia and, at others, their modern counterparts.[21] The burlesque
itinerary that Boccaccio's Friar Cipolla dishes up to the gullible villagers of
Certaldo in day six, story ten of the *Decameron* is littered with mangled
place-names (many of them filthy double entendres). The enthusiastic response to this crudely fabricated yarn bears out the narrator's characterization of the friar as a "latter-day Cicero or Quintilian" in terms of his
powers of persuasion, while his ineptitude with place-names illustrates the

novella's seemingly contradictory claim that Cipolla, for all of his oratorical
finesse, is "completely ignorant" (*"niuna scienza avendo"*).[22] In the fourteenth century, Boncompagno da Signa maintained that a foolproof memory for place-names could be attained only through a forbidding program of
study, which included the close examination of Scripture, *mappaemundi*,
encyclopedias, histories, and the works of "other philosophers and poets
who have discussed topics of this sort."[23] Two centuries later, Erasmus—
echoing Augustine—treated a command for place-names as low-hanging
fruit for anyone with the slightest pretensions to intellectual seriousness,
deriding simpletons who "turn the name of a tree into a quadruped . . . a
cithera player into a river, a town into a fruit."[24]

These attitudes help explain why the failure to recall place-names correctly could expose even bona fide travelers to charges of Cipolla-esque
mendacity. The scribe who helped Margery Kempe record her late-life pilgrimage across central Europe anticipated that withering criticisms might
be leveled against one or both of them on precisely this account:

> If the names of the places are not correctly written, let no man marvel,
> because she studied more about contemplation than about the names
> of places, and he that has written them down has never seen them and
> therefore excuse him.[25]

Manuscript evidence shows that medieval readers of travel writing cross-
referenced works by different authors in order to identify and correct erroneous place-names.[26] A reputation for toponymic fidelity has even shaped—
for better and for worse—the long-term reputations of certain medieval
travelers. Sixteenth-century mathematician Kaspar Peucer published Friar
Burchard of Mount Sion's *Description of the Holy Land* as a companion
piece to his own treatise on the calculation of geographical distance. Peucer criticized people's ignorance about the names and relative locations
of places, declaring it "not only an egregious barbarism, but also a token
of impiety." He held up the topographical scrupulosity of Burchard as a
model for his readers to emulate.[27] *Astley's Voyages*, an eighteenth-century
history of travel, averred that Odoric of Pordenone had never been to East
Asia, in part because his account garbled or perhaps fabricated "the names
of places." For this reason, Odoric appears in the index of the *Voyages* as:
"Oderic [*sic*], Friar, Travels of, *A great Liar. Ibid.*"[28] Ramusio found himself
on the defensive when it came to the erroneous place-names he found in
manuscripts of Marco Polo, a fault he laid at the feet of careless medieval

scribes.[29] To this day, Polo's tendency to use Persian, rather than Chinese, toponyms is cited as evidence that he did not actually visit China.[30]

For particularly learned pilgrims like Burchard of Mount Sion, a topographical place was also a topic of scholarship. One gets the sense that, as Burchard looked out upon a landscape, he reflexively approached it as a memory place, where he gathered his recollections of what had been written about it. Indeed, Burchard's methods of geographical investigation betray the influence of Scholasticism on how he experienced the physical reality of the Holy Land. Throughout his *Description*, Burchard leverages his scholastic training in order to identify, juxtapose, and adjudicate contradictory geographical claims. While visiting Sabaste, Burchard is hosted by a community of Greek monks, who tell him that their monastery was founded on the site where John the Baptist was imprisoned. Citing several authorities—including Josephus, Peter Comestor, and Eusebius—Burchard pronounces their claim "useless," observing that John the Baptist "was beheaded in Machaerus, which is today called Haylon."[31] Burchard does not stop at correcting his eastern Christian hosts. In the very same discussion of Sabaste, Burchard wields his first-hand analysis of the town's layout to challenge what Peter Comestor—one of the authorities that he has just cited to refute the Greek monks—has written about 1 Kings 20:10:

> [Comestor] seems to imagine that the city wall and the mountaintop were equal in height and that buildings were constructed over them. This was not the case; on the contrary, the city wall was at the foot of the mountain, strongly fortified with very strong towers, and the mountain was inside it rising gradually upwards and encircled by buildings, just as a bunch is filled with grapes, and when upright, rises gradually to a point.[32]

The implicit point of this otherwise curious digression seems to be that, even for a scholar as famed for his erudition as Peter "the Book Eater" Comestor, one's learning is not complete until one has reconciled the book of the memory against the book of the world.

The density of scholarly and poetic discourses that surrounded the Holy Land ensured that one did not have to be a university-trained theologian in order to feel the effects of textual mediation on one's travels. Medieval travelers experienced the places that they visited under the influence of liturgy, painting, drama, sermons, and personal reading (in much the same way that modern tourists navigate cities like New York or Paris under the influence of iconic photographs, television shows, motion pictures, and novels).[33] Consider the example of the Red Sea. Two intellectual-discursive traditions conditioned how many medieval pilgrims experienced that body of water. On the one hand, the Red Sea was the site of the miraculous emancipation of the Hebrew people in Exodus, an event that was linked—by typological association—to Christian salvation. At the same time, the Red Sea also conjured the allure of Oriental luxury—gold, spices, perfumes, gems—and all of the moral hazards that attended them.[34] This latter association (inherited from antiquity) was strengthened by the Red Sea's role as a medieval entrepôt for luxury goods from the Indian Ocean.[35] The intersection of these two discursive nebulas predisposed medieval pilgrims to approach the Red Sea with a mixture of wonder and trepidation.

In a surprising number of travel accounts, the Red Sea becomes the stage for a morality play, in which the pilgrim is tempted by worldly appetites. For Thietmar (ca. 1217), temptation came in the form of the dazzlingly colorful seashells and pebbles that adorned the shores of the Red Sea. After an initial period of enchantment, Thietmar suddenly resolved to rein in his admiration, for fear that it had become excessive.[36] Over a century later, Friar Niccolò da Poggibonsi unearthed a scintillating gem along the same shoreline, only to lose it shortly after, during his arduous desert trek toward Mount Sinai. Niccolò construes the loss of the treasured object as a divinely ordained punishment for his materialism.[37] Petrarch cautioned a friend who was traveling to the Holy Land not to get drawn into admiring the "Indian Spices and the merchandise of the East" while visiting the Red Sea but instead reflect on the liberation of the Hebrew people: "The former is the work of human cupidity and weakness, the second of piety and divine power."[38] For Pero Tafur, the Red Sea temptation is a possible chivalric adventure in India, a prospect that the knight ultimately rejects as trivial and reckless (see chapter 6). In all of these examples, one sees the cross-pollination of older ideas about memory's power to ward off the subversive enticements of travel with medieval techniques of memory training, in which place-names are used to store and cross-reference knowledge gained through reading and devotional instruction. More important, these examples illustrate the mental self-discipline demanded of the pilgrim, who must at all times focus his contemplative and mnemonic energies in the proper directions.

The metaphors of the book of the world and the book of memory even influenced the layout and decorative programs of medieval travel books. Consider two deceptively simple illuminations, each from a different manuscript of *The Book of John Mandeville*:

Figure 4. Mandeville between the Tree of the Sun and the Tree of the Moon. From *Le livre des merveilles* (ca.1400–1420). Bibliothèque nationale de France, ms. fr. 2810, f. 220r. (Photograph: BNF, Paris.)

The first image—from the *Livre des merveilles*—appears to document Mandeville's visitation of a place along his itinerary (fig. 4). Flanked by two trees, the genuflecting knight contemplates a book while mischief-meaning beasts lurk in the wings, licking their chops in his general direction. Readers familiar with the *Book* will recognize the twin arbors as the Tree of the Sun and the Tree of the Moon. The prophetic powers of the legendary trees enticed Alexander the Great to the ends of the earth in an effort to learn about—and thereby evade—the hour of his death.[39] Since Mandeville twice mentions that he aspired—but failed—to visit the trees himself, one might conclude that the illuminator has misread the text.

Nothing of the kind has occurred. By condensing two registers of reality into a single image, the illuminator succeeds in translating the moral argument that the *Book* wages through its repeated allusions to Alexander's visitation of the oracular trees. In an aside not found in William of Boldensele—the principal source of the *Book*'s descriptions of Egypt—Mandeville reports that the Egyptian sultan's famous garden outside Cairo is one of only two places on earth where the balm of Gilead can be grown successfully. The other place "is in India Major in that desert where Alexander spoke to the Tree of the Sun and the Tree of the Moon. But I have not seen it . . . for there are too many dangerous routes to navigate."[40] The second reference to the trees occurs during the *Book*'s depiction of India. Once again, Mandeville observes that he did *not* traverse the perilous, beast-filled desert that separates the trees from the habitable regions of the world.[41] Unlike Alexander, Mandeville accepts the inevitability of his mortality and does not hazard his life—or the lives of traveling companions—in order to gain knowledge that might forestall it. The illuminator renders Mandeville's posture (head bowed, knees bent) and his costume (a pilgrim tunic so spare that it exposes his left leg) in a way that underscores his piety and geographical humility. The image deliberately conflates an inaccessible place on the globe with its corresponding "reality" as a memory place in Mandeville's mind in order to express the *Book*'s ethical concerns about which circumstances do—and which do not—justify particularly perilous journeys.

For a viewer familiar with the conceits of the book of memory and the book of the world, the second Mandeville miniature (fig. 5) invites a surprisingly rich range of interpretations. On the left margin of the page, Mandeville sits on the ground, and—in Jane Goodall fashion—takes note of the behavior of the Blemmye, a legendary race of acephalous creatures with faces on their torsos. As is true of other illuminations in the same manuscript, Mandeville sports the characteristic hat, tunic, scrip, and bourdon of the pilgrim. One way to interpret this image is that it is making a documentary claim about Mandeville's note-taking practices.[42] Since the surrounding text says nothing about Mandeville's experiences among these people, it is possible that the image aims to represent the otherwise invisible labor that went into the knight's travel account. In such an interpretation of the image, Mandeville's notebook can also be seen as a literalization of the book of memory, as a materialization of intellectual labor.

Nor is this all. Like the physical world and the human memory, the pages of medieval manuscripts are also organized into "places." Marginal notes and illuminations were mnemonic aids, guides that led readers back to this or that passage in a book. One of the most common mnemonic drawings found in medieval manuscripts is the *maniculus*, a disembodied hand that points toward a noteworthy passage. The marginal inscription "nota" (the imperative form of the Latin *notāre*—to remember) served the same purpose.[43] This manuscript of Mandeville's *Book* adopts the common practice of building such notes into its design on the reader's behalf. Various marginal images show Mandeville pointing toward a textual passage, extending his index finger in a manner obviously modeled after the *maniculus*. The picture of the note-taking Mandeville could be counted as a variation on this mnemonic motif, one that enjoins readers to engage the *Book* with the same enthusiasm and intellectual care that characterized the travels of its author.

Figure 5. Mandeville among the Blemmye (ca. 1425–50). British Library, Harley 3954, f. 42r. (Photograph: © The British Library Board.)

The fact that Mandeville is pictured as a pilgrim reinforces the didactic interpretation of this image. Broadly speaking—and in an emphatically literal sense—the medieval pilgrim traveled *in order to* remember. As a self-professed pilgrim to the Holy Land, Mandeville had undertaken a journey that medieval readers would have associated with a uniquely challenging form of memory work. Sustained by an increasingly formalized set of rituals, the memory work of Jerusalem pilgrims built on the same learned notions of *place* that imbued these two visual depictions of Mandeville with ethical significance.

PILGRIMAGE AS MEMORY WORK

By the later Middle Ages, pilgrimage had long been identified with the penitential mortification of the flesh. An equally long tradition portrayed it as a rigorous labor of the mind—and of the memory, in particular. The memory work of medieval pilgrims was based on a more flexible notion of the mind-body dichotomy than the one presumed by many modern readers. The practices of the medieval pilgrim begin with the assumption that remembrance is achieved not only through the movements of the mind but also through the movements of the body, of other people's bodies, and even of inanimate objects.

The pilgrimage of thanksgiving is one corner of a larger constellation of pilgrim rituals that illustrate the contours of this material, embodied, intersubjective, and interobjective conception of memory. Chaucer's *Canterbury*

Tales depicts the pilgrimage to the tomb of Thomas à Becket as a remembrance of past mercies in the form of a physical journey:

> And specially from every shires ende
> Of Engelond to Caunterbury they wende,
> The hooly blisful martir for to seke
> That hem hath holpen whan that they were seeke.[44]

Having reached their destination, actual pilgrims expressed their gratitude to the shrine's saints through votive offerings. Ex-voto offerings—made of wax, wood, or precious metal—were shaped to resemble an object that had something to do with the kind of succor that a given saint had provided the grateful devotee. Pilgrims cured of cataracts might donate a pair of wax eyes; those recovering from arthritis a leg or arm; those who had prayed successfully to conceive a child, wax genitalia; and so on.[45] According to Jean de Joinville, Queen Margaret of France vowed to undertake a pilgrimage to the Church of Saint Nicholas in Varangéville after a tempest began to batter the ship that conveyed her back to France from the Seventh Crusade. Joinville, who was also aboard the imperiled vessel, may have acted as an official witness to the queen's pledge, which would explain why she later "remembered" her pilgrimage vow by sending him in her place. As part of this vicarious pilgrimage, Joinville was entrusted with rendering the queen's offering to Nicholas on her behalf: an ornate miniature ship made of silver, which included figures of the queen, the king, their three children, and the mariners whom the saint had helped deliver from pelagial doom.[46]

Medieval pilgrimage to the Holy Land gave rise to an intensive, complex, *and singularly misunderstood* brand of memory work. On the other side of Reformation polemic, the pilgrim's devotions—her counting of steps, columns, and lanterns; her measurement of shrines and reliquaries; her repetitive intonation of hymns and tabulation of indulgences; and so forth—are easily written off as tedious, superstitious exercises requiring little thought. However, these rituals were meant to serve as the basis of a program of intellectual discipline that demanded the full, focused engagement of the pilgrim's memory during and after the journey. The rituals of Holy Land pilgrimage were ultimately rooted in learned speculation about human psychology and cognition. As a result, even if a late medieval pilgrim was "illiterate" by the standards of the university, his or her experience was nevertheless mediated by scholarly theory and practice. The learned origins of pilgrim ritual were recognized and seized upon by poets such as Dante and Christine de Pizan—and by travel writers eager to imbue their dubious literary pursuits with an air of respectability.

The memory work of the Holy Land pilgrim consisted of three interlocking tasks: (1) the *ritual commemoration* of important events from salvation history in the places where they had transpired; (2) the *formation* of a unique, vivid, and durable pictorial memory for each of the sacred places in which the pilgrim worshipped; and (3) the lifelong *reconstruction* of these pictorial memories for the purposes of meditational reading, scholarship, and prayer. One can find references to all three exercises in late antique and early medieval accounts of Holy Land pilgrimage. However, beginning in the thirteenth century, these three memory tasks are increasingly understood as articulated *phases* of a single process, which took as its goal nothing less than the intellectual and ethical transformation of the pilgrim.

The first phase, *ritual commemoration*, leveraged the emotional resonance of place in order to unlock the pilgrim's prior knowledge of salvation history in uniquely vivid ways. Burchard of Mount Sion described the visceral power of the pilgrim's recollections of scripture as though they were projected into the mind's eye of the traveler by a kind of genius loci— as though the pilgrim's memory actually belonged to the sacred site itself: "The memory of each and every one of these places is still as complete and clear as it was on the day when things were done in their presence."[47] Here, as elsewhere, Burchard builds on the foundations laid by Jerome. In a famous letter describing the pilgrimage of Paula, Jerome depicted his spiritual companion as she visited the holy places of Jerusalem, drawing on her knowledge of scripture to populate the landscape before her bodily eyes with vivid remembrances of events long past. In an arresting passage, Jerome recalls the ardor of these devotions:

> Before the Cross she threw herself down in adoration as though she beheld the Lord hanging upon it: and when she entered the tomb which was the scene of the Resurrection she kissed the stone which the angel had rolled away from the door of the sepulcher. Indeed so ardent was her faith that she even licked with her mouth the very spot on which the Lord's body had lain, like one athirst for the river which he has longed for. What tears she shed there, what groans she uttered, and what grief she poured forth, all Jerusalem knows.[48]

Compared to the seemingly unfettered itinerary of Paula, the ritual commemoration of late medieval pilgrims was highly formalized. The liturgical organization of Holy Land pilgrimage may already have been standard in the age of Paula and Jerome and is documented in many medieval chronicles and travel accounts.[49] However, the 1330s mark a turning point in the development of pilgrimage to Jerusalem and its environs. It was in this decade that the sultan of Egypt granted the Franciscan community on Mount Zion the exclusive right to guide Latin Christian pilgrims around Jerusalem.[50] The vicissitudes of Latin Christian relations with the sultan of Egypt left the tour vulnerable to change around its edges, but—by and large—the Franciscans institutionalized a relatively stable set of rituals that reflected their order's interest in meditational devotion and the instruction of the laity. At each significant church, city gate, or ruin, Franciscan guides prompted pilgrims to meditate on a historical event associated with the place in question. These meditations were set into motion by relevant liturgical chants, scriptural readings, or sermons.[51] At the close of the fifteenth century, the Jerusalem tour would achieve its greatest degree of formalization in the Stations of the Cross.[52]

The *Liber peregrinationis* (ca. 1288–89) of Dominican friar Riccoldo of Montecroce suggests that the devotional practices of at least some Latin Christian pilgrims to Jerusalem bore a Franciscan stamp even before the 1330s. Riccoldo—a Florentine who professed special affection for Francis of Assisi—mentions his involvement in organizing the kinds of ritual activities that would later become standard features of the Franciscan tour. Especially worthy of note is Riccoldo's participation in staging a live tableau of the Nativity in Bethlehem, a relatively new devotional practice associated with Saint Francis, who was widely credited with instituting it in Greccio, Italy, during the town's Christmas festivities.[53]

Intriguingly, the prose style of *Liber peregrinationis* appears to mimic the physical experience of ritual commemoration. Dominated by brief sentence structure and conspicuous syntactic patterns, Riccoldo's prose creates the impression of an ideal pilgrimage, in which the act of walking conforms itself to contemplative practice. Riccoldo pauses to "gloss" each stop along his route, ruminating on its historical importance and its significance to his own life:

> Galilee: found the location of the wedding and the place and shape of the jars. There, we chanted and proclaimed the gospel and the wedding at Cana [John 2:1–11]. There, I asked Christ who had turned water into wine to turn my water of insipidity and infidelity into the wine of remorse and spiritual savor. From there we travelled fifteen miles straight ahead to the village of Genesareth, which is on the Sea of Galilee. There, while descending the mountain which towers over the sea, we chanted

the gospel about the two demoniacs Christ cured by expelling a legion of demons from them and which he then drove into a herd of swine [Matthew 8:28–34]. In that place I asked the Lord to liberate me from the harassment of demons.[54]

The cadence of the passage suggests the halting, inescapably embodied, nature of the pilgrim's memory work. The link between physical and mental self-possession is also clear in the words of John Poloner—who visited the Holy Land in 1422: "Let it be noted that from the site of Calvary to the aforementioned court [where Christ was tried], it is 450 paces, which I counted with the greatest diligence, to the best of my ability."[55] The disciplined focus exhibited by Riccoldo and Poloner provides a vivid contrast to the wanton self-abandonment of stereotypical pilgrims, which—if medieval moralists are to be believed—expressed itself as a noisy, unregulated, and chaotic movement through space.[56]

If ritual commemoration regulates the body's movements through space, it does so in the interest of ensuring the quality of memory over time. In other words, ritual commemoration is not just commemorative, but also mnemonic, in its aims. In fact, it laid the groundwork for the second phase of the pilgrim's memory work: the *formation* of a unique mental picture for each of the places visited along the itinerary. Since late antiquity, visitors to Jerusalem had counted paces between chapels, columns, and shrines, using hands, arms, feet, or lengths of cord.[57] These activities promoted a deliberate, unhurried engagement with the pilgrim's surroundings, and physical immediacy with the sacred. They had the added mnemonic advantage of appealing simultaneously to the optical and tactile senses. Moreover, the instruments used to measure distances were kept as souvenirs and sometimes used as mnemonic props after the conclusion of the pilgrimage. Nompar de Caumont included his measuring implement in the inventory of sacred relics he had acquired in the Holy Land, and Margery Kempe used her measuring tape to bear visual witness to the dimensions of Christ's tomb to those who had never traveled to Jerusalem.[58]

Perhaps less intuitive from a modern perspective, ritual measurement and related devotional acts were considered mnemonically effective because they elicited deeply felt emotional responses. Recall that Felix Fabri attributes his failure to picture the Holy Land in his mind to the fact that he was compelled "to run around the holy places without understanding *and feeling* what they were."[59] Like many other medieval travel writers, Riccoldo of Montecroce discerns intellectual use value in the strong emotions stirred by places such as the Holy Sepulcher, which he believed would imprint "the memory of [Christ's] passion . . . more firmly" in his mind.[60] The importance of affective sensation to the memory work of pilgrims recalls the teachings of rhetoricians, who maintained that memories formed in heightened emotional states were more likely to be vivid and enduring.[61] As medieval teachers told their students, effective memorization was aided by bodily self-control and strong emotional connections to the object of study; ritual commemoration provided both.

It was in the last phase of memory work that the truly transformative potential of pilgrimage was thought to reside. If done successfully, the *reconstruction* of the place memories formed during pilgrimage could enrich devotional activity and scholarly reading for life. By conjuring mental images of the Holy Land, the erstwhile pilgrim heightened the pleasure of devotional and scholarly pursuits. Thietmar went on pilgrimage out of an "ardent desire to see personally those things which, at different times, I heard from the scriptures in cloudy and obscure language."[62] Seeing them enhanced Thietmar's subsequent ruminations on sacred scripture. Riccoldo of Montecroce hoped that the image of the crucifixion that his pilgrimage had seared into his brain would make him more eager to suffer martyrdom during his missionary activities in Muslim lands. At Mount Calvary, Margery Kempe experienced the first of her recurring bouts of involuntary weeping, which she identified as a key turning point in her mystical career.[63] Denied any comparable life-changing experience, the disappointed Fabri set out on his second pilgrimage to the Holy Land.

The value accorded to the pilgrim's reconstruction of place memories got an important boost from late medieval trends in lay piety, especially meditational prayer, popularized by the devotional guidebooks of Bonaventure, Ludolph of Saxony, and others. This influence was mutual.[64] The popularity of virtual pilgrimage guides, the European-wide vogue for replicas of the Church of the Holy Sepulcher, and the development of "Jerusalem" pilgrimages in various localities within Europe testify to the broad cultural impact that the memory work of pilgrimage had on devotional practice at the close of the fifteenth century.[65] A striking example of this influence is found in the decorative programs of certain books of hours, which include marginal illuminations of pilgrim badges.[66] At least one owner of a book of hours sewed actual pilgrim badges into the margins of the volume, locating them alongside relevant prayers.[67] Many badges had an instantly recognizable association with a particular pilgrimage center—for example, the palm frond of Jerusalem, the scallop shell of Santiago de Compostela, and the Veronica of Rome. Their appearance in books of hours—texts explicitly designed for memorial and meditational use—suggests that the close association of badge to place allowed such souvenirs to be used as mnemonic prompts in the reconstructive phase of the pilgrim's memory work.

Echoes of the memory work of the Jerusalem pilgrim are discerned far afield of devotional practice, as well. Dante not only understood the memory work of the pilgrim as a three-pronged process but also associated it with the pedagogy of the language arts classroom. In *Purgatorio*, Dante and Beatrice witness a perplexing spectacle involving a giant, a harlot, and a griffin-drawn chariot. Beatrice explains the allegorical implications of the scene to the befuddled Dante, but not before issuing the following command:

> I'd also have you bear my words within you—
> if not inscribed then at least outlined (*dipinto*)—just as
> the pilgrim's staff is brought back wreathed with palm.[68]

These lines allude to the pilgrim's custom of tying a frond of the Jericho palm around his or her walking stick, a practice that eventually gave rise to Jerusalem's palm-shaped badge and to the English word *palmer*. For Beatrice, the Jerusalem pilgrim provides a benchmark for academic rigor, a model for how the overwhelmed student rises to the challenge of committing a teacher's lessons to memory. The memory work of pilgrimage pops up once again in the final cantos of *Paradiso*, as Dante struggles to perceive the blindingly bright heights of the heavenly Jerusalem. Dante compares himself to "a pilgrim in the temple he / has vowed to reach" who, having paused to refresh himself, "looks / and hopes he can describe what it was like."[69] The idea that the successful pilgrim regulates his travels in a way that optimizes the faculty of memory may even be behind Dante's famously idiosyncratic use of the epic invocation in canto 2 of *Inferno*. Defying the precedent of Virgil and other classical poets, Dante does not open his poem with the invocation but rather postpones it until the second canto. The invocation emerges at the precise moment in the poem when Dante and Virgil are about to embark on their downward voyage into the underworld. Just before Dante prays for the muses to help him narrate his journey, he expresses his confidence that the powers of his formally trained memory (*mente*) will be an unerring guide.[70]

Christine de Pizan's 1403 dream vision *Le chemin de long estude* (The road of long study) draws on the *Divine Comedy*, and strengthens Dante's association between the learned visionary quest and the memory work of the earth-bound pilgrim. The middle portion of the *Chemin* recounts Christine's guided tour of the earth's notable sites, under the tutelage of the Cumaean Sybil. Christine's main source of geographical information is *The*

Book of John Mandeville (a fact that, in Mandevillean fashion, she does not acknowledge).[71] Nevertheless, Christine's depiction of the psychology of the pilgrim is clearly more indebted to Dante. Initially, the Sybil has to reassure her reluctant charge that she should not fear separation from home, since travel yields both short- and long-term delights. The traveler derives pleasure during the journey through the observation of places she has read about and subsequently through the recollection of those places after the journey has concluded:

> I will show you many notable
> Places, which, upon seeing them, will delight you
> And for the rest of your life
> You'll take delight whenever you picture them.[72]

To that end, Christine takes "great pleasure / in investigating everything calmly."[73] At the Church of the Holy Sepulcher, Christine follows the example of the pilgrim described in *Paradiso*, resting her body before she studies the sacred shrine she has journeyed to see—and to remember:

> I saw and kissed the Holy Sepulcher
> And rested there a while.
> When I had made my offerings
> And said my prayers
> I looked at how it was built
> In the form of a semicircle, and in fact
> I took its measurements,
> Which I have to this day.[74]

Christine and Dante appropriate the rituals of pilgrimage with intuitive ease because the devotions of the Holy Land pilgrim drew on the same mental faculties involved in the composition of literary works. The overlap between the pilgrim's memory work and the mental effort involved in composition fostered one of the most consequential and misunderstood developments in the literature of medieval travel: the *synthetic tradition* of writing about the Holy Land.

THE SYNTHETIC TRADITION

In the Middle Ages, the most common justification for writing about one's pilgrimage to the Holy Land was that it allowed those who could not travel there in person the opportunity to contemplate its sacred landscapes in the mind's eye. In contrast to the flighty, insubstantial ramblings of the pilgrim's tale, the written account transformed the raw material of the traveler's memory into something systematic and visualizable, for the edification and wholesome delight of readers. Though he wrote about the Holy Land in Greek, twelfth-century travel writer John Phocas summed up the goals of his Latin Christian counterparts concisely: "We must attempt . . . as best we can, to paint a picture using words on our canvas, and to those who love God to give a full written account of what we saw directly with our own eyes."[75] Painting such a verbal picture was not for the faint of heart. The travel writer first needed to commit things to memory during the journey. Memory was also involved in the even more difficult work of *imposing order* on the otherwise unruly swarm of images, facts, and experiences during the process of composing the travel account.

These basic assumptions provided the foundations for the *synthetic tradition* of travel writing about the Holy Land. The synthetic tradition is comprised mostly of works written in Latin by clerical authors. The first stirrings of the tradition are detectable in twelfth-century writers such as Theoderic and John of Würzburg. The tradition achieves its full articulation in the thirteenth century, in the works of Thietmar, Wilbrand of Oldenburg, and Burchard of Mount Sion; it persists into the following two centuries in the writings of authors such as Niccolò da Poggibonsi, Anselmo Adorno, and Felix Fabri. Works belonging to the synthetic tradition exhibit the following traits:

1. A statement to the effect that the text is an image painted with words, designed to enable readers who have not been to the Holy Land to "picture" it in their minds.

2. A discussion or dramatization of the difficulty involved in creating such a verbal map.

3. An insistence that the finished book is the result of writing undertaken after the author returned home from his journey, sometimes with the help of library research and/or notes taken during his travels.

4. A tendency to equate the endurance of the journey's discomforts and the resistance of its temptations with the subsequent labor involved in composing the account. In many cases, this entails associating—or even conflating—the writing process with the memory work of pilgrimage.

Many of the first authors to link the activity of travel writing to the memory work of pilgrimage did so in self-defense. The pilgrim's tale was a disreputable genre of discourse, widely dismissed as boastful, frivolous, and lying. For this reason, Wilbrand of Oldenburg took pains to distance his written account from the proverbially useless chatter of devotional travelers. He did so by likening the spirit in which he undertook the composition of his account to the devout memory work of pilgrimage: "I therefore propose to write imbued not at all with the vain and pernicious arrogance of pomposity, but instead with the state of fixed contemplation of the Holy Places and cities."[76]

Similarly, Thietmar found it necessary to defend himself against possible charges of "vainglory" for indulging in travel writing. Thietmar insists that he is not so stupid as to have endured the perils of road and sea and land (*viarum et maris et terre pericula*) and spiritual and bodily fatigue (*tam spiritus quam corporis fatigatione*) only to turn around and damn himself by attempting to win earthly fame as an author.[77] On the contrary, Thietmar states that he has written his account in order to prolong the spiritual benefits of the memory work of his pilgrimage:

> Because when engrossed in reading (*lectioni*), the pleasure drawn from such delectable things smells to me of thyme and tastes of honey, I considered it not unuseful to commit to writing (*scripto commendar*) what I saw and accurately learnt from truthful witnesses lest suddenly by the smoke of oblivion I should not preserve artificially by the little aide-memoire (*amminiculo memorie*) of something written down that which I was not able to remember naturally.[78]

He adds that if the book he has written as an aid to his personal devotions ends up in the hands of other devout souls, all the better:

> If anyone picks up this work and wishes to take pleasure in it with me, he will not get annoyed with me because of it and impute to me the sap of arrogance when he sees that the sequence of these writings has been compiled not pompously, but simply (*scripti seriem non pompatice, sed simpliciter viderit compilatam*), with the particular purpose of banishing idleness and reflecting (*recogitandum*) on the places of the Holy Land and those wonderful things done by the power of God.[79]

Thietmar is perhaps the first medieval travel writer to refer to his literary activities as those of a compiler rather than an author. This disavowal of the authority and prestige of the *auctor* is consistent with the humble pose that he strikes elsewhere. At the same time, Thietmar's self-identification as a compiler suggests that he saw the memory work of pilgrimage and the labor of composition as analogous cognitive operations. Thietmar's "flowery" invocations of thyme and honey evoke a particular genre of compilation: the *florilegium*, which took its name from the beelike labor of extracting noteworthy passages from various flowers/books, and gathering them—like so much honey—into one honeycomb/volume. Although the forms and topics of the monastic florilegium varied greatly, the generic name applied broadly to any collection of noteworthy textual passages used—to borrow Thietmar's turn of phrase—as an "amminiculo memorie," a prop, or support, for the memory.[80] *Recogitandum* suggests a process similar to the literary practice of *compilatio*, insofar as both entail a purposeful recollection that surveys, extracts, and recombines in one place content previously stored in separate places, be it in one's library or in one's memory.

The kinship between the memory work of pilgrimage and the labor of composition is even more evident in the terms used by Felix Fabri. Fabri characterizes his inability to conjure vivid memory images of the places he has seen as a failed attempt at *cogitatio*, a word that provides the root for Thietmar's *recogitandum*. In the Middle Ages, the precise meaning of *cogitatio* varied according to context. Today, translators tend to render the term with a general, all-purpose word such as *thought*. However, Fabri inherited a set of propositions about *cogitatio*, which—though different from one another—all referred to a more experimental and creative process than the activities conjured by *thought*. Carruthers, building on the work of Harry A. Wolfson, argues that *cogitatio* corresponds to what Aristotle called the *deliberative imagination*, "the power of constructing with conscious judgment a single image out of a number of images."[81] Though there was a rational dimension to Aristotelian cogitation, it was nevertheless a process that engaged the sensory soul, which is why it was emotionally charged. Augustine also conceived of *cogitatio* as a constructive activity, a willed summoning and synthesis of previously atomized memory content. For Augustine, *cogitatio* enabled dim and unconnected memories to "be collected and gathered together from their dispersions"; he also defined it as "the mind's putting together of things that are dispersed."[82] Augustine likened cogitation to manual labor, claiming that "*cogo* and *cogito* are of the same relation as *ago* and *agito*, *facio* and *factito*."[83] The influential rhetorical textbook *Ad Herennium*, attributed to Cicero, provides a third important context for Fabri's use of *cogitatio*. In the *Ad Herennium*, *cogitatio* is the faculty responsible for fashioning the imaginary architectural backgrounds used as mnemonic loci, or artificial memory places.[84]

A careful reading of Fabri shows that, for him, the failure of his first pilgrimage resides in his inability to "cogitate" in the Aristotelian and Augustinian senses of that term, a capacity that he implicitly contrasts to the mental operation called *cogitatio* in the *Ad Herennium*:

> So after I had returned to Ulm and began to *think about (cogitare)* the most holy sepulcher of our Lord and the manger wherein He lay, and the holy city of Jerusalem and the mountains which are round about it, the *appearance, shape, and arrangements (species, formae et habitudines)* of these and of other holy places escaped my mind *(fugerunt a me)*. . . . Wherefore I was grieved beyond measure that I had undergone such *sufferings, toils, and perils (miserias, angustias, et labores)* and had spent such great sums of money and so much time, without receiving any fruit of knowledge *(cognitione)*. Oftentimes when I tried to solace myself by *turning my thought to Jerusalem and the holy places (me converti ad cogitandum de Jerusalem et locis sanctis)*, and was only able to *conjure up a vague image of them (dubiosa imaginatio mihi occurreret)*, I have said to myself in a rage: "I prithee cease from *thinking about those places (de illis locis cogitare)*, for you have only been there *in imagination (putas enim te ibi fuisse)*."[85]

The meaning of this passage hinges on the distinction between mental images of places that are painstakingly reconstructed with reference to past experience (*cogitatio* in some of the ways that it was theorized by Aristotle and Augustine) and the imagination's fabrication of places that were never seen or that do not actually exist (*cogitatio* in the pseudo-Ciceronian sense). Several meditational treatises and travel accounts—including one written by Fabri—encouraged readers who had never been to the Holy Land to draw on the mnemonic techniques of rhetoric in order to develop imaginary backdrops for their mental re-creations of biblical events. Meditants were encouraged to use elements of places familiar to them from experience to construct these virtual places.[86] Fabri takes exception to having to resort to such techniques, since he could have done so without undergoing the psychic, somatic, and fiduciary expenditures of travel. Fabri implies that the sacrifices involved in pilgrimage should yield a *different kind* of knowledge (*cognitione*) of the Holy Land than the pilgrim had prior to the journey, one based in something more concrete than the flitting phantasms produced by the imagination.[87]

The parallel that Thietmar and Fabri draw between the memory work of pilgrimage and the process of prose composition is, in fact, authorized by the view that both involve cogitation. Following classical precedent, monastic educators construed rhetorical invention (*inventio*)—the initial phase of composition—as a meditational activity. Monastic views on the process of *inventio* were absorbed by the late medieval university, and thereby influenced liberal arts pedagogy long after the monastery had been eclipsed as Europe's predominant educational institution.[88] *Inventio* entailed the "discovery" of the contours of one's subject matter (*res*)—its beginning, middle, and end. During rhetorical invention, the would-be author scanned memory's inventory, experimentally combining its contents in different configurations until the best possible shape for the work was found. As a meditational practice, *inventio* resembled the pilgrim's mental reconstruction of the Holy Land's landscape in the concentration that it demanded, in the intensity of the emotions it could ignite, and in its imagistic nature.

A well-known passage from Geoffrey of Vinsauf's thirteenth-century *Poetria nova* shows that *inventio* was theorized in explicitly pictorial—even cartographic—terms. Geoffrey compares the process of discovering the shape of one's subject matter to the work of the mapmaker. In Geoffrey's reckoning, the cartographer begins by picturing where he will locate Cádiz, the city on the Straits of Gibraltar, which marks the boundary between the Mediterranean and the Atlantic, Africa and Europe. Cádiz is also the site of the Pillars of Hercules, the point once thought to mark the end of the world. For poets, knowing where to locate their metaphorical Cádiz entails a definitive decision about where to begin and end one's treatment of the subject matter, in order not to stray beyond those self-imposed limits:

> Let the mind's interior compass first circle the whole extent of the material. Let a definite order chart in advance at what point the pen will take up its course, or where it will fix its Cadiz. As a prudent workman, construct the whole fabric within the mind's citadel.[89]

For travel writers, the gap between the literal and figurative dimensions of Geoffrey's map metaphor was narrowed considerably. One anonymous English travel writer opened his synthetic account of the Holy Land by conjuring an anthropomorphized map of the Mediterranean: "I depicted in imagination the Greek sea as the image of a man (*Mare grecum in hominis effigie ymaginando depinxi*) . . . [who] turns [his] face to the western world, having [his] body in an enclosed space of two thousand miles. At the head is Apulia . . . one of the arms embraces Apulia."[90] Theoderic asked his readers to imagine Jerusalem's location within the Holy Land as though the city were an "eye in the middle of a head."[91] Travel writers avail themselves of a number of other conceits designed to help readers picture individual places—and their corresponding textual descriptions—as part of a larger, bounded whole.

The challenges of *inventio* gave way to the related problem of *dispositio*: the approach used to systematize the text's presentation of its content. Some synthetic travel writers—such as Thietmar and Wilbrand of Oldenburg— used their actual itineraries as the primary structuring principle for their accounts, presenting places in the order that they had encountered them in real life. Others preferred a sequence of hypothetical itineraries based on an artificial organizing principle. John of Würzburg used the chronology of Christ's incarnation, death, and resurrection to order his descriptions of Jerusalem's holy places—with occasionally disorienting disregard to their relative topographical positions. In the fifteenth century, Alessandro Ariosto and Francesco Suriano structured their accounts as pedagogical dialogues, so that the subject matter of their treatises emerged as it became relevant in the fictionalized back-and-forth with their respective interlocutors.[92] Burchard of Mount Sion adopted a highly abstract approach to organizing his *Description*. Burchard points out that he *could have* organized his verbal map around the geographical center of the Holy Land but chose instead to picture/invent/devise an alternative, artificial center in the town of Acre.[93] Burchard explains that he made this choice because his readers are more likely to be familiar with Acre—the last crusader stronghold to fall to Muslim armies—than with any other locality in the region.

The language used by Burchard suggests that he views the Holy Land as a university text, which he subjects to the scholastic practices of *divisio* and *compilatio*. In the *inventio* phase, Burchard first pictures (*cogitaui*) Acre as what Geoffrey would call his "Cádiz," and then uses the cardinal directions and the winds to divide (*divisi*) the region into twelve different parts, and organize (*ordinare*) each of its significant places into one of those divisions. He then discusses each of these twelve sectors and the places that they contain, so that readers can both picture the Holy Land and know where in the book they can seek out the description of any given place within it:

> Considering, however, how I might usefully describe these things, so that they might be easily [grasped/perceived] by readers in their imaginations (*possent a legentibus imaginatione facili comprehendi*), I [pictured/contrived] a central point (*cogitaui centrum*) among them and [set] out (*ordinare*) all the land around it in due measure. And for this center I have chosen the city of Acre, as it is better known than other places (*plus aliis notam*). However, it is not located in the center (*medio*) but at the western border on the sea. From [this center] I [drew/extended] (*protraxi*)

four lines corresponding to the four [directions/parts] (*partibus*) of the world and each quarter I have divided (*diuisi*) into three, so that those twelve divisions (*diuisiones*) might correspond to the twelve winds of heaven; and in each division (*diuisionibus*) I have placed the cities and places mentioned more especially in scripture, so that the location and disposition of individual places might more easily be [found/learned], and the part of the world in which they [are situated] (*ut singulorum locorum situs et dispositio posset de facili reperiri, ad quam partem mundi esset collocata*).[94]

For Burchard and other synthetic travel writers, there is artistry in arrangement. Their ability to entertain different ways of ordering their works shows that—even if they have experienced the Holy Land as a linear, time-bound series of places—they are capable of ranging over their memories of the region with confidence and dexterity. The artificiality of formal structure becomes, in other words, a display of virtuosity.

Authors like Burchard construe memory's relationship to writing and writing's relationship to travel in ways that defy the expectations of modern readers, and the critical reception of their works has suffered for it. Today, the dominant, commonsense way of thinking about the relationship between the journey and the travel narrative is best described as "mimetic." The mimetic conception of travel writing presumes that the travel writer first goes on a journey and—once that journey is completed—subsequently "represents" or "reproduces" the experience of travel in the form of narrative content. In the synthetic tradition, however, the subjective experience of travel *includes* the process of creative recollection that takes place at home during the process of composition. The synthetic account is not a postmortem analysis but rather a continuation—and even a culmination—of the pilgrimage. In the mimetic view of travel writing, memory records information to a greater or lesser degree of fidelity. In the synthetic tradition, memory not only preserves knowledge and experience, it also—and perhaps more importantly—*transforms* knowledge and experience in a way that makes it valuable to readers. The manner in which an author's memory achieves this transformation of experience into text becomes a mode of creative, individualistic expression, often at the "cost" of the well-plotted narratives and character development privileged by the mimetic paradigm. Even in cases where the resulting text is dominated by grammatically impersonal descriptions of places, the synthetic account bears the unique impress of the memory and intentions that shaped it for the benefit of others. One hastens to add that the commentary tradition on Aristotle encouraged medieval scholars to see experience as essentially linked to recollection. Thus, for Aquinas, the sum of the "stuff" that happens to a human does not constitute experience; instead, experience comes into being only through recollection; or—as he put it—experience is the synthetic outcome of "the comparison of many singular things received in the memory" ("*ex multis memoriis unius rei accipit homo experimentum de aliquo*").[95]

The fate endured by John of Würzburg's *Descriptio* at the hands of modern editors illustrates what happens when the aesthetic norms of the mimetic tradition are treated as the end to which all travel writing ought to strive. At least two of John's editors radically reordered the content of the *Descriptio*, to bring it in line with their expectations of what a travel narrative should look like. Tobler rearranged the account so that the descriptions of places followed the order in which a pilgrim in the twelfth century might have visited them.[96] However, John set out to produce a book that could help pilgrims recognize the traces of the biblical past in a Jerusalem that had been transformed by the ravages of crusade and subsequently by the rebuilding projects of its new Latin Christian rulers (see chapter 4). John's decision to use the chronology of Christ's life to organize his verbal map of Jerusalem was part of a larger effort to restore a sense of the city's ontological continuity across time in the aftermath of radical change. From the point of view of the mimetic paradigm, it might seem as if one were doing John a service by "correcting" his text in the way that Tobler did. However, the formal organization of the *Descriptio* is the expression of an individual sensibility, one that reflects its author's understanding of the significance of his experiences. This is precisely what is lost in Tobler's reordering of the text.

When modern literary critics insist on a strict polarization of experience and text, they refuse to hear what many medieval travel writers explain in plain language: that memory is the nexus where text and experience intertwine, and that travel writing is the socially oriented fruit of that intertwining.

For this very reason, it is worth reevaluating current accounts of the role that post-pilgrimage research played in the process of travel writing. Many travel writers—including Burchard of Mount Sion, Ludolph von Suchem, and Felix Fabri—acknowledge that they leaned on the works of their predecessors in order to verify doubtful points or repair gaps in their recollections. Countless other travel writers availed themselves of vast swaths of others' work without acknowledging their debts.[97] Such practices are usually explained through general statements about the differences between medieval and modern conceptions of originality and intellectual property. Such explanations are fine, as far as they go. But the foundational assumptions of the synthetic tradition provide a richer context for understanding the textual borrowings of medieval travel writers. As Fabri suggests, the work undertaken in the library is one of the most laborious aspects of the pilgrim's memory work:

> I did not undertake as much labor (*laborem*) in traveling from place to place (*de loco ad locum peregrinando*), as I have had in running to and fro from book to book (*de libro ad librum discurrendo*), in reckoning, reading and writing, and correcting and synthesizing (*concordando*) what I have written.[98]

Such a claim makes sense in a literate culture that understands the absorption of the works of others into one's own thought as a mode of experience as self-defining as travel, and travel itself as an activity that is prolonged through the act of writing.[99]

One final point: though the synthetic travel writer is often viewed as the antithesis of adventurous explorer, several clues point to the influence that this bookish lot of pilgrims exerted on the conception and reception of the works of travel writers such as Marco Polo and John Mandeville. According to the *Divisament dou monde*, Polo surpasses rival long-distance specialists at the court of Khubilai Khan by seeking out exotic points of interest and carefully committing them to memory. The word that the *Divisament* uses for the mental effort expended during these marvel-hunting missions is *entent*—the Franco-Italian equivalent of the Latin *intentus*, a term applied to the disciplined concentration that characterized serious reading and memorization.[100] Then, there is the *Divisament*'s organization into a series of hypothetical itineraries, which recalls earlier works such as the widely copied *Description* of Burchard of Mount Sion. The influence of the synthetic tradition could also explain the *Divisament*'s repeated avowals that it will relate its material "in order." This refrain has confounded scholars, who have been unable to discern the underlying logic that dictates the arrangement of the text's materials.[101] Yet, this emphasis on orderliness may simply signal that the *Divisament* is not indiscriminately rattling off Polo's stray recollections as they occurred to him but has rather harnessed the synthetic powers of memory to present a vast, unknown world to readers in a clear, coherent, visualizable way. Admittedly, none of this is decisive proof of direct influence. Tipping the scales slightly in favor of the influence argument is the probability that Polo was introduced to the ritualistic memory work described by Riccoldo of Montecroce during his visit to Jerusalem in the 1270s.

In the end, whether or not the *Divisament* was influenced by the methods of an author such as Burchard, its translators and editors approached the work with expectations promoted by the synthetic tradition. One early French rendition of the *Divisament* seems to attribute Polo's superiority as a long-distance specialist to his mastery of rhetoric while also underscoring the causal link between Polo's self-regulation on the road and the aesthetically delightful nature of his reports to Khubilai Khan:

> And he, as a man who was wise and knew the ways of his Lord, exerts himself greatly (*se penoit moult*) to know and to understand all of the things that he saw (*de savoir et d'entendre toutes choses*) that would please the Great Khan, so that when he returned he would tell everything in an orderly fashion (*li contoit tout ordoneement*), to the end that his Lord loved him very much, and Marco pleased him very much.[102]

Ramusio declared it "miraculous" (*meravigliosa*) that Polo was able to compose a book such as the *Divisament*, "seeing that such an accomplishment was possessed by very few in his day, and that he had a large part of his nurture among those uncultivated Tartars, without any regular training in the art of composition."[103] The contrast that Ramusio strikes between Polo's compositional prowess and the alleged illiteracy of Khubilai's subjects grows out of seeds planted by the *Divisament*, which proposes that the best kind of traveler is one who uses the memory training learned through the study of rhetoric to read, extract, and make something coherent out of the wondrous variety of the book of the world.

As I suggested in the previous chapter, Mandeville's allusion to his gout was a way to show that the strenuous travails of his journey carried over into the labor of composing his account. The illuminator of a textless Bohemian manuscript seems to have understood this as well. The young, energetic Mandeville is depicted traveling the world in several of the manuscript's illuminations. One very different image portrays the inveterate voyager as a nearsighted old man, hunched over a draft of his *Book* (fig. 6). The gout-afflicted knight adopts the meditational posture characteristic of the working writer: legs crossed, pen and knife in hand, a blank page before him, staring off into space. The writing process is made to look all the more laborious by the suggestion of the fatigue and nearsightedness of the retired knight.

The perseverance of this painted Mandeville embodies the ideals of the synthetic tradition. The process of prose composition forced the travel writer to impose order on the scattered, shadowy, and—at times—contradictory

Figure 6. Mandeville laboring over his *Book* (ca. 1400–1425). British Library, Add. 24189, f. 4. (Photograph: © The British Library Board.)

content of memory. To be of use to readers, the recollections of the travel writer had to be first preserved, then gathered, sifted through, verified, supplemented, combined, recombined, and systematized to produce a synthetic, comprehensible whole. This was painstaking work, its results uncertain. Synthetic travel writers viewed success in their endeavors as the hallmark of a well-regulated journey and—in a world full of silly, light-minded, and boastful pilgrims—as a mark of distinction.

WRITING IN TRANSIT I: NOTE-TAKING AND AUTHORIAL SELF-PRESENTATION

The synthetic tradition placed the labor of post-pilgrimage writing at the heart of what it meant to travel well. Niccolò da Poggibonsi and Felix Fabri extend this line of thought to include the writing that the traveler does *during* the journey. Earlier synthetic travel writers mention, or strongly imply, taking notes during their explorations of the Holy Land. However, Niccolò and Fabri are uncharacteristically specific about the media, techniques, and motivations that underpin their approaches to writing in transit. The way that these travel writers discuss their note-taking habits is, in fact, *qualitatively* distinct, insofar as it becomes a pillar of their authorial self-presentation.

Niccolò da Poggibonsi's *Libro d'Oltramare* (Book of the overseas regions) opens on an apprehensive note, with a prayer that reads like a devotional revision of the epic invocations of Virgil and Dante. In terms of its length and apparent urgency, Niccolò's plea for mnemonic inspiration puts both poets to shame. The Franciscan calls on God and a goodly cross section of his celestial court, including the Virgin Mary, Saint Francis, Saint Catherine, Saint Barbara, and "all [God's] male and female saints." This phalanx of intercessors is asked to

> bestow their grace so that I will be able to describe and enumerate (*dire . . . e contare*) the holy places overseas in order (*per ordine*) and without misstep (*sanza fallimento*), just as I visited/investigated (*visitai*) them.[104]

During his journey, Niccolò had done his part to ensure the successful recollection of what he had seen. At Jerusalem, he tells readers, "I procured a *braccio* [arm-length] measurement, along with a *passo* ["pace"] measurement, and walking, I measured the distances, lengths, and widths of everything in order (*per ordine*) as you will hear; I took all the measurements and immediately wrote [them] down" using "a pair of tablets that I carried by my side."[105] Elsewhere, the *Libro* reveals that these were gypsum-plaster tablets and Niccolò used them to record his observations "day by day"[106] Indeed, his approach to note-taking is an important element of his authorial persona—a sign of his foresight, discipline, and seriousness of purpose: "It

well becomes a man to be wise, and prudent in his foresight, and be very
shrewd in conserving his memory; and, in order not to fail [in this regard],
I wrote down everything about the places overseas."[107] Niccolò emphasizes
the discipline and effort demanded of his meticulous note-taking: "I tired
myself out in [doing] this" (*"in questo m'affaticava"*).[108] The additional
onus imposed by the habit of writing in transit may explain why Niccolò
took the unusual step of branding the fruits of his toil with an authorial
acrostic:

> But so that no person might claim my bodly exertions (*fatica corporale*)
> for himself [nor] the labor (*travaglio*) that I have had on account of this
> book, and so that no one can claim to have made it other than I, brother
> Niccolò; whoever would want to find my name, and also the name of
> my father Corbizo, and where I was from, he will find it all [spelled out
> in] the first illuminated letter of each chapter beginning from this point
> forward, letter by letter, in order.[109]

Tablets were the obvious choice for a note-taking traveler like Niccolò
da Poggibonsi, who—in his own words—set out to remember "everything"
and to remember it perfectly. In fact, Niccolò was hardly the first travel
writer to resort to tablets when taking notes in the field. Adamnán of Iona
(d. 704) made use of a floor plan of the Holy Sepulcher, etched into wax
tablets by Irish bishop and saint Arculf, who had visited Jerusalem as a pilgrim.[110] As Niccolò testifies, tablets were small enough to be carried in a
sack by one's side and kept on hand for whenever the need to record something might suddenly present itself. Moreover, the writing surface of tablets
was protected from the elements by a compact case (usually made of box-
wood or ivory), which also added a measure of stability in the absence of a
desk. There was an obvious economic advantage to tablets as well, since the
writing surface could be erased with the blunt end of the stylus and then
refilled once their content had been copied onto a more permanent support. The most common material used to manufacture this erasable surface
was wax, though slate came to be preferred by late medieval composers of
music.[111] The "gypsum" surface that bore Niccolò's notes was made of a
length of parchment stretched over the tablet case and then covered with
layers of mineral plaster.[112] Moreover, in many of the daily situations in
which travelers found themselves, writing with a stylus on tablets was far
easier than wielding quill and ink, which easily spilled and smudged. Paper
and parchment, meanwhile, could be scattered to the winds or ruined by
water. Such considerations were not lost on Baudri de Bourgueil, who dedi-

cated loving poems to the wax tablets that enabled him to compose verses while mounted on his horse.[113] As we will see shortly, Felix Fabri made much of the fact that he had learned to wield wax tablets while riding an ass and even a camel (an animal whose unhorsely gait—then, as now—can cause dizziness and nausea in the uninitiated).

At two points in the *Libro*, Niccolò calls particular attention to his use of tablets and instruments of measurement; the timing of these references is calculated to reinforce his image as a traveler who is "wise and prudent" in matters related to memory. The first occurs just before the *Libro*'s description of Jerusalem, the holiest—and most mnemonically intensive—destination on the Holy Land itinerary.[114] The second precedes the account of Niccolò's excursion through the desert to Mount Sinai and Saint Catherine's monastery. This voyage was, like the visitation of Jerusalem, a pilgrimage-within-the-pilgrimage, abounding in sacred sites and curiosities. It was, at the same time, an excursion so remote, arduous, and potentially lethal that many Latin Christian pilgrims to the Holy Land did not undertake it.[115] The discomforts of the desert did little to aid the pilgrim's memory work. At such mnemonically demanding junctures of the pilgrimage, it will not suffice for Niccolò to wait until the end of the day to record his observations in the relative comfort of his lodgings. The careful pilgrim must record his impressions in the field, and do so—as Niccolò maintains—"immediately."

Niccolò dramatizes his note-taking habits in ways that shed light on less pious aspects of his character, as well. At Venice, he measures an elephant tusk, an object that he tries (and fails) to lift. Elsewhere, he shrinks from measuring the carcasses of giant sea tortoises being sold by merchants "for the dread I had of them." Luckily, even though Niccolò was so terrified by the prospect of touching the creatures "that I could not bring myself to measure them," one of his companions *could*. It is for this reason that the dimensions of one of the dead beasts are recorded in the *Libro*.[116] In addition to reminding us that medieval people viewed measurement as both an optical and a haptic operation, this episode illustrates how intimately enmeshed Niccolò's travels are in the mercantile culture of medieval Italy. It was probably merchants who gave Niccolò the idea that gypsum tablets might be useful for his purposes. At the turn of the fifteenth century, painter Cennino Cennini's *Book of the Art of Painting* recommended such tablets for apprentices learning how to draw, characterizing them as the "kind that merchants keep accounts on."[117]

Recent research into the manuscript tradition of the *Libro* lends new interest to Cennini's passing comment and raises the possibility that there is an additional rhetorical motivation for Niccolò's specificity about the kind of tablet he has used. Kathryn Blair Moore has shown that Niccolò's *Libro* is the long-unacknowledged source for the illustrated pilgrimage guide *Voyage from Venice to the Holy Sepulcher and to Mount Sinai*, first printed in Venice in 1518.[118] Moore demonstrates that the *Voyage* not only drew on the text of the *Libro* but also modeled its famous wood-block prints after illustrated manuscripts of Niccolò's work. Four of the ten extant manuscripts of the *Libro* contain illustrations, including the earliest (Florence: BNCF II. IV. 101), which dates from the second half of the fourteenth century, and may possibly be an autograph copy.[119] While Moore does not prove this last point conclusively, it is a question of considerable importance to the historiography of travel writing, because—if she is right—the *Libro* would be the first fully illustrated work of travel writing decorated by its author.[120] The precedent of Arculf's wax-tablet sketches of the Church of the Holy Sepulcher provides an additional glimmer of hope that future research on this question will prove that Niccolò did, in fact, adorn the *Libro* with his own drawings, which he first sketched in the field with the help of his gypsum tablets. If this turns out to be the case, then it is likely that Niccolò's specific mention of *gypsum* tablets—which Cennini associates with the training of apprentice painters—was intended to highlight his innovative inclusion of images in the *Libro*. For the moment, this must remain a tantalizingly open question.

Even more than Niccolò, Fabri sets himself apart from other travelers by dramatizing his commitment to writing in transit. Given the disappointment of his first pilgrimage, it's hardly surprising that Fabri imbues note-taking with a heroic aura:

> I never passed one single day while I was on my travels without writing some notes, not even when I was at sea, in storms, or in the Holy Land; and in the desert I have frequently written as I sat on an ass or camel; or, at night, when others were asleep, I would sit and put into writing what I had seen.[121]

Fabri subsequently states that he often took preliminary notes on wax tablets before transferring them to paper, an idea he may have taken from Arculf, whose account he read prior to setting out on his second pilgrimage.[122]

As is the case with Niccolò, Fabri's medium specificity expresses his seriousness of purpose. Since antiquity, wax tablets evoked several iconic associations. They were among the most common metaphors for the faculty of memory. They were also associated with the writing exercises of the grammar school classroom and—by extension—with the discipline of the intellect. Wax tablets were more generally linked to the activity of written composition and therefore became an instantly recognizable emblem of authorship and authority.[123]

Like Niccolò, Fabri mentions using tablets during the trek to Mount Sinai and Saint Catherine's. The account of his note-taking habit during the desert excursion underscores Fabri's commitment to ensuring the comprehensiveness of his recollections:

> In this valley I wrote the account of almost the whole journey from Gaza to this place; for while I sat on my ass, I had noted down the nature of the country and the direction of the roads in a waxen tablet (*tabula de cera*), which I carried in my girdle, and here I wrote out all this again in a [paper notebook] (*libello*), and rubbed it off the wax, that thereafter I might write more upon it. I very often dismounted from my ass, and wrote descriptions of routes, mountains, and valleys, because no one could retain all these things in his [memory] (*mente*) unless he wrote them down almost hourly.[124]

Fabri suggests that wax tablets do not simply record data; they stimulate—and even expand—the sentience of the traveler, enabling him to observe and experience more than he could have without their aid.[125] As one thoroughly read in medieval travel writing, Fabri no doubt noticed that most pilgrims' recollections of the Egyptian desert were not especially rich in detail. The blistering heat of the nine-day trek to Sinai and the shifting, seemingly infinite horizons of sand and sky created an environment little suited to extensive note-taking and place-based description. As a chronotope in medieval travel writing, the desert is a place where movement through space tends to be rewritten—in precious few words—in terms of the passage of time. Take, for instance, this four-day stretch from the diary of Ogier d'Anglure:

217. We left Saint Catherine on Wednesday, the tenth day of November and the eve of Saint Martin's day, right after mass, and made camp in the desert.

218. The following Thursday, we went on for the whole day.

219. The following Friday, we traveled all day.

220. The same on Saturday, we went on all day till vespers, when we came to a halt beside a well, where we found some refreshment for ourselves and watered our animals.[126]

When events occur in the desert, they tend to do so "suddenly"—as is the case with the following anecdote from Bertrandon de Broquière's 1432 pilgrimage:

> We thus traveled for two days in the desert, absolutely without seeing anything worth being related. Then, one morning, I saw, before sunrise, an animal running on four legs, about three feet long but scarcely a palm in height.[127]

The creature that emerged suddenly from the dunes was an unlucky monitor lizard. Against the advice of their Arab guides, Bertrandon's companions gave chase to the dangerous reptile and slew it with a sword. Fabri's fine-grained account of the names and relative orientations of mountains, valleys, and oasis towns is a study in contrast to these examples, one that would have been impossible without his wax tablets. In reinforcing the powers of memory, this portable writing technology liberates the mental energies of the traveler so that they can be redirected toward more minute and comprehensive forms of perception in an environment little suited to complex intellectual tasks.

Fabri's tireless note-taking is presented as something that influenced the quality of his interactions with fellow travelers. Each evening of the desert trek, Fabri transferred the notes he had taken on his tablets during the day onto paper. As part of this routine, Fabri often visited the tent of the group's Muslim guide, in order to clarify topographical doubts. On one of these occasions, the curious Fabri approaches the guide and some of his Muslim friends with "pen, ink, and paper" in hand.[128] Fabri asks about the name of the place where they have set up camp for the night, and the guide replies "Alborach." Fabri dutifully records the name and then reads it back, prompting peals of laughter from his Muslim interlocutors. As Fabri later discovers, the mysterious "Alborach" (i.e., Al-Burāq) is not a toponym at all but rather the name of the man-headed steed that conveyed Muhammad on his night journey from Mecca to Jerusalem (Qur'an, sura 17). Fabri—who never quite brings himself to do justice to this ribbing—conjectures that the guide attributes magical powers to the name and surreptitiously aimed to influence Fabri's behavior by tricking him into writing it down. This exchange calls attention to the potentially alienating effects of Fabri's commitment to writing as well as the discretion that he exercised in committing the contents of his wax tablets to paper.

The note-taking practices of Niccolò and Fabri are inspired by—and per-

haps in competition with—a form of travel writing that would come to rival
the synthetic tradition: the travel diary. The surprising popularity of travel
diaries among pilgrims to the Holy Land was fostered by the rise of urban
professional groups and the increased availability of paper. The diary raised
the bar in terms of what it meant to remember one's journey successfully,
and therefore what it meant to travel well. The effects of these changes were
first felt in the Holy Land pilgrimage but quickly spread to other kinds of
journeys.

WRITING IN TRANSIT II: THE TRAVEL DIARY

The pilgrimage to Jerusalem was the first kind of journey in which many
different travelers kept diaries; they did so in numbers that were unrivaled
during the Middle Ages. Internal textual evidence suggests that many extant pilgrim diaries were fair copies of versions jotted down in transit. Revision of this kind guaranteed greater legibility, an important consideration,
since pilgrim diaries were widely understood as memorials of the journey,
usually intended for a concrete audience of family, friends, neighbors, and
descendants.[129] Like the more familiar genres of the chronicle or the *ricor-
danze*, the travel diary emerged out of the record-keeping practices of city-
states, households, and ecclesiastical institutions. The travel diary is both
a memorial of the completed pilgrimage and a quantitative accounting—of
acquired assets (of indulgences, relics, souvenirs, wonders witnessed) and
expenditures (of time, money, bodily energy). Its bureaucratic origins flicker
periodically into view. It is not uncommon for diaries to include copies of
legal documents—charters, safe-conducts, contracts, and wills—related to
the pilgrimages that they record.[130]

The typical travel diary differs from the works of the synthetic tradition in a number of ways. Most diarists do not set out to transform the diachronic experience of the journey into a synchronic overview of the Holy
Land. As a series of dated entries, the diary is organized by the unfolding
of continuous, lived time. Whereas the synthetic tradition foregrounds the
labor of writing, the travel diary tends to take it for granted. Finally, for the
most part, the travel diary did not pretend to be an inherently learned or
literary pursuit.

Perhaps not surprisingly, when the travel diary emerged in the fourteenth century, it did so in Italy. Thanks to their close commercial ties
to Muslim communities across the Mediterranean, Italian city-states were
among the first producers of paper in Europe. The sophisticated economic
organization of city-states like Genoa and Venice—made all the more com-

plex by the need to administer a growing collection of overseas colonial possessions—increased the demand for paper, which, in turn, gave rise to new bookmaking formats, including the *quaderno*, or prebound paper note-book.[131] As Armando Petrucci has shown, the availability of such products greatly increased "the freedom to write" in medieval Italy, further loosening the clerical monopoly on the production and interpretation of texts.

The earliest Italian travel diaries were kept by both clerics and laymen, and their affinity to documentary writing is clear. Friar Jacopo da Verona's *Liber peregrinationis* (1335) is a hybrid work, which includes both a day-by-day account of the voyage from his native Verona to Jerusalem along with a synoptic description of Jerusalem typical of the synthetic tradition.[132] In 1384, Giorgio Gucci voyaged to the Holy Land with fellow Florentines Lionardo Fescobaldi and Simone Sigoli. All three wrote daily, dated records of their travels. The fact that Gucci—the treasurer of the pilgrim company's common fund—included an account of the group's expenses in his diary suggests that the journal may have doubled as a pragmatically motivated record.[133] Nicola de Martoni seems to have approached his diary as an extension of the legal writing he did as a notary. Nicola's recollection of the excitement that his fellow passengers felt when they first espied volcanoes off the coast of Sicily is striking in its bureaucratic scrupulosity: "Sed ego notarius Nicolaus videre non potui propter nimiam debilitatem visus" ("But I, Nicola, the notary, could not see [for myself], due to the excessive weakness of my sight").[134]

English and French pilgrims did not lag far behind Italians in keeping travel diaries, or—to be more accurate—in having others keep diaries on their behalf. In England and France, most of the earliest extant travel diaries document the pilgrimages of landowners and ecclesiastical officials; most are maintained by a member of the pilgrim's household. The 1392 pilgrimage of Englishman Thomas de Swinburne is commemorated in a Latin diary written by his chaplain, Thomas Brygg. The inclusion of a record of the journey's expenses suggests that at least part of the book originated as a household account. Written advice about how to maintain records of domestic expenses while traveling over shorter distances can be found in England as early as 1228.[135] It is also worth recalling that the most thorough contemporary source for the 1392 pilgrimage of Henry Bolingbroke (the future King Henry IV of England) is his wardrobe accounts.[136] The pilgrimage of French nobleman Ogier d'Anglure (1395) is recorded in diary form, as well. While the text does not document Ogier's expenses, it does include an early example of a Jerusalem inventory—a record of places visited by the pilgrim and a corresponding reckoning of the indulgences acquired at each shrine. In such lists, individual entries are usually introduced with the word *Item*—a verbal feature common to inventories of various kinds.[137] In 1418, Nompar de Caumont had someone maintain a daily record of his pilgrimage. In addition to the Jerusalem inventory, Caumont's diary keeps a daily log of distances traveled and a catalogue of all of the relics acquired by the nobleman over the course of his journey.

The earliest diaries of English and French landowners look ahead to the wealthy pilgrims of the fifteenth century, who commissioned diaries in much the same way that other pilgrims patronized paintings or chapels to commemorate their journeys.[138] Among those who employed others to write on their behalf are: Marquis Niccolò d'Este (1413), Philippe de Voisins (1490), and Richard Guylforde (1506).[139] Though he traveled much later (and to Rome rather than Jerusalem), Michel de Montaigne is interesting to consider in this context, since—although he was a devoted man of letters—he initially had a servant maintain the diary of his pilgrimage.[140] The self-discipline (and sometimes even the names) of the diarists who wrote for their pilgrim-patrons is rendered invisible, subordinated to tabulations of the patron's expenditures of time, wealth, and physical energy. This subordination of the labor of the diarist is vividly felt in the diaries of Richard Guylforde and Denis Possot (1532), whose scribes step out of the shadows at the moment when their masters die during the journey, and only then in order to explain their decision to carry on with their efforts.

By the end of the fifteenth century, the synthetic account and the diary are explicitly construed as competing forms of travel writing. Some authors expressly opt for one over the other, while others—in a manner reminiscent of Jacopo da Verona—hybridize the two. The diarist known as "Anonymous Parisian" probably had the synthetic tradition in mind when he wrote that he would describe the things he had seen on a day-to-day basis, and "non pas par manier de cosmographie ou aultres descriptions artificielles" ("not in the manner of a cosmography or other kinds of artificial description").[141] The nameless travel writer adds that writing things down daily as he sees them will make for a more trustworthy account, a method that ensures that he will not "adjouster ou obmettre de la verité" ("revise or stray from the truth").[142]

Meanwhile, authors such as Anselmo Adorno and Felix Fabri superimposed the day-based framework of the diary onto works that otherwise exhibit the synoptic and analytic approaches of the synthetic tradition. Adorno (under the apparent influence of Marco Polo) included a table of contents in which he divided his text into place- and topic-based chapters. In the table of contents, Adorno records the corresponding dates of the places that he describes, in an attempt to harmonize his synthetic approach to organizing the work with the conventions of the travel diary.[143] Fabri divided the *Evagatorium* so that each chapter represented a day of the year. As is the case with Adorno, Fabri's chapters do not confine their subject matter to the things that he saw on that day but instead range over a number of practical, historical, and geographical topics. The day-by-day progression of chapters is not, in other words, the sole—or even dominant—organizational principle. The diurnal structure does, however, underscore Fabri's claim that the *Evagatorium* is the product of disciplined, daily writing.

Interestingly, Fabri structured his *Sionpilger*—a devotional treatise written for cloistered nuns who could not go to Jerusalem in person—as a diary. He did so at the request of the nuns themselves. In language that recalls Anonymous Parisian, the nuns rebuffed Fabri's initial offer to copy Bonaventure's popular meditational guide for them. Instead of an abstract topographical treatise, the women insisted on having a book that was the product of Fabri's "pilgrimage" (*bilgerfart*) and all its travail, requesting that said book emphasize the "rough" (*raüchen*) day-to-day realities of travel.[144] As Albrecht Classen has noted, the *Sionpilger* can be an odd reading experience, since, on certain days, it is comprised of conventional meditational ruminations on the places of the Holy Land, and on others, it asks the nuns to imagine that they are aboard a storm-tossed pilgrim galley, trying to overcome terror and seasickness.[145] The *Sionpilger* seems less singular when it is read within the context of fifteenth-century travel writing on the Holy Land, which drew on the conventions of both the synthetic tradition and the travel diary.

The simple fact that travelers *could* keep a record of the journey in progress raised expectations about how much the traveler *ought* to remember. In the fifteenth century, Hans Tucher—a travel writer from Nuremburg who was read and praised by Fabri—advised Jerusalem-bound pilgrims to purchase paper, pen, and ink at Venice, so that they could record their observations during the journey's idle moments.[146] Burgundian knight Bertrandon de la Broquière makes repeated references to the "memorandum book" that he used to take the notes that served as the basis for the narrative of his overland journey home from Jerusalem.[147] Denis Possot claims to have had his "tablette" always on hand (*ayant toujours la tablette en main*) throughout his journey.[148]

If pilgrims to the Holy Land were the first travelers to insist in large numbers on the importance of taking notes, they were soon joined by others.

John Capgrave's *Solace of Pilgrims* has little to say about the daily rhythms of the author's pilgrimage to Rome. One exception to this general rule occurs at a moment when, back in his study in England, Capgrave fails to recall all of the relics housed in the Church of Saint Lawrence. Capgrave apologizes for having "no fresch rememberauns" of them, "because I did not write them down on account of the crowds of people that were there" ("for I wrote hem [them] nowt for the prees [press of people] that was there").[149] From 1403 to 1406, Ruy González de Clavijo participated in an embassy to the court of Tamerlane on behalf of King Enrique III of Castile. The account of this journey presents itself as the product of fervid note-taking, which began at the very moment of embarkation:

> Because the said embassy is arduous and to distant lands, it is necessary and prudent (*necesario e cumplidero*) to put in writing all of the places and lands through which the said ambassadors passed, and the things that happened to them so that they are not forgotten (*no cayan en olvido*) and so that they can be better and more truly told and known. To that end, in the name of God, in whose power lie all things, and of his mother the Virgin Mary, I began to write from the day that the ambassadors arrived at Port Santa María, near Cádiz, where they embarked in the carrack in which they had to go.[150]

Other travel writers expressed regrets that they had not written during, or at least soon after, their journeys. Ludolph von Suchem apologized for the brevity of his observations about the Holy Land and the places visited en route to it. Ludolph insists his descriptions would have been fuller "if, when in those parts, I had formed the intention of writing some account of them a little earlier."[151] The expectation that the travel writer would take careful notes during the journey even affected the reception of works that had been written prior to the emergence of this norm. Readers of *The Book of John Mandeville* inserted passages—occasionally in the author's voice—claiming that the English knight had kept thorough notes during his travels. Three copies of the Insular French version of Mandeville's *Book* state that the work is based on abridged memoranda ("memoires abregés fais par moi") that he kept during his journey.[152] A Middle English versification of the *Book* dating from the fifteenth century exaggerates Mandeville's notetaking efforts in the following—justifiably obscure—lines:

> And al that he sawe he vndirtoke
> And euer he wrote it in a boke,

And al that men hym tolde therto
He wrote it in a boke also. [153]

Something similar happened with the account of Marco Polo. The Z manuscript of the *Divisament dou monde*—a unique Latin translation perhaps rendered by someone who interviewed Polo—feels the need to explain that the Venetian traveler recorded only a few scattered details in writing during his time abroad.[154] In the sixteenth century, Ramusio alleges that what Polo managed to recollect when he finally returned to Venice was "little compared to the many and almost infinite things" he might have related had he taken notes. Ramusio adds—perhaps defensively—that Polo, believing that he might never see his native land again, recorded only "a few small things in his notebooks" while living in Asia.[155]

The *Evagatorium* of Felix Fabri suggests that, by the close of the fifteenth century, writing became so intertwined with travel of all kinds that it was viewed not only as a mnemonic necessity but as something that could be done with greater or lesser degrees of finesse. Fabri claims that Persian travelers to Jerusalem seek out German pilgrims in order to ask them why they believe that the biblical Magi are buried in Cologne rather than Persia. Fabri describes this custom in a way that suggests that it is misguided and uncritical: "They write down what they hear in answer word for word in their note-books, even as we note down the position of the Holy Land, of Jerusalem, and of the Church of the Lord's Sepulcher."[156] Elsewhere, Fabri chafes at the graffiti left behind by vainglorious nobles, who carve their names and heraldic crests into the walls of sacred sanctuaries.[157] He even calls into question the wisdom of travelers who write down what they believe they have seen in their explorations of subterranean caverns. Fabri maintains that many of the "mystical" phenomena experienced by spelunking pilgrims are hallucinations caused by dim lighting and poor air quality—a sentiment that anticipates the Cave of Montesinos episode in Cervantes's *Don Quixote*.[158] If the synthetic tradition had given rise to the conviction that literacy was an organic—and perhaps essential—component of travel, the social and methodological diversification of writing practices prompted Fabri and others to make fresh, qualitative distinctions among the literate endeavors of their fellow travelers.

CONCLUSION

Building on the deep foundations of scholarly and devotional tradition, pilgrims to the Holy Land spearheaded the conceptual integration of the arts

of literacy and travel. As the Middle Ages drew to a close, the literate labor of the Jerusalem pilgrim was informed by methods and practices drawn
from various spheres of cultural activity. This, in turn, contributed to a new
self-consciousness about *which* literate practices should ideally define the
ideal pilgrimage. Similar developments can be seen in late medieval debates
about how pilgrims ought to approach the task of geoethnographic investigation.

CHAPTER FOUR

The Pilgrim as Investigator

Today, the medieval pilgrim to Jerusalem is more known for his ritual devotions than for his investigative spirit. This is somewhat surprising. A growing body of scholarship testifies to the striking range of intellectual interests that animated Latin Christian approaches to writing about the Holy Land during the later Middle Ages.[1] Medievalists have also shed light on the rich literature of Muslim and Jewish pilgrimage to the region during the same period.[2] Meanwhile, early modernists have shown that the European enthusiasm for traveling to and writing about the Holy Land not only *survived* Columbus's bungled expedition to Asia but also flourished to a degree that we are only now beginning to comprehend.[3] Nevertheless, it proves hard to dislodge the hoary dogma that medieval pilgrims produced a bland, homogenous corpus of texts whose interests were idiosyncratic during the Middle Ages and decisively irrelevant to modernity.

Curiously, in the 1980s, influential books by Donald Howard and Christian K. Zacher called attention to the late medieval emergence of new approaches to writing about the Holy Land.[4] Both studies argued that, toward the end of the Middle Ages, pilgrims take greater interest in describing the nondevotional dimensions of their journeys. While the findings of Howard and Zacher should have dislodged long-standing caricatures of the medieval pilgrim, the reception of their research ended up entrenching those stereotypes even more deeply. This missed opportunity is partially attributable to how Howard and Zacher explained the underlying causes of what they observed. Both suggested that, over the course of the Middle Ages, pilgrims progressively emancipated themselves from the dour clerical disapproval of novelty, empirical observation, and secular interests. This was essentially a reinscription (writ small) of Jakob Burckhardt's discredited vision of the Renaissance as a period of enlightenment, founded on a radical break with the benighted mentalities of the Middle Ages (a zombie lately reanimated—and in saucy defiance of common sense—by Stephen Greenblatt).[5] The related thesis found in Hans Blumenberg's *The Legitimacy of the Modern Age* has also contributed to the longevity of these stereotypes, insofar as it has encouraged scholars to view curiosity and religious devotion as inherently oppositional impulses.[6]

In reality, the history of travel writing about the Holy Land is one characterized by skepticism toward—and curious, creative engagement with—official claims, political and social realities, and literary convention. This was not a matter of choice. Medieval visitors to Palestine—be they Christian, Jewish, or Muslim—seldom enjoyed the luxury of premade itineraries or univocal truths. The region was home to members of all three Abrahamic faiths. Each of these confessional groups consisted, in turn, of various sectarian communities. Over time, numerous written and oral traditions about the topography of the Holy Land accumulated, sometimes coming into open conflict with one another. Moreover, military contests in the region displaced local populations and resulted in the destruction or repurposing of sacred sites. Under such conditions, certainty about the history and geography of the region was a hard-won rarity.

If the evidentiary challenges of writing about the Holy Land were a historical constant, the constellation of ideological, social, and literary resources available to a given travel writer during the Middle Ages were historically and culturally particular. An understanding of which resources were on hand and how they were appropriated by any given travel writer is a prerequisite for any assessment of the historical "significance" of his or her work. While it is true that late medieval pilgrims tended to write at much greater length than their predecessors had about the contemporary realities of the Holy Land and of the places visited en route to it, that does not necessarily mean that these developments were "oppositional." There is even less warrant to presume that they are the product of a single, defining fault line in the history of the "Western" episteme. The expanding scope of the medieval pilgrim's investigations is the outcome of a number of factors, including the vicissitudes of cross-cultural conflict and exchange; the rise of new social groups, such as urban professionals, merchants, and the fraternal orders; shifting political and economic realities within Europe and the Mediterranean; and an array of technological, intellectual, and sociological phenomena signaled by the shorthand phrase "the spread of literacy."

This chapter considers significant turning points in the development of travel writing about the Holy Land, with a primary focus on the years 1100–1500. The trajectory traced by the chapter should not be understood as an evolutionary timeline, in which each section marks a phase of development that supersedes the ones that precede it, but rather one in which developments accrete and—at times—coexist unharmoniously. As an alternative to the rigid teleology that underpins the most widely known historiographical account of the travel writing of Holy Land pilgrims, this survey proceeds in a rhizomatic fashion, identifying major innovations in the methods and objects of pilgrim investigation, explaining the factors that facilitated their emergence, and—when possible—considering the meanings that travel writers and their medieval audiences attached to these novel features. Perhaps the three most consequential of these developments were: (1) the emergence of overt statements about the travel writer's investigative methods, (2) the increased energy devoted to investigating European and Mediterranean places visited en route to Jerusalem, and (3) the sense that the unfolding journey was itself an object worthy of scrutiny.

DOUBT AND THE RECOVERY OF PLACE (1099–1187)

From its inception, Christian pilgrimage entailed the laborious recovery of the biblical past. When Emperor Constantine visited Judea in 326, the Jerusalem of Jesus was beneath his feet.[7] Titus and Vespasian had destroyed the city's Second Temple in 70 CE. This calamity was followed in 135 by the brutal suppression of the Bar Kokhba revolt, which resulted in the wholesale destruction of Jerusalem. Hadrian built a new city over the shattered remains, renaming it "Aelia Capitolina," after himself.[8] According to legend, when Constantine wanted to access the site of Christ's burial nearly two hundred years later, he had to tear down a pagan temple built by his imperial predecessors to do so.[9] The first Christian emperor not only recovered the sacred tomb but ordered the Church of the Holy Sepulcher to be built around it. A second major archaeological discovery followed soon after, in 326–28, during the imperial visitation of Constantine's mother, Helena. At her son's urging, Helena conducted an inquiry into the location of Mount Golgotha, rumored to be the location of Christ's crucifixion.[10] Golgotha was eventually found beneath another crumbling pagan temple. The site's convenient proximity to the Holy Sepulcher allowed it to be incorporated within the church recently founded by Constantine.

As dramatic as these discoveries were, it would be the scholarly endeavors of Jerome (347–420) that would provide the era's most enduring model for recovering the Christian past of the Holy Land. During his residence outside Antioch and later Bethlehem, Jerome studied Hebrew and interviewed Jewish residents regarding local lore. These investigative pursuits informed his translation of the Bible into Latin, his scriptural commentaries, and his translation/revision of the *Onomasticon* of Eusebius.[11] Of particular importance to the Middle Ages, Jerome conceived of pilgrimage as a learned mode of travel, one that supplemented—and even perfected—scholarly pursuit. In his commentary on the book of Chronicles, Jerome remarks that a traveler "who has seen Judea with his own eyes and who knows the sites of ancient cities and their names, whether the same or changed, will gaze more clearly on the Holy Scripture."[12] Elsewhere, Jerome compared the intellectual value of pilgrimage to the Holy Land to the kinds of travel undertaken in pursuit of secular knowledge:

> Time forbids me . . . to recount the bishops, the martyrs, the divines, who have come to Jerusalem from a feeling that their devotion and knowledge would be incomplete and their virtue without the finishing touch, unless they adored Christ in the very spot where the gospel first flashed from the gibbet. If a famous orator blames a man for having learned Greek at Lilybaeum instead of at Athens, and Latin in Sicily instead of at Rome (on the ground, obviously, that each province has its own characteristics), can we suppose a Christian's education complete who has not visited the Christian Athens?[13]

Even Augustine—hardly known for his gushing advocacy of pilgrimage to the earthly Jerusalem—conceded that firsthand knowledge of what Jerome called "the Christian Athens" was an asset to interpreters of scripture.[14] More important, Jerome effectively fashioned the physical journey to the Holy Land as a literate—and hermeneutically oriented—mode of travel, organized around the identification and inspection of places one had previously known exclusively through books.

In the aftermath of the First Crusade (1095–99), the new Frankish rulers of the Holy Land were confronted with a glut of contradictory traditions regarding the history and topography of the region, which perplexed even the most learned among them. Uncertainty surrounded even the Church of the Holy Sepulcher. Fulcher of Chartres—an eyewitness chronicler of the First Crusade—was overcome by the swarm of competing legends that surrounded Christianity's holiest shrine: "I am not able, nor do I dare assert, nor am I wise enough to tell, of the many things that are kept therein, some of which are there now, and others already gone, lest I mislead those who hear of or read about these things."[15] According to Albert of Aachen, a single vessel located within the Dome of the Rock spawned a host of incompatible claims: "Some declare it the golden pot, some say the blood of the Lord is concealed in it, others manna."[16] In time, the rulers of the new Latin Christian Kingdom of Jerusalem would oversee a dramatic transformation of the Holy Land, in which saints' bodies and other relics were "discovered" and "translated" to new shrines, in which mosques were converted into churches, in which new architectural programs altered the face of cities.[17] Although these efforts helped consolidate the topographical knowledge of Latin Christian residents of the Holy Land, they occasioned confusion and resistance among pilgrims of various confessional persuasions.

The period that spans the founding of the Latin Kingdom of Jerusalem (1099) and Saladin's conquest of Jerusalem (1187) was one in which pilgrim-investigators frequently questioned official claims and reflected on the limitations of available evidence. John of Würzburg wrote his *Descriptio* (ca. 1160–70) so that future pilgrims would enjoy a luxury he had been denied: the ability to visit sites of biblical significance "without delay and difficulty" involved in finding them.[18] John observed that library research alone was insufficient preparation for navigating the contemporary Holy Land, which no longer resembled the region described in the once-authoritative pages of Bede's *De locis sanctis*.[19] To orient oneself in this transformed landscape, one literally had to read writing on the wall. The *Descriptio* offers conspicuously detailed descriptions of painting, sculpture, architecture, and—especially—epigraphy: "I worked hard to collect all of the inscriptions, whether in prose or in verse."[20] John hoped that his labors would assist future pilgrims to picture the events of the biblical past amid the changed and changing realities of the present day.

In contrast to later Dominican and Franciscan travel writing on the Holy Land, John's *Descriptio* does not extend its investigations to the beliefs and rituals of other confessional groups. This is due, in part, to the work's interest in mapping the topography of the contemporary Holy Land in terms of its past. Thus, even though John—like many other Latin Christian travel writers—relies heavily on the testimony of eastern Christians, he explicitly passes over the topic of their beliefs, practices, and cultural peculiarities in favor of describing the layout of the Church of the Holy Sepulcher.[21]

Theoderic, another twelfth-century travel writer, made liberal—if unacknowledged—use of John of Würzburg's *Relatio*. His *Peregrinatio* seconded John's assertions about the difficulty of finding the places mentioned in scripture. Theoderic found that residents of the Holy Land were little help in his investigations, since they did not recognize ancient place-names. He lamented that the ignorance of the locals could not be supplemented through archival work, since—he maintained—the Second Temple, destroyed by the Romans, had housed all of Jerusalem's property deeds.[22] The idea that one *might* hypothetically clarify the names of places through such documentary research, like John of Würzburg's analyses of images and inscriptions, was a creative attempt to bring clerical literacy to bear on a confused, fragmentary body of evidence.

In this era of uncertainty, Latin Christians were not alone in their quest for alternative archives. Having visited the Holy Land in 1165, Iberian rabbi Benjamin of Tudela warned Jewish readers about several unsettling developments in the region. Benjamin advised would-be pilgrims that they would no longer find the body of the Prophet Samuel in Rameh, since it had been removed by Christians and reinterred in a church in Shiloh.[23] The Frankish rulers had also converted the mosque at Hebron—which housed the sacred tombs of the Patriarchs—into the "Church of Saint Abraham." While in the past, Muslims allowed Jews to visit the tombs of Abraham and his family, Christians barred them from entering the building.[24] By way of consolation, Benjamin reports that the tombs venerated by Christians inside the Church of Abraham are, in actuality, fakes, erected by greedy priests in order to extract offerings from naive pilgrims. Benjamin asserts that the "authentic" tombs are really *beneath* the church, accessible to anyone willing to bribe the porter who guards the subterranean passage to them.[25] In support of this claim, Benjamin cites the testimony of local rabbis, as well as his own inspection of the Hebrew inscriptions that adorn the underground monuments.[26] Interviews with men of learning and the analysis of Hebrew inscriptions are, in general, the central evidentiary pillars of Benjamin's counterhegemonic topography.[27]

Intriguingly, disagreement about the authenticity of the tombs at Hebron would divide Muslim scholars two centuries after Benjamin contested official Christian claims about them. When Ibn Battuta visited Hebron (in Arabic, al-Khalīl) in the fourteenth century, the building that Benjamin had known as the Church of Saint Abraham was once again a mosque. Though this had been the case for over a century, some Islamic scholars inveighed against the Muslim veneration of the Tombs of the Patriarchs, decrying the practice as a recent innovation. The objections of Ibn Battuta's opponents were part of a broader resistance to pilgrimages not explicitly prescribed by the Qur'an.[28] Such practices were frequently impugned as Jewish or Christian contaminations of the faith. Ibn Battuta mounts a spirited defense of the legitimacy of visiting the Hebron tombs. Stressing that he has personally inspected the monuments "several times," Ibn Battuta leverages scholarly tradition, communal memory, and reverse charges of heresy against the naysayers:

> When I met, in this town, the pious and aged professor, as well as imām Burhān al-Dīn al-Ja'barī . . . I questioned him about the truth of al-Khalīl's (i.e. Abraham's) grave. . . . He replied to me, "All the scholars whom I have met accept as a certainty that these graves are the very graves of Abraham, Isaac, and Jacob . . . and the graves of their wives. No one raises objections to this but the followers of false doctrines; it is a tradition which has passed from father to son for generations and admits of no doubt."[29]

The circumspection surrounding the Tombs of the Patriarchs was no doubt fueled by the various claims and counterclaims that already surrounded the monuments in the age of Benjamin of Tudela.

When Saladin toppled the Latin Christian Kingdom of Jerusalem in 1187, he rebuilt and refortified it, altering its appearance considerably.[30] A number of sites formerly venerated by Christians were ruined. Others were repurposed as mosques and rendered off-limits to non-Muslims. Christian pilgrims could still visit the Church of the Holy Sepulcher, but initially, their access was not guaranteed. A decrease in the number of extant Latin Christian pilgrimage accounts in the century following Saladin's triumph probably reflects a broader uncertainty about the safety and feasibility of travel to Jerusalem. Those who did undertake the pilgrimage were by no means sanguine about what they saw. Wilbrand of Oldenburg ascended the mountains outside Jerusalem in 1211 and looked out onto "many destroyed and desolate villages and monasteries, whose names are unknown to me."[31]

During the thirteenth and fourteenth centuries, the scholarly recovery of places and Christian traditions preoccupied travel writers perhaps more acutely than it ever had. Dominican polemicist Riccoldo of Montecroce called Jerusalem "a city of catastrophe and destruction," and documented each of the many ruined churches he came across.[32] In the 1330s, Jacopo da Verona claimed that he composed his pilgrimage account even though several superficially similar texts already existed, because "things have changed very much in the overseas regions in such a short time, and to the great detriment of Christians."[33] Alongside the resurgence of the kind of scholarly investigation pioneered by Jerome emerged new, tactical fields of investigation oriented toward the future conversion of non-Christians and the reconquest of the Holy Land.

ESPIONAGE, MISSION, AND CRUSADE (1285 AND AFTER)

The thirteenth and fourteenth centuries have been justly identified as a watershed in history of travel writing about the Holy Land.[34] In contrast to their predecessors, late medieval travel writers manifested a keen interest in ethnography and the analysis of social life, both within and beyond the Holy Land. Dominican authors were among the most prominent early fulminators of these developments. The innovative works of Burchard of Mount Sion, Riccoldo of Montecroce, and William of Boldensele reflect the scholarly, disputatious, and universalizing ideals of their order. These Dominicans each put a distinctive new stamp on the investigative labor of pilgrimage, influencing the travel writing of both clerics and laypeople in the process.

Burchard of Mount Sion's *Description of the Holy Land* (ca. 1285–89) was the most influential thirteenth-century travel account written about the region. Composed initially in Latin (in a longer, then in a shorter, recension) and later translated into French and German, the *Description* survives in more than one hundred manuscript copies.[35] At first glance, Burchard's *Description* seems thoroughly conventional. It opens by citing Jerome's argument that visiting the Holy Land allows scholarly travelers to see "things they had learnt about from books."[36] The learned investigations of Burchard entail research, interviews, and personal observation. Burchard's authority is based in large part on his physically demanding treks across the Holy Land:

> I have inspected (*consideraui*), diligently recorded (*notaui diligenter*), and studiously described (*studiose descripsi*) in so far as I have been able that land through which I have frequently passed on foot; and I would wish the reader to know that I have included nothing in this description except what I saw with my own eyes when I was in the place itself or, when I was unable to gain access, what I saw standing on some mountain or in another suitable place; and I have noted down what I have learnt from Syrians, Saracens, or other inhabitants of the land, diligently questioning them.[37]

For Burchard, the fact that such an exhausting undertaking is necessary in the first place is a symptom of a larger problem. The *Description* repeatedly emphasizes Christians' ignorance about the places of the Holy Land, contrasting it to the far greater knowledge of Burchard's Muslim informants. In chapter 3, we saw that Burchard chose Acre as the artificial center of his imaginary map of the region because, among his Latin Christian readers, "it is better known than other places," even though—he pointedly adds—"this city was not ever part of the Holy Land."[38] With no little horror, Burchard observes that ignorance about sacred geography extends even to those Christians who enjoy the benefits of formal education. Burchard's description of Jerusalem veers off into a polemic against certain unnamed authors who claim that the city has shifted "to a different position" since the crucifixion (an argument advanced, for example, in the pilgrimage account of Wilbrand of Oldenburg and in *Ernoul's Chronicle*).[39] Elsewhere, Burchard resolves to pass over the topic of the Dead Sea quickly on the grounds that many other books have addressed it, only to pause and correct an error he has detected in the writings of his coreligionists. Eager to rebut the supposedly widespread Christian misconception that the Jordan River does not "mingle its waters" with the infamous Dead Sea, Burchard cites the more reliable testimony of the "Saracens" he has interviewed in the field.[40]

If Muslims are more trustworthy authorities than Latin Christian authors, the same does not hold true for the Greek Orthodox monks who have continued to dwell in the region after the fall of the Frankish kingdom. Chapter 3 alluded to Burchard's dismissal of a legend that identified a Greek Orthodox monastery at Saba with the prison that once held John the Baptist.[41] Burchard prefaces his debunking with the description of a site that neighbors this monastic community, which actually *can* be legitimately linked to the cousin and forerunner of Jesus: the Nabi Yahya Mosque. Named after John the Baptist, this church-turned-mosque housed the tomb of the saint (and, to this day, remains a site of devotion for both Muslims and Christians).[42] Through its juxtaposition of these authentic and spurious tourist attractions, the *Description* strongly implies that the Greek monks' fabulous tale is a compensatory fantasy, spun in order to cope with their forced displacement from the genuinely significant historical site next door.

This is one of many instances in which the *Description* implies that dominion over a given territory is the only certain guarantee of access to the truth about its past and present. As Burchard stresses in his prologue, his researches can but partially and temporarily restore Latin Christians' severed connection to the Holy Land. The only permanent remedy for this estrangement is crusade:

We may sigh over the dull-wittedness of the Christian people of our time, who having so many and such great examples delay in delivering from the hands of our enemies that land that Jesus Christ consecrated with His blood, the name of which resounds in all churches every day. For what hour is there of the day or night throughout the whole cycle of the year in which every devout Christian does not recall by singing, reading, psalmody, preaching and meditating all of those things that were done in this land and in its cities and localities?[43]

At the core of Burchard's revival of the bookish place-based inquiries of Jerome is a nostalgic yearning for a lost era, when Christians asserted their military dominance over the Holy Land and—as an outgrowth of this hegemony—displayed a scholarly command of its history and geography.

Burchard's call to arms did not fall on deaf ears. The *Description* was used not only for devotional and scholarly purposes but also for military-strategic ones. Burchard was an important source for Marino Sanudo Torsello's procrusading treatise *The Book of Secrets of the Faithful of the Cross* (ca. 1300–1321), which also included maps by Genoese cartographer Pietro Vesconte.[44] Sanudo helped launch espionage as a new investigative field for travel-writing pilgrims. In the wake of the Christian loss of Acre in 1291, the works of pilgrim-spies attended to matters that had not previously been central to descriptions of the Holy Land, including fortifications, military organization, governmental structures, social and political dynamics, commercial activity, and courtly life.

This tactical approach to investigation provided lay pilgrims such as Lionardo Frescobaldi, Emmanuel Piloti, and Bertrandon de la Broquière with an entrée into a tradition of travel writing previously dominated by clerics.[45] The status-leveling potential of the crusading enterprise is manifest in a fifteenth-century copy of Burchard's *Description*. At the time the manuscript was executed in the 1450s, its recipient, Philip the Good, Duke of Burgundy, was planning to mount a crusade against the Ottoman Empire. Bound with this lavishly produced version of Burchard's *Description* is the chivalric travel narrative of Bertrandon de la Broquière, the duke's carver, who traveled through Ottoman territory disguised as a Muslim (see fig. 3, in chapter 1). Bertrandon's spirited narrative doubled as a work of espionage, and described Ottoman territory in much greater depth than it did the Holy Land. The composition of this manuscript suggests that each work made a different—but equally valuable—contribution to nurturing the duke's crusading ambitions.

The *Liber peregrinationis* of Riccoldo of Montecroce is another of the thirteenth century's most successful and groundbreaking works of travel writing. The *Liber* devoted significant space to the kinds of questions that normally preoccupied travelers to East Asia. Riccoldo drew on his experience as a Dominican missionary in Persia to investigate the theological and ethnic diversity of the world beyond the Holy Land. Among the unconventional subjects he addressed were: Mongol beliefs about resurrection, the origins of Kurdish identity, the "heretical" teachings of Jacobites and Nestorians, and the Persian vogue for purchasing "pygmy" entertainers.[46] The *Liber*'s affinities with exotic travel writing are further suggested by a unique heading found in the oldest extant version of the work (Berlin: Staatsbibliothek, MS lat. 4º 466), which bears corrections made in Riccoldo's hand: "Contained briefly in this book are the kingdoms, peoples, provinces, laws, rites, sects, heresies and monsters which I came upon in the eastern regions."[47]

The ease with which Riccoldo pivots from the description of the Holy Land to an exoticizing account of the East reflects the global, universalizing ambitions of the Dominican Order. Riccoldo understood his travels—and those of his fellow friars—as part of a larger geopolitical struggle:

> All Christian people and all western people should gratefully remember that at the same time the Lord sent the Tartars to the Eastern countries in order to kill and destroy, he also sent his most faithful servants blessed Dominic and blessed Francis to the Western countries in order to illuminate, instruct, and edify. And as much as the latter have accomplished in their building up, the former increased in their destroying.[48]

Indeed, the tactical, globalizing perspective of Riccoldo cannot easily be distinguished from the military agendas of crusaders and secular rulers, whose grandiose ambitions were fostered by the cross-pollination of pilgrimage and exotic travel writing. An illustrative example is provided by the vernacular anthology compiled and translated by Hospitaler Jean de Vignay for would-be crusading king Philip VI of France (1328–50).[49] One manuscript copy of the collection (London: BL Royal MS 19 D I) gathers French versions of Marco Polo with three other texts translated by Jean de Vignay: the works of Odoric of Pordenone and John of Plano Carpini (from the epitome of Vincent of Beauvais) and a tract advising how to recapture the Holy Land (attributed to Burchard of Mount Sion but probably written or reworked by another anonymous Dominican). The fact that these texts are bound with two Alexander romances suggests the imperialist fantasies that underlie the manuscript's synthesis of formerly distinct categories of geographical and travel writing.[50]

Then there is John le Long's anthology of travel writing, discussed in chapter 1. John gathered into one volume French renditions of Riccoldo's

Liber with the exotic travel writings of Odoric of Pordenone, Hetoum of Armenia, Marco Polo, and—in later versions—John Mandeville. The anthology incorporated yet another important text about the Holy Land, also written by a Dominican: William of Boldensele's enormously influential *Liber de quibusdam ultramarinis partibus* (1336). William turned the interests of pilgrims and exotic travel writers inward toward the eastern Mediterranean and in the process helped spark new investigations into places even closer to home.

THE MEDITERRANEAN AND INWARD TURNS (1330–1500)

The variety of late medieval approaches to writing about the Holy Land defies crisp and definitive summation. In part, this is due to the dramatic increase in the number of extant pilgrimage accounts written during the later Middle Ages. Ursula Ganz-Blätter estimates that Jerusalem pilgrims wrote 262 accounts between 1301 and 1520, with roughly half of these texts dating from after 1460.[51] These works served a range of purposes, and were authored by clerics and laypeople alike.

One clear trend that emerges between 1330 and 1500 is a new focus on investigating the places visited en route to Jerusalem, particularly Mediterranean islands and ports of call. A number of factors contributed to this development. Despite the dangers posed by shipwreck and piracy (as well as periodic Christian-on-Christian aggressions among the Genoese, Catalans, and Venetians), maritime travel to the Holy Land provided a faster, safer option than the overland journey from western Europe. Genoa, Venice, and the crown of Aragon claimed a number of Mediterranean towns and islands as colonial possessions. Meanwhile, various French-speaking monarchs and aristocrats continued to assert dynastic claims on lands across the region, maintaining control over valuable territories such as Sicily and Cyprus. Despite papal embargoes against trade with the Egyptian sultan, Iberian and Italian merchants entered into lucrative commercial arrangements with the Muslim ruler and even settled in significant numbers in cities under his control.[52] Franciscan and Dominican missionaries followed the trails blazed by merchants and crusaders, founding Mediterranean churches and hospitals that would themselves become pilgrimage attractions. The presence of Latin Christian communities and business interests across the Mediterranean ensured that pilgrim ships bound for the Holy Land would make frequent, and sometimes protracted, stops along the way. Meanwhile, the introduction of paper into Europe made various forms of record keeping cheaper, including the travel diaries that allowed pilgrims to take notes on all of the ports and islands that they visited en route to Jerusalem.

The pilgrimage account of German Dominican William of Boldensele (also known as Otto von Nyenhusen) played a significant part in promoting the Mediterranean turn in travel writing on the Holy Land. William apparently absconded to Genoa in 1330, without authorization from his superiors.[53] From Genoa, he sailed along a common trade route to Constantinople before voyaging onward to the Holy Land via a series of Greek islands. Upon his return, William dedicated his *Liber* to his patron Cardinal Elie Talleyrand (who—incidentally—also numbered among Petrarch's correspondents).[54] Several of William's near contemporaries likewise recorded their impressions of the places they visited on the way to the Holy Land— including the Norwegian Franciscan known as Friar Maurice (1271–73), the Irish Franciscan Simon FitzSimons (1322–23), and Jacopo da Verona (1335).[55] Though not the first to investigate the charms of the Mediterranean region, William of Boldensele exerted a profound—if largely indirect—influence on subsequent travel writing. William's *Liber* was the main source for the pilgrimage portion of *The Book of John Mandeville*. Large swaths of the *Liber* were also reproduced nearly verbatim in Ludolph von Suchem's *Description of the Holy Land*, a book that was, in turn, an important source for Felix Fabri.

The *Liber* takes note of the relics, antiquities, and conditions of everyday life in places such as Cyprus, Ephesus, and Egypt. The first place described in William's *Liber* is Constantinople, at the time an unconventional choice for any kind of travel account. Exotic travel writers like William of Rubruck, Marco Polo, and Odoric of Pordenone passed over the city in virtual silence, perhaps because they considered it too well known to their readers. In the fourteenth century, Constantinople does not appear to have been a common stop for Jerusalem-bound pilgrims, who were more likely to sail along Venetian trade routes, reaching the Holy Land via Cyprus or Alexandria. Moving on from Constantinople, William of Boldensele subsequently describes "Troy," Ephesus, Rhodes, and Cyprus before settling finally into the Holy Land.

Notably, William's portrait of the eastern Mediterranean draws on investigatory practices developed by earlier pilgrims to the Holy Land. This is particularly evident in the *Liber*'s discussion of the Pyramids of Giza. William measured the perimeter of each monument's base and sought out Latin inscriptions that might yield clues to their enigmatic origins. What he observed prompted him to challenge the then-dominant identification of the pyramids with the granaries that Pharaoh built on the advice of Joseph, an assertion first recorded in the sixth century by Gregory of Tours.[56] Based on his investigations, William concluded that the pyramids were actually royal tombs. As evidence, he recorded a Latin verse inscription that had been etched into one of the structures, with an accompanying commentary that concludes: "These verses are obscure in their meaning, and I pondered them for some time . . . and it is true that these are tombs, as the above-written verses attest." For good measure, William adds that simpletons (*simplices*) refer to the structures as the Pharaoh's granaries, "but this cannot be true at all, for there is nowhere to store grain there."[57] In this passage, William combines earlier travel writers' attention to epigraphy with an equally long tradition of skepticism about the limitations of written authority and oral tradition.

William's theory about the pyramids' origins inaugurated a debate among European visitors to Egypt that would endure through the sixteenth century. Among the travel writers who contradicted William's judgment was the one most indebted to him: John Mandeville. Reversing the evidentiary hierarchy of William of Boldensele without naming him explicitly, Mandeville contends that "some say" (*Dient ascuns*) that the structures are "tombs" (*sepultures*) rather than Joseph's granaries, but that these unnamed people are wrong to doubt the "common word" that prevails throughout the country (*la comune renomee est par toute le païs*).[58] In answering William, Mandeville articulates clear convictions about the best practices of pilgrim investigation. The inquisitorial posture that William adopts toward the "comune renomee" is contested by Mandeville, who—in keeping with the secularizing notion of authority that we saw him champion in chapter 2—puts more faith in the local, traditional knowledge of laypeople than in the Latinity and book learning of clerics.

Egypt was one of the primary theaters in which travel writers like William and Mandeville investigated natural and social phenomena seldom mentioned by travel-writing pilgrims prior to the fourteenth century. William of Boldensele's Egyptian investigations typify the secularizing undercurrents of the Mediterranean turn. While fellow Dominican Riccoldo of Montecroce boasts of victories in disputations, William showcases the "singular favor" (*singularem gratiam*) vouchsafed him by the sultan, in the form of letters of permission granting the traveler unfettered access to holy places throughout his domain without any tribute, toll, or fee.[59] With a palpable pride, he recalls his swift journey on horseback through the desert to Mount Sinai, which—due to its unprecedented nature—made him the object of admiration among locals.[60] This last bit of self-celebration did not sit well with Mandeville, who—in referring to the same stretch of wilderness—declares that camels are the only animals that can survive the journey, since "there is nothing for horses to eat and drink there."[61]

Even though Mandeville parts ways with William of Boldensele on several points, in other respects, he expands on the worldly impulses of his source. *The Book of John Mandeville* greatly multiplies the number of Mediterranean marvels found in the pages of William's *Liber*. Mandeville discourses at length on the miraculous origins of Egyptian balm and on the best techniques for detecting its adulteration.[62] He embellishes William's allusions to the sultan, claiming to have served as a mercenary in the ruler's wars against the Bedouin.[63] The *Book* also introduces a number of implausible Mediterranean wonders inspired by chivalric fiction. Particularly notable is its fanciful description of the Dodecanese island of Kos. According to Mandeville, residents of Kos report that, long ago, the goddess Diana transformed the daughter of Hippocrates into a dragon. The enchanted maiden continues to haunt a cavern on the island, condemned to languish there in reptilian form until she is visited by a knight brave enough to kiss her on the mouth. The *Book* devotes most of its discussion of Kos to recounting the story of various knights who have tried—and failed—this test of valor.[64]

In finding equal measures of enchantment in East Asia and in places closer to home, Mandeville helped fuel a growing fascination with Mediterranean travel and geography. Mandeville's intimate depiction of the Egyptian sultan's court inaugurates a tradition of embedded ethnographic investigation on the part of chivalric travel writers. In one of the *Book*'s most studied sequences, the sultan voids his court in order to have a private audience with Mandeville.[65] To the English knight's astonishment, the sultan addresses him in "very good French" (*moult bien franceois*) and demonstrates a detailed understanding of current European affairs.[66] The ruler tries to dispel Mandeville's astonishment by confessing that he frequently sends courtier-spies to Europe, disguised as merchants. In the secrecy of the voided chamber, the sultan also avows his belief that Christianity will eventually triumph over Islam in the struggle over the Holy Land. This episode, which has no precedent in William of Boldensele, recalls Marco Polo's interactions with the Great Khan and Francis of Assisi's exchanges with the Egyptian sultan (both considered in chapter 1).

In any event, *The Book of John Mandeville* anticipated—and, in some cases, provided an imitable model for—investigations into the governance and courtly culture of Egypt and other non-Christian kingdoms. The *Andanças* of fifteenth-century knight Pero Tafur casts a curious eye on the af-

fairs of the Egyptian sultan, the Byzantine emperor, and the Ottoman sultan
(see chapter 6). The intimate exchanges between Tafur and the members
of the Egyptian and Byzantine courts bear a striking resemblance to the
dialogue between Mandeville and the sultan. The influence of Mandeville
likely informs *The Beauchamp Pageants*—a chivalric biography of Richard
Beauchamp, thirteenth Earl of Warwick (1382–1439). Rendered as a series
of captioned drawings, the unique manuscript of the *Pageants* (London, BL:
Cotton Julius IV e) includes a sequence of illustrations of the earl's pilgrimage to the Holy Land. One drawing shows Beauchamp making an offering at
the Church of the Holy Sepulcher. However, the work as a whole seems far
more interested in depicting Beauchamp's experiences as the honored guest
of "Sir Baltirdam," a lieutenant to the sultan of Egypt, devoting no fewer
than three drawings to it. As an enthusiastic reader of chivalric romances,
Baltirdam cannot pass up the opportunity to host the English earl, who
claims to be the descendant of legendary hero Guy of Warwick. The most
Mandevillean of the *Pageants* depicts an exchange between Beauchamp and
his host, in which the latter tells his guest "in secrete wise" that he believes
in the truth of Christian doctrine.[67] Arnold von Harff's debt to Mandeville is
more obvious still. Von Harff, a German knight from Cologne, appropriated
several passages from the *Book*, including two scenes—one with the sultan
of Egypt and the other with the Ottoman sultan—that are thinly revised
versions of Mandeville's audience with the Egyptian ruler.[68]

The influence of the *Book* extended beyond the circle of chivalric pilgrims. The pilgrimage account of notary Nicola de Martoni included a
lengthy rehearsal of the legend of Hippocrates's daughter, which he purportedly heard from a Franciscan friar on the island of Rhodes.[69] The humanist-
inspired nobleman Joos van Ghistele echoed the same Mandevillean yarn
in the posthumous Flemish account of his voyage to the Holy Land, which
he undertook in the 1480s.[70] The anecdote is also mentioned in Cristoforo
Buondelmonti' s *Liber insularum archipelagi* (1420). Along with Cyriac of
Ancona, Buondelmonti is given perhaps undue credit for "discovering" the
Mediterranean as a discrete, worthwhile field of geographical and antiquarian inquiry.[71] The enchanted maiden of Kos also appears in unabashedly fictional guise in the Mediterranean-focused romance *Tirant lo blanch* (1490),
cowritten in Catalan by Joanot Martorell and Martí Joan de Galba.

Like Mandeville, Ludolph von Suchem widened the scope of William
of Boldensele's Mediterranean explorations. Contradicting the stereotype
of the medieval pilgrim as a traveler whose horizons were constrained by
tradition, Ludolph expressly set out to contribute something original to the
existing body of travel writing on the Holy Land, pledging to write "not

only . . . about the lands beyond the seas, but also of the wonders which are beheld *in* the seas."[72] Keenly interested in Mediterranean ecology, Ludolph taps the expertise of some rather unlikely authorities, including the "truthful mariners" who convey him to the Holy Land. These sailors inform Ludolph about the names and seasonal behaviors of Mediterranean winds and describe an array of monstrous fish and other perils that they have encountered while at sea.[73] In Sicily, Ludolph marvels at the alien geology of Mount Etna and investigates allegations that the volcano is a gateway to hell.[74] In Sardinia, he interviews the island's oldest resident in order to determine if the recent storm that nearly wrecked his ship was truly, as some were maintaining, the worst ever experienced there.[75] This curiosity about the natural world finds particularly endearing expression in the canon's efforts to chart the annual migration path of the (European) swallow, which he pieces together by comparing observations made in Germany with the testimony of sailors and foreigners he meets while abroad.[76]

There is at least one sense in which the works of William of Boldensele, John Mandeville, and Ludolph von Suchem differ from later works that participate in the Mediterranean turn: they purport to be written from memory *after* the journey has concluded. Increasingly, pilgrims wrote throughout the voyage, recording their observations in travel diaries. The related phenomena of the Mediterranean turn and the travel diary herald the emergence of a new attitude toward travel writing, one in which the investigation of noteworthy places is accompanied by an ongoing analysis of the journey itself.

In the closing decades of the fifteenth century, a number of diarists write at some length about places very close to their respective homes. Arnold von Harff traces his itinerary from the moment he leaves Cologne. Pietro Casola, a native of Milan, includes detailed descriptions of stops in his itinerary, beginning with nearby towns such as Verona and Venice.[77] Felix Fabri starts recording his progress toward the Holy Land with observations about the small Alpine settlements that he visits on the way to Italy from his native Ulm.

The inward turn taken by works such as these includes a great deal of self-reflection about the manner in which the author undertakes the art of travel. The narrative of Florentine friar Alessandro di Filippo Rinuccini (1473) offers an especially dramatic illustration of this trend. In a few—vividly detailed—pages, the opening chapter of Rinuccini's account outlines his first, failed attempt to reach Jerusalem. Shortly after leaving his native city on horseback, Rinuccini enters a forest, where he is suddenly beset by a torrential cloudburst. Apprehensive about the poor visibility and the desolation of the surrounding wilderness, Rinuccini nearly comes undone at the sight of the loathsome creatures that teem in the mud beneath his horse's hooves. When he finally emerges from the forest, soaked and battered, he discovers that his traveling companions have called off the pilgrimage. In a manner reminiscent of Odoric of Pordenone's allegorically laden adventure in the demonic valley, Rinuccini presents this aborted, half-day journey to Jerusalem as an exemplary tale. It was an act of presumption and vanity, repents the friar, to have embarked on a penitential voyage on horseback rather than on foot.[78] The story of Rinuccini's first anticlimactic "pilgrimage" suggests that the pilgrim's investigations should begin even before he departs from home, his probing gaze turned inward toward the self.

One manifestation of this heightened self-reflexivity is the tendency to reflect on the ways that other travelers approach the labor of investigation. Felix Fabri recalls having once been in the company of a group of pilgrim-knights in the orchard of the Franciscan house on Mount Zion. Fabri and his lay companions ascend the garden's wall, in order to take advantage of its commanding vista onto the Mount of Olives and the Valley of Jehoshaphat. To Fabri's displeasure, the knights ignore the sacred panorama and fixate instead on the Mosque of Omar, also known as the Temple of Solomon. "Admiring" and "desiring to enter" the mosque, the knights "discoursed much one to another about how this temple had endured from the time of Solomon."[79] Tiring of listening to the knights speak "long and unprofitably" about such "a vain thing," Fabri asks them why they have not said anything about "the holy and wondrous sights" right before their eyes. One of the knights responds:

> We know this Temple of Solomon by common report, and we have nothing holier, nothing more glorious or more beauteous within sight. As for the mountains and valleys round about we do not care for them, nor do we know them.[80]

Echoing long-standing clerical condemnations of the "vain fables" of unlettered pilgrims, Fabri takes it upon himself to correct the misguided curiosity of his companions. The Dominican professes that the Temple of Solomon was destroyed long ago, and that the structure that currently fascinates the men is actually the fourth temple built on the site. He adds that, as a mosque, the edifice is nothing more than a "desecrated church" where "Mahomet the accursed is praised." Fabri redirects the knights' attention to the Valley of Jehoshaphat, where "all the world will be gathered on the Day of Judgment," and the Mount of Olives, "from whence Christ ascended into heaven." To Fabri's satisfaction, he and his fellow pilgrims enter into "a profitable discourse about the smallness of the valley . . . and about many of the like subjects."[81] At the outset of this vignette, Fabri characterizes the landscape that fails to rouse the knights' interest as "a delightful one to a man who knows the Scriptures," which suggests that the laymen's short-comings as travelers are due to their deficiencies as readers.[82] The learned Fabri attempts to teach his charges to view the Holy Land as he does, a feat that requires him to discipline their roving gazes.

This episode registers a clash between two different modes of inves-tigative labor: the chivalric/adventurous and the scholarly/clerical. The knights' fascination with the Mosque of Omar was something of a fashion-able trend among adventurous pilgrims, who—as Fabri notes elsewhere—contrived dangerous ruses in order to infiltrate and investigate the prohib-ited space.[83] Pero Tafur was just such a traveler (see chapter 6). The layman's interest with the Temple of Solomon grows out of chivalric traditions of pilgrim investigation that emerged with the Mediterranean turn. The edu-cation that prepares the chivalric traveler to dwell in Muslim courts or to brave death in the name of forbidden geographical knowledge involves a different set of dispositions and literacies than the erudite efforts through which Fabri seeks to master the topography of the Holy Land, and—in so doing—to master the self. Fabri's objections to the chivalric orientation of his companions' pilgrimage is, in fact, anticipated by Petrarch, another au-thor who participated in the Mediterranean turn without embracing all of its consequences. In a letter, Petrarch criticized his friend for planning to be dubbed a knight at the Holy Sepulcher. Petrarch maintained that this cus-tom, "though fashionable," was nevertheless an impious perversion of the sacred journey's aims.[84] The convictions of Fabri and Petrarch open up onto a far broader assortment of discrepant beliefs about how pilgrims ought to experience Jerusalem.

THE PROBLEM OF JERUSALEM (1330–1500)

During the 1330s, the Egyptian sultan granted the Franciscan community on Mount Zion the exclusive right to act as guides to Latin Christian pil-grims visiting Jerusalem. Thanks to the Franciscans, Latin Christian knowl-edge about the sacred city was, in effect, institutionally guaranteed for the first time in centuries. The formalization of the pilgrim's itinerary enabled what is perhaps the most derided convention of medieval travel writing: the "Jerusalem inventory," a spare list of shrines, distances, and indulgences that, to some scholars, typifies the antiempirical orientation of pilgrimage during the Middle Ages.

Pope Clement VI cleared the way for the advent of the Jerusalem inventory in 1343, by issuing the bull *Unigenitus Dei Filius*. Clement appealed to the conceit of the "treasury of merit" in order to defend the church's right to grant indulgences. The bull ushered in an era of inflation in the number of indulgences available to pilgrims. Christiane Deluz has argued that this development compromised the quality of pilgrimage to the Holy Land, redirecting pilgrims' attention away from its contemplative dimensions and toward the quantitative goal of maximizing pardon.[85] The evidence that best supports this hypothesis would appear to be the Jerusalem inventory itself, which, after 1350, becomes an increasingly common feature in accounts of travel to the Holy Land.[86] With its punctilious reckoning of pardons gained and distances surmounted, the Jerusalem inventory is right at home in the travel diary, which maintained obvious formal ties to the record-keeping genres out of which it emerged. In fact, the travel diary, like the mania for indulgences, can be viewed as part of the broader infiltration of commercial rhetoric into the language of late medieval piety, a development reflected in—and reinforced by—official discourses such as the "treasury of merit."

There is, however, reason to be skeptical of Deluz's hypothesis. It is very clear from reading the accounts of late medieval pilgrims that the visitation of Jerusalem continued to be the unrivaled emotional high point of the journey.[87] The most fascinating implication of this observation is that the personal climax of the Holy Land pilgrimage seemed no less personal or climactic to those who entrusted their memories of the experience to what we now view as an alienated—and alienating—form of writing.

But did the establishment of the Franciscan tour diminish the practice of critical inquiry into the topography of Jerusalem? Yes—and no. While Niccolò da Poggibonsi included a Jerusalem inventory in his account, he pained himself to record his measurements of the city and to report as accurately and completely as possible on the condition of its sacred places. Niccolò was not alone. On the second of his two pilgrimages to Jerusalem, William Wey armed himself with a list of eleven topographical questions that he had failed to settle during his initial visit. The points of confusion that Wey sought to clarify included the location of the tombs of David and Solomon, whether or not the pillar where Christ was bound and whipped still had visible traces of his blood on it, and whether it was true that the lamp above the Holy Sepulcher lit up of its own accord.[88]

Then, of course, there is Felix Fabri's second pilgrimage, undertaken to compensate for the superficiality of his first. Fabri's extensive research into more than a millennium of travel writing about the Holy Land disposed him to question long-established beliefs about the topography of Jerusalem. Fabri lodged a vociferous objection to an assertion found in many "little books"—namely, that Saint Helena supervised the construction of the Temple of Solomon / Mosque of Omar.[89] Though the mosque was officially off-limits to Christians, Fabri stole a few furtive glances into the building from the outside. On the basis of what he could perceive about the mosque's floor plan, Fabri concluded that its construction could not have been overseen by Helena—or by any Christian—because "in the infidel fashion . . . its main door opens up from the east, a thing that I have never seen in churches of Christ."[90] Even more surprising, Fabri conducts a prolonged investigation into no less a question than the *authenticity of the Holy Sepulcher*. Ultimately, he concludes that, even if the tomb was built well after the resurrection (as seems probable), it is, nevertheless, still worthy of veneration.[91]

Fabri's skeptical, inquisitive approach to Jerusalem contrasts sharply to other authors' treatments of the city. Though he never made the journey to the Holy Land in person, Petrarch wrote a virtual pilgrimage guide to the region, the *Itinerary to the Sepulcher of Our Lord Jesus Christ*. In many ways, the *Itinerary* resembles several other texts that grew out of actual, physical journeys to the Holy Land during the age of the Mediterranean turn. Petrarch famously expends more than half of his word count describing Italian localities along the Mediterranean coast and concludes his imaginary tour with a description of Alexander the Great's tomb in seaside Alexandria. Yet, even though Petrarch reminds his readers that Jerusalem is "the destination of your journey and of your desire" and is the reason why "you have undertaken such an arduous labor (*tantum laboris ac negotii suscepisti*),"[92] he says almost nothing about the city, since its multitude of sacred sites "would be too long for me to enumerate, and would be unnecessary for you, who are familiar with everything through the Gospel."[93] Jerusalem is the most anticipated stop on the imaginary itinerary traced by Christine de Pizan in her *Chemin de long estude*. Though Christine lingers longer in the holy city and its environs than she does any other place, this does not translate into a detailed topographical description: "I saw many wonders (*estranges choses*) in Judea, as in Jerusalem, about which I will say nothing because people often travel there as pilgrims, and the itinerary is well enough known."[94] In terms of people who actually traveled to the Holy Land, Thietmar was perhaps the first to express such a sentiment about Jerusalem.[95] Similarly, in the fifteenth century, Johannes Witte de Hese and Bertrandon de la Broquière had surprisingly little to say about Christianity's most sacred city. In 1479, Sebald Rieter passed over the topic of Jerusalem's geography entirely, referring readers to the pilgrimage account written by his father decades before.[96] Ludovico di Varthema, who extols the love of novelty as an admirable incitement to travel, does not describe Jerusalem at all and barely mentions Alexandria and Cairo, since he believes that Italians are already well acquainted with these places from the accounts of others.[97] Whether they are writing about physical or virtual travel, the authors mentioned above evince an attitude toward Jerusalem that would have shocked most travel-writing pilgrims between 1100 and 1350, who pained themselves to untangle the knotted skein of legend that cloaked the city in uncertainty. More than any other evidence, this diversity of attitudes toward Jerusalem discredits the sweeping generalizations that have come to characterize the travel writing of late medieval pilgrims and—in the case of many scholarly arguments—the travel writing of the Middle Ages.

CONCLUSION

Donald Howard puzzled over the title that Samuel Purchas gave his 1613 anthology of exotic travel writing: *Purchas His Pilgrimes*. Howard suggested that this curious editorial decision was thinkable only after the demise of the Holy Land pilgrimage "as an institution." For Howard, it was then, and only then, that it made sense to "think of 'pilgrimage' as an image of travel in general."[98] This assertion presumes that the tales of heroic geographical discovery prized by Purchas are fundamentally at odds with medieval pilgrimage's devout fixation on holy places and its (presumably) related abjuration of curiosity about the unknown. Zur Shalev has recently ventured an alternative to Howard's gloss on the title of Purchas's anthology: "Far from indicating the secularization of pilgrimage, Purchas's complex use of the term may in fact point to a sacralization of travel in general."[99]

This chapter and the one that precedes it have furnished evidence that justifies an even bolder assertion of Shalev's important corrective. Pilgrims to the Holy Land promoted a conception of travel as *literate labor*—as travail managed and undertaken with some productive, textual end in mind. The end-oriented nature of *labor* marks it as inherently intentional, and—by extension—as more "instantly" subject to ethical judgment than the related concept of *travail*. To approach travel as labor is to concede that it can be shoddy, fruitless, clumsy, bungled, squandered, or half-assed. Travel-as-labor poses the question of what, *exactly*, is produced in and through the journey, and whether that something is of any value *at all* to anyone. Though given their first full, sustained articulation by pilgrims to the Holy Land, these ethical concerns informed and were reframed by those who wrote about journeys to other parts of the world.

As this chapter, in particular, has shown, during the late Middle Ages, the travel writing of Holy Land pilgrims was fully integrated into the broader enterprise of investigating the diversity of the world. This does not appear to have changed significantly during the early modern period. Before creating the revolutionary world map that bears his name, Mercator rigorously applied himself to charting Palestine.[100] Mercator was, therefore, the species of geographer that Michel de Montaigne impugned in his essay "Of Cannibals," which criticizes those who, having gained a modicum of experience in the Holy Land, make pronouncements about the entire world.[101] If the road to Jerusalem paved the way to more global investigations, it also fostered the exploration of familiar climes. Having satisfied his doubts about the Holy Land, Felix Fabri became the first person to write a descriptive, scholarly geography of his native Ulm.[102] In the final part of this book, I consider two other travel writers whose explorations of the proximate benefited from the contributions of Jerusalem pilgrims, who helped pioneer the discovery of the exotic closer to home.

PART III

Discovering the Proximate

Prior to 1350, few authors composed travel narratives about journeys within Europe and the Mediterranean. Gerald of Wales's twelfth-century writings on Ireland and Wales are a rare and seemingly unprecedented exception in a literary landscape otherwise dominated by encyclopedic geographies and guidebooks or topographical descriptions focused narrowly on pilgrimage destinations such as Rome, Santiago de Compostela, and Saint Patrick's Purgatory (in Lough Derg, Ireland).[1] After 1350, there are many more travel accounts and travel narratives that grow out of relatively short-range journeys.

This corpus of texts is notable for its formal and temperamental diversity. The second part of *The Book of Margery Kempe*, for instance, is devoted almost exclusively to telling the story of Kempe's late-life pilgrimage across northern Europe. Meanwhile, part-time myth-buster Antoine de La Sale wrote about his journeys to third-tier pilgrimage attractions in the Apennines, simply to dispel the fantastic legends that surrounded them. Arnold von Harff used the three major Christian pilgrimages to Jerusalem, Rome, and Santiago de Compostela to anchor a chivalric travel narrative in which the author-protagonist visits exotic destinations such as the sphere of the moon while also writing in minute detail about linguistic and cultural regionalisms within Europe and the Mediterranean. Similar in spirit are the two narratives kept by followers of Bohemian knight and ambassador Leo of Rozmital, which document the nobleman's two-year journey through western Europe (1465–67), in the process describing the most notable cities, courts, pilgrimage sites, and tourist attractions between Prague and Portugal. The letters and journals of merchant and antiquarian Cyriac of Ancona (1391–ca. 1453) record his enthusiastic explorations of the eastern Mediterranean during the expansion of Ottoman power. Studied almost exclu-

sively as "Renaissance" works, Cyriac's protohumanist texts are puzzlingly
treated as though they belong to another epoch, as though they did not
spring from the soil of a late medieval literary culture in which exceptional-
ity was anything but exceptional in the field of travel writing.

Petrarch and Pero Tafur are good representatives of the variety of approaches that travel writers adopted when depicting itineraries once considered too banal to justify a written account. Both authors also typify the
increasingly subtle distinctions used to distinguish one traveler from another. In the later Middle Ages, it becomes possible to talk about "styles"
of travel, defined by considerations such as the motivation, intellectual disposition, and social standing of the traveler; the route, tempo, and duration
of the journey; and the investigatory methods, literary influences, and ideal
readership of those travelers who chose to write about their experiences.
For all of their differences, Petrarch and Tafur converge upon the opinion
that acculturating tours of Europe and the Mediterranean are superior to the
kind of itinerary that conferred legendary status on the likes of Marco Polo
and John Mandeville.

A number of factors contributed to the emergence of figures like Petrarch and Tafur. The enduring fame of long-distance specialists such as
Polo, Mandeville, and Odoric of Pordenone continued to furnish rhetorical
and investigative models for travel writers of all stripes. The same can be
said about the uniquely pervasive accounts of Holy Land pilgrimage, which
had a hand in mainstreaming the practice of travel writing as well as inquiries into marvels that might be found closer to home. In the fourteenth and
fifteenth centuries, travel within Europe and the Mediterranean assumed
a particularly prominent place in the conceptions of elite education and
self-realization. Chivalric biographies and chronicles by figures such as Jean
Froissart, Gutierre Díez de Games, and the Chandos Herald accorded travel
a conspicuous role in the ideal career of the knight while also subjecting
courtly ceremony and other regional peculiarities to ethnographic scrutiny.
Animated by the motifs of earlier romances, chivalric chronicles and biographies helped nourish the realist, geoethnographic impulses of fifteenth-
century novels of chivalry such as *Curial e Güelfa* and *Tirant lo Blanch*,
whose protagonists investigate and perform deeds of daring in recognizably
contemporary European and Mediterranean settings. An important part of
Petrarch's humanist legacy was the invention of a scholarly alternative—
albeit an ambivalent one—to the knight's heroic, and sporadically violent,
explorations of well-known cultural centers.

In a way that distinguishes them from most of the works discussed in
parts 1 and 2, the travel writing of Petrarch and Tafur is thoroughly inte-

grated into larger autobiographical and protonationalist projects. It therefore would seem to demand a different kind of contextualization. For this reason, I have devoted a chapter to each rather than attempting a broad overview of late medieval travel writing about Europe and the Mediterranean. Though sorely needed, such a survey would require a book of its own, since—in contrast to Holy Land pilgrimage and East Asian travel—there is no tradition of high-quality, synthetic scholarship on the literature of European and Mediterranean travel during the Middle Ages.

While Columbus and the rise of European colonialism have served as the genealogical center of gravity for many—arguably most—recent monographs on medieval travel writing, the findings of early modernists suggest that, in the grand scheme of things, accounts of European and Mediterranean travel may have exerted a greater influence on intellectual and cultural life than did writings about the conquest of the New World.[2] Even if one does not subscribe to this opinion, it is hard to dismiss it categorically, especially given the centrality of the Grand Tour to subsequent educational and literary history. And yet, as scholars, we currently have little understanding of the moment in the Middle Ages when self-conscious accounts of European and Mediterranean travel—energized by older traditions of travel writing—flourished as they never had before. What follows is hopefully a modest step in that direction.

CHAPTER FIVE

Becoming Petrarch

While investigating the holdings of Verona's cathedral library in 1345, Petrarch happened upon a manuscript of what was, at the time, a relatively obscure work: Cicero's *Ad Atticum*, a collection of the Roman philosopher's personal correspondence.[1] The discovery inspired Petrarch to anthologize his own letters. As a result, 563 of his epistles survive, organized for posterity into four self-curated works. The largest of these anthologies is the *Rerum familiarium libri* (commonly called the *Familiares*, or *The Letters on Familiar Matters*). The *Familiares* preserves 350 of Petrarch's Latin prose letters, written between 1325 and 1366, and organized into twenty-four books (in imitation of Homeric epic). The final book consists of letters addressed to ancient Roman men of letters, including Virgil, Horace, Cicero, and Quintilian—all of whom Petrarch numbered among his "friends." Petrarch began gathering, editing, collating, and—in some cases—*fabricating* the contents of the *Familiares* in 1350. The anthology was finalized in 1366 and dedicated to Petrarch's intimate friend, the Flemish monk and music theorist, Ludwig van Kempen, whom Petrarch addressed by the affectionate sobriquet "my Socrates."

This chapter considers a cluster of letters gathered in the first five books of the *Familiares*, all addressed to Petrarch's mentor and patron Cardinal Giovanni Colonna. Purportedly written at Colonna's behest over the course of ten years (1333–43), the letters document three Petrarchan journeys: his youthful exploration of Germany, France, Belgium, and the Netherlands in 1333 (*Familiares* I.4 and I.5), his first-ever visit to Rome in 1337 (*Familiares* II.12–15), and his second, disappointing sojourn in Naples in 1343 (*Familiares* V.2–6).

Prior to the groundbreaking work of Thomas Greene and Theodore J.

Cachey Jr., characterizations of the significance of travel in Petrarch's vo-
luminous oeuvre were founded almost entirely on readings of two letters
from the *Familiares*: the account of Petrarch's ascent of Mount Ventoux
(IV.2) and the so-called Letter to Colonna (VI.2), a topographical description of Rome's ruins rendered from memory and addressed to a different
Giovanni Colonna.[2] For over a century, discussions of Petrarchan notions
of travel were shaped by Burckhardt's framing of the problem. For Burckhardt, Petrarch's decision to climb to the summit of Mount Ventoux for no
other reason than to observe the surrounding landscape made him "a truly
modern man."[3] Lynn Thorndike's pointed observation that would-be me-
teorologist Jean Buridan climbed Mount Ventoux before Petrarch did little
to shake scholarly belief in the epoch-defining nature of the letter.[4] Thus,
two decades after Thorndike's essay, Hans Blumenberg espoused a modified
version of Burckhardt's thesis, depicting Petrarch's alpine exploration as a
premature intellectual revolution, one torn between the "modern" desire
for experiential knowledge and the "medieval" disapprobation of curiosity.[5] The philological discovery that Petrarch actually falsified the date of
Familiares IV.1 and the related suspicion that he may never have climbed
Mount Ventoux in the first place have perhaps furnished little incentive to
scholars who might otherwise have developed a more plausible account of
the letter's significance to the history of ideas about travel. Meanwhile, outside of Italian studies, book-length surveys of medieval travel writing have
decisively passed over Petrarch. This chapter hopes to offer a corrective to
this oversight by situating Petrarch's historically influential ideas about the
benefits, liabilities, and ideal methods of travel within the broader landscape of late medieval debate on these questions.

In the pages that follow, I argue that, in order to grasp the significance
of Petrarch's views on travel, one must foreground the political and cultural concerns that informed them. As Cachey has compellingly argued,
Petrarch's discussions of travel in the initial books of the *Familiares* are
"central to understanding" his midcareer agenda.[6] A considerable part of
this agenda was political in its orientation, focusing on the unification of
the Italian peninsula and the restoration of Rome as the world center of intellectual, spiritual, and imperial authority. Petrarch, who self-consciously
styled himself as a lifelong political exile, reflected on the experience of geographical displacement throughout his career.[7] Nevertheless, considerable
analytic advantage is gained in approaching Petrarch's travel letters as the
work of a *diasporic*, rather than exilic, author.

Thanks to a philosophical tradition of which Petrarch himself is a part,
to speak of *the exile* is to privilege metaphysics and autobiographical expe-

rience in a way that abstracts the author from the world, thereby making it more difficult to integrate aesthetic and ideological analyses of his work.[8] By contrast, *diaspora* embraces much of the same analytic terrain as *exile* while at the same time situating the individual subject within the context of a communal experience marked by complex histories of migration, multiple displacement, and creative, variegated identifications across space and time. Of course, the rise of *diaspora* as a keyword in the humanities and social sciences has not been without its critics. Some have questioned whether the term inevitably forces various culturally specific phenomena into the mold of Jewish historical experience, while others have worried that its various new definitions might render it meaningless.[9] To my mind, the term *diaspora* helpfully foregrounds the flexible ways of conceiving of travel's relationship to dwelling, and of preserving a sense of home, culture, and community outside of the framework of the sovereign state. These issues are arguably the root motivation of Petrarch's tireless letter writing and certainly informed his skeptical, evolving stance on the individual and collective significance of travel.

As a corpus, the travel narratives written for Colonna interrogate what it means for Petrarch—the son of an exile who, at the time, was making his home in modern-day France—to be an "Italian" author in an age in which "Italy" has become little more than a bloodless abstraction, incapable of inspiring its citizens to set aside their factional differences. The three journeys documented in these letters plot Petrarch's artistic and intellectual evolution along a deceptively tidy timeline: from the naively curious and internationally renowned author of vernacular lyric (book I), to the politically engaged reviver of Roman epic and oratory (book II), to the stay-at-home champion of solitude and quotidian self-discipline (book V). Each of these "epochs" is marked by a different perception of the kind of writer that Petrarch must become in order to influence public affairs; each epochal transition also raises the question of the role that travel might play in helping Petrarch become that kind of author. Indeed, epiphanies, thresholds, and transformations are persistent motifs in Petrarchan accounts of travel. Petrarch's dramas of recognition, reversal, and reinvention are marked by ambivalent—and, occasionally, overtly phobic—depictions of women. The uneasy rendering of sexual difference that suffuses these letters reaches a fever pitch in the account of the 1343 journey to Naples, during which Petrarch suffers a crisis of confidence, which, among other things, marks the beginning of a lifelong aversion to maritime travel.

After 1343, Petrarch will increasingly depict travel as a toilsome and pernicious distraction from the more pressing labor of living in diaspora, which he will equate with a regime of literary self-discipline based in the home. The main pillar of this ascetic life was the focused, daily application to reading and writing classical Latin.[10] In the literary form of the epistle, Petrarch found a surrogate that could endure the tedium and hardship of travel on his behalf, enabling him to advise rulers and to encourage a growing, geographically widespread network of friends to emulate his quasi-monastic commitment to the study and revival of ancient literary aesthetics—all without ever having to absent himself from his library.

BECOMING WORLDLY (PARIS AND AIX-LA-CHAPELLE)

Familiares I.4 and I.5 recount scenes from Petrarch's 1333 tour of northern Europe. Petrarch presents this journey as an educational rite of passage, in language that has understandably invited comparisons to the Grand Tour.[11] This is especially true of *Familiares* I.4, a self-ironizing account that focuses primarily on Petrarch's visits to Paris and Aix-la-Chapelle (today, Aachen, Germany). The mock heroism that pervades the letter suggests the perspective of an older man looking back on a period of youthful indiscretion. This ironic detachment supports Giuseppe Billanovich's conjecture that *Familiares* I.4 and I.5 were written (or at least heavily revised) around 1350–51, nearly twenty years after the journey that they purportedly document "in real time."[12]

In the conclusion of *Familiares* I.4, Petrarch rehearses a legend that he has heard from the cathedral clergy of Aix-la-Chapelle. Charlemagne, Petrarch is told, once became infatuated with a woman of low birth. Oblivious to the grumblings of his subjects, the ruler happily carries on with the scandalous affair until his mistress suddenly dies. Things go from bad to worse as the disconsolate Charlemagne treats his lover's corpse as though it were still alive, "fondling it night and day in an attitude of sadness and longing" (1:27).[13] The ruler also begins to neglect affairs of state. Things persist in this unpromising direction until the bishop of Cologne discovers the secret supernatural origins of the emperor's obsession. In a revelatory vision, the bishop learns that there is an enchanted ring concealed beneath the tongue of the mistress's cadaver. The bishop arranges to be alone with the corpse long enough to fish the demonic bauble out from "under the cold and lifeless tongue" (1:28).[14] The effects are immediate. Charlemagne shrinks away in disgust from the formerly all-consuming object of his desire. Unfortunately, he redirects his libidinal energies in the bishop's direction. Disconcerted, the bishop casts the ring into a swampy patch of Aix, where Charlemagne "by chance happened to be living" at the time (1:28).[15]

Charlemagne's longing settles on that fetid marshland, so that "even the smell of the place came to please him very much" (1:28).[16] The enchanted emperor therefore makes Aix his capital city and is eventually buried there. And so it is—sniffs Petrarch—that a once-insignificant backwater became the place where the holy Roman emperor is now crowned, a custom that will continue "as long as the reins of the Roman empire are in Teutonic hands" (1:28).[17] The political lesson that Petrarch extracts from this anecdote explains, in part, why he dedicated about half of *Familiares* I.4 to rehearsing what he otherwise considered a vain and unprofitable fable.

In the first place, the tale of pseudo-Charlemagne serves as a counterexample to many of Petrarch's core convictions about educational travel. The emperor's grotesque fixation on the fetid bogs of Aix provides a counterexample to the Stoic ideal of rising above personal attachments to place, especially one's native land. At least initially, *Familiares* I.4 presents the journey of 1333 as an actualization of this ideal:

> Recently I traveled (*peregravi*) through France for no particular purpose (*negotium*), you know, except for the youthful desire of seeing as much as possible (*visendi tantum studio et iuvenili quodam ardore*). (1:25)[18]

Throughout his writings, Petrarch extols the great knowledge-seeking travelers of antiquity—including Pythagoras, Plato, and Ulysses—who left behind the comforts of home to learn about the realities of the outside world. In fact, Petrarch explicitly identifies himself with Ulysses in the famous opening letter of the *Familiares*, observing that he has traveled farther and more frequently than the ancient Greek hero. In *Familiares* IX.13, Petrarch rebukes his friend Philippe de Vitry for claiming that any time spent anywhere in the world other than Paris must be endured as a kind of exile. While it is appropriate, Petrarch scolds, "for the good peasant to stay in his own country, to understand the quality of his land, the behavior of his cattle," travel is an essential component of the education of elite men, as the examples of Ulysses, Aeneas, and many others illustrate (2:40).[19] Petrarch adds:

> I would like to suggest that the Parisian Petit-Pont and its arch, not quite in the shape of a tortoise shell, is too appealing to you; the murmur of the Seine flowing under it delight your hearing too much; finally, the dust of France lies too heavily on your shoes. In my opinion, you seem to have forgotten the man who, when asked where he was from, answered that he was a citizen of the world (*mundanum*).[20]

To become worldly (*mundanum*), one must leave home behind. Or, more precisely, one must—like the tortoise with his Petit-Pont–shaped shell— carry his home with him everywhere he travels, as a central coordinate for understanding and evaluating the customs and conditions of other places.

As *Familiares* I.4 makes clear, the purpose of studying the conditions of foreign places is to arrive at a new perspective on one's own native land:

> At one point I reached Germany and the shores of the Rhine River care- fully viewing the customs of the people and delighting in the sights of an unknown country, comparing each new thing to ours. And though I saw many magnificent things on both shores I nevertheless did not repent being an Italian. Indeed to tell the truth the further I travel the greater is my [admiration/wonder] (*admiratio*) of my native soil. (1:25)[21]

Comparing these sentiments to the rebuke of Philippe de Vitry, one might be tempted to charge Petrarch with logical inconsistency. In his defense, Petrarch would probably respond by pointing out that there is a difference between a capricious and immobilizing attachment to home and a patri- otism that is arrived at rationally, after one has already absented oneself from the native land. Even so, this does not address the more dubious sug- gestion that Petrarch's travels have been a success because, in becoming worldly, he has become more deeply convinced of his cultural superiority as an Italian.

This impoverished justification of travel is just one of the facets of *Fa- miliares* I.4 that might lead one to doubt the educational dividends of Pe- trarch's journey. Immediately after he relates the legend of Charlemagne and the enchanted ring, Petrarch calls attention to the discrepancy between the intellectual merit of the anecdote and the word count that he has ap- portioned to its retelling. What starts off as an apology for bad travel writing turns into a criticism of travel:

> I have taken more time in telling the story than I [ought to have] (*debui*). But my extensive journey (*peregrinatio*) depriving me of the [whole- some pleasure] of books (*librorum solatio destituta*), and my constant moving about (*perpetuo motu*) making it easier to contemplate many things rather than great things (*facilius est multa cogitare quam gran- dia*), and being unable to fill my letter properly with serious things, I have crammed it as you can see with whatever was ready at hand. (1:28)[22]

If travel is the only means of establishing a mature perspective on home, it is also an activity characterized by commotion, intellectual deprivation, and unproductive expenditures of time and energy. *Perpetuo motu* conjures an image of frenzied, impulsive, and undisciplined movement, the negation of the Stoic and monastic ideals of solitude and *stabilitas*—central pillars of Petrarchan ethics.[23] Although this *perpetuo motu* yields an array of bizarre spectacles, these novel sights come at the cost of the *solatio*—a lofty, intellectually substantive, and salubrious kind of pleasure—that Petrarch could have experienced by staying home and contemplating the works in his library.[24]

Petrarch's Janus-faced portrait of educational travel is closely related to his unique approach to long-distance specialism. Cachey has explicitly drawn on the work of Mary W. Helms in order to characterize Petrarch as a "long-distance specialist"—a figure who gains prestige and profit by becoming a purveyor of rare geoethnographic knowledge.[25] Indeed, throughout his letters to Cardinal Colonna, Petrarch plays the part of Marco Polo, studying foreign places on behalf of a patron too burdened by responsibilities to travel himself. In *Familiares* I.5, Petrarch reminds Colonna that he has promised to "keep you well informed in writing, just as I do in speaking, of all the lands I visited and of everything I saw and heard" (1:31).[26] In a letter written to Colonna from Naples a decade later, Petrarch avows:

> I have known your attitudes for some time; you cannot endure not knowing about things because an implacable desire for knowledge stirs your noble spirit. I have tried to satisfy your desires whenever my fortune had me travel to the North or to the West. Now I have made a different journey, but in the same frame of mind and with the same intention of obeying. (1:238)[27]

Cachey's illuminating characterization of Petrarch as a long-distance specialist does, however, demand some qualification. Like many medieval authors, Petrarch steps into the shoes of the long-distance specialist with professions of reluctance, but not for the reasons one might expect. Petrarch voices no concerns about being branded as a braggart or a liar. This is largely due to the fact that, in contrast to the exotic travel writer or even the Jerusalem-bound pilgrim, Petrarch writes about places that are already known to his readers—or, if not known, then reasonably accessible to them. The value of the knowledge produced by Petrarch does not derive from some exceptionally toilsome or heroic triumph over geographical distance. Likewise, the singularity of *Familiares* I.4 is (rather decidedly) *not* a function of the singularity of the people, places, and things that it describes. Insofar as Petrarch is a long-distance specialist, he is one who specializes in the art of estranging the proximate rather than domesticating the mysteries of the faraway. As is the case with the other travel letters that Petrarch addressed to Colonna, *Familiares* I.4 traffics in sudden, surprising, and ideologically freighted shifts of perspective, which remap the zones of the world that are most familiar to readers.

Take, for instance, the account of Petrarch's first impressions of Paris. *Familiares* I.4 says next to nothing about Parisian monuments or mores. Instead of peddling the customary wares of the long-distance specialist, *Familiares* I.4 directs nearly all of its rhetorical energies toward narrating an arrival scene of mock-heroic proportions:

> I entered Paris, the capital of the kingdom which claims Julius Caesar as its founder, with the same kind of attitude shown by Apuleius while visiting Ipatea, a city of Thessaly. Similarly, in suspense and in thoughtful anticipation, viewing everything carefully, desiring to see and to discover whether what I had heard about the city was truth or fiction, I spent considerable time in it. When the light of day was spent I devoted my nights to the visit. At last, ambling around and gaping, I observed enough of it to discern the truth about it and the fiction. (1:26)[28]

The depiction of Paris turns almost entirely on a sly allusion to an episode from book 2 of Apuleius's *The Golden Ass*. Petrarch likens his expectant exploration of Paris to the scene in which Lucius (as Apuleius calls himself throughout the work) first inspects Hypata (Ipatea), the capital of Thessaly. In the prologue to *The Golden Ass*, readers learn that the book's narrator is a native of Thessaly who, having mastered Latin, now lives and works in Rome. Taking temporary leave of the imperial capital in order to visit relations in his homeland, Lucius encounters a fellow wayfarer who relates marvelous tales about the women of Hypata, famous for their knowledge of sorcery. Tingling with expectation, Lucius repairs with haste to the town in order to confirm rumors of heartless sorceresses and the hapless lovers that they transform into animals and inanimate objects:

> I am, as a rule, a man driven to distraction, wildly eager to learn by my own experience about things unheard of, signs and wonders, and I kept returning to the fact that I was surrounded by—was in the very heart of—Thessaly itself. The whole wide world in clear and unanimous voice sings of the spells and incantations of Thessaly as the cradle of the art of magic.[29]

In the scene referenced by Petrarch, Lucius ogles the banality of Hypata for the first time, scouring its horizons for any hint of wonder:

> There was nothing in that town that I believed to be what it really was when I saw it. No, absolutely everything had been shifted into another shape by some muttered graveyard spell, and as a result, I believed the stones that I was kicking were human once, but petrified; the birds that I was hearing had the same origin, but feathered; the trees that ringed the city and its lands were leafed out in just the same way; the waters in the public fountains flowed from the bodies of human beings. At any moment the statues and the images of the gods were going to step forward and walk, the walls were going to talk, the oxen and other such farm animals would deliver omens and portents, and from the very sky itself, from the disk of the radiant sun, would come an oracle out of the blue.[30]

Of course, when Lucius finally manages to track down a sorceress, he rues the consequences. *The Golden Ass* treats exoticism as a silly perspectival distortion, a mode of experiencing the world in which rational standards of judgment and discrimination are suspended.

On the one hand, Petrarch's invocation of Apuleius expresses a generalized critique of exoticism. As such, it is consistent with the famous climactic episode of *Familiares* IV.1, in which Petrarch rejects the allure of geographical curiosity in favor of self-examination. The arrival scene at Paris has even more in common with *Familiares* III.1, which—though included later in the anthology—was also purportedly written during the educational tour of 1333. The addressee of *Familiares* III.1 is Petrarch's intimate friend Tommaso of Messina, who is also the recipient of seven of the twelve letters in book I. *Familiares* III.1 documents Petrarch's efforts to comply with Tommaso's wishes that he investigate the location of the mythical island of Ultima Thule. Even with the advantage of being able to interview people who live close to the Atlantic Ocean (where the evasive island is said to lie), Petrarch fails to gain any clarity on the subject. Petrarch admits defeat and proceeds to question the ethical soundness of the fruitless inquiry:

> But let it be that way, because what we seek with hard labor (*laboriose querimus*) we may safely ignore. But let Thule lie hidden to the North, let the source of the Nile lie hidden to the South, provided that virtue, which is centrally placed, does not lie hidden. . . . Let us not expend too great a labor (*magnam operam*) in search for a place (*in inquisitione loci*),

which, if we found, we would gladly leave. The time has come to bring
this letter to a close and to expend our time on [better/loftier concerns]
(*curis melioribus*). (1:119)[31]

This critique of misplaced geographical curiosity recalls Mandeville's renunciation of firsthand knowledge of the Trees of the Sun and of the Moon
and Dante's depiction of the folly of Ulysses. Even more than Mandeville or
Dante, Petrarch foregrounds the ethical issue of the time and labor involved
in geographical discovery. What good would it do to spend months or years
toiling away at sea—or even in the library—just to be able to tell others that
you are the first to uncover the secrets of a place whose only appeal might
be the mystique that ignorant parties have built up around it?

The recent work of William J. Kennedy allows us to see the political and
social dimensions of Petrarch's critiques of exoticism in both *Familiares*
III.1 and I.4. From the midpoint of his career to the end of his life, Petrarch
routinely criticized "the sect of Aristotle." Petrarch admired aspects of Aristotle's thought but followed the example of Cicero and Augustine in pre-
ferring Plato, a philosopher who had focused his attention more consistently
on ethics. For Petrarch, Aristotle's interest in exotic animals epitomized the
misguided elements of the philosopher's thought.[32] More problematic still
were the Scholastics, whom Petrarch accused of fetishizing the intricate
subtleties of dialectic. Traditionally, scholars of Petrarch have treated his
anti-Aristotelianism as a matter of intellectual taste. Kennedy offers a compelling new sociological perspective on this Petrarchan bugbear, arguing
that the authority accorded to Petrarch by his coterie of admirers put him
on a collision course with university-based intellectuals, who appealed to
their institutional affiliations and their Aristotelian bona fides in order to
discredit the less conventional scholarly pursuits of the humanist/poet.[33]
For our purposes, it is particularly important that Petrarch associated the
allegedly excessive subtleties of the sect of Aristotle with the universities of
Paris and "Britain." In fact, the argument about the futility of searching for
Ultima Thule can be seen as a rewriting of the anti-Aristotelian positions
developed in *Familiares* I.7 and I.12, which are also addressed to Tommaso.
These two letters caricature the pettiness and intellectual triviality of "an
aged dialectician" who lives in "Britain." Petrarch's refusal to persist in the
quest for Ultima Thule—articulated while he was "on the shores of the
British Sea"—is one chapter in the annals of his conflicts with university
intellectuals. One such adversary was Paris-trained theologian Jean de Hes-
din, the target of Petrarch's "Invective against a Detractor of Italy" (1373).
Petrarch identifies his adversary as "some Scholastic" and spends much

of the treatise dismantling the image of Paris as the intellectual capital of Europe. At one point, Petrarch characterizes Paris's university as a "rustic little basket" made great only by the fact that it gathers together the harvest of foreign intellectuals.[34]

The association of Paris with the sect of Aristotle is an essential context for the self-ironizing arrival scene in *Familiares* I.4. In the end, Petrarch's allusion to Apuleius is not simply a criticism of exoticism in the abstract. Petrarch is also evoking the geographical prejudices of *The Golden Ass*, provincializing Paris by comparing it to Hypata. Whatever Paris may lack in knowledge of sorcery, it more than makes up for in the subtle arts of dialectic. Notwithstanding its pretensions to intellectual authority, the French capital—like the Thessalian one—is rendered marginal in relation to Rome (an idea that Petrarch also suggests when he introduces the city by pointing out that its legendary founder is Julius Caesar, conqueror of Gaul). In fact, Petrarch issued a public challenge to Paris's claims to cultural and intellectual supremacy in 1341, when he rebuffed the city's suggestion that it should host his coronation as poet laureate. Instead, Petrarch would accept the laurel crown—and Roman citizenship—atop Rome's Capitoline Hill.[35]

We are now in a position to sum up what *Familiares* I.4 suggests about Petrarch's views on long-distance specialism and educational travel. The first point is that the Petrarchan critique of exoticism is not "merely" philosophical but also informed by a hegemonic fantasy. In a way, William of Rubruck offers the closest parallel to Petrarch here. Chapter 1 discussed William's rejection of the prestige economy of long-distance knowledge as a viable bridge between Latin Christendom and the Mongol Empire on the grounds that exoticism covets many objects interchangeably—whether or not they attest to sublime and universal truths. As William sees it, to the marvel-hunting Mongol emperor, the spectacle of the Christian mass is just as good as a leopard trained to ride a greyhound. A comparable will to Roman universalism motivates Petrarch's ironic depictions of Aix-la-Chapelle (the ceremonial capital of the Holy Roman Empire) and Paris (the intellectual and cultural capital of Latin Christendom). If the educational value of Petrarch's tour is dubious, it is because he visits places where he is shown "many" (curious, lurid, and novel) things, but nothing in the way of the "great" things found in the classical Latin volumes of his library. Petrarch seems quite serious when he claims that what he has learned from travel is that, notwithstanding historical reversals of fortune, the "many" things that northern Europeans brag about are trivial when compared to the "great" things achieved in former times by his native land.

In concluding this consideration of *Familiares* I.4, it should be noted that there is more to the letter's expressions of chauvinism than initially meets the eye. In 1333, Petrarch was living in the household of Cardinal Colonna—the son of one of Rome's most powerful families. Colonna's position within the papal Curia compelled him to take up residence in Avignon, far away from the "native soil" praised in *Familiares* I.4. Petrarch calls attention to this fact at the end of *Familiares* I.5, when he notifies Cardinal Colonna that he has begun his return journey to Avignon, "where the Roman pontiff detains you and the rest of humanity" (1:32).[36] The rivalries that Petrarch sets up between Rome on the one hand and Aix and Paris on the other are, in a sense, proxies for the more significant contest over spiritual authority between Avignon and Rome. For most of his adult life, Petrarch would advocate vigorously for the return of the papacy to Rome from Avignon, where it was housed during the "Babylonian Captivity" of 1309–78. Petrarch viewed the restoration of the papacy to its "rightful" location as a precondition for the peace and prosperity of the Italian peninsula and of Europe, more broadly.

The 1333 date that Petrarch assigns to *Familiares* I.4 also calls attention to Petrarch's separation from Italy (he would not reside there again until he moved to Padua in 1343). In fact, at the time of his explorations of northern Europe, Petrarch had never even laid eyes on Rome. Thus, the "homeland" that he comes to treasure anew during his youthful travels is one that is an as-yet-unrealized ideal. *Familiares* I.4 presents Petrarch's travels as an awakening that enables him to imagine a unified Italy and a differently centered Europe, both united under the rule of Rome. The judgments passed on Aix, Paris, educational travel, and exoticism are determined by this diasporic agenda. In *Familiares* I.5, the same utopian yearnings condition Petrarch's perception of Cologne and prompt him to consider the role that his poetry might play in galvanizing political reform and cultural renewal.

BECOMING VIRGIL (COLOGNE)

Of the towns that Petrarch visited in the spring and summer of 1333, he had the most to say about Cologne. Almost the entirety of *Familiares* I.5 is devoted to his eventful arrival in the prosperous city. True to form, Petrarch initially focalizes Cologne through a classicizing lens, referring to it by its Latin name (Agrippina Colonia) and quipping, "I was astonished to find so much civility (*civilitas*) in such a barbarous land (*terra barbarica*)." The "astonishment" that he professes at the beginning of *Familiares* I.5 is a playful remapping of fourteenth-century Europe along the coordinates of ancient

Roman prejudice, particularly against anyone living north of the Apennines. This humorous conceit typifies the resourceful ways that Petrarch manipulates geoethnographic anachronism, toward ends both witty and polemical. Here, his knowing invocation of the binary civilization/barbarism has a thematic function, a well, calling attention to the fallen state of Rome, which, in Petrarch's lifetime, no longer enjoyed the luxury of viewing the rest of the world as pure periphery.

Petrarch quickly dispenses with the anachronistic binary of Roman civilization / Germanic barbarity and replaces it with another, more productive opposition: epic/lyric. This literary-generic opposition provides the organizing framework for *Familiares* I.5, facilitating the letter's synthesis of geoethnographic description, artistic autobiography, and political commentary. If there is a dramatic arc to the tale of Petrarch's sojourn on the banks of the Rhine, it is a coming-of-age story about a poet who is confronted with the intellectual and political limits of courtly lyric, the poetic genre that has earned him international renown. *Familiares* I.5 dramatizes the intuition that vernacular lyric is insufficient to the cause of uniting—imaginatively and politically—an Italian populace that is factionalized and dispersed. Petrarch's exploration of Cologne alerts him to the hollowness of fame won through courtly verse and foreshadows his politically invested attempts to revive Virgilian epic and Roman historiography in the late 1330s.

Familiares I.5 stresses Petrarch's status as an international literary celebrity. From the moment he arrives in Cologne, Petrarch is embraced by the town's literati, who seek him out at his inn and introduce him to local attractions. Petrarch remarks, "I had won friends there through my fame, rather than through my merit."[37] In an elliptical passage, Petrarch begins to unspool the logic behind this belittling allusion to his own literary achievements:

> You will be astonished to hear that those heavens rear poetic spirits, so that while Juvenal was astonished that "eloquent Gaul taught British orators," he would have been equally astonished that "learned Germany rears lively prophets." However, lest you misunderstood me, keep in mind that there is no Virgil here but many Ovids. (You might say that there was truth in the prediction made at the end of the *Metamorphoses* where he maintained that, depending on the good graces of posterity or on his own talent, wherever the power of Rome or indeed wherever the Roman name became established after conquering the world, he would be read with applause by a favorable public.) (1:29–30)[38]

We will return to the significance of the link between poetry and prophecy in a moment. First, it should be noted that, in this context, the pairing of Ovid/Virgil is a rewriting of the opposition fame/merit, and—relatedly—a surrogate for a third binary: lyric/epic. On the one hand, we are being told that Petrarch's German fans are admirers—and perhaps practitioners—of courtly lyric. As the letter draws to a close, it becomes increasingly clear that Ovid/Virgil also represent the youthful and mature stages of Petrarch's literary career. *Familiares* I.5 pinpoints the first stirrings of Petrarch's transition between those two phases.

Ovid was a profound and acknowledged influence on Petrarch's early lyric poetry.[39] However, Petrarch would come to view his admiration of Ovid—like the writing of vernacular lyric—as a youthful indiscretion. This dim view of Ovid explains why, despite Petrarch's debts to the author of the *Metamorphoses*, there is no letter addressed to him in book XXIV of *Familiares*. There is, however, a reference to Ovid in *Familiares* XXIV.1. This letter remarks that, to the young, impressionable Petrarch, Ovid seemed more authoritative "the more licentious his Muse" (3:309).[40] Petrarch's *De vita solitaria* contrasts Ovid to Virgil, criticizing the former for his inability to rise above earthly appetites and enjoy the higher pleasures of solitude. Petrarch singles out Ovid's ignoble response to exile for special condemnation, attributing it to the Roman poet's "lascivious, unsteady, and extremely effeminate temper." Petrarch further alleges that Ovid took "pleasure in the company of women to such an extent that he placed in them the sum and apex of his happiness (*felicitatis sue apicem summamque*)."[41] As Gur Zak has observed, Petrarch drew a causal relationship between Ovid's overvaluation of eroticism and the supposedly "low" or "weak" style of Ovidian verse, which Petrarch contrasted to the "strong" and "heroic" style of Virgil.[42] The allusion to Ovid in *Familiares* I.4 seems to be another instance in which ideas developed later on in Petrarch's career were projected back onto the account of his youthful travels. In the context of *Familiares* I.4, the name of Ovid stands in for a bundle of aesthetic and moral vices that Petrarch would later associate with courtly lyric.

By contrast, Petrarch spoke of Virgil as the most important role model for the more mature phases of his literary career. In *Familiares* XXIV.11, Petrarch addresses Virgil as the consummate master of "heroic," or "epic," poetry. He also refers to Virgil as one of two classical "luminaries of eloquence"—the other being Cicero (3:340). Petrarch admired Cicero not only for his prose style but also for his engagement in civic affairs. In comparing the eloquence of Virgil to that of Cicero, Petrarch is painting the former as a civic-minded poet. Tellingly, Petrarch spends much of *Familiares* XXIV.11 updating Virgil on the disastrous state of public affairs in contemporary Italy. For Petrarch, the shift from Ovid to Virgil is one that is at once stylistic and ethical. This evolution entails the mastery of erotic impulses and the redirection of those energies toward matters related to the public good. Relatedly, renouncing Ovid to become Virgil involves writing about serious subject matter in a style that aims to win the admiration of the discerning few (those capable of reading classical Latin) rather than seeking fame by pandering to the taste of the masses.

The difficulty involved in renouncing Ovid to become Virgil is dramatized in the most dazzling sequence of *Familiares* I.5. After Petrarch's German admirers fetch him from his inn, they take him to the banks of the Rhine to observe an annual ritual performed by the city's women. The dramatic tension of the vignette derives from Petrarch's struggle to gain a suitable perspective on the beguiling spectacle:

> The entire shore was covered with a huge and remarkable crowd of women. I was struck dumb. Good God, what beauty, what costumes! Anyone could have fallen in love were his heart free. I stood on a somewhat higher location in order to understand what was going on. There was a remarkably controlled crowd. The women were cheerful, part of them girt with fragrant flowers, with their sleeves folded back above the elbows as they washed their white hands and arms in the water and conversed through foreign whispers. I never understood more clearly what Cicero liked about the ancient proverb that "among the known languages everyone is to some degree deaf and dumb." (1:29)[43]

The stately, decorous eroticism of this scene recycles some of the most instantly recognizable topoi of courtly lyric. Among the most obvious: the whiteness of the women's hands and arms; the profusion of floral wreaths and garlands; and the arousing, inscrutable exchange of whispers among the women. This accumulation of courtly commonplaces alerts the reader to the fact that Petrarch's polished Latin prose is a "translation" of aesthetic conventions native to vernacular verse.

The influence of vernacular lyric on this scene does not stop there. The subjective standpoint from which "Petrarch" (the traveler) views this gathering of women is that of the courtly lover / lyric poet. The brief, vital aside "Anyone could have fallen in love were his heart free" is an obvious allusion to Laura, whom Petrarch saw for the first time in 1327. The inaccessible Laura is—at least initially—the absent center of this episode, the figure who defines the coordinates of Petrarch's subjective experience of the spectacle.

When "Petrarch" ascends to higher ground in order to comprehend the meaning of the enigmatic gathering of women, he literalizes a mode of subjectivity synonymous with courtly lyric and codified by Occitan troubadour Jaufré Rudel, under the name *amor de lonh*. This mode of lyric subjectivity is characterized by: a sense of estrangement from one's surroundings and oneself; the hyperintellectualization of—or disinterest in—attainable and universally enjoyed sources of pleasure; and a tendency toward fanciful, speculative flights of self-scrutiny. The key figure in this mode of lyric subjectivity is the absent or inaccessible beloved, whose distance (or disdain) establishes the coordinates for the lover's engagement with the world. The literary-generic origins of this Petrarchan vignette explain a detail that might otherwise be mistaken for a ham-handed attempt at mimesis. It runs counter to common sense that, having climbed to a higher elevation farther away from the river, Petrarch gains a more sensual, fine-grained perspective on the women. Yet, this is exactly what his rhetoric suggests. The soft, seductive appeal of German whispers—arguably, the most captivating detail of Petrarch's description—is not a trait that inherently belongs to the women; on the contrary, it is the effect of the distance that Petrarch imposes between them and himself. This is precisely Petrarch's point. In many a courtly lyric, the price one pays for knowledge (coded as *analytical distance* from the world and the self) is the perpetual deferral of erotic satisfaction (coded as *physical distance* from the beloved).[44] This structural pattern guarantees that, in lyric scenarios, the lover's movement from one location to another is an event that gives rise to new ontological, epistemological, and ethical possibilities.

In the case of the Cologne episode, Petrarch distances himself physically from an exotic tableau that the rhetoric of his letter has already rendered familiar through poetic commonplace. When Petrarch moves to higher ground, his attention is drawn to the one element of the spectacle that the conventions of vernacular lyric cannot domesticate: linguistic difference. To be more precise, Petrarch transposes the most mystified antimony of courtly lyric—sexual difference—onto this scene in a way that construes linguistic difference as absolute, unbridgeable distance. In *Familiares* I.5, the lyric lover's archetypal alienation from the world is used to dramatize an irredeemable limitation of the courtly lyric: its vernacularity.

With Petrarch's allusion to Cicero, the nature of this limitation comes into focus. The consolatory recollection that even Cicero, master of Latin eloquence, had to bow before the reality of linguistic difference marks a turning point in *Familiares* I.5. The irresolvable clash between the Italian and German languages—itself a recasting of the mystique that defines the relationship between the lyric lover and the courtly lady—finds its "synthesis" in the Latin of Virgilian epic. In a key moment, Petrarch turns away from the sight of the women and toward his male guides, in order to gain some long-deferred understanding of what he has seen:

> As I admired what I saw without knowing what it was, I inquired of one of the persons near me by means of a short verse of Virgil: "what is the meaning of the rush to the river? What do those souls seek?" I was told that it was a very old ritual of the people, widely accepted, especially by the women. They believed that any calamity that might befall throughout the year could be avoided by their washing in the river on that day and that therefrom more joyful things would happen. (1:30)[45]

Standing on the summit of a hill, Petrarch turns away from erotic temptation, literalizing his rejection of the example of Ovid, who made the company of women "the sum and apex" of all his pleasure. The eruption of Virgil's *Aeneid* into a scene previously filtered through the conventions of courtly lyric breaks the spellbound silence of the traveler and marks a shift in his attitude toward what he is observing:

> Smiling at this, I cried: "Oh happy inhabitants of the Rhine whose afflictions are cleansed by it! You send your ills across to the Britons by means of the Rhine; we would gladly send ours to the Africans and Illyrians. But we realize our rivers are more lazy." After a good laugh we departed rather late. (1:30)[46]

The mock-epic style of Petrarch's response dons the rhetorical habit of the apostrophe (literally, a "turning away" from a text's previous preoccupations), addressed, in theory, to the bathing women, but, in practice, to his male friends—as if the women in question were absent entirely. The homosocial culmination of this episode highlights the intellectual and ethical superiority of Latin epic.

The link that Petrarch forges between poetry and prophecy underscores the political dimensions of the triumph of epic over lyric. Recall that Petrarch credits Ovid with "predicting" nothing more than the longevity of his own literary fame and, implicitly, the eternal appeal of less-than-serious poetry among the masses. For many of Petrarch's contemporaries, Virgil's reputation as a prophet rested on claims that his fourth *Eclogue* predicted the birth of Christ.[47] However, Petrarch seems to treat the *Aeneid* as Virgil's prophetic book. The lines that rescue Petrarch from his ignorance of the German language are taken from book VI of Virgil's epic—the scene in which Aeneas and the Cumaean Sybil approach the River Acheron. It is on the other side of this aquatic threshold that Aeneas will receive prophetic foreknowledge of the greatness of the Roman Empire he will help found. Living in the fourteenth century, Petrarch understood that the *Aeneid*'s prediction of "empire without end" would not be borne out by history. What matters here is not the accuracy of the Virgilian "prophecy," but rather its potential to inspire political action among the weary and discouraged, as it did in the case of Aeneas.

The remainder of *Familiares* I.5 seems designed to illustrate the initial assessment that Cologne is a place that has no Virgil—just a flock of Ovids. The depiction of Cologne is steeped in images drawn from courtly lyric. Genteel eroticism and the blandishments of youthful pleasure suffuse the city. Petrarch contrasts the insouciance and prosperity of Cologne to the grim, dysfunctional realities of contemporary Rome:

> I saw a Capitoline which was an imitation of ours; except that whereas deliberations of peace and law are heatedly held in the Senate in Rome, here in the evening, handsome young men and girls together sing the praises of God in endless harmony. In the Roman forum, the clattering of wheels and of arms and the groans of prisoners can be heard everywhere; here reign peace and joy and the voices of gay people. In short, in Rome the military hero triumphs; here, the hero of peace triumphs. I saw a very beautiful temple, as yet unfinished, which they properly call *maximus*. There I reverently beheld the bodies of the Magi transported from the East to the West in three stages, those very same about whom we read that once they came to the manger of the heavenly king with their gifts. (1:31)[48]

This contrasting diptych recalls the visual idioms of Ambrogio Lorenzetti's famous fresco cycle *The Allegory of Good and Bad Government*, which adorns the interior of Siena's Palazzo Pubblico (fig. 7). Painted in the 1330s, Lorenzetti's cycle juxtaposes the image of a peaceful, prosperous polity with the portrait of a dystopian city ravaged by war, famine, and violent crime. The depiction of urban prosperity draws on the same courtly aesthetic that shapes Petrarch's depiction of Cologne. However, the analogy between Petrarch and Lorenzetti is most instructive at the point at which it breaks

Figure 7. Ambrogio Lorenzetti, *Good Government* (ca. 1338–39) (detail). Fresco. Palazzo Pubblico, Siena. (Photograph: Erich Lessing / Art Resource, New York.)

down. In Petrarch's tale of two cities, there is actually a *third*, invisible, term of comparison: ancient Rome. This virtual city—or, as it was once known, *the* city (*Urbs*)—makes Cologne, for all of its pleasantness, seem unsatisfying by comparison.

It is hard to account for the qualified—and occasionally backhanded— praise that *Familiares* I.5 extends to Cologne. What fault could one possibly find with favorable economic conditions, sensible Teutonic governance, civic harmony, and good times? Petrarch suggests that the courtly pleasantness of the town is a lesser good than the epic grandeur embodied by the Roman Empire. For instance:

On the following several days, I went about the city from morning to night with the same guides. It was a pleasant enough experience, not so much because of what I witnessed, as from the recollection of our more renowned leaders who had left such illustrious monuments of Roman virtue so far from the fatherland. (1:30)[49]

In a vernacular poem written shortly after his visit to Cologne, Petrarch offered a more precise critique of German prosperity. Written in support of a proposed crusade, the poem goads contemporary Germans to action by contrasting their alleged complacency in matters of holy war to the "Teutonic rage" that their ancestors displayed in their clashes with the Roman Empire.[50] This is an example of Petrarch's tendency to speak of crusading in secularizing terms, as a revival of Roman cultural and imperial supremacy.[51] The constellation of ideas that shape Petrarch's advocacy of crusading may also underlie his allusion to German barbarity at the beginning of *Familiares* I.5 as well as the underwhelmed posture that he adopts toward Cologne as the letter progresses.

In the end, *Familiares* I.5 is less about Cologne than it is about the first uncertain stirrings of a poetic metamorphosis. In the letter's climactic episode, Laura is displaced as the absent center through which Petrarch charts the world. She is replaced by an even more elusive ideal: the Rome that produced Virgil. The drama that plays out on a hill above the Rhine portends Petrarch's politically engaged revivals of Roman epic and historiography. At the time of his tour through northern Europe, Petrarch had been working on his scholarly edition of Livy's *Decades* for five years. During the journey of 1333, he also discovered a manuscript of Cicero's *Orations*. It would be his first journey to Rome in 1337, however, that would mark the decisive beginning of a more activist phase of his literary career.

IN SEARCH OF LOST TIME (ROME)

The account of Petrarch's long-awaited introduction to Rome is the subject of four consecutive letters of the second book of the *Familiares* (numbers 12–15). Considering the momentous autobiographical import that Petrarch assigned to this event, these four letters have surprisingly little to say about his first explorations of the city. Only *Familiares* II.14—the briefest of the lot—remarks in any way on Petrarch's experience of Rome. *Familiares* II.12 focuses on the heavily militarized nature of the Roman countryside, and *Familiares* II.13 and II.15 describe the warm hospitality extended to Petrarch in the rural estates of Colonna's siblings. It is therefore not especially difficult to understand why posterity has tended to bypass *Familiares* II.12–15 in favor of letters that discuss subsequent Petrarchan journeys to Rome, such as *Familiares* XI.1, in which Petrarch tells Giovanni Boccaccio of a debilitating injury that he incurred en route to the city in 1350, or the even more famous *Familiares* VI.2, also known as "The Letter to Colonna."

On its own, even *Familiares* II.14 cuts a negligible figure. Its rhetorical force derives almost entirely from the place that it occupies within a plot arc engineered through Petrarch's strategic arrangement of the letters in the first two books of the *Familiares*, particularly the entries addressed to Cardinal Colonna and the cardinal's brother Giacomo. When viewed within the framework of the letters to the Colonna brothers, it becomes clear that *Familiares* II.14 is the climax of a plot arc that will give rise to one of the most enduring modern motifs of learned travel writing.

Petrarch actually sets the stage for his fateful 1337 journey to Rome in the final paragraphs of *Familiares* I.5. On his return journey to Avignon, Petrarch crosses paths with one of Cardinal Colonna's messengers, who shares the distressing news that Giacomo Colonna has set out on a journey to Rome. Petrarch, dismayed that his departing friend has not waited for him, concludes the account of his northern European tour on a disenchanted note. The final lines of *Familiares* I.5 suggest that the journey that has denied Petrarch the chance to go to Rome amounts to little more than wasted travail:

> Therefore, my intention is to stop here until the heat, which up to this point I had not felt, subsides. I hope that the rest will rid me of the weariness I had not felt until I had spoken with this messenger. There is no greater weariness than that of the mind, and if the weariness or tediousness of this journey continues afflicting me, I will return to the Rhone as a means of conveyance. (1:32)[52]

These dejected musings are followed by *Familiares* I.6, which reproaches Giacomo for journeying to Rome without Petrarch. *Familiares* II.9 was subsequently addressed to Giacomo sometime between the journeys of 1333 and 1337. In this letter, Petrarch responds to the gentle mockery of his correspondent, who has faulted him for failing to visit him in Rome. *Familiares* II.12 and II.13 discuss the days that the Rome-bound Petrarch is forced to spend in the Roman countryside before completing the final leg of his highly anticipated journey. Collectively, these letters to the brothers Colonna create a sense of destiny painfully delayed; they also retrospectively cast the journey to Rome in 1337 as the deferred culmination of the tour of 1333.

On the other side of this narrative buildup is the laconic *Familiares* II.14, which at last relates Petrarch's eagerly awaited first encounter with Rome. In contrast to the "over-long" accounts of Paris, Aix, and Cologne, the sublimity of Rome does not invite loquacity: "For the present I know not where to start, overwhelmed as I am by the wonder of so many things and by the greatness of my astonishment" (1:113).[53] In few—but highly stylized—words, Petrarch describes his hushed reaction as he looks down onto the ruins of the Roman Forum from the heights of the city's current governmental center, the Capitoline Hill. The elevated prose style of the passage—achieved through parallel syntax, alternations in verb tense, and *antanaclasis*—offers insight into what differentiates Petrarchan wonder from "naive" exoticism:

> Vere maior fuit Roma, maioresque sunt reliquie quam rebar. Iam non orbem ab hac urbe domitum, sed tam sero domitum miror. (II.14.3)

> In truth, Rome was greater, and greater are its ruins than I imagined. I no longer wonder that the whole world was conquered by this city but that I was conquered so late. (1:113)

In the first sentence, the shift from preterit to present tense underscores Petrarch's juxtaposition of two different senses of the same word: Rome was once great/powerful (*maior*) because it imposed its will militarily on nearly all of the known world; the remains of that formerly great imperial capital are today great/large-and-extensive (*maioresque sunt*). The rhetorical conceit is continued in the second sentence: the city whose military force once empowered it to rule (*domitum*) the world overwhelms (*domitum*) Petrarch when he contemplates the vestiges of its greatness. In both cases, the semantic difference between the first and second incarnations of the same word suggests that a previously unfathomable historical gulf has been overcome in Petrarch's experience of wonder.

It is worth pausing here to observe that, in the letters addressed to the Colonna brothers, Petrarch becomes the first in a long line of cultured tourists who will depict his first sight of Rome as a portentous, self-defining, and long-deferred encounter. In 1581, Michel de Montaigne braved the predawn cold—and courted a fresh bout of colic—just to ensure favorable light for his deeply anticipated approach to the city.[54] Edward Gibbon remarked, "At the distance of twenty-five years I can neither forget nor express the strong emotions which agitated my mind as I first approached and entered the *eternal City*."[55] As with Petrarch, the literary career of Gibbon took a defining turn atop Capitoline Hill: "It was at Rome, on the fifteenth of October 1764, as I sat musing amidst the ruins of the Capitol . . . that the idea for writing the decline and fall of the city first started to my mind."[56] Then there's Goethe: "My anxiety to reach Rome was so great, and grew so every moment that to think of stopping anywhere else was out of the question;

even in Florence, I stayed only three hours." He added: "We may almost say that a new life begins when a man once sees with his own eyes all that before he but partially heard or read of."[57] Freud traveled to Italy five times between 1895 and 1898 but could not bring himself to visit Rome, despite his burning urge to do so. This so-called Rome-neurosis became one of the most fascinating occasions for self-analysis in *The Interpretation of Dreams* (1900). A year after the publication of this foundational work, Freud at last made it to Rome, which, in his dreams, had appeared to him in the guise of "the promised land": "It was an overwhelming experience for me, the fulfillment of a long-cherished wish."[58] The miniature intellectual autobiography found in the appendix of E.R. Curtius's *Essays on European Literature* credits the indelible memory of Curtius's first journey to Rome for his 1930 decision to abandon his focus on modern French literature in order to study antiquity and the Middle Ages.[59] This is a minute sample of hundreds, and maybe even thousands (?), of similar cases. With striking regularity, the first encounter with Rome is not only a fateful turning point in the life of the intellectual, it is also one that is attained laboriously, and—in many cases— only after excruciating delay.

As Petrarch liked to tell it, the story of his intellectual trajectory took a defining turn after the journey of 1337. In 1338, Petrarch devised his first plan for the *Africa*, a Latin epic in hexameter. Set during the Second Punic War, the *Africa* recounted Scipio Africanus's heroic military campaign against the forces of Hannibal. As a companion to this neo-Virgilian epic, Petrarch also undertook the *De viris illustribus*, an anthology of exemplary lives based on figures from antiquity. These works were meant to rekindle pride in Italian cultural achievement and move elite male leaders to emulate Roman virtue. Word of Petrarch's new project quickly reached King Robert I, the Wise, of Naples (1277–1343), who became a patron and the intended dedicatee of the *Africa*. In 1341, Robert summoned Petrarch to his court in Naples, where he submitted the poet to a three-day qualifying exam. Petrarch's reward for passing this arduous test was the right to revive the ancient Roman title of poet laureate. On April 8, 1341—Easter Sunday— Petrarch was decorated with the laurel crown in the auditorium of the Senatorial Palace on Capitoline Hill. He was also granted Roman citizenship.

The occasion was suffused with spiritual and temporal symbolism, signaling the promise of social, cultural, and political resurrection. Petrarch foreshadows the politicized redirection of his literary horizons in *Familiares* II.14, a letter allegedly written in situ and dated "Rome, ides of March, on the Capitoline."[60] In alluding to the assassination of Julius Caesar, this (almost certainly fabricated) dateline foretells a mutually reinforcing literary and political resurrection, a rebirth of the age of Caesar Augustus, the emperor who, in Petrarch's coronation speech of 1341, is credited with nurturing the unrivaled literary achievements of the age of Virgil.[61]

None of this would come to pass. Neither the pope nor the Holy Roman emperor returned to Rome during Petrarch's lifetime. In 1343, King Robert died. The *Africa* would never be completed. Petrarch's hopes for a political reformation of Rome were temporarily fanned in 1347, when notary Cola di Rienzo seized control of the Capitoline and pronounced the end of the aristocratic rule that had plunged the city into a perpetual state of factional war. Within a few years, even these revolutionary reforms would fail, leaving Petrarch to regret his initial support of them. The narrative of Petrarch's second journey to Naples in 1343 augurs a period of disillusion and introspection that would alter his understanding of both travel and the political consequences of his Virgilian revival.

A CASE OF CAMILLA; OR, ONE IS NOT BORN— BUT RATHER BECOMES—A ROMAN

When Petrarch revisited Rome and Naples in 1343, he did so under inauspicious circumstances. Cardinal Colonna charged him with a difficult (and ultimately fruitless) diplomatic mission, which involved negotiating the release of captives imprisoned by King Robert's granddaughter and successor, the infamous Queen Giovanna of Anjou. In book V of the *Familiares*, Petrarch collected four of the letters that he wrote to Colonna over the course of his bootless stay in Naples (numbers 3–6). Their overall cast is gloomy. In Petrarch's earlier letters to Colonna, travel—whatever its drawbacks—is nevertheless associated with inspiration, self-realization, and the project of diasporic homecoming. This is not the case with the letters of book V, which decry the shocking moral, political, and cultural decadence of Naples.

Nestled among these bleak reflections is *Familiares* V.4, which tells of Petrarch's excursion to nearby Baia, a favorite seaside spa resort of the ancient Romans. This side trip afforded Petrarch the chance to visit sites associated with Virgil's *Aeneid* with some of his oldest friends. He remarks: "I do not recall a happier day in my life, not only because of my friends' company and the variety of notable sights but because of the recent experience of many sad days."[62] However, even the news of this happy excursion to Baia sounds a note of despair. In this letter, Petrarch reflects on the gulf that separates his experiences as a traveler from those of ancient Roman wayfarers, for whom travel was a vital and seemingly effortless technique of self-fashioning.

The toponym "Baia" provides *Familiares* V.4 with a ready-made chrono-tope, one whose straightforward moralism carries much of the letter's philo-sophical water. Classical authorities, Petrarch observes, represent Baia as paradise for hedonists:

> I am not ignorant of the fact that this was a place of dwelling more worthy of human pleasures than of the gravity of the Romans. For that reason, Marius, naturally a rather rough man, and Pompey and Caesar, more noble in character, are all praised for building on the mountains from where, as was fitting for such men, they were not immersed in, but rather protected themselves from, effeminate elegance, the obstrep-erousness of sailors, and distained the pleasures of Baia from aloft [*ex alto*]. (1:240)[63]

Petrarch's praise of these three Roman generals recalls the topographic sym-bolism of *Familiares* I.4. Like Petrarch (and unlike Ovid), these Roman gen-erals enact their rejection of "effeminate elegance" and common pleasures by taking to the hills. At this point in the letter, Petrarch recalls one other exemplum of masculine self-restraint related to Baia: that of Scipio Africa-nus, the protagonist of the *Africa*. According to Petrarch, the example of Scipio is even more praiseworthy than the ones he has already mentioned:

> Scipio Africanus, however, an incomparable man, who did all things vir-tuously and cared nothing for pleasure not only disdained life on the hills of Baia, but determined never to see this place, which he considered inimical to his ways, a resolution very much in keeping with the rest of his life. He therefore avoided even a view of the place and preferred to live in Literno rather than Baia. I know that his small villa is not far from here, and there is nothing that I would look upon more eagerly. (1:240)[64]

The mention of Scipio Africanus introduces a critical problem. The Baia of Petrarch's day continues to draw the dissolute crowds that were shunned by his Roman role models: "Now many people of all ages and both sexes throng from neighboring cities to the waters" (1:240).[65] While it might be within Petrarch's power to emulate Marius, Pompey, and Caesar and re-move himself to hills surrounding Baia, his inability to contrive a way to reach nearby Literno prevents him from modeling himself after the even more noble ideal embodied by Scipio. By implication, this also means that Petrarch cannot follow in the footsteps of Seneca, whose admiring pilgrim-age to Scipio's villa is the subject of epistle 86 of his *Letters to Lucilius*, the other ancient epistolary anthology that inspired the *Familiares*. Seneca's visit to Literno and Scipio's determination "never to see" Baia presuppose unimpeded mobility—the latitude to choose one location over another. Denied this degree of mobility, Petrarch is forced to confront the constraints placed on his ethical self-determination by the dangerous and cumbersome nature of fourteenth-century travel.

The circumstances that constrain Petrarch's freedom of movement rear their heads at other points in *Familiares* V.4. The tour of Baia and its environs is itself the result of compromise and abandoned aspirations. Petrarch originally plans to escape the malaise of Naples by making a longer journey to Apulia. He alters his itinerary when the apparently well-intentioned widow of King Robert urges him to go on a briefer excursion:

> Influenced by the useless waiting and the long weariness, I had decided to explore Mt. Gargano and the port of Brindisi and that length of sea that lies above, not so much for the sake of seeing those places as from a wish to leave this place. Through the personal persuasion of the elder queen I did not do so, but instead changed my plans for a longer trip and decided to visit closer and certainly more wonderful places. (1:238)[66]

Petrarch later juxtaposes the compromises and negotiations that characterize his modest excursion to Baia with the ease of ancient Roman travel. Commenting on the thermal baths that Rome built at Baia, Petrarch declares:

> Henceforth, I shall be less astonished by the walls of Rome and her fortresses and her palaces, when such care was taken by Roman leaders, so far from the homeland (although the homeland for outstanding men is everywhere). They often took wider pleasures in places more than a hundred miles from home as if they were suburbs. (1:239)[67]

Here, and elsewhere, the constrained ambit of Petrarch's wanderings is treated as a symptom of civilizational decline. Petrarch had already forged a link between bad governance and the perils faced by overland travelers in *Familiares* II.12. In an outraged letter addressed to the city of Florence in 1349 (*Familiares* VIII.10), Petrarch accused the commune of failing to maintain peace and justice. Petrarch was responding to the death of his friend Mainardo Accursio, who had recently been murdered by thieves on a main road outside Florence. Throughout his letters, Petrarch associates ease of overland travel with good governance, and although this causal relationship is not directly stated in *Familiares* V.4, the letters that surround it encourage one to see Petrarch's historical comparison of ancient and modern mobility as a political critique.

These troubling ruminations furnish the context for the most extraordinary episode in all of Petrarchan travel writing. As *Familiares* V.4 draws to a close, Petrarch encounters an uncanny foil in the dashing figure of Maria, a virgin warrior from the town of Pozzuoli. In contrast to Petrarch, Maria enjoys a freedom of movement that recalls a more heroic age: "She spends her nights under the open sky and travels fully armed" (1:241). Petrarch refers to the virgin soldier as a latter-day Camilla, who, according to Virgil, ran so quickly that she could sprint across a body of water without wetting her heels. Maria's extraordinary mobility is a precondition for her emulation of Virgilian *pietas*:

> Her primary concern is with arms, and her mind disdains the sword and death. She wages a hereditary war with her neighbors in which already a large number have perished on both sides. . . . She is quick to engage in war, slow to disengage, she attacks her enemy boldly, and she weaves ambushes carefully. She endures hunger, thirst, cold, heat, wakefulness, and weariness with incredible patience. (1:241)[68]

According to Petrarch, tales of Maria's prowess have even fueled local tourism to Pozzuoli:

> There are many fabulous stories (*fabulis*) told about her; I am reporting only what I saw. Powerful men from different parts of the world assembled, men hardened by warfare whom chance caused to stop there although they were directed elsewhere. Having heard the reputation of the woman, they were driven by the desire to test her strength. (1:241)[69]

At this point, the letter takes an unexpected turn, as Petrarch reveals that he and his friends are among the men who have challenged Maria to a contest of strength. The results are predictably mortifying:

> She was walking in front of the doors of the church in deep meditation, which caused her not to notice our approach. We approached to ask her to supply us with some kind of proof of her strength. At first excusing herself for some time because of pain in her arm, she finally ordered that a heavy stone and an iron beam be brought to her. After she had thrown it into the center of the group, she urged them to try lifting and competing. To be brief, a long contest ensued among equals, and everyone tried

his hand as if in great rivalry while she acted as observer, judging the strength of each of the men. Finally with an easy try, she showed herself much superior to all, causing stupefaction in others and shame in myself. (1:242)[70]

It is curious that Petrarch, the full-time scholar, identifies himself as the only one among his company who feels shame, rather than stupefaction, in the aftermath of this contest. This detail is characteristic of the admiring, yet anxious, tenor of Petrarch's portrait of Maria, which is best characterized as uncanny. As described by Freud, the uncanny scenario occurs when a formerly familiar element of psychic life that has been either consciously disavowed or primordially repressed returns in the guise of something not quite alien enough for comfort. As it turns out, this is precisely how Maria enters into *Familiares* V.4. Petrarch follows his initial description of the virgin warrior with the revelation that he has met her before, during his 1341 journey to Naples. When they meet again in 1343, he does not recognize her:

> Among such continuous hardships she has changed considerably in a short time. Not too long ago when my youthful desire for glory (*iuveni-lis studium glorie*) led me to Rome and Naples and to the King of Sicily, she attracted my attention as I saw her standing there unarmed. When she approached me today armed and surrounded by armed men in order to pay her respects, I was taken by surprise and returned her greeting as if to an unknown man (*ignoto viro*) until warned by her laughter and by the gestures of her companions. I finally managed to recognize (*recognovi*) under the helmet (*sub casside*) the fierce and unpolished virgin (*torvam et incultam virginem*). (1:241)[71]

The fascinating novelty of the virgin warrior thrusts the issue of sexual difference to the foreground, tempting one to conclude that the central anxiety of this vignette is that Petrarch seems like "the woman" when set alongside Maria. However, the inversion of sexual roles is simply the idiom through which the repressed kernel of this encounter expresses—and dissimulates—itself. It is fairly clear that when Petrarch mistakes the known *virgo* for *ignoto viro*, it is not his virility, but rather his *Virgility*, that is on the line. Here and elsewhere in *Familiares* V.4, the figure of Maria calls into question Petrarch's own choice to pursue renown and effect political change through the revival of Virgilian epic—by "singing" of arms rather than wielding them. When Maria and Petrarch last met, only one of them had publicly built their life around a revival of Roman heroism; when they are reunited, the poet is confronted with a more fully realized version of his revivalist fantasies.

It is significant that Petrarch's misrecognition of Maria is wrong on two accounts. He mistakes her not only for a man but also for a stranger, a *viro ignoto*—an *unknown* man. This second prong of the misrecognition is itself wrong on two accounts. Petrarch unwittingly greets Maria as though she were unknown *to him* but also addresses this famous latter-day Camilla as though she were a nobody—"a virtual unknown" rather than someone who attracts visitors to her from "various parts of the world" (*diversis mundi partibus*). In a cycle of letters that wallow in Petrarch's lack of diplomatic influence at the very court where he was once a favorite son, the real issue raised and submerged in this episode is Petrarch's refusal to recognize that, to his supposed compatriots, *he* might be the *viro ignoto*: an outsider; a stranger; an obscure, unremarkable, unrecognized, *unknown* man.

This anxiety is underscored by the close associative link that the letter forges between Maria and the late King Robert. The laureation was the greatest public acknowledgment of Petrarch's literary achievement. The conclusion of *Familiares* V.4 suggests that what makes Maria both fascinating and disconcerting is that she has returned to Petrarch's life in the form of a second Camilla, but at a moment when the sword and helmet are disproportionately prized in comparison to the pen and the laurel crown. This unwelcome thought prompts Petrarch to break his earlier promise not to rehearse any of the foolish fables that people relate about Maria. The tall tale for which he makes this exception is one that involves his recently deceased royal sponsor:

> It is said that Robert, the greatest of men and of kings, once sailing along these shores with a large fleet, stopped at Pozzuoli intrigued by the wonders of such a woman and desirous of seeing her. In my opinion, this does not seem to be quite believable because living so close to her he could have summoned her. But perhaps he landed there for some other reason, being desirous of viewing something new and being naturally eager for all kinds of knowledge. But let the burden of proof for this matter, as with everything else I have heard, lie with its tellers. (1:242)[72]

The political valences of medieval exoticism provide illuminating context for this passage. As we saw in chapter 1, the prestige economy of long-distance knowledge construes the sovereign as an unmoved mover, a micro-cosmic center that pulls the world's diversity into his or her orbit. Behind this supposedly worthless "fable" about Maria and Robert is the horrify-ing possibility that the same king who summoned Petrarch to his court in Naples in order to subject him to the laureate exam *did*, in fact, abandon his court in order to see the virgin warrior, compromising the majesty of his crown—and Petrarch's—in the process. In repeating what he considers to be a patent fabrication, Petrarch gives voice to the very fears that he attempts to disavow through its retelling.

The pitiable picture of the late king of Naples humbling himself before a provincial woman warrior resonates with the phobic imagery of the sur-rounding letters. *Familiares* V.6 relates the shocking event that exposed Pe-trarch to Naples's recent revival of gladiatorial games. While riding through the streets of the city, Petrarch is intercepted by friends who insist that he accompany them to some unspecified entertainment. As they near their destination, Petrarch looks up to see a crowd, huddled around some kind of spectacle:

> Suddenly, as if something very delightful had occurred, thunderous ap-plause resounded. I looked around and to my surprise saw a most hand-some young man lying at my feet, transfixed by a sharp pointed sword which emerged from his body. I stood there astounded, and my whole body shuddering (*Obstupui, et toto corpore cohorrescens*). I spurred my horse and fled from the infernal spectacle. (1:250)[73]

In this dizzying moment, Petrarch is nearly undone by an uncanny return of ancient Rome. He recoils at this revival of epic violence, which confronts him in a form unmediated by philological detachment and classicizing po-etics. As the letter from Baia suggests, Petrarch identified with—and fash-ioned his domestic and intellectual self-discipline after—an idealized image of the Roman general. This traumatic event exposes the highly selective nature of his imaginative identifications. In the moment that the impaled body crashes down before his feet, Petrarch finds himself face to face with *the* defining elements of the ancient Roman ethos, which he has studiously sanitized and disavowed in—and through—his literary endeavors.

Worse still, the episode forces Petrarch to realize that the death of Rob-ert has not just limited his political influence in Naples but has also di-minished his cultural authority as the foremost expert on matters related to antiquity. The loss of this prerogative impresses itself on Petrarch when he fails to convince the Neapolitans of the barbarity of their gladiatorial revival: "I have already wasted many words speaking of it with the obstinate citizens" (1:250). Petrarch concludes his invective against the practice by remarking that it is no wonder that the cardinal's friends continue to be unjustly imprisoned in Naples, "where killing men is considered a game, a city which Virgil indeed does call the most delightful of all" (1:250).[74]

The Neapolitan letters present Petrarch as a traveler who is repeatedly jarred by uncanny dislocations in the heart of the Italian homeland. Taken as a whole, they problematize travel—even within Italy—as a mode of ethical self-fashioning and political activism. In *Familiares* V.5, Petrarch describes a storm that has wreaked unparalleled destruction on Naples during his visit. Shaken by the ferocity of the tempest, Petrarch informs Colonna of his intentions to minimize future travel by sea:

> I beseech you not ever again to order me to place my trust in winds and seas. This is something in which I would obey neither you, the Pope, or my own father if he were to return to life. (1:247)[75]

As Cachey has noted, Petrarch's reaction to this storm marked a turning point in his career, after which he will excuse himself from many journeys proposed to him by others, citing his incapacity to endure the travails of travel.[76]

Shaken by doubts about the significance of his revival of the Roman epic and confronted with the limits of travel as a means of ethical self-fashioning, Petrarch will shift his focus to the art of dwelling as his preferred expression of diasporic masculinity. The daily labor of reading and writing offered Petrarch a sounder path to self-realization than the indulgence of his youthful wanderlust. The frequent changes of residence that marked Petrarch's mature life were not undertaken for the sake of curiosity but rather to ensure that he would have the necessary time and income to devote himself to his all-consuming commitments to literature and classical scholarship. These developments did not put an end to Petrarch's intervention in public affairs. In the domestic letter, Petrarch discovered a technique for performing the work of diaspora that had none of the disadvantages of travel. More important, Petrarch used the medium of the letter to assemble and educate a diasporic network of "Roman" correspondents. Many of these latter-day Romans—including Petrarch's "Socrates"—were not of Italian descent. Petrarch did not entirely give up hope that inspiring others to mimic his revival of classical virtue might contribute to political change, but his correspondence with friends was, to an even greater degree, a source of consolation in a world that might just as likely ignore his calls for reform.

BEYOND TRAVEL

In a letter dispatched from Venice in 1368, Petrarch urged his friend Papal Secretary Francesco Bruni to find the time each day to labor over his Latin prose style. The letter is included as the third entry of the second book of Petrarch's epistolary anthology the *Seniles*, or the *Rerum senilium libri* (Letters of old age). The (all-too-relatable) topic of *Seniles* II.3 is "[On] how laborious and dangerous it is to write, yet one must write, and in what manner" (*quanti laboris et periculi sit scribere; scribendum tamen, et qualiter*).[77] The encouraging letter acknowledges the host of frustrations that face the serious-minded writer: lack of time, job obligations, endless revision, and the critical grumblings of the envious. Drawing on a store of learned topoi, Petrarch compares the craft of writing to other arts that must be mastered through trial and error, including sculpture and navigation.

Midway through *Seniles* II.3, Petrarch confesses that he is returning to his letter, having been earlier enticed away from his writing desk. As Petrarch was writing the first half of the epistle, he began to nod off, but was startled back to consciousness by the boisterous sounds of a merchant ship departing from the Venetian harbor. Intrigued, Petrarch leaves his letter writing and ascends to the upper floor of his house in order to watch the vessel set sail. After marveling at the size of the ship and at the vast distances it will traverse, Petrarch turns his thoughts to the peril involved in maritime travel, which so many merchants and shipmen undertake for the sake of financial profit.[78] He writes:

> I returned to my pen with my mind deeply shaken. Silently, I kept turning over this one thought: alas, how costly and, at the same time, how cheap life is to mortals.[79]

The letter concludes with a bleary-eyed Petrarch persisting in his writing until well past midnight, triumphing over the fatigue caused by the professional obligations that have filled his day.

In the first half of the letter, Petrarch uses navigation as an analogy to illustrate the patience, hard work, and inconvenience involved in mastering the craft of writing. Having introduced this conceit, he then draws a moralistic contrast between the travail of the writer and that of the professional traveler. The point of these comparisons seems to be that not every form of self-discipline is equally commendable. Though the merchant and the mariner inspire awe because they confront unthinkable travails as a matter of routine, they do so for motives that are dubious, and perhaps even reckless. *Seniles* II.3 levels, then, a fairly conventional criticism against those who subject themselves to the perils of travel unnecessarily or for misguided reasons. The more unique dimension of Petrarch's views on this subject is his conviction that scholarship and writing are a morally superior redirection of the ascetic impulse that spurs men to know the world and realize the self through travel.

Petrarch articulates this ethical position in a more straightforward way in his most sustained engagement with the conventions of medieval travel writing, the *Itinerarium ad Sepulchrum Domini Nostri Yehsu Christi* (Itinerary to the sepulcher of Our Lord Jesus Christ). Petrarch wrote the *Itinerary* over the course of three days during the spring of 1358, for his friend Giovanni Mandelli.[80] Assuming the form of a lengthy epistle, the treatise traces a virtual journey from Genoa to the Holy Land, devoting most of its attention to the Italian coastline and the islands of the Mediterranean. The *Itinerary* was designed to accompany Mandelli on his physical pilgrimage, to be used as a guidebook and as a surrogate for the company of Petrarch, who had disappointed his friend by declining the invitation to join him on the journey. The rigors of overseas travel were far too daunting, Petrarch argued, and would disrupt his scholarly pursuits. Petrarch promised Mandelli that, in the future, he would not hesitate to accompany him if the proposed journey remained "within the confines (*finibus*) of Europe or Italy."[81]

While the *Itinerary* does not criticize the practice of traveling to the Holy Land, it extols the virtues of staying home and imagining the journey to Jerusalem instead. As he does at one juncture in *Seniles* II.3, Petrarch strategically collapses the distinction between the travails of travel and the labor of writing, telling Mandelli:

> But we have already traveled far enough, and enough has been written. You have come this far by oars and by foot on sea and on land: I, plowing this paper with a swift pen. I don't know if you are tired of traveling; certainly I am tired of writing, especially since I have advanced at greater speed. Your journey of three months I have completed in three days. . . . You must return home, while I to my studies.[82]

It might seem as if Petrarch is simply echoing the consensus belief that one did not have to travel bodily to Jerusalem in order to reap the benefits of pilgrimage. This was, after all, the foundational assumption of the synthetic tradition, whose authors sought to provide readers with the contemplative pleasures of the Holy Land pilgrimage without having to undertake the perilous and expensive voyage overseas. If, in theory, virtual pilgrimage was no less devout or meritorious than physical pilgrimage, it was also commonly held that material travel yielded valuable forms of knowledge that could be gained in no other way.

The most remarkable facet of Petrarch's arguments about pilgrimage in the *Itinerary* is the assertion that physical presence in a place does not necessarily confer any epistemological advantage on the traveler. Petrarch acknowledges that he might seem slightly mad for writing a guide to places he has never actually visited "were it not for the fact that we sometimes know many things that we have never seen and many things that we have seen we do not know."[83] Montaigne would stake out a similarly skeptical position in his essay "On Cannibals." Petrarch and Montaigne form part of a minoritarian tradition that claims James Mill as one of its descendants. In his *History of British India* (1817), Mill averred: "A duly qualified man can obtain more knowledge of India in one year in his closet in England than he could obtain during the course of the longest life, by the use of his eyes and ears in India."[84]

In the case of Petrarch, skepticism about what one actually learns by abandoning the labors of study in favor of travel is already a feature of the letters collected in book I of the *Familiares*. These doubts become more pronounced with each new batch of letters to Colonna and reach an urgent pitch with the 1343 sojourn in Naples. The idiosyncratic rationale behind Petrarch's eventual aversion to travel is best explained by the diasporic orientation of his political consciousness, which predisposed him to develop a pragmatic, flexible, and intricately dialogic notion of the relationship between mobility and dwelling. In Petrarch, the Middle Ages gets a traveler who maintains that there is good and bad taste in itineraries—and a reluctant wayfarer, who views the decision to stay at home as one of travel's many techniques, and not as its negation.

CHAPTER SIX

The Chivalric Mediterranean of Pero Tafur

Pero Tafur (ca. 1410–ca. 1487) was a knight and alderman from the Andalusian town of Cordova (in southern Castile) and the author of an engaging travel narrative that has recently attracted increased scholarly attention. Tafur left Cordova in 1435, voyaging for four years across the Mediterranean and subsequently northern Europe. Sometime after the fall of Constantinople to the Ottomans in 1453, Tafur finalized his account, a text that has survived in only one copy and is now commonly known as the *Andanças é viajes de Pero Tafur por diversas partes del mundo avidos* (Wanderings and journeys undertaken by Pero Tafur in diverse parts of the world). Tafur dedicated his narrative to bibliophile and apparent travel-writing enthusiast Don Fernando de Guzmán, a native of Seville and the chief commander of the Order of Calatrava, a military organization dedicated to the conquest of Muslim-controlled territory within Iberia.[1]

As is the case with the travel writing of Petrarch, the interest of the *Andanças* resides in the unusual perspective that it offers on places that were probably already known to its first readers. Indeed, the majority of Tafur's itinerary unfurls along Genoese and Venetian trade routes traversed on a regular basis by a broad spectrum of people.[2] If Petrarch's engagement with classical texts was the defining feature of the unique light that he shed on familiar places, for Tafur this literary touchstone is chivalric fiction— filtered through the frontier mentality of the Iberian *reconquista*.

The *Andanças* vacillates between two, often conflicting, positions regarding the significance of its author's journey (both adapted from chivalric literature). On the one hand, it depicts Tafur's travels as a perilous test of his knightly prowess. Scattered throughout the *Andanças* are episodic adventures, in which Tafur must risk his life to uphold the cultural boundaries between Christianity and Islam. These chivalric travails map the Mediterranean as a series of contested frontiers, in a manner redolent of *reconquista*. On the other hand, Tafur also depicts his journey as an elite educational opportunity founded on his intimacy with Muslim and Greek Orthodox hosts. Indeed, the ethnographic authority of the *Andanças* largely derives from Tafur's embedded investigations in multiconfessional courts. The adventure mode of the *Andanças* presents the Mediterranean as a hostile and fragmented place, and the labor of travel as a series of death-defying, boundary-enforcing deeds. The courtly ethnographic mode of the account paints a different picture: of a world in which elite, interfaith hospitality transcends ethnic and confessional difference, and in which travel is justified by the lessons learned through prolonged, intimate contact with peers who belong to "outside" groups.[3]

As a traveler, Tafur finds himself torn between idealizations of the knight as the sworn enforcer of boundaries and long-standing traditions of cultural reciprocity at interfaith courts. The tensions that strain Tafur's chivalric travels reflect a growing Iberian unease with the cross-cultural and interfaith exchanges that had long prevailed in the medieval Mediterranean and that had endowed Castilian culture with many of its defining attributes. This circumspect stance is an early expression of the drive for religious and ethnic purity that would come to define Spain as a nation during the reign of the "Catholic Monarchs." Seen from the point of view of a different history—that of postmedieval travel writing—the bifurcation of the adventurous and sentimental/educational modes of travel prefigures two later archetypes: the intrepid explorer and conqueror of uncharted territories on the one hand and, on the other, the gentleman traveler who—like Petrarch—confines his edifying wanderings to Europe and the Mediterranean.

TRAVEL AS ELITE SELF-SACRIFICE

Like many travel writers of the later Middle Ages and the "age of discovery," Tafur was influenced by chivalric romance, a literary genre in which adventurous knights achieve fame through deeds of daring undertaken far from home.[4] The opening words of the *Andanças* situate its author's journey within a tradition of chivalric excellence:

> El estado de cavallería, o muy virtuoso señor, ovo siempre comienço más çierto é más duradero de que otra cosa, de la virtud, porque el tal exerçiçio es mas apropiado á los nobles, é la nobleza tiene á la mesma virtud por mayor e mejor fundamento. É tanto tiempo puede alguno ser dicho noble, quanto siguiere las costumbres de otros sus anteçesores,

los quales, non se apartando de áctos virtuosos, mas dando algun buen
prinçipio por luenga continuaçion de proeza, meresçieron ser cabeçeras
é governadores de muchos.[5]

[The estate of knighthood, o most virtuous lord, has always been the
most certain and lasting of things because of virtue, because the exercise
of virtue is most appropriate for nobles, and nobility takes, therefore,
virtue as its foundation. And one can be considered noble as long as he
follows the customs of his ancestors, who, not departing from virtuous
acts and always contributing to the preservation of prowess, earned the
right to be the rulers and governors of the masses.]

Tafur's account celebrates travel as one of the virtuous deeds (*áctos virtuosos*) that tests and builds knightly prowess (*proeza*). As Tafur makes clear,
travel is, therefore, an undertaking that justifies the hereditary privileges of
the nobleman and the unequal social relations on which they are founded.

This disquisition on the origins of knighthood is thoroughly conventional. Throughout Europe, landed warriors argued that their elevated
social station had been secured by their forefathers' selfless displays of
military courage, while the subordinate position of the peasantry was the
consequence of its congenital vice.[6] In the Iberian kingdoms, chivalric self-
sacrifice found a culturally specific outlet in the campaign of *reconquista*.
As John Edwards has observed, the *reconquista* demanded that knights hazard their lives, which, in theory, placed other social groups in their debt.[7]
For many, discharging this debt involved a seemingly indefinite submission
to political inequality and economic exploitation. Centuries after the crown
of Aragon had "reconquered" all of its former territory from Muslim kings,
knights in Catalonia continued to claim that their privileges derived from
their ancestors' bravery in resisting the Moorish invasions of the eighth
century. The peasantry's justification of their rebellion during the Catalan
Civil War (1462–86) contested the historical narrative that painted their
forefathers as pusillanimous capitulators to this ancient incursion; indeed,
the rebels advanced a counterhistory that depicted Catalonia's Christian
peasants as the descendants of freeborn Muslims who had fought bravely,
but were ultimately vanquished, during the *reconquista*.[8]

The moth-worn lineaments of Tafur's rhetoric should not, however, di-
vert attention away from the unique use to which they are put—namely, to
exalt chivalric travel above all other forms of Mediterranean mobility. Many
worldly travelers flicker across the pages of the *Andanças*, but none is more
celebrated than the knight-errant. Drawing on the narrative conventions of

romance, the *Andanças* stages a series of death-defying adventures that test the prowess and resolve of its author/protagonist. Cumulatively, these tales of daring equate chivalric travel with the self-sacrificing defense of confessional and territorial boundaries. At the center of most of these vignettes are Christian captives and/or *renegados* (converts to Islam). Throughout the *Andanças*, the apostate and the captive are the objects of self-serving rescue fantasies, figures used to demonstrate the indispensability of the knightly estate and the unique authority of chivalric travel.

The frequent appearance of Christian converts—or potential converts— to Islam illustrates the extent to which the *Andanças* is shaped by the contested borderland between Castile and the emirate of Granada (which would finally capitulate to the forces of Ferdinand and Isabella in 1492). The influence of this contact zone is particularly apparent in Tafur's depictions of symbolically resonant places such as Jerusalem and Troy. Juan Carlos Ochoa has noted the remarkable extent to which Tafur emphasizes the chivalric, rather than biblical, past of Jerusalem.[9] The knight's account of his stay in Jerusalem manipulates romance's episodic structure in order to imbue his journey with an aura of heroism. One evening, Tafur—in search of adventure—enlists the aid of a Portuguese *renegado* to help him infiltrate Jerusalem's "Temple of Solomon" (the Mosque of Omar), a site prohibited to Christians on pain of death:

> É aquella noche yo rogué a un moro renegado, que fué natural de Portugal, que le daría dos ducados é me metiese aquella noche en el templo de Salomon, é fízolo ansí. . . . Yo entré con él vestido en su ropa é ví todo el templo, el qual es una nave sola toda de oro musayco labrada, é el suelo é paredes de muy fermosas losas blancas, é tantas lámparas colgadas, que paresçe que se juntan unas con otras, é el çielo de arriba todo llano cubierto de plomo. Çiertamente dizen que este fué, quando Salomon lo fizo, la mejor obra que uvo en el mundo, despues fué destruydo é rehedificado, pero çiertamente oy es una de las buenas que ay en el mundo; si yo fuera conosçido por xpiano luego fuera muerto. Este templo pocos dias que era yglesia sagrada, é un privado del Soldan fizo tanto con él, que la tomó é fizo mezquita. Aquel moro renegado que allí me levó, me bolvió a Monte Syon, donde los frayles me esperavan, si non que yo fuese muerto, pues que á tal hora non venía, é ovieron grant plaçer con my venida, é non menós a los cavalleros de mi compañía. (63–64)

> [And that night I implored a Moorish renegade, a native of Portugal, to sneak me into the Temple of Solomon in exchange for two ducats, and

he did. . . . I entered with him dressed in his clothing and saw all of the temple, which consists of one nave, all decorated with gold mosaic work and the floors and walls made of beautiful white flagstones, and so many lanterns that it appears that one converges with the next and the roof flat and covered with lead. Truly, they say that when Solomon constructed this building, it was the finest in the world. Later, it was destroyed and rebuilt, but without a doubt it is one of the finest buildings in the world today. Had I been recognized as a Christian there, I would have been killed. Not long ago, this temple was a sacred church, but one of the sultan's favorites convinced him to seize it and turn it into a mosque. The renegade Moor who took me there returned me to Mount Zion, where the friars were awaiting me, thinking that I may have been dead since I had not returned by that late hour, so they were very pleased by my coming and no less so were the other knights of my company.]

This vignette draws on a perennial romance motif: the knight's surreptitious and/or incognito infiltration of forbidden spaces. The potentially lethal peril that hangs over the episode individualizes the knight, distinguishing his way of knowing Jerusalem from that of the nameless Portuguese renegade, the famously international community of Franciscans on Mount Zion, and even the other knights of his "company," about whom the *Andanças* has little else to say.

There is nothing inevitable about this anecdote. Many Christian pilgrims visiting Jerusalem resented the restrictions placed on their movements but did not use them as a springboard into a defiant adventure.[10] Pietro Casola, for example, simply notes with regret that he can provide readers with only secondhand knowledge of the Mosque of Omar, due to the harshly enforced taboo that restricted Christian access to the building.[11] Felix Fabri chided his knightly companions for fantasizing about seeing the interior of the forbidden building rather than contemplating the sacred landscape around them (see chapter 4). Even when Christian pilgrims managed to maneuver their way into a mosque, they did not necessarily frame their actions as deeds of daring.[12] Mandeville, amplifying a passage he read in the travel account of William of Boldensele, presented his access to the mosques of the Holy Land as a token of the special regard in which the sultan held him.[13] Italian merchant Giorgio Gucci and his companions infiltrated a mosque in Bethany in 1384, but his account says little about how this was achieved or what the interior looked like.[14]

Tafur's scopophilia in the Mosque of Omar articulates a desire to remap Jerusalem—if only at the level of chivalric fantasy—from the perspective

of Christian dominance and in an idiom peculiar to the militarized frontier
that separated Granada and Castile. Mosques assumed a powerful symbolic
valence in the age of *reconquista*. The capture of a Moorish-controlled town
was ritually ratified by the conversion of its congregational mosque into a
church.[15] As is true today, the most famous former mosque in all of Iberia
was that of Cordova, Tafur's native city. Built and expanded under the aus-
pices of the Umayyad Caliphate, Cordova's mosque was consecrated as a
church and dedicated to the Virgin Mary when the town fell to Castilian
forces in 1236. Many of the mosque's stylistic elements survived unaltered,
including its Qur'anic inscriptions, geometrical mosaics, and striped horse-
shoe arches. During Tafur's lifetime, a powerful faction in Cordova attempted to deny Muslim residents the right to gather in any mosque located
in the city center.[16] In fact, the last recorded duty rendered by Tafur as an
alderman was to supervise construction of a new mosque in the wake of
this controversy.[17] Political symbolism and ideological fantasy suffuse Tafur's detailed rendering of the Mosque of Omar and the perilous adventure
through which he accessed it.

The mosque episode is, moreover, typical of the way that the adventure
mode of the *Andanças* emphasizes the threatening dimensions of Islam as
a means of distinguishing its author's experiences from those of countless
other travelers. Take, for instance, the following vignette, in which Tafur
sustains a shamelessly Homeric injury off the coast of Troy:[18]

> É yendo por el canal çerca del Dardinelo, que fué puerta de Troya, unos
> onbres nos fazían señas que nos llegásemos á la ribera, é el patron dixo,
> quél sabíe bien que aquellos eran xpianos cativos, que vinían por es-
> capar en aquel navío, é que non curásemos dellos; yo le rogué mucho
> que echase el batel en el agua é fuésemos por ellos, que si otra cosa fuese
> non seríe maravilla que Dios nos diese la mala ventura; Entré yo en él é
> otros cuatro conmigo, é fuémos a la tierra é en allegando que queríamos
> resçebir los cativos, vienen turcos en pos dellos é comiençan pelear con
> ellos é con nosotros . . . é allí fuí ferido en el pié de una frecha, pero bien
> se fizo, pues non perdimos nada é servimos a Dios. (186–87)

> [And as we headed to the channel close to the Dardanelles, which was
> once the port of Troy, some men made signs to us from the shore that we
> should land the ship, and the shipmaster said that he was sure that those
> were Christian captives that had come to escape aboard our boat and that
> we should pay no heed to them. I implored him to launch a small boat
> in the water so that we could go and rescue them, for otherwise it would

be little wonder if God sent us misfortune. I entered the small boat with four other men and we went to the shore and as we approached to receive the captives a group of Turks came behind them and began to fight with them and with us. . . . There, I was wounded in the foot with an arrow, but it was all for the best, since we lost nothing and served God.]

In this adventure, shipmen and captives appear as peripheral figures in a self-centering narrative; they are, in fact, drawn as stock characters easily recognizable to readers of chivalric romance. Like the tearful community of Franciscans in Jerusalem, the shipman inhabits the margins of the Trojan adventure plot, serving as an index of its peril. Both parties have fictional counterparts in characters such as Perceval's mother in Chrétien de Troyes's *Perceval* and King Arthur in the anonymous thirteenth-century *Queste del Saint Graal*, who function in their respective narratives as figures whose resistance to the chivalric quest affords the protagonist the opportunity to explain why he must defy their wishes and embrace his heroic destiny. The captives, meanwhile, are inscribed into this feat of daring as defenseless creatures awaiting knightly intervention. Tellingly, Tafur never actually specifies how many of them were, in reality, rescued as a result of his efforts, nor how they ended up in their predicament to begin with. For Tafur's purposes, what matters about the shipmaster and the captives is their inability and/or unwillingness to enforce the boundaries of Christendom against the incursions of Islam.

Behind this Trojan rescue fantasy lurks a long Iberian tradition of exploiting the plight of the captive in order to rationalize the privileges of the nobility.[19] The landowning elite positioned themselves as the defenders of unarmed Christians, who might otherwise be forced to convert to Islam. The ideological importance of the "helpless" captive contributed to a general denial of agency and religious conviction in discussions of Christian conversion to Islam. Dwayne E. Carpenter observes that the thirteenth-century Siete Partidas, a legal code compiled under King Alfonso X, lists four motives why Christians become Muslims: because they like Moorish lifestyles, because of the death of a family member, because they have lost all of their money, or because they want to escape the law; religious belief factors nowhere in these ruminations.[20] Similarly, the municipal records from the Andalusian border town of Jaén tend not to parse the doctrinal convictions of those Christians who, despite the desires of their "rescuers," wished to remain in Granada as Muslims.[21] Refusal of—or at least confusion regarding—the agency of so-called *renegados* is registered in one document's strange concatenation of reflexive and transitive verbs: thus, the case of one Fernando, who "se cortó su natura e dixo que era moro, e lo tornaron moro" ("cut his own member, said he was a Moor, and then they made him a Moor").[22] Somehow, not even the demonstrable resolve suggested by self-circumcision can effect Fernando's conversion—it is the government of Granada that "made him a Moor."[23]

The specter of inevitable, forced apostasy is what authorizes Pero Tafur to purchase Christian slaves, an act long prohibited by canon law. At the Genoese slave market of Kaffa, Tafur buys two women and a man, whose children he claims to "possess" in Cordova at the time he writes his narrative (162). According to Tafur, the pope has authorized the ownership of Christian slaves in order to prevent their sale to the sultan of Cairo, who will force them to "renounce the faith" (162).[24] This rationalization is a more explicit articulation of the assumptions that structure the fantasies of trespass and rescue that recur throughout the *Andanças*. The *Andanças*'s chivalric vignettes showcase the sublime quality of the knight's negotiation of geographical and confessional boundaries, which is founded on a willingness—even a drive—to sacrifice life and body. For Tafur, this chivalric death drive is the foundational precondition of all knightly deeds and, by extension, the sine qua non of what it means to *travel*.

In fact, what counts as *travel* in the *Andanças* is so thoroughly defined by these ideologies that Tafur's confidence in the inevitable convertibility of his slaves expresses itself in the rhetorical erasure of their agency as travelers. Even though these slaves cross the exact same political boundaries as Tafur, according to the *Andanças*, they do not *travel* to Venice but are "carried" and then "held" there by Tafur's friend while the knight seeks adventure in northern Europe:

> Al tiempo que yo me partí de Veneja, para yr andar por las tierras de los xpianos, dexé todas las cosas que traya del Levante, ansí esclavos como dinero é todas las otras cosas que avía comprado, en poder de miçer Doménego Vent' un mercador de allí mucho mi amigo. (218)

> [At the time that I left Venice to wander through Christian lands, I left all of the things that I had carried with me from the Levant, including slaves and money and all of the other things that I had bought, in the control of Master Doménego Vent', a merchant from there (i.e., Venice) and a very good friend of mine.]

This, despite the fact that slaves were some of the most widely traveled and cosmopolitan of people.[25] A typical itinerary for a slave who ended up in western Europe might include birth in Crimea, indoctrination into Christianity at Kaffa, service in a Florentine household, then resale to other corners of Europe.[26] The logic through which the *Andanças* sacralizes knightly travel is based on the assumption that the self-sacrificing deeds (*trabajos*) of the *hildago* are of staggeringly more value than the work (*trabajo*) of his social inferiors—so much more so that the second group, and perhaps their children, were expected to labor their entire lives in order to balance accounts.

Seen from the vantage point of the adventurous episode, the Mediterranean is a fractured terrain, in which the significance of the knight's journey is defined by the ongoing struggle between Christian and Muslim powers. The *Andanças* develops a second perspective on the Mediterranean voyage of its author, one that locates the unique benefits of knightly travel within the rarefied, multiconfessional world of courtly hospitality. This second line of argument exists in uneasy relationship to the adventure mode of the *Andanças*, which—in the process of subliming chivalric travel—subordinates cross-cultural dialogue to the aims of territorial contest.

COURTLY HOSPITALITY
AND ETHNOGRAPHIC AUTHORITY

Pero Tafur's emphasis on chivalric hospitality is, to no small degree, part of the *Andanças*'s larger rhetorical agenda of distinguishing the knightly journey from the broader sphere of Mediterranean mobility. Tafur argues that visiting foreign lands ("visitar tierras extrañas") hones chivalric prowess; anticipating the Grand Tour by centuries, he also adds that studying the governance and mores of distant realms grants the noble traveler the knowledge he needs to exercise his inherited political power:[27]

> De la tal visitaçion, raçonablemente se pueden conseguir provechos cercanos á lo que proeza require, ansí engrandeçiendo los fijosdalgo sus coraçones donde sin ser primero conosçidos los intervienen trabajos y priesas, como deseando mostrar por obras quien fueron sus anteçesores, quando solamente por propias fazañas puede ser déllos conoçedora la jente estrangera. É no ménos porque, si acaesçe fazer retorno despues del trabajo de sus caminos á la provinçia donde son naturales, puedan, por la diferencia de los governamientos é por las contrarias qualidades de una naçion á otra, venir en conosçimiento de lo más provechoso á la cosa pública é estableçimiento della, en que principalmente se deben trabajar los que de nobleza no se querrán llamar enemigos. (1–2)

[Through such visitation, one can reasonably attain the benefits that prowess demands, thereby strengthening the hearts of noble men in places where they are not known, as they are impeded by challenges and hardships and they—desiring to show through their works who their ancestors were—gain renown through their deeds among foreign people. And no less because if they happen to return to the regions where they were born after the labor of their travels, they are able, because of their knowledge of different governments and the contrasting traits of different nations / races / ethnic groups, to come home with an understanding of those things that most benefit the common good and the maintenance thereof, which should be the top priority of those who do not wish to be considered the enemies of nobleness/nobility.]

The knight's lessons in comparative civics depend on the ministrations of his hosts, the men of influence who govern the lands he visits. The production of useful knowledge about the world therefore takes place necessarily within the rarefied world of courtly hospitality, an assumption that is crystallized in the *Andanças*'s choice of the verb *visitar.*

Derived from the Latin *vidēre*, "to see," the medieval Castilian verb *visitar* meant "to visit" in the social sense of the word and also "to inspect or investigate."[28] *Visitar* and its nominative form *visitación* suggest a close—perhaps even inseparable—relationship between the quality of the hospitality extended to the traveler during his visit (*visitación*) to a foreign land and the quality of his description *of* that land, which is in itself the outcome of the knight's embedded ethnographic investigation (*visitación*). A critical commonplace presumes that travel narrative is torn between two competing impulses: the drive to show ("an elephant looks like such and such") and the drive to tell ("I went here and this or that happened").[29] Tafur's use of *visitar* suggests a continuous, or even seamless, understanding of the relationship between narrative and description.

Indeed, in the *Andanças*, tales of stylized hospitality and the description of distant kingdoms are mutually reinforcing components of Tafur's chivalric self-presentation. Their mutual imbrication is particularly evident in the work's treatment of Egypt. The *Andanças* describes Cairo at great length. Tafur's breathless catalogue of Egyptian exotica is punctuated by notices of the richness, the importance, and the generosity of his host and guide, the sultan's chief interpreter:

Yo estuve en Babylonia çerca de un mes mirando muchas cosas muy estrañas, mayormente a las de nuestra naçión. E çiertamente yo ove grant

dicha en aver tal guía como aquella del truxamán mayor que él avíe grant
plaçer en trabajar comigo en aquello que yo quería. (85)

[I was in Egypt around a month looking at many very strange things.
And certainly I had great fortune in having such a guide like that chief
interpreter because he took great pleasure in working to help me with
whatever it was that I desired.]

This statement is an example of Tafur's larger tendency—noted by Barry
Taylor—to present himself as a courtly "insider."[30] In the description of
his Egyptian host, Tafur shows how the institution of elite hospitality transcends the very confessional differences that, in other settings, he imagines
as perilous frontiers:

> Él ovo mucho placer comigo, porque asimesmo él era de Sevilla, que sey-
> endo niño fue levado a Jerusalén con su padre, que era judío, e murió el
> padre e él tornóse moro, e primeramente le lamaron Haym e agora Saym.
> Él quiso saber de mí, quién yo era e cómo venía, e yo no le encobrí nada
> de mi fecho, por me aprovechar de él e de su consejo, e así lo fizo. Yo fui
> tan bien tratado de él en su casa, dexándome andar entre sus mugeres e
> fijos como si fuera fijo propio, e dizíeme que esta era la mayor onrra que
> él me pudíe fazer e que bien paresçía que yo era de su naçión, pues sus
> fijos tanto me querían. Seríe este onbre de noventa años, mas por eso no
> dexava de fazer generación, que, aun estando yo allí, le parió una de sus
> mugeres un fijo. Éste tenía quatro mugeres cristianas de aquellas que
> compran en la mar Mayor, por quanto avríen por grant desonrra casar
> con mora de natura. (78–79)

[He took much pleasure in me because he himself was from Seville, having been as a child taken to Jerusalem by his father, who was Jewish,
and when his father died, he turned Moor, and before they called him
Haym and now Saym. He wanted to know about me, who I was and
from where I came, and I concealed nothing of my deeds, in order to take
advantage of him and his advice, and so it was that he offered it. I was so
well treated by him in his house, with him allowing me to socialize with
his wives and his children as though I were his own son, and he would
tell me that this was the highest honor that he could do me, and that it
appeared to him that I was of his race/nation/bloodline, because his children loved me so much. This man must have been about ninety years

old, and moreover he did not stop reproducing, because while I was still there, one of his wives gave birth to a son. He had four wives, all Christians of the kind that are bought on the Great Sea, because it would be a great dishonor to marry a native Moor.]

Tafur presents Saym as someone who recognizes the restrictive realities of confessional difference, only to recast them as opportunities for homosocial bonding. From Saym's perspective, the "honor" that he shows Tafur consists of his voluntary transgression of cultural norms—in this case, allowing a male, a foreigner, and a Christian, to mix freely with the women of his household. Intriguingly, Tafur blunts the force of the potentially unpalatable fact that the interpreter's wives are Christians by entering into an ethnographic excursus on why Egyptian men prefer Christian (rather than "Moorish") wives. Tafur also records his host's assertion that it seems as though the two men are of the same *"nación"*—a word whose connotations include notions of bloodline, linguistic group, ethnic or geographical origin, and confessional identity. The measured rendering of these unlikely arrangements—and the unflinching discussion of polygamy, Christian apostasy, and interfaith marriage—could not be farther removed from the polarizing rhetoric of the chivalric adventure.

Pero Tafur's closeness to Saym is key to understanding his representation of Egypt as a whole. The knight's description of the sultan's elephants, for example, demands to be understood within the context of the narrative of hospitality that surrounds it. The depiction of the royal elephants begins, logically enough, by reporting on the animals' physical appearance: their size, color, and shape. Somewhat more idiosyncratic is the acute interest that Tafur demonstrates in the everyday lives of the creatures:

Estas bestias paresçe como que tengan entendimiento, tantas burlas fazen que á las vezes traen aquella trompa llena de agua é échala encima a quien quiere, e fázenlos jugar con una lança, echándola en alto e recibiéndola, y otros muchos juegos. E cuando están en celo, lévanlos desde amaneciendo e métenlos en el río por que se resfríen, en otra manera no los podrían mandar. Estos tienen el cuerpo muy duro e, si resçiben alguna ferida, pónenle donde le dé la luna e luego otro día es sano. El que los manda lleva un ferreçuelo engastado en un palo e escárvale tras el oreja e llévalos donde quiere, porque allí tienen el cuero muy delgado e, áun una mosca que se asiente allí le da pena. Estos se goviernan de paja e çebada, como acá los cavallos. (87–88)

[These beasts appear as though they have reason, so many tricks they play; at times they fill their trunks with water and spray it over anyone they choose. They also play with a lance, tossing it up in the air and catching it, and many other games. And when they are in heat, they are carried at dawn and placed in the river so that they can cool off; otherwise, it would be impossible to control them. They have very hard bodies and if they receive a wound, they are placed in the moonlight and the next day they are cured. The one who rides them carries an iron barb attached to a stick and he pricks them behind the ear and takes them wherever he wants, because in that spot their hide is very thin, so that even when a fly alights there it causes them pain. They are given straw and barley to eat, just as horses are here.]

In essence, this passage is an event—the time Tafur was honored as a foreign knight through the chief interpreter's private tour of the menagerie—rewritten as a description.[31] In other words, the elephants are not the sole object of this description. An equally important emphasis is placed on rendering the singular standpoint from which the traveler observes the animals. The account of the elephants' capers and japes suggests an interview with the animals' keepers, probably secured through and translated by the chief interpreter.[32] The resources and labor that sustain the lives of the sultan's elephants are, meanwhile, an index of the ruler's wealth and power. In a manner typical of long-distance specialism, the magnificence of the sultan reflects favorably on Tafur, who has been honored by special access to the king's pets and to the men who care for them. The tales of hospitality that frame Tafur's geoethnographic descriptions ensure that, even when the knight seems to fade into the background of the text, his presence is nevertheless registered through a certain quality of descriptive detail, one that calls attention to the socially mediated standpoint from which Tafur came to know the object being described.

The *Andanças's* tendency to ground geoethnographic authority in interfaith hospitality is obviously at odds with the vision of knightly travel that it advances through its adventure mode. The perilous deed calls upon the knight to mark the absolute boundary between two hostile civilizations even as he physically crosses over to the other side. The courtly ethnographer, on the other hand, relies on practices that potentially subvert the symbolic integrity of the boundary-enforcing warrior. This is true not only of Tafur's interactions with Muslim leaders but also of the time that he spends in the stately orbit of John VIII Palaeologus, the emperor of Constantinople.

Tafur's relationship to the emperor and his courtiers is the occasion for the
Andanças's most sustained examination of the tensions that strain its conception of elite travel.

THE CONTRADICTIONS OF ELITE TRAVEL

Constantinople occupies a special place in Tafur's mapping of the chivalric
world. The Byzantine capital of the *Andanças* is the setting of a long tradition of amity between Castilian and Greek knights. John VIII Palaeologus,
the Byzantine emperor, extends Tafur a warm reception to his court.[33] The
ruler enters the *Andanças* as an admirer of Castilian chivalry and as a patron of its poetic manifestations:

> Despues de dos dias que yo estuve reposando, fuí á fazer reverençia al
> emperador de Constantinopla, é vinieron todos los castellanos á me
> acompañar, é yo púseme á punto lo mejor que pude, é con el collar des-
> cama, que es la devisa del rey Don Juan, é embié por un trujaman del
> Emperador, que llamavan Juan de Sevilla, castellano por naçion; é dizen
> quel Emperador, allende de ser Trujaman, porque le cantava romançes
> castellaños en un laud. (139)

> [After resting for two days, I went to do reverence to the emperor of Con-
> stantinople, and all of the Castilians came with me, and I presented my-
> self as well as I could, and with the collar of the Order of Escama, which
> is the device of King Juan, and I sent for an interpreter of the emperor,
> whom they called Juan of Seville, Castilian by birth. And they say that
> the emperor appointed Juan interpreter because he used to sing Castilian
> verses/ballads to him accompanied by the lute.]

The inclusion of the Castilian interpreter's name and the story of his place
at court sets the stage for Tafur's request that the emperor have the city's
archives searched for evidence that the Tafur family is descended from the
imperial bloodline. The results of these researches yield an elaborate tale of
chivalric *translatio* worthy of Chrétien de Troyes's *Cligès*. According to Tafur, the emperor unearths documentary proof that the founder of the Tafur
clan was a Byzantine prince who went into exile in Spain in the wake of a
protracted dynastic dispute (141–47).

In another extraordinary episode set in Constantinople, Tafur is invited
to dine with a Greek-speaking knight. At the end of the meal, the host dismisses his family and his servants in order to speak to Tafur privately. Then:

Él entró en su cámara é púsose un collar de oro descama de la divisa del
Rey nuestro Señor, é salió á mí é fabló en nuestra lengua castellana é
dixo: cavallero, vos seades mucho bien venido, vedes aquí mi casa é los
que en ella es presto á vos como á mi hermano propio, porque de vuestro
Rey yo resçebí mucha honor é merçedes, é de los cavalleros de vuestra
tierra todo buen acogimiento, é si yo non vos e fablado en plaça vuestra lengua, es porque nosotros avemos á grant menospreçio en ninguna
manera dexar nuestra lengua por fablar la estraña, mas por el amor que
yo tengo con vuestra naçion é á vos, de aquí adelante, quando nos falláre-
mos solos, fazé razon que en todo tenes un castellano á par de vos. (150)

[He went to his bedroom and put on a gold collar of the Order of Escama,
the device of the King, our lord, and he came out to me and he spoke in
our native Castilian tongue, saying: Knight, you are very welcome. You
see here my house and all that is in it, know that all of it is at your dis-
posal as if you were my own brother, because from your king I received
much honor and many graces, and from the knights of your country very
good hospitality. And if I do not speak to you in your language in public
places, it is because for us it is a shameful thing to leave our native language for another under any circumstances, but for the love that I have of
your people and for you, from now on, whenever we find ourselves alone,
you will have a Castilian at your side.]

As with the episode involving Saym, this nameless Greek knight flouts pro-
hibitions intended to enforce distinctions between his own ethnic/confes-
sional group and outsiders such as Tafur. However, the Greek knight also
seems to acknowledge that his tribute to Castile falls somewhat short of
what the occasion demands. A common investment in honorable conduct
brings knights of different nations together. Nevertheless, local variations
on the concept of honor—in this case, the dishonor that accrues to Greeks
who abandon their native tongue in favor of another—establish zones of
prohibition that constrain chivalric reciprocity.

A similar scene is played out later in the *Andanças*, when Tafur encounters Emperor John VIII Palaeologus in Italy, at the Council of Ferrara
in 1438. This time, it is Tafur who must reconcile his gratitude toward the
Greek ruler with the expectations of his countrymen. The Council of Ferrara was convened by Pope Eugenius IV in order to discuss the possible re-
unification of the Catholic and Greek Orthodox Churches. John VIII Palaeologus sailed to Italy to facilitate this entente because he saw the potential
alliance with the pope as a shield against the threat of Ottoman advance.

While attending this official diplomatic meeting, Tafur encounters a group of fellow Castilians, who have been sent to Ferrara as royal envoys. Of the emperor, Tafur writes:

> Este día me despedí dél é fuí á reposar, é quitéme la barva, que traya muy luenga, por ruego de los castellanos; é otro dia vestido á la manera nuestra, fuí a ver al Emperador, é como me vido, dixo que le pesaba mucho por lo que yo avía fecho en tajarme la barva, que es la mayor onrra é el mayor bien que los onbres tienen; yo le respondí: señor, nosotros por lo contrario lo tenemos, que sino por grant dapño jamás nunca la traemos; ansí que en esto fablamos una grant pieça. (221)

> [That day I said good-bye to him and I went to take a nap, and, at the petition of the Castilians, I trimmed my beard, which I was wearing quite long. And on another day I dressed in our manner and went to see the emperor, and as he saw me, he said it pained him greatly that I had shaved off my beard, which he said was the greatest source of pride and the best thing that men have. I responded to him, "Lord, we believe the contrary, and only in the case of a very grave injury do we wear a beard," and so on this theme we conversed a goodly amount of time.]

The *Andanças* does not say why Tafur has permitted his facial hair to grow so long. The beard could be the result of negligence, a pilgrimage vow,[34] or perhaps even a calculated attempt to adopt the styles of eastern Mediterranean courts.[35] Regardless of the intentions behind this alleged lapse in grooming, Tafur's defense of shaving puts him at odds with the emperor, who has so far played an important role in the Spanish knight's chivalric self-presentation.

The disagreement between Tafur and his erstwhile host should be viewed in light of the former's ultimately disenchanted take on Greek society. Although the *Andanças* relies on John VIII Palaeologus to establish its protagonist's illustrious pedigree, it also presents him as an unlucky ruler, who presides over an empire whose collective lack of masculine virtue leads to its capture by the Ottoman Turks. At one point, Tafur expressly claims that the Greek defeat of 1453 is a token of the *pecado* ("sin") of the populace (*Andanças*, 144). At another point, he mocks a miracle story about a past war on Constantinople. According to local legend, an angel relieved a young boy who had been left to keep watch over one of the walls of the besieged city, which prompts Tafur to quip: "pero poderse ía dezir agora quel niño era venido, é el Angel avíe dexado su guarda" (180) ("but now it could be said that the boy has come back to the wall while the angel has left its guard"). The image of a boy sentinel seems to be offered up as a parodic twist on the boundary-securing Christian warrior of Tafur's adventurous vignettes. Tafur also alleges that Greek men flock to churches to engage in sodomitic orgies (175–76) and casts doubt on more of the imperial capital's self-aggrandizing urban legends (180). In aggregate, these criticisms suggest that the well-intentioned emperor's subjects are simply not up to the task of defending the territorial integrity of Christendom. In this way, Greek knights are the antithesis of their Castilian counterparts, even as they are also their ancestors and peers.

This ambivalence suggests that there is more at stake in Tafur's rejection of the Greek beard than first meets the eye. While the Greeks' preference for long beards was widely noted by travel writers, including Mandeville and Petrarch,[36] in Tafur's Iberia, the beard had powerful symbolic valences related to the *reconquista*, as a boundary marker between Islam and Christianity. During the royal entry of King Juan II of 1454, men in the Andalusian border town of Jaén donned "prosthetic beards" ("*barvas postizas*") in order to play Moorish knights.[37] "*Barvas postizas*" were also on parade the previous year, when the town staged a mock battle between Christian and "Moorish" knights; the tournament culminated in the defeat of the latter party and the "baptism" of the person playing the king of Morocco.[38] Teofilo F. Ruiz has argued that the entertainments of Jaén had a boundary-marking function, articulating a set of symbolic relationships between the town and the rural buffer zone that separated it from the neighboring emirate of Granada.[39] A similar border-marking practice is at work in the famous *Catalan Atlas* (ca. 1375) (figs. 8 and 9). The maps included in the *Atlas* render Europe as an empty space in which political boundaries are signaled through heraldic signs; by contrast, the maps of Asia and Africa teem with animal and human figures, with large depictions of bearded monarchs featuring prominently.

For Tafur, the unchecked growth of his facial hair inhibits his performance of an elite "Castilian" identity in a politically fraught environment where a successful performance is essential: to represent (in the diplomatic sense) Castile (metonymically understood as its king), one had to represent (in the mimetic sense) Castile (metonymically understood as its Christian male elite).[40] As the work of Ernst H. Kantorowicz made clear long ago, the bodies of male rulers in the Middle Ages came to signify something much larger than themselves—namely, the entire political order of which they were the head.[41] Mary Douglas has suggested that there is an inverse proportion between the mundanity of an action and its symbolic potency in ritual

Figure 8. Northern Africa (detail). From *The Catalan Atlas* (ca. 1375). Bibliothèque
nationale de France, ms. ESP 30. (Photograph: BNF, Paris.)

practice.[42] If one were to view the ritual transubstantiation of the trivial
into the sublime from a slightly different angle, one could say that there is
a direct proportion between the symbolic importance of a given body and
the threat posed to the symbolism of that body by mundane activities. In
late medieval Spain, the margins of the male body—especially the beard
and the foreskin—were called upon to represent and magically uphold cultural boundaries. Muslims living in Christian parts of Spain were distinguished by legally mandated haircuts, and the thirteenth-century Customs
of Tortosa ordered all Muslim men to wear beards.[43] The circumcision of the
Christian body, on the other hand, would be seen as incontrovertible proof
of one's status as a *renegado*.[44]

The troubled reign of King Enrique IV of Castile (ruled 1454–74) illustrates the volatile symbolic role that the Muslim/Christian divide played
in the self-fashioning of elite men. Enrique's adversaries dubbed him *el rey
impotente*, a particularly vicious sobriquet that crystallized several allegations leveled against him, including his failure to defend the frontier, his
penchant for Islamic culture, the illegitimacy of his daughter, and his homo-
sexual leanings. Alonso de Palencia mercilessly mocked the king for having playfully volleyed a couple of arrows at the walls of Granada before
retreating with his wife back to Jaén.[45] This charge of royal weakness vis-à-
vis Granada was particularly damning, since popular imagination—fed by a
steady diet of chivalric ballads set in Andalusia—associated male heroism
with the defense of the Christian/Muslim frontier.[46] Meanwhile, the "Islamic" features of Enrique's court raised eyebrows among domestic adver-

Figure 9. Depiction of Musa Keita I of Mali (ca. 1280–ca. 1337) (detail). From
The Catalan Atlas (ca. 1375). Bibliothèque nationale de France, ms. ESP 30.
(Photograph: BNF, Paris.)

saries and foreign visitors alike. Political tensions crescendoed in 1465 with
the Farce of Ávila, in which an effigy of the king was dethroned and cast
to the ground to resounding cries of "A tierra, puto!" ("To the ground with
you, faggot!").[47]

The important thing to take away from the example of Enrique is that
Tafur was exploring the Mediterranean at a historical juncture in which the
syncretic tendencies of courtly culture came into tension with Iberia's increasingly exclusionary notions of individual and communal identity. Historians have traced these developments back to the Jewish pogroms that
convulsed the peninsula in 1391. The century that followed this calamity witnessed the Castilian nobility's fraught attempt to define themselves
as a group. The number of families claiming noble ancestry increased dramatically; textual theorizations of what it meant to be noble proliferated;
texts related to heraldry and family history were produced in ever greater
numbers; and controversies raged over the conferral of noble status on *conversos*, Jewish converts to Christianity.[48] The rise of the Inquisition promoted the infamous link between nobility and *limpieza de sangre* ("purity
of blood"). To be a noble was to be culturally "pure," to have one's lineage
free of the "stain" of Islamic or Judaic ancestry. The conquest of Granada
and the expulsion of the Jews in 1492 might be seen as the culmination of

a long-stirring realignment of sentiment about the religious multiplicity
that had defined Castile and the "Spains" united under Isabella and Ferdinand. Reactionary "neo-Gothic" discourses began to seek the essence of
national identity in the lands that hugged the Pyrenees, a region home to
the Visigothic bloodline of the crown and historically untouched by Moorish invasion.[49] As a chronotope for nativist history, the Visigothic interior
furnished an alternative to Spain's porous Mediterranean shores, enabling
the fantasy of a national identity that had always been—at least in its ideal
expressions—culturally monolithic and Christian.

The *Andanças* is, in this regard, a prescient work. Less than a decade
after Tafur's death, the Spain united by Ferdinand and Isabella would con-
quer Granada, expel all Jews from the kingdom, and aim to convert the
entire world to Christianity through exploration and conquest. The Inquisition redoubled efforts to ferret out those converts to Christianity whose
convictions and allegiances were suspect, including people whom it sought
to disqualify from noble status. In an environment in which claims to nobility were evaluated in the interest of smothering ethnic and religious multiplicity, a hermeneutics of suspicion plagued the interpretation of courtly
signs.[50] Juan del Encina's play *La égloga de Mingo, Gil y Pascuala* (ca. 1494)
comically stages this semiotic instability. The play's three eponymous
characters are recognizable types drawn from pastoral poetry: the first, a
simple, unrefined shepherd; the second, a squire who abandons the court to
go slumming in the countryside; and the third, a beautiful shepherdess who
becomes the squire's love interest. All of them eventually abandon rustic
pleasures for courtly comforts, but not without a fight. Reluctant to relin-
quish his accustomed way of life, Mingo must first be convinced of the superiority of the courtier's vocation. In the following dialogue, Gil attempts
to teach the shepherd how one is to dress in polite company:

GIL: Echa el bonete a un lado, assí como aqueste mío.
MINGO: ¡Ha, pareceré jodío![51]

[GIL: Put your hat to one side. Now, do as I do.
MINGO: Ha! What? And look like a Jew?]

This satirical agon was staged in the household of Juan del Encina's patron, Fadrique Álvarez de Toledo y Enríquez, the Second Duke of Alba, a
staunch ally of the Catholic kings and a participant in the Castilian conquest of Granada. Something more than just a gentle ribbing of noble spectators, Mingo's skeptical view of the court's refinements is a comic rewrit-

ing of the restless, paranoid gaze of the Inquisition. A less developed form of this accusatory posture marks the limits of chivalric exchange among Christians in Pero Tafur's Mediterranean.

There is another, equally interesting, way to understand the tensions that strain the *Andanças*'s idealization of the knightly journey—as the incomplete synthesis of two later kinds of elite male travel: that of the conquistador and that of the gentleman-scholar. The outlines of this latter type are sketched in Petrarch's letters, continued along a familiar French-Italian axis in the writings of Renaissance scholars, and formalized in the institution of the Grand Tour. Notwithstanding the importance that Tafur attaches to the maintenance and expansion of Christendom's boundaries, his notion of travel has more in common with this learned tradition of intracontinental and Mediterranean travel than it does with the fearless expansionism of Columbus and Cortés. This affinity is particularly obvious in what has become the most famous episode of the *Andanças*, in which Tafur rejects the prospect of chivalric adventure in East Asia in favor of a tour of that includes many of the same cultural centers that Petrarch had explored in his youth.

THE ROAD NOT TAKEN

During his stay in Egypt in 1437, Pero Tafur contemplated a further voyage into India. While mulling over this prospect on the shores of the Red Sea, Tafur crossed paths with Nicolò di Conti, a Venetian merchant who was returning from a decades-long sojourn in East Asia. Nicolò's journey purportedly included a visit to the court of Prester John as well as stops in Java, Sumatra, and the Indian subcontinent. When Tafur first met Nicolò, the merchant was accompanied by his wife and children, all of them "tornados moros, que los fizieron renegar en la Meca" ("turned Moors on account of the fact that they were made to renounce [Christianity] in Mecca") (97). Tafur traveled from the Red Sea to Cairo in the company of Nicolò, and en route the merchant enraptured the knight with tales of self-immolating widows, cannibals, necromancers, precious stones, and strange flora and fauna. Tafur even claims that Nicolò gave him some pages of writing on these subjects, which the *Andanças* translates into Castilian and presents at great length in the third person. This chance encounter left a singular impression on the chivalric traveler, who devoted several pages of his account to transcribing the merchant's anecdotes. The inclusion of Nicolò's observations violates Tafur's general rule of not describing places he has not seen himself—a principle that leads him, for example, to pass over the city of

Damascus in silence, even though he has heard many reliable reports of its splendors (66).

Nicolò eventually achieved celebrity through a second interview—this one with influential humanist Poggio Bracciolini. Poggio would include his rendition of Nicolò's account of Asia as book IV of his *De varietate fortunae* (On the vicissitudes of fortune, 1447), a volume that, as a whole, proved far less successful than this one part. In fact, the collaboration of Nicolò and Poggio circulated independently among intellectual circles, which ensured its nearly immediate impact on maps and learned cosmographies, some of which were owned and studied by Columbus.[52]

As Joan-Pau Rubiés has noted, modern scholarship on Conti has tended to compare the interviews of Tafur and Poggio, only to dismiss the former as wanting. Rubiés offers an important rereading of the two versions of the Venetian merchant's reminiscences, in which he advocates for the value of Tafur's while also illustrating how Poggio's humanist interests in Ptolemaic geography, moral philosophy, and classical topics such as the nature of civility prompted him to craft Nicolò's testimony in a more self-evidently structured way than Tafur had.[53] Consistent with his stated preoccupation with content rather than form, Rubiés pays more attention to the topics addressed by these two accounts than he does the larger narrative frameworks in which Conti's claims are embedded. As a result, even though he challenges dismissive assessments of Tafur, Rubiés still frames the comparison between the knight and Poggio in starkly contrasting terms. However, to approach the appearance of Conti in the *Andanças* within the broader narrative arc of the work troubles the rigid binary between chivalric adventurer and humanist scholar, particularly as it relates to the topic of elite educational travel.

Take, for example, the manner in which Tafur's Nicolò speaks about Prester John. In locating the kingdom of Prester John in India (as opposed to Abyssinia), Nicolò admittedly offers Tafur a vision of the world that had long sustained the ambitions of crusaders and chivalric adventurers. The legendary ruler first entered into public consciousness in the twelfth century, when the famous forgery "The Letter of Prester John" began to spread throughout Europe. The letter so captivated readers that it exists in over 250 manuscripts, in languages as diverse as Latin, German, Welsh, and Hebrew.[54] Many travel writers from the thirteenth through the sixteenth centuries claimed to have made contact with Prester John, while others insisted that he did not exist. Like the perennial Latin Christian dream of entering into an alliance with the Great Khan, interest in Prester John was sparked by the military goal of capturing Muslim-controlled lands by attacking them from the East and the West. In 1403, King Enrique III of Castile sent Ruy González de Clavijo to the court of Tamerlane, in the hope of securing an alliance that would give him leverage against North Africa and the Ottoman Empire. At the end of the century, Columbus would present his first voyage to "Asia" as an offshoot of Isabella and Ferdinand's victorious conquest of Granada, touting the possibility that the maritime campaign might lead to the conversion of India to Christianity, a political alliance with the Great Khan, and perhaps even the eschatologically symbolic reconquest of Jerusalem.[55]

Notwithstanding the tactical or chivalric aspirations that might underlie Tafur's interest in Prester John, the *Andanças* ultimately exploits the figure of Nicolò to distance itself from the adventure drive that will eventually become the hallmark of the conquistador. Tafur confides his plan to travel to India to Nicolò, only to be met with a thorough dismissal of his proposal. The *Andanças* renders Nicolò's objection—uncharacteristically—in direct discourse:

En lo que á ti toca, yo te ruego por Dios é por el amor que te e, pues eres xpiano é de la tierra donde yo soy, que non entremetas en tan grant locura, porque el camino es muy largo é trabajoso é peligroso, de generaciones estrañas sin rey é sin ley é sin señor. ¿E cómo pasarás tú sin salvoconduto o a quién temerá el que te quisiere matar? Después, mudar el aire e comer e bever estraño de tu tierra, por ver gentes bestiales que no se rigen por seso, e que, bien que algunas monstruosas aya, no son tales para aver placer con ellas. Pues ver montones de oro é de perlas é de piedras, ¿qué aprovechan, pues bestias las traen? (97)

[Turning to what touches on you, I beg you for the love of God and for the love that I bear you, since you're a Christian and from my native land, that you not undertake such a rash adventure, because the way there is long, and painstaking, and dangerous, full of strange peoples who are without king, without law, without a lord. And how will you pass through them without a safe-conduct or without someone who will be feared by those who would attempt to kill you? On top of this, to change the air and food and drink of your native land for strange ones, just to see bestial people who do not govern themselves according to reason, and fine—there might be some freakish things to see, but they are not so great as to take pleasure in them. Anyway, to see mountains of gold and of pearls and of gems, what good are they at all, since it is beasts that wear them?]

In a travel narrative that celebrates the knight's life-threatening exploration of the Mosque of Omar, it is strange to hear the argument that knowledge of India is not likewise worth dying for. Indeed, in its transcription of another traveler's account, in its description of lands not seen by Tafur himself, and in its protagonist's unwillingness to perform deeds of chivalry, the exchange with Nicolò di Conti seems at odds with the several foundational principles of the *Andanças*. Notably, Nicolò's speech abandons the dominant antimony through which the *Andanças* maps the world—Christendom-Islam—in favor of another organizing distinction: civilization-barbarity. Nicolò conjures a phobic image of Asia in which incomparably wealthy kingdoms are separated from one another by vast, barbaric wastelands, lacking any sense of law, order, or reason. This landscape is fashioned out of ancient Roman discourses about the nature of civility and civilization, which were taken up and elaborated by numerous medieval intellectuals and travel writers.[56] Unlike his famous Venetian predecessor Marco Polo, Nicolò recalls the "mountains of gold and of pearls and of gems" he has seen with disdainful ennui. In the absence of courtly refinement and good governance, this embarrassment of exotic riches—the dream of Polo and so many early modern conquistadors—is little more than a pile of rocks.

Without denying Tafur's obvious affinities to subsequent chivalric adventurers, it is also clear that he never sounds more like Petrarch than when he records and tacitly endorses the world-weary assertions of Nicolò di Conti. Nicolò's admonition is an argument against travel for travel's sake, one that Tafur seconds when he—like Poggio—opts to record the merchant's testimony rather than voyage to Asia in person. In redirecting the remainder of his itinerary toward northern Europe, Tafur also sides with Petrarch. Not every journey is worth taking. In most cases, distant, dangerous voyages are better left to the merchants and shipmen who foolishly undertake them in dubious pursuit of novelty and profit. For both Petrarch and Tafur, the ethical force of their experience as travelers finds its clearest articulation in the road *not* taken.

Coda: Beyond 1500; or, Travel's Labor's Lost

A lthough the time frame surveyed by this book stops at 1500, the effort to find meaning in the travail of travel did not. Many of the phenomena that I have discussed continued to flourish and evolve long after the notional denouement of the Middle Ages. The practice of writing in transit provides a prime example. Many early modern travelers would not have dreamed of voyaging without erasable tablets or a notebook of some sort. During his "trauailes heere in the Low Countries," Henry Peacham wrote verses "without other helpe then a bad memorie, and my Table booke," while John Harrison recorded his "meditation coming downe the Rhyne . . . in my table booke."[1] In 1789, Count Leopold Berchtold maintained that the "inquisitive traveller should never be without paper, pen, and ink, in his pocket," adding that the truly diligent wayfarer records impressions throughout the day in a "pocket-book" before transferring them to a more official "journal" at night.[2] It's not just that postmedieval travelers continued to keep notebooks and diaries, but also that they debated the value of doing so along lines developed during the Middle Ages. As Wes Williams has shown, several early modern pilgrims extolled the fidelity of their travel accounts on the grounds that they had been composed day by day as the journey unfolded and were not crafted and embellished at home after the fact.[3] If some viewed daily writing "in the field" as more reliable than other approaches to travel writing, others criticized the triviality of the wayfarer's jottings. Ben Jonson, Daniel Defoe, Jonathan Swift, and Jane Austen numbered among the travel diarist's many postmedieval satirists.

Similarly, medieval cultural debates established the coordinates of subsequent arguments about educational travel. In 1703, Martin Martin decried the frivolity of acculturating tours of Europe. Martin, who wrote two accounts of his travels within his native Scotland, lamented that it had "become customary in those of Quality to travel young" to the Continent and to return with nothing more than "the bare names of famous libraries, stately edifices, fine statues, curious paintings . . . and the like." Meanwhile, these same young people "spend little thought or time on the place of their nativity."[4] Elsewhere, Martin extended this line of argument in a direction that more obviously echoes the opinions of Petrarch and Pero Tafur:

> If we hear at any time a description of some remote corner in the Indies cried in our streets, we presently conclude we have some Divertisement in reading of it, when in the mean time, there are a thousand things nearer us that may engage our thoughts to better purpose. . . . It is a piece of weakness and folly merely to value things because of their distance from the place where we are born: thus, men have traveled far enough in the search of foreign plants and animals, and yet continue strangers to those produced in their own natural [i.e., native] climate.[5]

Jean-Jacques Rousseau's *Émile; or, On Education* (1762) concludes with a disquisition on the pedagogical value of travel. Rousseau enters into this topic via a perennial uncertainty: "It is asked whether it is good for young people to travel, and there is much dispute about it."[6] His conception of travel as a method-governed art shaped by previously acquired habits of learning is, moreover, strikingly medieval in tenor: "Travel—taken as part of education—ought to have its rules. To travel for the sake of traveling is to wander [*errer*], to be a vagabond."[7] In elaborating this position, Rousseau touches on a number of concerns that preoccupied the late Middle Ages, as well: What intellectual and moral benefits are derived from travel? How might the choice of itinerary and the quotidian material practices of the journey facilitate (or thwart) the attainment of those benefits? Is it better to read about the world through travel writing or to visit foreign lands in person? To what extent should one lend credence to travel narratives, and what is the proper place of that genre within the established canon of learning? These questions—inflected by the particularities of Rousseau's time, place, and temperament—were no less important to the authors and readers of medieval travel writing, who were the first to pose several of them.

Some of the most fascinating medieval echoes in later debates about travel are not the result of direct literary influence but can nevertheless be seen as evidence of the Middle Ages' success in reinventing travel as literate labor. Jane Austen, for instance, probably never read the works of the synthetic tradition, and yet the ideal traveler imagined by Elizabeth Bennett in *Pride and Prejudice* (1813) bears a striking resemblance to the dutiful, memory-oriented pilgrim of the Middle Ages:

> Oh! what hours of transport we shall spend! And when we do return, it shall not be like other travellers, without being able to give one accurate idea of anything. We will know where we have gone—we will recollect what we have seen. Lakes, mountains, and rivers shall not be jumbled together in our imaginations; nor when we attempt to describe any particular scene, will we begin quarreling about its relative situation. Let our first effusions be less insupportable than those of the generality of travellers.[8]

In this passage, Austen responds to preoccupations about the advent of mass tourism in much the same way that Felix Fabri did in his initial group tour of the Holy Land: by imagining an alternative kind of journey, one that is strictly governed by a consideration of how it will be remembered and narrated in the future. If the medieval pilgrim and the nineteenth-century novelist sound an analogous tune, it is because both share the conviction that they inhabit a world in which material practice—that is, the speed of transit and the impersonality of the group tour—has sapped the experience of travel of its intellectual and affective fullness. Both also believe that memory is at once the target of this assault as well as the only means by which it can be resisted.

Confronted with many other possible postmedieval exhibits, it is hard not to conclude that the best justifications for the temporal terminus of this current study are pragmatic rather than intellectual. In a world where the dictates of pragmatism held less sway, the nineteenth century would arguably be the most interesting and fruitful place to end a book-length study of the medieval invention of travel. The perfection of the steam engine is perhaps the single development that most contributed to the extinction of the expectations and paradigms discussed in this book. Indeed, the railroad and the steamboat occasion a historical rupture many magnitudes greater than the one that scholars have traditionally attributed to the "rediscovery" of Ptolemy or the expeditions of Columbus.

This was apparent to many who witnessed the initial effects of steam-powered travel. In his classic study *The Railway Journey*, Wolfgang Schivelbusch demonstrated that even the early locomotive engine—which attained maximum speeds of roughly thirty miles per hour—seemed to herald an irreversible revolution in terms of how humans experienced time, space, and place.[9] William Wordsworth and John Ruskin articulated what have become the canonical reactions to this new technology. Wordsworth famously lamented the transformation that train travel wrought on the alpine landscape of the Simplon Pass. Once a sublime destination accessible only at great pains via steep roads and rickety bridges, the pass became—to Wordsworth's mind, at least—a perfunctory day-trip for indifferent tourists:

> Instead of travellers proceeding with leisure to observe and feel, [there] were pilgrims of fashion hurried along in their carriages not a few of them perhaps discussing the merits of the last new Novel or poring over their Guide books or fast asleep.[10]

Ruskin's *Modern Painters* encapsulated this Romantic malaise for the Victorian age with the dictum "All travelling becomes dull in inexact proportion to its rapidity." Like Wordsworth, Ruskin decried the passivity of train travel: "Going by rail road I do not consider as travelling at all; it is merely 'being sent' to a place, and very little different from becoming a parcel."[11] Denied the physical labors of travel, Ruskin's railway adventurer was also shut off from "real knowledge" of the places he or she traveled in order to know. Such "authentic" knowledge depended on an appreciation of the "sublimity given to all places . . . by the true sense of the spaces of earth that separate them." Ruskin deemed such an experience of place impossible in an era in which the traveler no longer journeyed through the world on foot.[12]

It is perhaps too easy to dismiss these criticisms as so much reactionary pearl clutching on the part of the overfed. And, indeed, one cannot help but wonder what medieval travelers might have to say about this nostalgia for an age when travel was *more* laborious. However, the context provided by the Middle Ages affords a more sympathetic (and more illuminating) perspective on figures such as Wordsworth and Ruskin. Wordsworth and Ruskin were heirs to a notion of *travel*, which—for all of its internal variations—found coherence in the links that it forged between knowledge production, literate self-discipline, and the inevitability of travail. In societies where technological advance rendered this third factor exceptional, a ligament that once connected modernity to centuries of human experience was severed. Unmoored from its medieval coordinates, *travel* was reinvented as leisure—its tie to literate labor loosened and its primordial associations with torture and toil all but forgotten.

NOTES

ABBREVIATIONS

In the notes, I have abbreviated the titles of the following frequently cited publications:

CWT   Henry Yule, ed. and trans. *Cathay and the Way Thither.* 2nd ed. Revised by
       Henri Cordier. Hakluyt Society, 2nd ser., nos. 38–41. 4 vols. London: Hakluyt
       Society, 1914–16.

HC   J.B. Harley, David Woodward, et al., eds. *The History of Cartography.* 6 vols.
       Chicago: University of Chicago Press, 1987–2015.

JMEMS *Journal of Medieval and Early Modern Studies.*

MA   Christopher Dawson, ed. *Mission to Asia: Narratives and Letters of the
       Franciscan Missionaries in Mongolia and China in the Thirteenth and
       Fourteenth Centuries.* Trans. "a nun of Stanbrook Abbey." New York: Harper
       and Row, 1966.

PJ   Denys Pringle, ed. and trans. *Pilgrimage to Jerusalem and the Holy Land, 1187–
       1291.* Farnham, Surrey, UK: Ashgate, 2012.

PPTS   *The Library of the Palestine Pilgrims Text Society.* 13 vols. London, 1887–97.
       Repr., New York: AMS Press, 1971. Citations refer to AMS reprint edition.

SF   Anastasius van den Wyngaert, ed. *Sinica Franciscana: Itinera et relationes
       Fratrum Minorum Saeculi XIII et XIV.* Vol. 1. Quaracchi-Florence, Italy:
       Collegium S. Bonaventurae, 1929.

PREFACE

1. Joan-Pau Rubiés, *Travel and Ethnology in the Renaissance: South India through
European Eyes, 1250–1625* (Cambridge: Cambridge University Press 2000), 78. Several
studies of exotic travel writing that do not voice Rubiés's view explicitly reinforce it
tacitly through the relatively slight attention that they pay to works written between *The
Book of John Mandeville* (ca. 1350–71) and the first voyage of Christopher Columbus.

INTRODUCTION TO TRAVAIL AND TRAVEL WRITING

1. Ibn Battuta, *The Travels of Ibn Battuta, AD 1325–1354*, 4 vols., trans. H.A.R. Gibb (Farnham, Surrey, UK: Ashgate, 2010), 1:10–12.

2. *CWT*, 2:229.

3. Nicolas (Nicola) de Martoni, *Liber peregrinationis ad Loca Sancta*, in "Relation du pèlerinage à Jérusalem de Nicolas de Martoni, notaire italien (1394–1395)," ed. Léon LeGrand, *Revue de l'Orient latin* 3 (1895): 566–669 (at 627).

4. Fra Niccolò da Poggibonsi, *Libro d'Oltramare*, in *Pellegrini Scrittori: Viaggiatori toscani del trecento in Terrasanta*, ed. Antonio Lanza and Marcellina Toncarelli (Florence: Ponte Alle Grazie, 1990), 37–38, 127–29.

5. Margery Kempe, *The Book of Margery Kempe*, ed. Lynn Staley (Kalamazoo, MI: Medieval Institute Publications, 1996), 222.

6. The case is slightly different in German, where *reisen*—"to travel"—is related to the activity of mobilizing an army, which is, of course, no mean feat. Brief ruminations on the connection between medieval travel and travail are found in Scott D. Westrem, ed., *Broader Horizons: A Study of Johannes Witte De Hese's Itinerarius and Medieval Travel Narratives* (Cambridge, MA: Medieval Academy of America, 2001); Norbert Ohler, *The Medieval Traveller*, trans. Caroline Hillier (Suffolk, UK: Boydell, 2010), x–xv; and Jean Verdon, *Travel in the Middle Ages*, trans. George Holoch (Notre Dame, IN: University of Notre Dame Press, 2003). My characterization of *travail* draws on: Ernest Klein, *A Comprehensive Etymological Dictionary of the English Language*, 2 vols. (New York: Elsevier, 1966), s.v. "travail, n"; P. Meyer, "L'etymologie du prov. trebalh," *Romania* 17 (1888): 421–24; and Charles Du Fresne, G.A.L. Henschel, P. Carpentier, Christoph Adelung, and Léopold Favre, eds., *Glossarium mediae et infimae Latinitatis*, 10 vols. (Graz, Austria: Akademische Druck-U. Verlagsanstalt, 1954), s.v. "trepalium."

7. Kellie Robertson and Michael Uebel, eds., *The Middle Ages at Work* (New York: Palgrave, 2004), 4, observe that, in English, *labor* has connotations of pain and sacrifice that *work* does not. *Travail*, *labor*, and *work* can be seen as three different vantage points from which to view the same process. Influenced by Nicola Masciandaro, *The Voice of the Hammer: The Meaning of Work in Middle English Literature* (South Bend, IN: University of Notre Dame Press, 2007), I treat *work* as a view of the productive process that has its eye trained almost exclusively on the final result or object of the laborer's effort. *Labor* frames the productive process more subjectively, focusing on the producer's sacrifices of time, energy, health, and material resources while still usually gesturing to some degree toward the end product of the process. *Travail* is the least object oriented of the three terms, emphasizing pain and expenditure, often to the total exclusion of the end result. This constellation of English words has been helpful to my understanding of medieval travel writing, but it is not meant to replace the complicated and evolving uses of *travail* and related terms in the various languages discussed in this book.

8. Robert Bartlett, *The Making of Europe: Conquest, Colonization, and Cultural Change, 950–1350* (Princeton, NJ: Princeton University Press, 1993), 18–21, 101–5.

9. David Abulafia, *A Mediterranean Emporium: The Catalan Kingdom of Majorca* (Cambridge: Cambridge University Press, 1994); Felipe Fernández-Armesto, *Before*

Columbus: Exploration and Colonisation from the Mediterranean to the Atlantic, 1229–1492 (Philadelphia: University of Pennsylvania Press, 1987).

10. Fernández-Armesto, *Before Columbus*; P.E. Russell, *Prince Henry "the Navigator": A Life* (New Haven, CT: Yale University Press, 2000).

11. Steven Epstein, *Genoa and the Genoese, 958–1528* (Chapel Hill: University of North Carolina Press, 2001); Janet L. Abu-Lughod, *Before European Hegemony: The World System, A.D. 1250–1350* (Oxford: Oxford University Press, 1989), 102–34; Maria Georgopoulou, *Venice's Mediterranean Colonies: Architecture and Urbanism* (Cambridge: Cambridge University Press, 2001).

12. Abu-Lughod, *Before European Hegemony*; J.R.S. Phillips, *The Medieval Expansion of Europe* (Oxford: Oxford University Press, 1988).

13. Jonathan Sumption, *Pilgrimage: An Image of Mediaeval Religion* (London: Faber and Faber, 1975), 168–71; Diana Webb, *Pilgrims and Pilgrimage in the Medieval West* (London: I.B. Tauris, 1999), 133–47.

14. Ibn Battuta, *Travels*, 4:916.

15. Ibid., 4:925.

16. Martoni, *Liber peregrinationis*, 667–69.

17. Dante, *Inferno*, trans. Allen Mandelbaum (New York: Bantam, 2004), 26.79–142; cf. Dante, *Paradiso*, trans. Allen Mandelbaum (New York: Bantam, 2004), 27.67–96.

18. Giles Constable, "Opposition to Pilgrimage in the Middle Ages," *Studia Gratiana* 19 (1976): 125–46; Webb, *Pilgrims and Pilgrimage*, 246–53.

19. Caterina Bruschi, *The Wandering Heretics of Languedoc* (Cambridge: Cambridge University Press, 2009), 69–72.

20. On the resistance to female pilgrimage, see Susan Signe Morrison, *Women Pilgrims in Late Medieval England* (London: Routledge, 2000); and Leigh Ann Craig, *Wandering Women and Holy Matrons: Women as Pilgrims in the Later Middle Ages* (Leiden, Netherlands: Brill, 2009).

21. Kellie Robertson, *The Laborer's Two Bodies: Literary and Legal Productions in Britain, 1350–1500* (New York: Palgrave, 2006); Shayne Aaron Legassie, "Chaucer's Pardoner and Host—On the Road, in the Alehouse," *Studies in the Age of Chaucer* 29 (2007): 183–223.

22. Valentin Groebner, *Who Are You? Identification, Deception, and Surveillance in Early Modern Europe*, trans. Mark Kyburz and John Peck (New York: Zone Books, 2007).

23. William IX, Duke of Aquitaine, *Les chansons de Guillaume IX, duc d'Aquitaine (1071–1127)*, ed. Alfred Jeanroy (Paris: H. Champion, 1913), 8–13.

24. See G. Ward Fenley, "Faus Semblant, Fauvel and Renart le Contrefait: A Study in Kinship," *Romanic Review* 23 (1932): 323–31; Timothy L. Stinson, "Illumination and Interpretation: The Depiction and Reception of Faus Semblant in Roman de la Rose Manuscripts," *Speculum* 87 (2012): 469–98.

25. Caesarius of Heisterbach, *Dialogus miraculorum*, 2 vols., ed. J. Strange (Cologne, 1851), 2:131.

26. Juan Ruiz, Arcipreste de Hita, *El libro de buen amor*, ed. Alberto Blecua (Madrid: Cátedra, 2008), 298–301, lines 1198–1209.

27. Manuel R. Lapa, ed., *Cantigas d'escarnho e de mal dizer: Dos cancioneiros medievais Galego-Portugueses* (Vigo, Spain: Editorial Galaxia, 1965), 324.

28. Geoffrey Chaucer, *The House of Fame*, in *The Riverside Chaucer*, 3rd ed., gen. ed. Larry D. Benson (Boston: Houghton Mifflin, 1987), 372, lines 2122–24.

29. Alexandra Gillespie, *Print Culture and the Medieval Author: Chaucer, Lydgate, and Their Books (1473–1557)* (Oxford: Oxford University Press, 2006), 189–202.

30. Anne Hudson, ed., *Two Wycliffite Texts: The Sermon of William Taylor 1406, the Testimony of William Thorpe 1407* (Oxford: Early English Text Society, 1993), 64. I have modernized the orthography slightly.

31. Antoine de La Sale, *Le Paradis de la Reine Sibylle*, ed. Fernand Desonay (Paris: Droz, 1930).

32. Sumption, *Pilgrimage*, 257.

33. Santo Brasca, *Viaggio in Terrasanta di Santo Brasca, 1480, con l'itinerario di Gabriele Capodilista, 1458*, ed. Anna Laura Lepschy et al. (Milan: Longanesi, 1966), 128.

34. See chap. 3, p. 118.

35. See chap. 2, p. 66–74.

36. See chap. 5, p. 174.

37. Arnold von Harff, *The pilgrimage of Arnold von Harff, knight, from Cologne through Italy, Syria, Egypt, Arabia, Ethiopia, Nubia, Palestine, Turkey, France, and Spain, which he accomplished in the years 1496 to 1499*, ed. and trans. Malcolm Letts (Surrey, UK: Ashgate, 2010), 2; Arnold von Harff, *Rome–Jerusalem–Santiago: Das Pilgertagebuch Des Ritters Arnold von Harff (1496–1498)*, ed. Helmut Brall-Tuchel and Folker Reichert (Cologne: Böhlau Verlag, 2007), 34: "Es gibt ja viele mutwillige unbändige Kläffer und Ehrabschneider, die tatsächlich glauben, dass kein anderes Land unter der Sonner sei als jenes, in dem sie leben. Und darum meinen sie, was die Pilger berichten, sei gelogen."

38. For details, see chap. 4, p. 152.

39. Eric J. Leed, *The Mind of the Traveler: From Gilgamesh to Global Tourism* (New York: Harper Collins, 1991), 5–7.

40. Silvia Montiglio, *Wandering in Ancient Greek Culture* (Chicago: University of Chicago Press, 2005), 24–50.

41. On the origins and development of penitential pilgrimage, see Cyrille Vogel, "Le pèlerinage pénitentiel," in *Pellegrinaggi e culto dei Santi in Europa fino alla Iª crociata: [convegno] 8-11 Ott. 1961* (Todi, Italy: Accademia Tudertina, 1963), 37–94.

42. Kempe, *Book of Margery Kempe*, 222.

43. On the plasticity of the concept of pilgrimage, see Dee Dyas, *Pilgrimage in Medieval English Literature, 700–1500* (Woodbridge, Suffolk, UK: D.S. Brewer, 2001); and Julia Bolton Holloway, *Jerusalem: Essays on Pilgrimage and Literature* (New York: AMS Press, 1998). The term *pilgrimage* was already flexible in late antiquity, as shown by Maribel Dietz, *Wandering Monks, Virgins, and Pilgrims: Ascetic Travel in the Mediterranean World, A.D. 300–800* (University Park: Pennsylvania State University Press, 2005).

44. Jonathan Riley-Smith, *The First Crusaders, 1095–1131* (Cambridge: Cambridge University Press, 1997), 1–11, 24–39, 80–97.

45. See chap. 3.

46. Gerhart B. Ladner, "Homo Viator: Mediaeval Ideas on Alienation and Order," *Speculum* 42, no. 2 (1967): 233–59.

47. William Langland, *Piers Plowman: The B Version*, ed. George Kane and E. Talbot Donaldson (Berkeley: University of California Press, 1988), 329, Passus V, lines 529–30.

48. Felix Fabri, *The Wanderings of Felix Fabri*, 3 vols., trans. Aubrey Stewart, in *PPTS*, 7–9 (citation at 7:54–55). Interestingly, Fabri may help explain why Langland, *Piers Plowman*, at V.516, says that the Palmer is "apparailled as a paynym [pagan] in pilgrymes wise."

49. Hudson, *Two Wycliffite Texts*, 64–65.

50. Ibid., 63.

51. Thomas Aquinas, *Political Writings*, ed. and trans. R.W. Dyson (Cambridge: Cambridge University Press, 2004), 50.

52. Franco Mormando, *The Preacher's Demons: Bernardino of Siena and the Social Underworld of Early Renaissance Italy* (Chicago: University of Chicago Press, 1999), 114–19, 121–28, 294–95.

53. See chap. 5, p. 200.

54. Translation mine. Miguel Gual Camarena, *El primer manual hispánico de mercadería (siglo XIV)* (Barcelona: Consejo Superior de Investigaciones Científicas, Instituto de Geografía, Etnología e Historia, 1981), 57:

E per ço com en l'art de la mercaderia, entre les altres arts mesculines, és la millor e pus profitossa que nagunes de les altres arts. . . . Mercader deu aver primerament la sua persona adreta e sana per . . . sostenir los grans traballs e perills que per moltes vaguades han ha sostenir aquells qui de aquest art s'entrameten.

55. James Buzard, *The Beaten Track: European Tourism, Literature, and the Ways to Culture, 1800–1918* (Oxford: Oxford University Press, 1993).

56. The former view is held by Caren Kaplan, *Questions of Travel: Postmodern Discourses of Displacement* (Durham, NC: Duke University Press, 1996); and Janet Wolff, "On the Road Again: Metaphors of Travel in Cultural Criticism," *Cultural Studies* 7, no. 2 (1993): 224–39. The latter, "protravel," position was espoused in James Clifford, *Routes: Travel and Translation in the Late Twentieth Century* (Cambridge, MA: Harvard University Press, 1997).

57. Magister Gregorius, *The Marvels of Rome*, trans. John Osborne (Toronto: Pontifical Institute of Medieval Studies, 1987), 33; Magister Gregorius, *Narracio de mirabilibus urbis Romae*, ed. R.B.C. Huygens (Leiden, Netherlands: Brill, 1970), 41.

58. Gregorius, *Marvels*, 20; Gregorius, *Narracio*, 29: "Ceterum peregrinorum et Romanorum super hac re vanas fabulas penitus declinabo eamque originem huius operis assignabo, quam a senioribus et cardinalibus et viris doctissimis didici."

59. Gregorius, *Marvels*, 35; Gregorius, *Narracio*, 29.

60. Gregorius, *Marvels*, 26; Gregorius, *Narracio*, 20.

61. Edward W. Said, *Orientalism* (London: Penguin, 1978; repr., 1995); Suzanne Conklin Akbari, *Idols in the East: European Representations of Islam and the Orient, 1100–1450* (Ithaca, NY: Cornell University Press, 2009); Mary B. Campbell, *Witness and the Other World: Exotic European Travel Writing, 400–1600* (Ithaca, NY: Cornell University

Press, 1988); Stephen Greenblatt, *Marvelous Possessions: The Wonder of the New World* (Chicago: University of Chicago Press, 1991); Geraldine Heng, *Empire of Magic: Medieval Romance and the Politics of Cultural Fantasy* (New York: Columbia University Press, 2003); Shirin A. Khanmohamadi, *In Light of Another's Word: European Ethnography in the Middle Ages* (Philadelphia: University of Pennsylvania Press, 2014); Kim M. Phillips, *Before Orientalism: Asian Peoples and Cultures in European Travel Writing, 1245–1510* (Philadelphia: University of Pennsylvania Press, 2014); Rubiés, *Travel and Ethnology.* A handful of important essay collections have modeled a greater range of possible approaches to exotic travel writing without necessarily advocating for this expansion as a methodological principle, particularly: Scott D. Westrem, ed., *Discovering New Worlds: Essays on Medieval Exploration and Imagination* (New York: Garland, 1991); Palmira J. Brummett, ed., *The "Book" of Travels: Genre, Ethnology, and Pilgrimage, 1250–1700* (Leiden, Netherlands: Brill, 2009); Sylvia Tomasch and Sealy Gilles, eds., *Text and Territory: Geographical Imagination in the European Middle Ages* (Philadelphia: University of Pennsylvania Press, 1998); John M. Ganim and Shayne Aaron Legassie, eds., *Cosmopolitanism and the Middle Ages* (New York: Palgrave, 2013).

62. K. Phillips, *Before Orientalism*, 51.

63. This observation is so common that I will simply cite the most memorably worded example: "As a literary form, travel writing is a notoriously raffish open house where very different genres are likely to end up in the same bed. It accommodates the private diary, the essay, the short story, the prose poem, the rough note and polished table talk with indiscriminate hospitality." Thanks to Jonathan Raban, *For Love and Money: Writing-Reading-Travelling, 1968–1987* (London: Picador, 1988), 253–54.

64. Walter Benjamin, "The Storyteller," in *Illuminations: Essays and Reflections,* trans. Harry Zohn (New York: Random House, 2007), 83–110, at 85.

65. Michel de Certeau, *The Practice of Everyday Life,* trans. Steven F. Rendall (Berkeley: University of California Press, 1988), 115.

66. Fredric Jameson, *The Political Unconscious: Narrative as a Socially Symbolic Act* (London: Routledge, 1983), 93.

67. A good illustration is found in Henry Ansgar Kelly, *Ideas and Forms of Tragedy from Aristotle to the Middle Ages* (Cambridge: Cambridge University Press, 1993). K. Phillips, *Before Orientalism*, 51–54, has recently made the same observation about medieval classifications of travel writing. The impossibility of generalizing about the defining traits of medieval travel writing is the opening salvo of Paul Zumthor's "The Medieval Travel Narrative," trans. Catherine Peebles, *New Literary History* 25, no. 4 (1994): 809–24.

68. For observations about the relative durability and systematicity of documentary genres, see Alfred Hiatt, "Genre without System," in *Middle English: Oxford Twenty-First Century Approaches to Literature,* ed. Paul Strohm (Oxford: Oxford University Press, 2007), 277–94, at 290–92.

69. While acknowledging the "multiform" nature of medieval travel writing, Jean Richard, *Les récits de voyages et de pèlerinages* (Turnhout, Belgium: Brepols, 1981), classifies texts according to certain dominant rhetorical features. An even more rigorously narratological set of criteria underpins Michèle Guéret-Laferté, *Sur les routes de l'Empire Mongol: Ordre et rhetorique des relations de voyage aux XIIIᵉ et XIVᵉ siècles* (Paris:

H. Champion, 1994), which—in contrast to Richard—develops a rationale for considering apparently heterogeneous texts as a single corpus. Antonio García Espada, "Marco Polo, Odorico of Pordenone, the Crusades, and the Role of the Vernacular in the First Descriptions of the Indies," *Viator* 40, no. 1 (2009): 201–22, argues that, when treated with subtlety, manuscript contexts and other evidence of medieval reader response provide a fruitful way to classify medieval travel writing (a category that García Espada himself is admittedly circumspect about). My book draws on many of these scholars' heuristic conceptions of genre without subscribing to any of them exclusively.

70. Joan-Pau Rubiés, "Travel Writing as a Genre: Facts, Fictions, and the Invention of a Scientific Discourse in Early Modern Europe," *Journeys* 1 (2000): 5–33 (at 7).

71. Jan Borm, "Defining Travel: On the Travel Book, Travel Writing and Terminology," in *Perspectives on Travel Writing*, ed. Glenn Hooper and Tim Youngs (Aldershot, UK: Ashgate, 2004), 14.

72. M. Campbell, *Witness and the Other World*, 5–6.

INTRODUCTION TO PART ONE

1. Translation mine. Giovanni Boccaccio, *Trattatello in laude di Dante*, ed. Pier Giorgio Ricci, in *Tutte le opere di Giovanni Boccaccio*, ed. Vittore Branca, 10 vols. (Milan: Mondadori, 1964), 3:423–538, §113:

> —Donne, vedete colui che va ne l'inferno e torna quando gli piace, e qua su reca novelle di coloro che là giù sono?—Alla quale una dell'altre rispose semplicemente:—In verità tu dèi dir vero: non vedi tu come egli ha la barba crespa e il color bruno per lo caldo e per lo fummo che è là giù?—Le quali parole udendo egli dir dietro a sé, e conoscendo che da pura credenza delle donne venivano, piacendogli, e quasi contento che esse in cotale oppinione fossero, sorridendo alquanto, passò avanti.

2. Ignorant of basic literary concepts such as title, genre, *divisio*, and allegory, the women misconstrue Dante's fictive, allegorical pilgrimage as a recurring deed of real-life heroism. As Boccaccio would later argue in his *Expositions* on the *Comedy*, Dante christened his poem with its seemingly incongruous generic title precisely in order to underscore the moral-allegorical significance of the upward trajectory of his journey from hell to paradise. See Giovanni Boccaccio, *Boccaccio's Expositions on Dante's "Comedy,"* trans. Michael Papio (Toronto: University of Toronto Press, 2009), 41–43.

CHAPTER ONE

1. *OED Online*, s.v. "exotic, a. and n.," *The Oxford English Dictionary*, 2nd ed. (Oxford: Oxford University Press, 1989), accessed 30 April 2014, http://dictionary.oed.com/.

2. John Gerard, *The herball; or, Generall historie of plantes. Gathered by Iohn Gerarde of London Master in Chirurgerie very much enlarged and amended by Thomas Iohnson citizen and apothecarye of London* (London: printed by Adam Islip, Ioice Norton, and Richard Whitakers, 1633), 1610.

3. Particularly influential on this current study are Mary Louise Pratt, *Imperial Eyes: Travel Writing and Transculturation* (New York: Routledge, 1992); James Clifford, ed.,

Writing Culture: The Poetics and Politics of Ethnography (Berkeley: University of California Press, 2010).

4. Edward W. Said, *Culture and Imperialism* (New York: Vintage Books, 1994), xxi.

5. Ibid., 132.

6. Anne McClintock, *Imperial Leather: Race, Gender, and Sexuality in the Colonial Contest* (New York: Routledge, 1995), 207–30.

7. Gayatri Spivak, *Outside in the Teaching Machine* (New York: Routledge, 1993), 179–200; Graham Huggan, *The Postcolonial Exotic: Marketing the Margins* (London: Routledge, 2001).

8. Mary W. Helms, *Ulysses' Sail: An Ethnographic Odyssey of Power, Knowledge, and Geographical Distance* (Princeton, NJ: Princeton University Press, 1988). As Helms illustrates throughout, "distance" is culturally and historically relative, and often an index of the peril and travail involved in getting from one place to another.

9. Ibid., 1–19.

10. For praise of William: Khanmohamadi, *In Light*, 59–62; M. Campbell, *Witness and the Other World*, 112–20; Leonardo Olschki, *Marco Polo's Asia: An Introduction to His "Description of the World" Called "Il Milione"* (Berkeley: University of California Press 1960), 69; and C. Raymond Beazley, *The Dawn of Modern Geography: A History of Exploration and Geographical Science*, 3 vols. (London: Frowe, 1897–1906), 2:375–79. Peter Jackson, "William of Rubruck in the Mongol Empire," in *Travel Fact and Travel Fiction: Studies on Fiction, Literary Tradition, Scholarly Discovery and Observation in Travel Writing*, ed. Zweder R.W.M. Martels, 54–71 (Leiden, Netherlands: Brill, 1994), 53–55, foregrounds the violent call for crusade while at the same time characterizing the account as "more human" than that John of Plano Carpini. An exceptionally straightforward reckoning with the conclusion of the *Itinerarium* is found in Adnan Husain, "Mission to Crusade: Friar William of Rubruck's Journey to the Mongols," in *The Middle Ages in Texts and Texture: Reflections on Medieval Sources*, ed. Jason Glenn, 245–58 (Toronto: University of Toronto Press, 2011).

11. M. Campbell, *Witness and the Other World*, 114.

12. Henri Cordier and Henry Yule, *The Book of Ser Marco Polo, the Venetian: Concerning the Kingdoms and Marvels of the East*, 2 vols. (London: J. Murray, 1903), 1:107.

13. On these stylistic issues, see Valeria Bertolucci Pizzorusso, "Enunciazione e produzione del testo nel *Milione*," *Studi mediolatini e volgari* 25 (1977): 8–10; John Larner, *Marco Polo and the Discovery of the World* (New Haven, CT: Yale University Press, 1999), 48–51; Dietmar Rieger, "Marco Polo und Rustichello da Pisa: Der Reisende und sein Erzähler," in *Reisen und Reiseliteratur im Mittelalter und in der Frühen Neuzeit*, ed. Xenja von Ertzdorff et al., 289–312 (Amsterdam: Rodopi, 1992); Cesare Segre, "Chi ha scritto il *Milione* di Marco Polo?," in *I viaggi del Milione: Itinerari testuali, vettori di trasmissione e metamorfosi del Devisement du monde di Marco Polo e Rustichello da Pisa nella pluralità delle attestazioni*, 5–16 (Rome: Tiellemedia, 2008); Simon Gaunt, *Marco Polo's "Le Devisement du Monde": Narrative Voice, Language and Diversity* (Cambridge: D.S. Brewer, 2013), 41–78.

14. For overviews of these generic debates, see K. Phillips, *Before Orientalism*, 44–58, and Gaunt, *Marco Polo's "Le Devisement,"* 28–31.

15. William Chester Jordan, *Louis IX and the Challenge of the Crusade: A Study in Rulership* (Princeton, NJ: Princeton University Press, 1979), 33–34. On the mendicant orders' interactions with Mongol rulers, see Igor de Rachewiltz, *Papal Envoys to the Great Khans* (Stanford, CA: Stanford University Press, 1971); Jean Richard, *La Papauté et les missions d'orient au moyen âge (XIIIᵉ–XVᵉ siècles)*, Collection de l'École française de Rome 33 (Rome: École française de Rome, 1977); and Peter Jackson, *The Mongols and the West, 1221–1410* (Harlow, UK: Pearson, 2005).

16. *MA*, 220; *SF*, 331:

> Antiquitus transiverunt per istas regiones viri fortes, et prosperati sunt; habuerunt tamen fortissimos resistentes, quos Deus modo delevit de terra. . . . Fidenter dico si vellent vestri rustici, non dicam Reges et milites, ire sicut vadunt Reges Tartrorum et talibus esse cibariis contenti, possent acquirere totum mundum.

17. On Bacon's criticism of crusading, see Amanda Power, *Roger Bacon and the Defence of Christendom* (Cambridge: Cambridge University Press, 2013), 251–59.

18. *SF*, 171: "Visum fuit michi recte quod ingrederer quoddam aliud seculum."

19. Such considerations are part of what Igor Kopytoff has called "the cultural biography of things." For elaboration, see "The Cultural Biography of Things: Commoditization as Process," in *The Social Life of Things: Commodities in Cultural Context*, ed. Arjun Appadurai, 64–91 (Cambridge: Cambridge University Press, 1986), 66–68.

20. Paul Freedman, *Out of the East: Spices in the Medieval Imagination* (New Haven, CT: Yale University Press, 2008), 130–45.

21. In a famous discussion of *commodity fetishism*, Karl Marx (*Capital*, vol. 1, trans. Ben Fowkes [London: Penguin Classics, 1990]) observes: "It is nothing but the definite social relation between men themselves which assumes here, for them, the fantastic form of a relation between things. . . . The products of the human brain appear as autonomous figures endowed with a life of their own, which enter into relations both with each other and with the human race" (165). One could distinguish medieval and modern exoticism along similar lines, since the commodity fetish functions by means of logical reversals analogous to the ones outlined in Huggan, *Postcolonial Exotic*: "Although the word 'exotic' currently has widespread application, it continues—possibly because of this—to be commonly misunderstood. For the exotic is not, as is often supposed, an inherent quality to be found 'in' certain people, distinctive objects, or specific places; exoticism describes, rather, a particular mode of aesthetic perception—one which renders people, objects and places strange even as it domesticates them" (13).

22. On exotic gifts and premodern tributary economies, see Anthony Cutler, "Significant Gifts: Patterns of Exchange in Late Antique, Byzantine, and Early Islamic Diplomacy," *JMEMS* 38, no. 1 (2008): 79–101; and Anthony Cutler, "Gifts and Gift Exchange as Aspects of the Byzantine, Arab, and Related Economies," *Dumbarton Oaks Papers* 55 (2001): 247–78.

23. Murasaki Shikibu, *The Tale of Genji*, trans. Royall Tyler (New York: Penguin, 2003), 136.

24. Benjamin of Tudela, *The Itinerary of Benjamin of Tudela: Travels in the Middle Ages*, trans. Marcus Nathan Adler (New York: Nightingale, 2004), 97.

25. *The Arabian Nights*, trans. Husain Haddawy (New York: Norton, 1990), 464–65.

26. Petrarch, *Letters on Familiar Matters*, 3 vols., trans. Aldo S. Bernardo (Ithaca, NY: Italica Press, 2005), 1:183; Petrarch, *Lettres familières / Rerum familiarium*, 6 vols., ed. Ugo Dotti et al. (Paris: Les Belles Lettres, 2002–15), 2:39.

27. Möngke, the first khan of the Toluid line, had recently ascended to the throne with the help of his mother, Sorghanghtani Beki (d. 1252), at the expense of Batu and kept a wary eye on him and other rivals. For more on the dynastic politics of the Mongol Empire, see Thomas Allsen, "The Rise of the Mongolian Empire and Mongol Rule in North China," in *The Cambridge History of China*, vol. 6, ed. Herbert Franke and Denis C. Twitchett (Cambridge: Cambridge University Press, 1994), 321–413.

28. Passages in the *Itinerarium* suggest that news of Friar Andrew of Longjumeau's journey had prompted William of Rubruck to minister to Christians who had been subjugated during the Mongol conquests of Hungary and Armenia (*MA*, 135–36; *SF*, 289–90).

29. *MA*, 64.

30. *MA*, 202; *SF*, 306.

31. *MA*, 106; *SF*, 188: "Bene cavi quod nunquam dixi me esse nuncium vestrum. Tunc quesiverunt quid esset in bigis, utrum esset aurum vel argentum vel vestes preciose que defferrem Sartach."

32. For background, see Rosalind B. Brooke, *Early Franciscan Government* (Cambridge: Cambridge University Press, 1958), 86–88, 147–51, 248–51; John Moorman, *A History of the Franciscan Order from Its Origins to the Year 1517* (Oxford: Clarendon Press, 1968), 116–19, 307–19.

33. *MA*, 107; *SF*, 188: "Et omnia que videbant super famulos nostros: cultellos, cirothecas, bursas, corrigias, omnia admirantes et volentes habere. . . . Tunc dicebant quod essem baratator."

34. *MA*, 205; *SF* 310:

Ipsi autem tenebant tres vestes sive tunicas et dixerunt nobis: "Vos non vultis recipere aurum vel argentum et stetistis hic diu orantes pro ipso Chan, ipse rogat ut ad minus recipiatis unusquisque vestrum simplicem vestem, ne vacui recedatis ab eo." Tunc oportuit nos recipere eas ob reverentiam ipsius, quia multum habent pro malo quando contempnuntur munera eorum. Prius frequenter fecerat inquiri a nobis quid vellemus, et semper respondebamus idem, in tantum quod ipsi christiani insultabant ipsis ydolatris, qui nichil aliud querunt nisi munera.

35. *MA*, 133; *SF*, 221: "In principio despiciebat nos multum ductor noster et fastidiebat eum ducere tam viles homines."

36. *MA*, 133; *SF*, 196: "Si arripiebat eos appetitus purgandi ventrem, non elongabant se a nobis quantum possit faba iactari, imo iuxta nos colloquentes mutuo faciebant immunditias suas, et multa alia faciebant que errant supra modum tediosa."

37. *MA*, 129; *SF*, 216: "Et aliquando habuit socius meus tantam famem, quod dicebat mihi quasi lacrimando: 'Videtur michi quod nunquam comederim.'"

38. *MA*, 161; *SF*, 257:

Venimus ad domum nostram frigidam et vacuam. Lectiscrinia providebant et coopertoria, afferebant etiam nobis materiam ignis et dabant carnem unius arietis parvi et macilenti tribus nobis, cibum pro sex diebus. . . . Iste era cibus noster, et bene suffecisset nobis si permisissent nos comedere in pace. Sed tot sunt famelici, quibus non providetur de cibo, qui quam cito videbant nos parare cibum, ingerebant se super nos, quos oportebat comedere nobiscum. Ibi expertus sum quantum matirium sit largiri in paupertate.

39. Francis of Assisi, *Early Documents*, 4 vols., ed. Regis Armstrong, Wayne Hellman, and William Short (New York: New City Press, 1999–2003), 2:602–4. For background and medieval sources on this journey, see John Tolan, *Saint Francis and the Sultan: A Curious History of a Christian-Muslim Encounter* (Oxford: Oxford University Press, 2009).

40. Francis of Assisi, *Early Documents*, 2:603–4.

41. *MA*, 225; *SF*, 353: "hoc mirabile factum."

42. *MA*, 153; *SF*, 248: "Nos de longe venimus; primo si placet vobis, cantabimus laudes Deo qui nos salvos de tam longinquo usque huc perduxit."

43. See especially Lorraine Daston and Katherine Park, *Wonders and the Order of Nature, 1150–1750* (Cambridge: Zone Books, 1998); Caroline Walker Bynum, "Wonder," in *Metamorphosis and Identity*, 37–75 (Cambridge, MA: MIT Press, 2001); and Paula Findlen, *Possessing Nature: Museums, Collecting, and Scientific Culture in Early Modern Italy* (Berkeley: University of California Press, 2010).

44. The best overview of this conceptual terrain is found in Bynum, "Wonder," 42–53, 71–72.

45. Ibid., 48–52.

46. Ibid., 40–70. Note that, at the level of terminology, marvels and miracles were often conflated under the category *mirabilia*.

47. Ibid., 65–68.

48. *PJ*, 101.

49. *MA*, 118–19; *SF*, 202–3:

> Ego autem indutus preciosioribus vestibus, accepi in pectore pulvinar quod erat valde pulchrum, et bibliam quam dederatis michi, et psalterium pulcherrimum quod dederat michi domina Regina, in quo erant picture valde pulchre. . . . Tunc ingressi sumus cantando: *Salve regina*. In introitu autem hostii stabat bancus cum cosmos et cum ciphis, et convenerant omnes uxores eius, et ipsi Moal ingredientes nobis cum comprimebant nos. Ille Coiac tulit ei turribulum cum incenso, quod ipse respexit tenes in manu diligenter. Postea tulit ei psalterium quod valde respexit et uxor eius sedens iuxta eum; postea tulit bibliam. Et ipse quesivit si Evangelium esset ibi. Dixi: "Etiam tota sacra Scriptura."

50. On ecclesiastical and monastic marvel-collecting, see: Daston and Park, *Wonders and the Order of Nature*, 67–83; Pierre Alain Mariaux, "Collecting (and Display)," *A Companion to Medieval Art: Romanesque and Gothic in Northern Europe*, ed. Conrad Rudolph, 213–32 (Malden, MA: Blackwell Press, 2006).

51. Peter of Limoges, *The Moral Treatise on the Eye*, trans. Richard Newhauser (Toronto: Pontifical Institute, 2012), 162.

52. Cited in Mariaux, "Collecting (and Display)," 219.

53. H.W. Jansen, *Apes and Ape Lore in the Middle Ages* (London: Warburg Institute, 1952), 30; Shayne Aaron Legassie, "The Lies of the Painters: Artisan Trickery and the Labor of Painting in Boccaccio's *Decameron* and Sacchetti's *Trecentonovelle*," *JMEMS* 43, no. 3 (2013): 487–519 (at 503–5).

54. von Harff, *Pilgrimage*, 98–99.

55. *MA*, 118; *SF*, 201-2:

Quod et fecimus, honerantes bigam unam libris et capella, et aliam pane et vino et fructibus. Tunc fecit omnes libros et vestes explicari. Et circumstabant nos in equis multi Tattari et christiani et sarraceni. Quibus inspectis, quesivit si vellem omnia ista dare domino suo. Quo audito expavi et displicuit michi verbum. Dissimulans tamen respondi: "Domine, rogamus quatinus dominus vester dignetur recipere panem istum et vinum et fructus non pro exennio, quia exiguum quid est, sed pro benedictione ne vacua manu veniamus coram eo. . . . Vestes enim sacrate sunt, et non licet eas contingere nisi sacerdotibus." Tunc precepit quod indueremus nos ituri coram domino suo, quod et fecimus.

56. *MA*, 120; *SF*, 203-4:

Unum erat michi solatium, quod quando presensi cupiditatem eorum, ego subtraxi de libris bibliam et sententias et alios libros quos magis diligebam. Psalterium domine Regine non fui ausus subtrahere, quia illud fuerat nimis notatum propter aureas picturas que erant in eo.

57. Kopytoff, "Cultural Biography of Things," 73-77.

58. Philip D. Curtin, *Cross-Cultural Trade in World History* (Cambridge: Cambridge University Press, 1984), mounts a world-historical survey of this predilection on the part of merchants.

59. Here, it is useful to think of the archaic—ritual and juridical—notions of the sacred explored in the writings of Agamben and Bataille, particularly in Giorgio Agamben, *Homo Sacer: Sovereign Power and Bare Life*, trans. Daniel Heller-Roazen (Stanford, CA: Stanford University Press, 1998); Georges Bataille, *The Accursed Share*, 2 vols., trans. Robert Hurley (New York: Zone Books, 1988).

60. On the prohibition against anyone other than consecrated priests touching consecrated liturgical vessels, see Gratian, *Decretum*, "De consecratione," *Dist I*, can. 41-42. From Gratian, *Decretum: First Recension*, ed. Anders Winroth, https://sites.google.com /a/yale.edu/decretumgratiani/home.

61. Thomas Aquinas, *Summa theologica*, vol. 5, pt. 3, *Second Section and Supplement*, trans. Fathers of the English Dominican Province (New York: Cosimo, 2007), Q 83, art. 3, p. 2510. (Emphasis mine.)

62. See Thomas T. Allsen, *Culture and Conquest in Mongol Eurasia* (Cambridge: Cambridge University Press, 2001), 83-186.

63. Ibid., 198.

64. Leonardo Olschki, *Guillaume Boucher, a French Artist at the Court of the Khans* (Baltimore: Johns Hopkins Press, 1946), 28-44.

65. *MA*, 166; *SF*, 264:

Hanc crucem attulerat quidam Hermenus qui venerat cum monacho, ut dicebat de Ierusalem, et erat argentea appendens forte quatuor marchas et habebat iiij gemmas in angulis et unam in medio; ymaginem Salvatoris non habebat quia erubescunt hoc Ermeni et nestorini ut appareat Christus affixus cruci.

66. *MA*, 165; *SF*, 263:

Tunc monachus fecit eam surgere de lecto et fecit eam adorare crucem, ter genua flectendo et frontem dando ad terram, ipso stante cum cruce ad latus occidentale domus et illa ad orientale. Hoc facto mutaverunt loca, et monachus ivit cum cruce ad orientem et illa ad occidentem; et ipse precepit audacter ei, quamvis esset ita debilis quod vix posset stare super pedes, ut iterum se prosterneret ter adorando crucem ad orientem more christianorum, quod et fecit. Et docuit eam facere signum crucis ante faciem suam.

67. *MA*, 169; *SF*, 267:

Et miseri illi sacerdotes nunquam docuerunt eam fidem, nec monuerunt ut baptizaretur. Ego autem sedebam ibi mutus non valens aliquid dicere, sed ipsa docebat me adhuc ydioma. Nec reprehendunt sacerdotes in aliquo sortilegio; ibi enim vidi quatuor gladios a vagina extractos usque ad medietatem, unum ad capud lectuli domine, alium ad pedes et alios duos ad utrumque latus hostii unum. Vidi et ibi unum calicem argenteum de calicibus nostris, qui forte fuerat captus vel raptus in aliqua ecclesia Hungarie, et erat suspensus ad parietem plenus cineribus, et super cinerem illum erat unus niger lapis, et de talibus nunquam docent eos sacerdotes quod mala sint.

68. Supple discussions of this episode are waged in Khanmohamadi, *In Light*, 79–82; and Jackson, "William of Rubruck."

69. *MA*, 160; *SF*, 256:

Ipsa enim die fecerat convivium Manguchan; et mos eius est quod talibus diebus, quibus divini sui dicunt ei festos vel sacerdotes nestorini aliquando sacros, quod ipse tunc tenet curiam. Et talibus diebus primo veniunt sacerdotes christiani cum suo apparatu et orant pro eo et benedicunt cifum suum; istis recedentibus, veniunt sacerdotes sarraceni et faciunt similiter; post hos veniunt sacerdotes ydolatre idem facientes. Et dicebat michi monachus quod solum credit christianis, tamen vult ut omnes orent pro eo. Et ipse mentiebatur quia nullis credit sicut postea audietis; tamen omnes sequuntur curiam suam sicut musce mel, et omnibus dat, et omnes credunt se esse familiares eius et omnes prophetant ei prospera.

70. This section will focus primarily on what is thought to be the earliest version of the work, the Franco-Italian version commonly known as the "F." The text of the F version comes from Marco Polo, *Milione* = *Le divisament du monde: Il milione nelle redazioni Toscana e Franco-Italiana*, ed. Gabriella Ronchi with Cesare Segre (Milan: Mondadori, 1982).

71. Just about every detail of this timeline—from dates to assertions of fact—has been the subject of controversy. The most notorious example is Frances Wood, *Did Marco Polo Go to China?* (Boulder, CO: Westview, 1996). Wood's controversial and largely discredited answer: no. For rebuttals, see Igor de Rachewiltz, "Marco Polo Went to China," *Zentralasiatische Studien* 27 (1997): 34–92; Larner, *Marco Polo*, 58–63; and Peter Jackson, "Marco Polo and His 'Travels,'" *Bulletin of the School of Oriental and African Studies* 61 (1998): 82–101. These discussions also include acknowledgments of the contradictions in the timeline suggested by the *Divisament*.

72. Consuelo Wager Dutschke, "Francesco Pipino and the Manuscripts of Marco Polo's 'Travels'" (PhD diss., University of California, Los Angeles, 1993), 276–82, estimates 135. Larner, *Marco Polo*, 109–15, puts the number at 150. For more on the manuscript tradition, see John Critchley, *Marco Polo's Book* (Aldershot, UK: Variorum, 1992), 157–77. Though improved in some details by Dutschke, Luigi Foscolo Benedetto's *Il milione: Prima edizione integrale, a cura di Luigi Foscolo Benedetto* (Florence: Olschki,

1928)—a critical edition of the Franco-Italian version of the *Divisament*—is still a trove
of unique insights. Initiates looking for an English translation are best served by Marco
Polo, *The Description of the World*, 2 vols., ed. and trans. A.C. Moule and Paul Pelliot
(London: George Routledge and Sons, 1938).

73. Dutschke, "Francesco Pipino" (206–61), estimates that approximately a third
of extant manuscripts of the *Divisament* are copies of Pipino's translation. The best
overviews of the reception of the *Divisament* are: Suzanne C. Akbari and Amilcare A.
Iannucci with John Tulk, eds., *Marco Polo and the Encounter of East and West* (Toronto:
University of Toronto Press, 2008); Critchley, *Marco Polo's Book*; and Larner, *Marco
Polo*. For Columbus's copy, see Marco Polo, *El libro de Marco Polo (ejemplar anotado por
Cristóbal Colón y que se conserva en la Biblioteca Capitular y Colombina de Sevilla)*,
trans. Juan Gil (Madrid: Testimonio, 1986).

74. Polo, *Divisament*, 305:

> Seignors enperaor et rois, dux et marquois, cuens, chevaliers et b[o]rgio[i]s, et toutes
> gens que volés savoir les deverses jenerasions des homes et les deversités des deverses
> region dou monde, si prennés cestui livre et le feites lire. Et qui trovererés toutes les
> grandismes mervoilles et les grant diversités de la grande Harminie et de Persie et des
> Tartars et <de> Indie, et de maintes autres provinces, sicom notre livre voç contera por
> ordre apertemant, sicome meisser Marc Pol, sajes et noble citaiens de Venece, raconte.

75. Polo, *Divisament*, 434: "Et sachiés que unques ne fu, ne croi que soit, nulz homes
que si grant seulas ne si grant delit poist <avoir> en cest monde com cestui fait, ne que si
en aust le p<o>oir de fer."

76. Polo, *Divisament*, 418–19: "Et voç di que le grant sire, que launques l'en li content que fust un biaus arbres, il le fasoit prendre con toutes le racies et co<n> moute
[t]er[r]e et le fasoit porter a cel mont con les leofant. Et fust l'albre grant quant il vou-
sisti . . . et en ceste mainere hi avoit les plus biaus arbres dou monde."

77. Polo, *Divisament*, 318:

> Quant il retornoient a lui et li disoient l'anbasee por coi il estoit alés et no li savoient
> dir autres noveles de les contrees ou il estoient alés, il disoit elz qu'il estoient foux et
> non saichan[ç] et disio[t] que miaus ameroit oir les noveles et les costumes et les usajes
> de celle estra<n>jes contree qu'il ne fasoit oir celç por coi il li avoit mandé, et Marc, ke
> bien savoie tout ce, quant il ala en cele mesajarie, toutes les nuvités et tutes les stranges
> chauses qu'il avoit, met[t]toit son entent por coi il le seust redire au grant kaan.

78. Polo, *Divisament*, 319:

> Et il achevoit moult bien la beisogne et li savoit dir mai<n>tes novités et maintes
> estranges chouses. Et le grant kan il plasoit tant l'afer de meser Marc que il le vo<lo>it
> grant bien et li fasoit si grant onor et le tenoit si pres de soi que les autres baron en
> avent grant enoie. Or ço fui la raison por coi meser Marc seç plus de celes couses de
> celle contree que nulz autres home, qu'il cher<c>e plus de celes estranges parties ke
> nulz omes ke unques nasquist.

79. Sharon Kinoshita, "Marco Polo's *Le Devisement dou Monde* and the Tributary
East," in *Marco Polo and the Encounter of East and West*, ed. Suzanne Conklin Akbari
and Amilcare A. Iannucci with John Tulk, 60–86 (Toronto: University of Toronto Press,
2008), 71–72.

80. Polo, *Divisament*, 309: "E trovent grant mervoilles et diverses coses les quelç ne voç conteron ci por ce que messier Marc, fil de meser Nicolau, que toutes cestes choses vit ausint, le voç contera en ceste livre avant apertemant."

81. Polo, *Divisament*, 309–10:

VI. Comant les II Frers Vindrent au Grant Kaan
Et quant mesere Nicolau et mesere Mafeu furent venu au grant seignor, il les recevi honorablement et fait elç grant joie et gran feste: il a mout grant leesse de lor venue. Il les demande de maintes coses: primermant de les emperaors, comant il mantent lor segnoire et lor tere in justice et comant il vont a bataile et tous leur afer; et après lor demande des rois et des princes et d'autres baron.

VII. Comant le Grant Kaan Demande as II Frers des Affer des Cristienç
Et aprés lor demande de meser l'apostoille et de tous les fais de le yglise romane et de tous les costumes des latin. Et messere Nicolau e meser Mafeu lui distrent toute la verité de chascun por soi bie<n> et ordreemant et sajemant come sajes homes qu'il estoient ke bien s[a]voient la lengue de Tartarç <ce> [est] la tartaresce.

82. Polo, *Divisament*, 316: "Et ce que il trovent en la voie ne voç firon mencion [or], por ce que noç le voç conteron en notre livre avant."

83. Ibn Battuta visited this shrine as well. See Ibn Battuta, *Travels*, 4:849–54.

84. On the syncretism that characterizes this episode, see Eugenio Burgio, "Marco Polo e gli 'idolatri,'" in *Le voci del medioevo: Testi, immagini, tradizioni*, ed. Nicolò Passero and Sonia Barillari, 31–62 (Alessandria, Italy: Edizioni dell'Orso, 2005); and Michael Calabrese, "Between Despair and Ecstasy: Marco Polo's Life of the Buddha," *Exemplaria* 9 (1997): 189–229.

85. Polo, *Divisament*, 576: "en autre partie dou monde." This is an apparent reference to the belief that his skull was buried on Mount Calvary, beneath the site of Christ's crucifixion.

86. Though the *Divisament* treats the disagreement about the relics as one that pits "Muslims" against "idolaters," Sri Pada was a pilgrimage destination for medieval Muslims, Hindus, and Buddhists perhaps as early as the eleventh century. Buddhists associated the peak with the Buddha, Hindus with the deity Shiva. Moreover, the claim that Adam tarried on the mountain after his exile from Eden was not exclusively a "Muslim" belief but also one held by some Christians. In the fourteenth century, both Ibn Battuta and Franciscan missionary John Marignolli completed the Sri Pada pilgrimage. Marignolli devoutly knelt down beside a Muslim pilgrim from Spain to measure the footprint attributed to Adam. See Markus Aksland, *The Sacred Footprint: A Cultural History of Adam's Peak* (Bangkok: Orchid Press, 2001).

87. Polo, *Divisament*, 576:

Le g<r>ant kaan adonc comande que toutes les jens, e regulés et autres, aleisent encontre celles reliquies, que lor estoit fair entendant que fuernt de Adan. E porcoi voç firoie lonc conter? sachiés tout voirmant que toutes les jens de Ganbalu alent encontre a ceste relique; e les regulés le recevent e les aportent au grant can que molt les recevi con grant joie e con grant feste e con grant reveren[c]e.

88. Larner, *Marco Polo*, 47–51, 56–57.

89. Benedetto, *Milione*, xix–xxiii.

90. The miraculously self-igniting oil lamps were noted by Christian pilgrims as early as the ninth century. See Marius Canard, "La destruction de l'Église de la Résurrection par le calife Hakim et l'histoire de la descente du feu sacré," *Byzantion: Revue Internationale des Études Byzantines* 35 (1965): 16–43.

91. Polo, *Divisament*, 317.

92. Francesco Pipino, *De consuetudinibus et conditionibus orientalium regionum (translatio latina operis noti sub titulo "Il Milione")*, online resource, ed. J. V. Prášek et al. (Turnhout, Belgium: Brepols, 2011), p. 1, line 31–p. 2, line 7, http://clt.brepolis.net /LLTA/pages/TextSearch.aspx?key=MPOLOMILI_.

93. Polo, *Divisament*, 305–6: "Car je voç fais savoir que, puis que notre sire Dieu pasme de seç mainç Adam notre primer pere jusque a cestui point, ne fu cristienç, ne paiens, ne tartar, ne yndiens, ne nulç homes de nulle generasion, que tant seust ne cherchast de les deverses partie dou monde et de les grant mervoilles come cestui messire Marc en cherche et soi."

94. Polo, *Divisament*, 306: "Et por cet dit il a soi meisme que tropo seroit grant maus se il ne feist metre en ecriture toutes les granç mervoilles qu'il vit et qu'il oi por verités, por ce que les autres jens que ne le virent ne <ne> sevent, le sachent por cest livre."

95. Michel Zink, *The Invention of Literary Subjectivity*, trans David Sices (Baltimore: Johns Hopkins University Press, 1999), 58.

96. Polo, *Divisament*, 346: "Or voç ai contés de ceste plaigne et de les gens que font fer la scurité por rober; et s[i] voç di que messier Marc meesme fut el come pris da celle gens en celle oscurité; mes il escampe a un castiaus qui est apellés Canosalmi, et de seç conpains furent pris aseç et furent vendus et de tielz mors. Or voç conteronç avant des autres chouses."

97. Claire Richter Sherman, *The Portraits of Charles V of France (1338–1380)* (New York: New York University Press, 1969), 17–18.

98. See Dhira B. Mahoney, "Courtly Presentation and Authorial Self-Fashioning: Frontispiece Miniatures in Late Medieval French and English Manuscripts," *Mediaevalia* 21, no. 1 (1996): 97–160; Erik Inglis, "A Book in the Hand: Some Late Medieval Accounts of Manuscript Presentations," *Journal of the Early Book Society for the Study of Manuscripts and Printing History* 5 (2002): 58–97.

99. Joyce Coleman, "The First Presentation Miniature in an English-Language Manuscript," in *The Social Life of Illumination: Manuscripts, Images, and Communities in the Late Middle Ages*, ed. Joyce Coleman, Mark Cruse, and Kathryn A. Smith (Turnhout, Belgium: Brepols, 2013), 403–38.

100. Benedetto, *Milione*, xxxix, lvi–lviii.

101. On this disambiguation, see Gaunt, *Marco Polo's "Le Devisement,"* 58–60.

102. Translation mine. Marco Polo, *Il "Milione" Veneto: Ms. CM 211 della Biblioteca civica di Padova (Medioevo veneto)*, ed. Alvaro Barbieri and Alvise Andreose (Venice: Marsilio, 1999), 134:

> Or ve ò chontado de quel piano e de quelle zente che fa vegnir la oschurità per robar. . . . E sì ve digo io, Marcho, ch'e' fu' una fiada in grande pericolo d'eser prexo da quella zente in quella oschurità, ma e' schanpì a uno chastello che era lì apresso avea nome Chalosebini, ma piuxor dei mie' conpagni fono prexi, e tali morti e tali fono venduti.

103. Anne D. Hedeman, *The Royal Image: Illustrations of the "Grandes Chroniques de France," 1274–1422* (Berkeley: University of California Press, 1991), 11–17.

104. Benedetto, *Milione*, xxxiv–xxxv.

105. Translation mine. Antonio Rubió y Lluch, ed., *Documents per l'historia de la cultura catalana mig-eval publicats per Antonio Rubió y Lluch*, 2 vols. (Barcelona: Institut d'estudis catalans, 1921), 2:221: "Molt car avoncle, nos nos delitam molt en legir e axi propiament en frances com en nostra lengua matexa, perque us pregam que ns vullats enviar tres libres escrits en lenguatge frances, ço es les canoniques de França, Titus Livius, e Mendievila."

106. Translation mine. Ibid., 2:225: "lo libre de Johan de Mendrevile [*sic*] e lo romanç de Mexaut." Between 1374 and 1382, Joan I wrote four different letters to Ramon de Perellós in order to request a copy of the account of Odoric of Pordenone. See Eugenia Popeanga, "El relato de viajes de Odorico de Pordenone," *Revista de Filología Románica* 9 (1992): 37–61. Perellós, the Viscount of Roda, was not only an enthusiast of exotic travel writing and descriptions of the Holy Land but also the author of an account detailing his own journey to Saint Patrick's Purgatory, yet another instance of how authors writing about intra-European travel were inspired by works that grew out of journeys to East Asia and Jerusalem.

107. David Woodward, "Medieval *Mappaemundi*," in *HC*, 1:315.

108. Tony Campbell, "Portolan Charts from the Late Thirteenth Century to 1500," in *HC*, 1:371–463; Patrick Gautier Dalché, *Carte marine et portulan au XIIᵉ siècle: Le liber de existencia riveriarum et forma maris nostri Mediterranei (Pise, circa 1200)* (Rome: École française de Rome, 1995).

109. On form and sources, see *Mapamundi: The Catalan Atlas of the Year 1375*, ed. Georges Grosjean (Zurich: Urs Graf Verlag, 1978); Jean Michel Massing, "Observations and Beliefs: The World of the *Catalan Atlas*," in *Circa 1492: Art in the Age of Exploration*, ed. Jay A. Levenson, 27–33 (New Haven, CT: Yale University Press, 1991).

110. Jerry Brotton, *Trading Territories: Mapping the Early Modern World* (Ithaca, NY: Cornell University Press, 1998), 31.

111. R.A. Skelton, "A Contract for World Maps at Barcelona, 1399–1400," *Imago Mundi* 22 (1968): 107–113.

112. Suzanne Röhl, "*Le livre de Mandeville* à Paris autour de 1400," in *Patrons, Authors and Workshops: Books and Book Production in Paris around 1400*, ed. Godfried Croenen and Peter Ainsworth (Leuven, Belgium: Peeters, 2006), 281–95, at 282. Charles also donated books and scientific instruments related to medicine and astrology. For a superb study of this manuscript and its sociological context, see Marcia Kupfer, "'. . . lectres . . . plus vrayes': Hebrew Script and Jewish Witness in the *Mandeville* Manuscript of Charles V," *Speculum* 83, no. 1 (2008): 58–111.

113. For background, see Brigitte Buettner, "New Year's Gifts at the Valois Courts, ca. 1400," *Art Bulletin* 83, no. 4 (2001): 598–625 (at 602).

114. On this travel writing anthology and its translator, see John Larner, "Plucking Hairs from the Great Cham's Beard: Marco Polo, Jan de Langhe and Sir John Mandeville," in *Marco Polo and the Encounter of East and West*, ed. Suzanne Conklin Akbari and Amilcare A. Iannucci with John Tulk (Toronto: University of Toronto Press, 2008), 133–55.

115. Mandeville says nothing about the circumstances surrounding his departure from England, yet he is shown taking leave of its king. The *Livre* depicts Odoric of Pordenone departing for his journey from the papal curia, an episode that is not narrated in the text.

116. François Avril, "*Le livre des merveilles,* manuscrit 2810 de la Bibliothèque Nationale de France," in *Marco Polo, Le livre des merveilles: Extrait du Livre des merveilles du monde,* Ms. fr. 2810, de la Bibliothèque nationale de France, ed. Marie-Hélène Tesnière, François Avril, and Marie-Thérèse Gousset (Tournai, Belgium: Renaissance du livre, 1999), 291–324.

117. Millard Meiss, *French Painting in the Time of Jean de Berry: The Boucicaut Master* (London: Phaidon, 1968), x.

118. Ibid.

119. Buettner, "New Year's Gifts," 602.

120. Ibid., 600.

121. Tuddenham served as sheriff of Norfolk and Suffolk and as keeper of the king's wardrobe. See Helen Castor, "Tuddenham, Sir Thomas (1401–1462)," in *Oxford Dictionary of National Biography,* online ed., 2008.

122. John Capgrave, *Ye Solace of Pilgrims,* ed. C.A. Mills (London: Frowde, 1911), 1.

123. Ibid.

124. Translation mine. Anselmo Adorno, *Itinéraire d'Anselme Adorno en Terre Sainte (1470–1471),* ed. Jacques Heers and Georgette de Groër (Paris: Centre national de la recherche scientifique, 1978), 28: "inter omnes viatores gloria summa."

CHAPTER TWO

1. Anthony Grafton with April Shelford and Nancy Siraisi, *New Worlds, Ancient Texts: The Power of Tradition and the Shock of Discovery* (Cambridge, MA: Belknap Press of Harvard University Press, 1992), 13. A comparable assertion is made in Greenblatt, *Marvelous Possessions,* 45–47.

2. For an overview, see Hugh D. Walker, "John of Monte Corvino (1247–1328)," in *Trade, Travel, and Exploration in the Middle Ages: An Encyclopedia,* ed. John B. Friedman and Kristen M. Figg (New York: Garland Pub., 2000), 306–7.

3. Italian from *SF,* 340–45 (quotation at 340). English from *CWT,* 1:209–21 (at 1:209–10). (I have purged Yule's translation of deliberate archaisms.)

4. Two invaluable starting places for understanding medieval ideas about authorship are Marie-Dominique Chenu, "Auctor, Actor, Autor," *Bulletin du Cange* 3 (1927): 81–86; Alastair J. Minnis, *Medieval Theory of Authorship: Scholastic Literary Attitudes in the Later Middle Ages,* 2nd ed. (Philadelphia: University of Pennsylvania Press, 2009), esp. 1–12, 94–103, 156–57.

5. Minnis, *Medieval Theory,* 11–12.

6. Roger Bacon, The *"Opus majus,"* vol. 1, trans. Robert Belle Burke (Philadelphia: University of Pennsylvania Press, 1928), 320–21. For an overview of Bacon's attitudes toward geography, travel, and mission, see Power, *Roger Bacon.* On the apocalyptic cast of missionaries, crusaders, and travel writers, see Brett Whalen, *Dominion of God: Chris-*

tendom and Apocalypse in the Middle Ages (Cambridge, MA: Harvard University Press, 2009), 148–76.

7. Quoted in Power, *Roger Bacon*, 232.

8. See George Cary, *The Medieval Alexander* (Cambridge: Cambridge University Press, 1956); John Andrew Boyle, "The Alexander Romance in the East and West," *Bulletin of the John Rylands University Library of Manchester* 60 (1977): 13–27.

9. *CWT*, 3:218.

10. Poggio Bracciolini, *The Travels of Nicolo Conti in the East, in the Early Part of the Fifteenth Century (Translated from the Original of Poggio Bracciolini)*, trans. J.W. Jones (London, 1857), 4.

11. Bracciolini, *Travels of Nicolo Conti*, 34.

12. Petrarch, *Letters of Old Age (Rerum senilium libri)*, 2 vols., trans. Aldo S. Bernardo, Saul Levin, and Reta A. Bernardo (New York: Italica Press, 2005), 1:62.

13. Ibid.

14. *MA*, 80.

15. *SF*, 211; *MA*, 215: "IIII^{or} mensibus potest circumdari, et non est verum quod dicit Ysidorus quod sit sinus exiens ab occeano. Nusquam enim tangit occeanum, sed undique circumdatur terra."

16. *SF*, 269; *MA*, 170: "Quesivi de monstris sive de monstruosis hominibus de quibus narrat Ysidorus et Solinus. Ipsi dicebant michi quod nunquam viderant talia, de quo multum miramur si verum sit."

17. *CWT*, 3:213. For context, see Alessandro Scafi, *Mapping Paradise: A History of Heaven on Earth* (Chicago: University of Chicago Press, 2006).

18. *CWT*, 3:254–55.

19. Ibid., 3:227, 3:240–41.

20. Benedetto, *Milione*, cxciv.

21. Dutschke, "Francesco Pipino," 160–205.

22. Tony Campbell, "Portolan Charts from the Late Thirteenth Century to 1500," in *HC*, 1:371–463 (at 1:427–28).

23. Klaus Ridder, *Jean de Mandevilles "Reisen": Studien zur Überlieferungsgeschichte der deutschen Übersetzung des Otto Von Diemeringen* (Munich: Artemis Verlag, 1991), 226–27.

24. Ibid., 227: "Vnd do etteliche stücke lihte vngelöplich sint do han ich frömeder meistere von naturen zů zůgnůsse zů latine geschriben die man wol mag lesen der sú hören wil die die meistere pfaffen von naturen wol verston süllent."

25. See Jacques Heers, *Marco Polo* (Paris: Fayard, 1983), 165–85; Steven Epstein, *Purity Lost: Mixing Relationships in the Eastern Mediterranean* (Baltimore: Johns Hopkins University Press, 2006), 113–23.

26. See David Wallace, *Premodern Places: Calais to Surinam, Chaucer to Aphra Behn* (Malden, MA: Blackwell Publishing, 2006), 203–38; Phillips, *Medieval Expansion of Europe*, 102–16.

27. Josafa Barbaro, "Travels of Josafa Barbaro," in *Travels to Tana and Persia*, trans. William Thomas (London: Hakluyt Society, 1873), 1–2.

28. Domenico Silvestri, "Los islarios de la época del humanismo: El *De insulis* de

Domenico Silvestri," ed. and trans. José-Manuel Montesdeoca Medina (PhD thesis, Universidad de la Laguna, 2000), 6–10.

29. Ibid., 8:

> Quarum insularum aliquas posuissem nisi quod inter veterum autorum historias et fabulas miscere novorum, nec multum nostris temporibus probatorum, nil aliud esset quam mendaciis veritati fidem minuere et quamquam vera essent que Odorigus scribit tamen sequi mens est illosque imitari quorum fidem antiquitas et autoritas magis capit, vel que testimonnio vive vocis comperio.

30. Ibid.: "Fantinum venetum militem strenuum virum."

31. M. Campbell, *Witness and the Other World*, 12. Worth reading is the critique of Campbell's notion of the witness in Andrea Frisch, *The Invention of the Eyewitness: Witnessing and Testimony in Early Modern France* (Chapel Hill: University of North Carolina Department of Romance Languages, 2004), esp. chaps. 1 and 2. My own analyses in this chapter have been sharpened by Frisch's insights into the collaborative, institutional nature of medieval testimony. However, Frisch's overly broad claim that medieval travel writers tend to rely on what she calls "ethical" testimony (i.e., character witness and communal opinion) rather than "epistemic" or eyewitness testimony is based on readings of only two medieval travelers—Marco Polo and John Mandeville—and does not attend to the various ways that their medieval readers revised their texts to conform to different notions of truth. Her study provides a good example of how difficult it is to generalize about medieval constructions of authority in matters related to geoethnographic knowledge, a problem that is the product of ongoing debates about this issue during the Middle Ages.

32. Minnis, *Medieval Theory*, 10.

33. This detail is found in a deposition taken from Benedict the Pole in Cologne, known as the *Relatio*. See *SF*, 137. Translated in *MA*, 80.

34. Maria Cristiana Lungarotti, "Le due redazioni dell'*Historia Mongalorum*," in *Storia dei Mongoli*, ed. Enrico Menestò et al., 79–92 (Spoleto, Italy: Centro Italiano di studi sull'alto medioevo, 1989).

35. On Vincent's use of John, see Gregory S. Guzman, "The Encyclopedist Vincent of Beauvais and His Mongol Extracts from John of Plano Carpini and Simon of Saint-Quentin," *Speculum* 49, no. 2 (1974): 287–307.

36. Benedict the Pole, *Relatio*, in *SF*, 135–43; C. de Bridia, *Hystoria Tartarorum C. de Bridia Monachi*, ed. Alf Önnerfors (Berlin: De Gruyter, 1967). For a discussion of the text and its relationship to the Vinland Map controversy, see Gregory Guzman, "The Vinland Map Controversy and the Discovery of a Second Version of the *Tartar Relation*: The Authenticity of the 1339 Text," *Terrae Incognitae* 38 (2006): 19–25.

37. *MA*, 3; *SF*, 27: "Omnibus Christi fidelibus ad quos presens scriptum pervenerit."

38. *MA*, 4; *SF*, 28: "Sed si aliqua scribimus propter noticiam legentium que in vestris partibus nesciuntur, non debetis propter hoc nos appellare mendaces, quia vobis referimus illa que ipsi vidimus vel ab aliis pro certo audivimus quos esse credimus fide dignos. Immo est valde crudele ut homo propter bonum quod facit ab aliis infametur."

39. *MA*, 3; *SF*, 27–28:

> Et quamvis a Tartaris vel ab aliis nationibus timeremus occidi vel perpetuo captivari, vel fame, siti, algore, estu, contumeliis et laboribus nimiis quasi ultra vires affligi, que

omnia multo plus quam prius crediderimus, excepta morte vel captivitate perpetua, nobis multipliciter evenerunt, non tamen pepercimus nobis ipsis, ut voluntatem Dei secundum domini Pape mandatum adimplere possemus, et ut proficeremus in aliquo christianis, vel saltem scita veraciter voluntate et intentione ipsorum, possemus illam patefacere christianis, ne forte subito irruentes invenirent eos impreparatos, sicut peccatis hominum exigentibus alia vice contigit, et facerent magnam stragem in populo christiano.

40. *The Chronicle of Salimbene de Adam*, ed. and trans. Joseph L. Baird, Giuseppe Baglivi, and John Robert Kane, Medieval and Renaissance Texts and Studies, vol. 40 (Binghamton, NY: Medieval and Renaissance Texts and Studies, 1986), 197–98.

41. See pp. 70–71.

42. *MA*, 70; *SF*, 128: "Et ne aliqua dubitatio quin fuerimus ad Tartaros, apud aliquos oriatur nomina illorum scribimus qui ibidem nos invenerunt."

43. David Foote, "How the Past Becomes a Rumor: The Notarialization of Historical Consciousness in Medieval Orvieto," *Speculum* 75, no. 4 (2000): 794–815; Laurie Nussdorfer, *Brokers of Public Trust: Notaries in Early Modern Rome* (Baltimore: Johns Hopkins University Press, 2009), 1–31.

44. A biographical sketch of John is found in the introduction to Enrico Menestò et al., eds., *Storia dei Mongoli* (Spoleto, Italy: Centro Italiano di studi sull'alto medioevo, 1989), 49–67.

45. See André Vauchez, *Sainthood in the Later Middle Ages*, trans. Jean Birrell (Cambridge: Cambridge University Press, 1997); Dyan Elliott, *Proving Woman: Female Spirituality and Inquisitional Culture in the Later Middle Ages* (Princeton, NJ: Princeton University Press, 2004).

46. *MA*, 3–4; *SF*, 28: "Unde quecumque pro vestra utilitate vobis scribimus ad cautelam, tanto securius credere debetis, quanto nos cuncta vel ipsi vidimus oculis nostris, quia per annum et quattuor menses at amplius ambulavimus per ipsos pariter et cum ipsis, ac fuimus inter eos vel audivimus a christianis, qui sunt inter eos captivi et ut crediums fide dignis."

47. *MA*, 71; *SF*, 129–30: "Rogamus cunctos qui legunt predicta, ut nichil minuant nec apponant, qui nos omnia que vidimus vel audivimus ab aliis quos credebamus fide dignos, sicut Deus testis est, nichil scienter addentes, scripsimus previa veritate."

48. *MA*, 71–72; *SF*, 130.

49. Gervase of Tilbury, *Otia imperialia* = *Recreation for an Emperor*, ed. and trans. S.E. Banks and J.W. Binns (Oxford: Oxford University Press, 2002), 526–27: "Uarietas mendaces effecit de locorum ueritate picturas quas mappam mundi uulgus nominat, plerumque enim pictor, ut alias testis, cum de suo adicit, partis mendacio totam testimonii seriem decolorat, ut in *Decretis*, C. tercia, q. ix., 'Pura et simplex.'"

50. For details on Odoric's biography, see de Rachewiltz, *Papal Envoys*, 179–86; and Andrea Tilatti, ed., *Odorico da Pordenone: Vita e miracula* (Padua: Centro Studi Antoniani, 2004), 9–76.

51. Odoric of Pordenone, *The Travels of Friar Odoric: A 14th Century Journal of the Blessed Odoric of Pordenone*, trans. Henry Yule (Grand Rapids, MI: W.B. Eerdmans, 2002), 63–64. Where necessary, I have adjusted Yule's translation for the sake of accuracy. My interventions are signaled with brackets. *SF*, 413: "Licet multa et varia de ritibus

et condicionibus huius mundi a multis enarentur, tamen est sciendum quod ego frater Hodoricus de Foro Iulii volens transfretare et ad partes infidelium volens ire ut fructus aliquos lucrifacerem animarum, multa magna et mirabilia audavi atque vidi que possum veraciter enarrare."

52. "raris et a seculo quasi inauditis." Quoted in *CWT,* 1:5n3.

53. On the earliest Latin recensions of the work, see Paolo Chiesa, "Per un riordino della tradizione manoscritta della *Relatio* di Odorico de Pordenone," *Filologia Mediolatina* 6–7 (1999–2000): 311–50; and Paolo Chiesa, "Una forma redazionale sconosciuta della *Relatio* latina di Odorico da Pordenone," *Itineraria* 2 (2003): 137–63.

54. Rubiés, *Travel and Ethnology,* 53n49. Given the collaborative nature of deposition (which I discuss below), I do not think there is any reason to suspect this is an interpolated sequence, since there is no original, single-authored text to begin with.

55. Odoric, *Travels,* 92–93; *SF,* 436–37.

56. Odoric, *Travels,* 94–96; *SF,* 436–37.

57. Odoric, *Travels,* 158–60; *SF,* 491–92.

58. Modern critics have disagreed about the tone and truth claims of this passage, with some maintaining that it is meant to be read allegorically. See Odorico da Pordenone, *Libro delle nuove e strane e meravigliose cose,* ed. A. Andreose (Padua: Centro Studi Antoniani, 2000), 240n1.

59. This paragraph is based on two lengthy entries on Odoric in Bernardus de Bessa et al., *Chronica XXIV Generalium Ordinis Minorum: Cum pluribus appendicibus inter quas excellit hucusque ineditus liber de laudibus S. Francisci Fratris Bernardi a Bessa* (Quaracchi-Florence, Italy: Ex Typographia Collegii S. Bonaventurae, 1897), 477–79, 499–504.

60. Odoric, *Travels,* 160; *SF,* 494: "Multa etiam alia ego dimisi que scribi non feci, cum ipsa quasi incredibilia apud aliquos viderentur, nisi illa propriis oculis perspexissent."

61. Here I draw on the conception of "aura" found in Walter Benjamin, "The Work of Art in the Age of Mechanical Reproduction," in *Illuminations: Essays and Reflections,* trans. Harry Zohn (New York: Random House, 2007), 217–51.

62. Odoric, *Travels,* 160; *SF,* 494: "Ego Fr. Odoricus de Foro Julii de Ordine fratrum Minorum testificor et testimonium perhibeo reverendo patri Fr. Guidoto Ministro provincie S. Anthonii, cum ab eo fuerim per obedientiam requisitus, quod hec omnia que superius scripta sunt, aut propriis oculis ego vidi aut ab hominibus fide dignis audivi."

63. Josephine W. Bennett, *The Rediscovery of Sir John Mandeville* (New York: Modern Language Association of America, 1954), 38–39.

64. Odoric, *Travels,* 160; *SF,* 494: "Predicta autem ego Fr. Guilgelmus de Solagna in scriptis redegi sicut predictus Fr. Odoricus ore proprio exprimebat anno Domini MCCCXXX de mense madii, Padue in loco S. Anthonii. Nec curavi de latino difficili et ornato stilo, sed sicut ille narabat sic ego scribebam ad hoc ut omnes facilius intelligerent que scribuntur vel dicuntur."

65. James A. Brundage, *The Medieval Origins of the Legal Profession: Canonists, Civilians, and Courts* (Chicago: University of Chicago Press, 2010), 397–99 (quote at 398).

66. Marianne O'Doherty, "The *Viaggio in Inghilterra* of a *Viaggio in Oriente:* Odorico

da Pordenone's Itinerarium from Italy to England," *Italian Studies* 64, no. 2 (2009): 198–220 (at 204–16).

67. The notary in question is Guecello rather than William. See W.D. Macray, *Bodleian Library Quarto Catalogues, ix. Digby Manuscripts, a Reproduction of the 1883 Catalogue with Notes by R. W. Hunt and A. G. Watson* (Oxford: Bodleian Library, 1999), pt. 2, 10.

68. A. Andreose, "Tra ricezione e riscrittura: La fortuna romanza della *Relatio* di Odorico da Pordenone," in *Medioevo romanzo e orientale: Il viaggio nelle letterature romanze e orientali, VII Convegno della Società Italiana di Filologia Romanza, Catania-Ragusa 24–27 settembre 2003*, ed. Giovanna Carbonaro et al. (Soveria Mannelli, Italy: Rubbettino, 2006), 5–21 (at 6).

69. Translation mine. Giulio Cesare Testa, '"Questo mio librecto . . . ,"' in *Odorichus de rebus incognitis, Odorico da Pordenone nella prima edizione a stampa del 1513*, ed. Lucio Monaco and Giulio Cesare Testa (Pordenone, Italy: Camera di Commercio, 1986), 9–32 (at 28–29).

70. Alison Cornish, *Vernacular Translation in Dante's Italy: Illiterate Literature* (Cambridge: Cambridge University Press, 2010), 16–43.

71. For this reason, it is incorrect to assert that "after Marco Polo, the authority of the traveler replaced that of the book; the book was only authoritative if the traveler whose report it contained was authoritative, too." For this argument, see Jaś Elsner and Joan-Pau Rubiés, introduction to *Voyages and Visions: Towards a Cultural History of Travel*, ed. Jaś Elsner and Joan-Pau Rubiés (London: Reaktion Books, 1999), 1–57 (at 37).

72. This section takes as its base text the Insular French version found in John Mandeville, *Le livre des merveilles du monde*, ed. Christiane Deluz (Paris: CNRS Éditions, 2000), cited as Mandeville, *Livre* (ed. Deluz). The corresponding English translation will come from *"The Book of John Mandeville" with Related Texts*, ed. and trans. Iain Macleod Higgins (Indianapolis: Hackett, 2011), cited as Mandeville, *Book* (ed. and trans. Higgins). Occasional adjustments to Higgins's translation are signaled with brackets. For dating, manuscript tradition, and debates about authorship/language of composition, see M.C. Seymour, *Sir John Mandeville*, Authors of the Middle Ages 1 (Aldershot, UK: Variorum, 1993); the introduction to Mandeville, *Livre* (ed. Deluz), esp. 28–81; and the introduction to Mandeville, *Book* (ed. and trans. Higgins).

73. For discussion of sources, see the introduction to Christiane Deluz, *Le Livre de Jehan de Mandeville: Une "géographie" au XIVe siècle* (Louvain-la-Neuve, Belgium: Institut d'études médiévales de l'Université catholique de Louvain, 1988), pt. 1, chaps. 3 and 4; and the thorough scholarly apparatus of G.F. Warner, ed., *The Buke of John Maundeuill* (Westminster, UK, 1889).

74. On Scandella (who, like Odoric of Pordenone, was a native of Friuli), see Carlo Ginzburg, *The Cheese and the Worms: The Cosmos of a Sixteenth-Century Miller* (Baltimore: Johns Hopkins University Press, 1980). On reception history, see Rosemary Tzanaki, *Mandeville's Medieval Audiences: A Study on the Reception of the Book of Sir John Mandeville (1371–1550)* (Aldershot, Hampshire, UK: Ashgate, 2003); Bennett, *Rediscovery*; and Ladan Niayesh, ed., *A Knight's Legacy: Mandeville and Mandevillian Lore in Early Modern England* (Manchester, UK: Manchester University Press, 2011).

75. Donald Howard, "The World of Mandeville's Travels," *Yearbook of English Stud-*

ies 1 (1971): 1–17 (at 3); Bennett, *Rediscovery*, 46–57; Iain M. Higgins, *Writing East: The "Travels" of Sir John Mandeville* (Philadelphia: University of Pennsylvania Press, 1997), 206–16; Greenblatt, *Marvelous Possessions*, 157n4.

76. Mandeville, *Book* (ed. and trans. Higgins), 166; Mandeville, *Livre* (ed. Deluz), 446: "les oilz si movables et sy scintillantz . . . et tant de pulencie qe a peine le poet endurer."

77. Mandeville, *Book* (ed. and trans. Higgins), 167; Mandeville, *Livre* (ed. Deluz), 447: "or et argent et pierres preciouses et joyaux a grant foisoun de cea et dela."

78. Mandeville, *Book* (ed. and trans. Higgins), 167; Mandeville, *Livre* (ed. Deluz), 447: "II prudhommes freres menours qe estoient de Lombardie."

79. On the pilgrim's parting ritual, see Sumption, *Pilgrimage*, 168–75; M. Cecilia Gaposchkin, "From Pilgrimage to Crusade: The Liturgy of Departure, 1095–1300," *Speculum* 88, no. 1 (2003): 44–91.

80. Mandeville, *Book* (ed. and trans. Higgins), 166; Mandeville, *Livre* (ed. Deluz), 445–46: "En celle vallé y a mult d'or et mult d'argent par quoy mointz mescreantz et mointz christiens auxi y entrent sovent pur aler querre du tresour qe y est. Mes poy ent retornent especialment de mescreantz, ne auxi de christiens qe vont pur coveitise del avoir qar ils sont tantost estranglés du diable."

81. Mandeville, *Book* (ed. and trans. Higgins), 166; Mandeville, *Livre* (ed. Deluz), 446: "assautz . . . et . . . manaces et en l'air et en terre, et des cops, et des tonairs, et de tempestes. Et toudis ceo doute l'em qe Dieu ne prigne vengeaunce de ceo qe l'em ad maffait encontre sa volunté."

82. Mandeville, *Book* (ed. and trans. Higgins), 77; Mandeville, *Livre* (ed. Deluz), 258:

Ou pur poverté q'ils n'ount de quoy, ou pur ce q'ils ne ount compaignie sufficiante, ou pur ceo q'ils ne poent endurer la peine, ou q'ils doutent trop a passer le desert, ou q'ils se hastent trop de retorner pur lour femmes et pur lour enfantz, ou pur ascuns causes resonables.

83. For more on this point, see pp. 107–8 of this book.

84. Mandeville, *Book* (ed. and trans. Higgins), 181; Mandeville, *Livre* (ed. Deluz), 470.

85. Mandeville, *Book* (ed. and trans. Higgins), 184–85; Mandeville, *Livre* (ed. Deluz), 478–79:

Qar si jeo devisoie tant quantquez y est par dela, un autre qe se peneroit et travailleroit le corps pur aler en celles marches et pur cercher le pays seroit empeschez par mes ditz a recompter nulles choses estranges, qar il ne porroit rien dire de novel en quoy ly oyantz puissent prendre solacz. Et l'em dit toutdis qe choses novelles pleisent. Sy m'en taceray atant sanz plus racompter nulles diversetez qe soient par dela, a la fin qe cis qe vourra aler en celles parties y troeve assez a dire.

86. See *Anglo-Norman Dictionary*, s.v. "empescher," http://www.anglo-norman.net/.

87. Mandeville, *Book* (ed. and trans. Higgins), 6; Mandeville, *Livre* (ed. Deluz), 93:

Et sachez qe jeo eusse cest escrit mis en latin pur plus brifment deviser, mes pur ceo qe plusours entendent mieux romancz qe latin jeo l'ai mis en romancz pur ceo qe chescun l'entende, et luy chivaler et ly seignurs et ly autre noble hommes qe ne scievent point de latin ou poi et qe ount esté outre mer sachent et entendent si jeo die voir ou noun. Et si jeo erre en divisant par noun sovenance ou autrement qe ils le puissent adresser et amender, qar choses de long temps passés par la veue tournent en obly et memorie de homme ne puet mie tut retiner ne comprendre.

88. Higgins, *Writing East*, 55.

89. Mandeville, *Book* (ed. and trans. Higgins), 185; Mandeville, *Livre* (ed. Deluz), 479.

90. Higgins, *Writing East*, 247.

91. Roland Barthes, "The Reality Effect," in *French Literary Theory Today*, ed. T. Todorov (Cambridge: Cambridge University Press, 1982), 11–18.

92. C.L. Paul Trüb, *Heilige und Krankheit* (Stuttgart: Klett-Cotta, 1978), 282–83.

93. Arnaut Daniel, *Canzoni: Edizione critica, studio introduttivo, commento e traduzione*, ed. Gianluigi Toja (Florence: G.C. Sansoni, 1960), lines 41–42. Translation mine.

94. Tzanaki, *Mandeville's Medieval Audiences*, 138.

95. On the posited link between wealth, diet, and gout in premodern medicine, see Roy Porter and G.S. Rousseau, *Gout: The Patrician Malady* (New Haven, CT: Yale University Press, 1998), 13–23.

96. Thomas G. Benedek and Gerald P. Rodnan, "Petrarch on Medicine and the Gout," *Bulletin of the History of Medicine* 37 (1963): 397–416.

97. Higgins, *Writing East*, 249.

98. For an overview of the versions of the *Book* produced in England, see M.C. Seymour, "The English Manuscripts of *Mandeville's Travels*," *Edinburgh Bibliographic Society Transactions* 4 (1966): 169–210.

99. John Mandeville, *The Defective Version of "Mandeville's Travels,"* ed. M.C. Seymour (Oxford: Early English Text Society, 2002), 136.

100. John Mandeville, *"Mandeville's Travels": Translated from the French of Jean d'Outremeuse*, 2 vols., ed. Paul Hamelius, Early English Text Society, Original Series (London: Kegan Paul, Trench, Trübner, 1919–23), 1:210.

101. Higgins, *Writing East*, 254–55. As noted in chap. 5, this same upheaval leaves a large footprint on the travel writing of Petrarch.

102. Michel Foucault, "Of Other Spaces: Utopias and Heterotopias," trans. Jay Miscowiec, *Diacritics* 16, no. 1 (1986): 22–27 (at 24).

103. Mandeville, *Mandeville's Travels* (ed. Hamelius), 1:209.

104. John Mandeville, *The Book of John Mandeville*, ed. Tamarah Kohanski and C. David Benson (Kalamazoo, MI: Medieval Institute Publications, 2007).

105. Foucault, "Of Other Spaces," 27.

106. For dating and manuscript description, see John Mandeville, *The Bodley Version of "Mandeville's Travels,"* ed. M.C. Seymour (London: Early English Text Society, 1963), xviii.

107. Translation mine. Ibid., 175: "Et fecit cardinalem michi demonstrare quoddam instrumentum rotundum curiose et modo mirifico compositum, in eo contiens per sculpciones vel depicturas pene omnia regna et genera nacionum, mirificum quod appellauit *Speram Mundi* . . . . Et ibi inueni omnia genera tam virorum quam bestiarum contentorum in libello meo prenotato, valefaciensque domino Pape optinens ab eo suam benediccionem, asserenti et confirmanti ea in libro meo descripta esse vera."

108. See C.W.R.D. Moseley, "Behaim's Globe and *Mandeville's Travels*," *Imago Mundi* 33 (1981): 89–91. Globes of various kinds preexisted the *Erdapfel*, many of them produced for the same royal and aristocratic courts that also collected works of late medieval travel writing. See Elly Dekker, "Globes in Renaissance Europe," in *HC*, 3:36–73.

109. Translation mine. There is no critical edition of the Liège manuscripts, but a

study of three can be found in Guy De Poerck, "Le corpus mandevillien du ms Chantilly 699," in *Fin de Moyen Age et Renaissance: Mélanges de philologie offerts à Robert Guiette*, ed. Guy De Poerck (Antwerp: De Nederlansche Boekhandel, 1961), 31–48 (at 39): "Ian de grasce dessus dit mil trois chents et lvij al xxxvᵉ an que je men partis de mon pays dedens la noble cyté de Lyege en la basse sabloniere [saveniere] en lostel Hannekin dit le volt, a la requeste et proyere de honnorable [homme venerable] et discreit maistre Jehan de Bourgoigne dis a le barbe phizitien qui en ma maladie moy vizitoit, et en vizitant moy recognut et raviza sy com chil qui mavoyt veu en la court le souldan de Egypte avœc le quel il demoroyt quant je fuy la."

110. For documentary specifics, see Rita Lejeune, "Jean de Mandeville et les Liégeois," in *Mélanges de linguistique romane et de philologie médiévale offerts à M. Maurice Delbouille*, vol. 2, ed. Jean Renson (Gembloux, Belgium: J. Duculot, 1964), 409–37, esp. 427–28.

111. For context and two transcriptions of Mandeville's epitaph—which, like the church, no longer survives—see Mandeville, *Mandeville's Travels* (ed. Hamelius), 2:1–11.

112. See De Poerck, "Le corpus," 38, 43–44.

113. John Mandeville, *Sir John Mandevilles Reisebeschreibung: In deutscher Übersetzung von Michel Velser*, ed. Eric John Morrall (Berlin: Akademie-Verlag, 1974), 178.

114. The Fisher King is said to suffer from "a debilitating disease called podagra": "ein siechtuom heizet pögrät / treit er, die lem helfelös." See Wolfram von Eschenbach, *Parzival*, ed. Karl Lachmann, trans. Peter Knecht, intro. Bernd Schirok (Berlin: Walter de Gruyter, 2003), 501, lines 26–27. English translation mine.

115. Mandeville, *Bodley Version*, 147, is typical of most Middle English versions (but not the Cotton) in referring to Mandeville's affliction as a "certeyn cause" that constrains him.

116. Monica H. Green, "Salerno on the Thames: The Genesis of Anglo-Norman Medical Literature," in *Language and Culture in Medieval Britain: The French of England, c. 1100–c. 1500*, ed. Jocelyn Wogan-Browne (York, UK: York Medieval Press, 2009), 220–31. It is worth noting that manuscript variants of the gout passage in the Insular French version suggest that sometimes even fluent readers of Insular French were confused by Mandeville's terminology. See Mandeville, *Livre* (ed. Deluz), 479, note *n*.

117. Translation mine. The French for the Continental version comes from John Mandeville, *"Mandeville's Travels," Texts and Translations*, 2 vols., ed. Malcolm Letts (London: Hakluyt Society, 1953). From 2:392–93: "Je port l'enseingne noire comme charbon plus de xviii ans. Mainte personne la veue. Mais puis que je me suy repenti de mes pechies et que j'ay mis paine a Dieu servir selon ma fragilité, ceste tache est alee a neent, et est la pel plus blanche que nulle part. Mais toutesuoies le coup y pert bien, et perra tant comme la charoingne durra."

118. See Groebner, *Who Are You?*, 31–64.

119. A spirited account of the rougher side of dubbing is offered by Stephanie Trigg, *Shame and Honor: A Vulgar History of the Order of the Garter* (Philadelphia: University of Pennsylvania Press, 2012).

120. Translation mine. Thanks to Kathryn Starkey for help with two tricky turns of phrase. Mandeville, *Reisebeschreibung*, 161: "Item, e ich fúrbas kum, so wil ich Michel Velser, der diß búch zetútsch hät bracht, ain wenig sagen, und das laß sich niemen ver-

driessen. Es ist wär, alles das ich hab in disem bůch gelessen, so hon ich nit gelessen das inminem sinne als ungelöblich wär als diß matery."

121. For documentary research on Velser, see E.J. Morrall, "Michel Velser and His German Translation of Mandeville's *Travels*," *Durham University Journal* 55 (1962): 16–22.

122. Mandeville, *Reisebeschreibung*, 161: "Do fräget er mich von was sach es seyte. Do seyte ich im es. Do sprach er: 'Komest du gen Kier in die statt, so wölt ich dir zögen in unser liebry ain buch das unser gardion an dem töt bett gemachett hett. Da sich wunder und frag was er sag, wann er vil land hät erfaren enthalb meres.' Und kúrtzlich ich sach das bůch, und das litt an ainer ketten su Kier in der statt in der Barfůssen Clöster. Wan der múnch was von Kier von ainem geschlecht die haissend Raschier."

123. See Tzanaki, *Mandeville's Medieval Audiences*, 8–9, for a discussion of interpolations into a copy of the Vulgate Latin version, boasting that Mandeville endured more than Odoric.

124. Facing-page English translations of each work can be found, respectively, in Westrem, *Broader Horizons*; Nancy F. Marino, ed. and trans., *El libro del conoscimiento de todos los reinos (The Book of Knowledge of All Kingdoms)* (Tempe: Arizona Center for Medieval and Renaissance Studies, 1999).

INTRODUCTION TO PART TWO

1. Barbara Korte, *English Travel Writing from Pilgrimages to Postcolonial Explorations*, trans. Catherine Matthias (London: Palgrave Macmillan, 2000), 25–26.

2. Jaś Elsner and Joan-Pau Rubiés, introduction to *Voyages and Visions: Towards a Cultural History of Travel*, ed. Jaś Elsner and Joan-Pau Rubiés (London: Reaktion Books, 1999), 1–56, supply a representative specimen of this argument. Many of these idealizations draw on the classic study: Victor W. Turner and Edith Turner, *Image and Pilgrimage in Christian Culture* (New York: Columbia University Press, 2011).

3. Sidonie Smith, *Moving Lives: Twentieth-Century Women's Travel Writing* (Minneapolis: University of Minnesota Press, 2001), 3.

CHAPTER THREE

1. Plato, *Laws* XII, 950 d–e. Cf. *Protagoras* 342c–d: "And so that their young men won't unlearn what they are taught, they do not permit them to travel to other cities (the Cretans don't either)." In Plato, *Complete Works*, ed. John M. Cooper et al. (Indianapolis: Hackett, 1997), 1590, 774.

2. In Latin: "certum conscribere Evagatorium." Felix Fabri, *Evagatorium in Terrae Sanctae, Arabiae et Aegypti peregrinationem*, 3 vols., ed. C.D. Hassler (Stuttgart: Kosten des Literarischen Vereins, 1843–49), 1:61. English quotation from *PPTS*, 7:49.

3. *PPTS*, 7:48–49; Fabri, *Evagatorium*, 1:61: "sub quadam caligine tenebrosa, ac si in somnis ea vidissem."

4. *PPTS*, 7:50; Fabri, *Evagatorium*, 1:62.

5. *PPTS*, 7:48; Fabri, *Evagatorium*, 1:61: "et per loca sancta cucurrimus absque intellectu et sine affectu."

6. *PPTS*, 7:48; Fabri, *Evagatorium*, 1:61.

7. *PPTS*, 7:24; Fabri, *Evagatorium*, 1:42: "Sicut studens lectionem aliquam memoriae commendare intendes, primo perfunctorie lectionem praevidet et postea repetit mature et tractim tempus accipiens sufficiens imprimendi sic et in proposito feci, et nullo modo contentus fui de visis, nec ea, quae videram, memoriae commendaveram, sed servavi futurae peregrinationi."

8. On meditation and reading, see Brian Stock, *Augustine the Reader: Meditation, Self-Knowledge, and the Ethics of Interpretation* (Cambridge, MA: Harvard University Press, 1996), 1–18; Mary J. Carruthers, *The Craft of Thought: Meditation, Rhetoric, and the Making of Images, 400–1200* (Cambridge: Cambridge University Press, 1998), 3–5; Mary J. Carruthers, *The Book of Memory: A Study of Memory in Medieval Culture* (Cambridge: Cambridge University Press, 1990), 162, 171–76.

9. Isidore of Seville, *The Etymologies of Isidore of Seville*, ed. and trans. Stephen A. Barney et al. (Cambridge: Cambridge University Press, 2006), 39.

10. See Jonathan Culler, "Apostrophe," in *The Pursuit of Signs*, 135–54 (Ithaca, NY: Cornell University Press, 1981); Mary Carruthers, "Rhetorical 'Ductus,' or, Moving through a Composition," in *Acting on the Past: Historical Performance across the Disciplines*, ed. Mark Franko and Annette Richards, 99–117 (Hanover, MA: Wesleyan University Press, 2000).

11. On the book of the world, see E.R. Curtius, *European Literature and the Latin Middle Ages*, trans. Willard R. Trask (New York: Harper & Row, 1953), 315–26. On the book of memory, see Carruthers, *Book of Memory*.

12. On *divisio*: Carruthers, *Book of Memory*, 79–86, 103–7; Rita Copeland, *Rhetoric, Hermeneutics, and Translation in the Middle Ages: Academic Traditions and Vernacular Texts* (Cambridge: Cambridge University Press, 1991), 206–26; Malcolm Parkes, "The Influence of the Concepts of *Ordinatio* and *Compilatio* on the Development of the Book," in *Medieval Learning and Literature: Essays Presented to Richard William Hunt*, ed. J.J.G. Alexander and M.T. Gibson, 115–41 (Oxford: Clarendon Press, 1976).

13. Brouria Bitton-Ashkelony, *Encountering the Sacred: The Debate on Christian Pilgrimage in Late Antiquity* (Berkeley: University of California Press, 2005), 65–70; Susan Weingarten, *The Saint's Saints: Hagiography and Geography in Jerome* (Leiden, Netherlands: Brill, 2005).

14. Augustine, *On Christian Doctrine*, trans. D.W. Robertson Jr. (New York: Prentice-Hall, 1958), 65.

15. Patrick Gautier Dalché, *La "descriptio Mappe Mundi"* (Paris: Études augustiniennes, 1988), 93–96.

16. Lesley B. Cormack, "Maps as Educational Tools in the Renaissance," in *HC*, 3:622–36; Marcia Kupfer, "Medieval World Maps: Embedded Images, Interpretive Frames," *Word & Image: A Journal of Verbal/Visual Enquiry* 10, no. 3 (1994): 262–88 (at 269–73).

17. Carruthers, *Book of Memory*, 138–43, 271–80; Frances A. Yates, *The Art of Memory* (London: Routledge, 1956), 2–25.

18. Carruthers, *Book of Memory*, 18–20, 205–11.

19. Carruthers, *Book of Memory*, 71–80, 122–55; Yates, *Art of Memory*, 8–18, 296–97, 328–38.

20. Catalan friar Francesc Eiximenis recommended that preachers organize the points they wanted to address in a sermon by locating each topic within a notable town along the route from Rome to Santiago de Compostela. See his "On Two Kinds of Order That Aid Understanding and Memory," in *The Medieval Craft of Memory: An Anthology of Texts and Pictures*, ed. Mary Carruthers and Jan M. Ziolkowski, 189–204 (Philadelphia: University of Pennsylvania Press, 2002), 200–201.

21. Gervase of Tilbury, *Otia imperialia*, 526–29.

22. Giovanni Boccaccio, *Decameron*, ed. Vittore Branca, 2 vols. (Milan: Mondadori, 1985), 1:540.

23. Boncompagno da Signa, "On Memory," in *The Medieval Craft of Memory: An Anthology of Texts and Pictures*, ed. Mary Carruthers and Jan M. Ziolkowski, 103–18 (Philadelphia: University of Pennsylvania Press, 2002), 113–14.

24. Erasmus, "Ratio seu methodus compendio perveniendi ad veram theologiam," in *Opera omnia*, 9 vols. (Basel, 1540), 5:66–77: "ex arbore faciant quadrupedem . . . e citharoedo fluvium, ex oppido fruticem."

25. Kempe, *Book of Margery Kempe*, 217: "Yf the namys of the placys be not ryth wretyn, late no man merveylyn, for sche stodyid mor abowte contemplacyon than the namys of the placys, and he that wrot hem had nevyr seyn hem, and therfor have hym excusyd."

26. See, for example, Dutschke, "Francesco Pipino," 78–83.

27. Kaspar Peucer, *De dimensione terrae et geometrice numerandis locorum particularium intervallis ex Doctrina triangulorum Sphaericorum & Canone subtensarum Liber . . .* (Wittenberg, 1554), 3: "non regionum situs & intervalla considerare, non solum agrestis barbaries est, sed etiam impietas."

28. John Green and Thomas Astley, *A New General Collection of Voyages and Travels . . .* , 4 vols. (London: printed for T. Astley, 1745), 4:620.

29. Ramusio claimed that "countless errors" marred the manuscripts of the work, causing people to believe that that the names "of cities and provinces were fictitious and fanciful" and that Polo's account was therefore a "fable." See Giovanni Battista Ramusio, *Navigazione e viaggi*, 6 vols., ed. Marcia Milanesi (Turin: Einaudi, 1978–83), 3:22: "Il libro del quale, per causa de infinite scorrezioni ed errori, è stato molte decine d'anni riputato favola, e che i nomi delle città e provincie fussero tutte fizioni e imaginazioni senza fondamento alcuno, e per dir meglio sogni."

30. On these arguments, see Larner, *Marco Polo*, 59–61.

31. *PJ*, 241–320 (at 266–67).

32. Ibid., 267.

33. Here, I am indebted to the insights of John Urry, *The Tourist Gaze: Leisure and Travel in Contemporary Societies* (London: Sage Publications, 1990).

34. Let Jerome stand in for many other possible examples. In his letter to Oceanus on the occasion of Fabiola's death (letter LXXVII), Jerome praised the deceased for her austere lifestyle after the death of her husband, contrasting her to "Gentile widows" who "are wont to paint their faces with rouge and white lead, to flaunt in silk dresses, to deck themselves in gleaming jewels, to wear gold necklaces, to hang from their pierced ears the costliest Red Sea pearls, and to reek of musk" (445). When, in letter XXII, he discusses the

salvation of the soul at death, he conjures the image of "the Red Sea . . . and Pharaoh with his hosts drowned beneath its waves" (155). See Jerome, *Select Letters of St. Jerome,* ed. T.E. Page et al., trans. F.A. Wright (New York: Putnam, 1903).

35. Abu-Lughod, *Before European Hegemony,* 241–42.

36. *PJ,* 95–133 (at 122–23).

37. Niccolò, *Libro,* 126.

38. Francis Petrarch, *Petrarch's Guide to the Holy Land: Itinerary to the Sepulcher of Our Lord Jesus Christ = Itinerarium Ad Sepulchrum Domini Nostri Yehsu Christi: Facsimile Edition of Cremona, Biblioteca Statale, Deposito Libreria Civica, Manuscript BB.1.2.5,* ed. and trans. Theodore J. Cachey Jr. (Notre Dame, IN: University of Notre Dame Press, 2002). Because there are no standard page numbers in Cachey's translation, references to this work correspond to the chapter and paragraph numbers found in the margins of this edition. Citation at 18.4–18.5.

39. See chap. 2, pp. 80–81.

40. Mandeville, *Book* (ed. and trans. Higgins), 31.

41. Ibid., 176–77.

42. As is convincingly argued in Sarah Salih, "The Medieval Looks Back: A Response to 'Troubled Vision,'" in *Troubled Vision: Gender, Sexuality, and Sight in Medieval Text and Image,* ed. Emma Campbell and Robert Mills, 223–231 (New York: Palgrave Macmillan, 2004).

43. On the memory-friendly spatial arrangement of medieval manuscripts, see Carruthers, *Book of Memory,* 248–54.

44. Geoffrey Chaucer, *Canterbury Tales,* in *The Riverside Chaucer,* 3rd ed., gen. ed. Larry D. Benson (Boston: Houghton Mifflin, 1987), at fragment I, lines 15–19, p. 23.

45. On ex-voto offerings, see Eamon Duffy, *The Stripping of the Altars* (New Haven, CT: Yale University Press, 1992), 197–99; Ronald C. Finucane, *Miracles and Pilgrims: Popular Beliefs in Medieval England* (London: J.M. Dent, 1977), 97–99.

46. M.R.B. Shaw, trans., *Chronicles of the Crusades* (London: Penguin Books, 1963), 294–95.

47. *PJ,* 241–42.

48. Jerome, *Select Letters and Works,* in *A Select Library of Nicene and Post-Nicene Fathers of the Christian Church,* 2nd ser., vol. 6, trans. Philip Schaff and Henry Wace (New York, 1890), CVIII.9, p. 459.

49. For a view of pilgrim practices during late antiquity, see E. Wipszycka, "Les pèlerinages chrétiens dans l'antiquité tardive: Problèmes de définition et de repères temporels," *Byzantinoslavica* 56 (1995): 429–38; E.D. Hunt, *Holy Land Pilgrimage in the Later Roman Empire, AD 312–460* (Oxford: Clarendon Press, 1984), 110–17.

50. See Sabino de Sandoli, "La libération pacifique des lieux saints au XIVᵉ siècle," *Studia Orientalia Christiana Collectanea* 21 (1988): 73–159.

51. Mariano da Siena includes texts of the prayers in his *Viaggio fatto al Santo Sepolcro, 1431,* ed. Paolo Pirillo (Pisa, Italy: Pacini editore, 1991), 105.

52. Herbert Thurston, *The Stations of the Cross: An Account of Their History and Devotional Purpose* (London: Burns and Oates, 1906).

53. *PJ,* 361–75 (at 370).

54. Ibid. Original Latin in Riccoldo de Montecroce, *Pérégrination en Terre Sainte et*

au Proche Orient: Lettres sur la chute de Saint-Jean d'Acre, ed. and trans. René Kappler (Paris: Honoré Champion, 1997), 38:

> Gaililee ubi Christus fecit initium signorum aquam conuertendo mutando in uinum; est autem Cana Galilee quarto uel quinto miliario a Naçaret; Ibi extra casale inuenimus puteum. Vnde ministri hauserunt aquam implentes ydrias. Ibi inuenimus locum nuptiarum et loca et formulas ydriarum. Ibi cantauimus et predicauimus euangelium nuptiarum. Ibi rogaui Christum quod sicut aquam in uinum conuerterat, ita aquam mee insipiditatis et indeuotionis conuerteret in uinum compunctionis et spiritualis saporis.

55. "Et est notandum, quod a loco Calvariae usque ad idem praetorium sunt ccccl passus, quos omni diligentia, qua potui, numeravi." In T. Tobler, ed., *Descriptiones Terrae Sanctae, ex saeculo VIII. IX. XII. et XV* (Leipzig, 1874), 229.

56. See the introduction, pp. 8–9.

57. The so-called Piacenza Pilgrim was taking and recording measurements of sacred places in the sixth century. See John Wilkinson, *Jerusalem Pilgrims before the Crusades* (Warminster, UK: Aris and Phillips, 2002), 139. On pilgrim measurement, see Zur Shalev, "Christian Pilgrimage and Ritual Measurement in Jerusalem," *Micrologus* 19 (2011): 131–50.

58. Nompar de Caumont, *Voyaige d'oultremer en Jhérusalem . . . l'an 1418*, ed. Édouard Lelièvre de La Grange (Paris, 1858), 137.

59. Emphasis mine. See n. 5 of this chapter.

60. *PJ*, 362.

61. Carruthers, *Book of Memory*, 167–68.

62. *PJ*, 95. The Latin: from Thietmar, *Liber peregrinationis*, ed. J.C.M. Laurent (Hamburg, 1857), 10: "Multum enim estuaui et ardenter desideraui videre personaliter, que in nube et enigmate aliquotiens audieram scripturarum."

63. Kempe, *Book of Margery Kempe*, 75–76.

64. See, for example, the discussion of Ludolph's *Vita Christi* in Michelle Karnes, *Imagination, Meditation, and Cognition in the Middle Ages* (Chicago: University of Chicago Press, 2011), 151–53. At 152–53, Karnes includes a two-page block quote in which Ludolph's meditational guide laments the Muslim domination of the Holy Land and the failure of the crusading enterprise. Karnes characterizes this passage as "striking"; it is a thinly revised version of a passage from Burchard of Mount Sion, which we will consider in chap. 4, pp. 149–50.

65. For an overview of these developments, see Colin Morris, *The Sepulchre of Christ and the Medieval West: From the Beginning to 1600* (Oxford: Oxford University Press, 2005), 328–62.

66. Carruthers, *Book of Memory*, 246.

67. Jill Stevenson, *Performance, Cognitive Theory, and Devotional Culture: Sensual Piety in Late Medieval York* (New York: Palgrave Macmillan, 2010), 105–13.

68. Dante, *Purgatorio*, trans. Allen Mandelbaum (New York: Bantam, 2004), 33.76–79, pp. 310–11: "voglio anco e se non scritto, almen dipinto, / che 'l te ne porti dentro a te per quello / che si reca il bordon di palma cinto." Dante assures Beatrice that what she tells him will be imprinted in his mind like a seal in wax, a common image for describing the formation of a memory.

69. Dante, *Paradiso* (trans. Mandelbaum), 31.43–45, pp. 280–81: "si ricrea / nel tempio del suo voto riguardando, / e spera già ridir com'ello stea."

70. Dante, *Inferno* (trans. Mandelbaum), II.4–39.

71. Paget Toynbee, "Christine de Pisan and Sir John Mandeville," *Romania* 21 (1892): 228–39.

72. Translation mine. Christine de Pizan, *Le livre du chemin de long estude: Publié pour la première fois d'après sept manuscrits de Paris, de Bruxelles et de Berlin*, ed. Robert Püschel (Berlin, 1881), lines 1187–90:

Si te monstreray maint notable
Lieu qui au veoir t'iert delitable
Et toute ta vie en aras
Joie apres, quant veu l'aras

73. Translation mine. Ibid., lines 1213–14: "grant plaisir / De tout visiter a loisir."

74. Translation mine. Ibid., lines 1261–68:

Vi la saint sepulcre et baisay
Et la un pou me reposay.
Quant j'oz fait mes oblacions
Et dites mes devocions,
Je regarday comme il est fait
A demi compas, et de fait
Le hault et lé le mesuray
Et encore la mesure ay.

75. John Wilkinson, Joyce Hill, and W.F. Ryan, eds., *Jerusalem Pilgrimage, 1099–1185* (London: Hakluyt Society, 1988), 315–36 (at 315).

76. *PJ*, 61–94 (at 61).

77. *PJ*, 95–96; Thietmar, *Liber*, 11:

Cum itaque mihi soli in hoc scripto cupiam in Domino delectari, arrogantiam longe facio et vanam gloriam; presertim cum de hiis, qui laudem querunt hominum et inanem captant gloriam, dicat ewangelium: "Amen, dico vobis, receperunt mercedem suam." Stultum enim nimis et absurdum iudicarem, si tanta ac talia tot viarum et maris et terre pericula tam spiritus quam corporis fatigatione perpessa et retributionem eternam, quam a Deo ad vitam eternam expecto, laude hominum, vana gloria, immo, vt verius dicam, nichilo commutarem.

78. *PJ*, 95–96; Thietmar, *Liber*, 11:

Verum quia mihi aliquando lectioni operam danti redolet thimum, sapit fauum in tam delectabilibus delectari, non inutile duxi, que viderem et a veridicis veraciter intelligerem, scripto commendare, ne obliuionis fumo surrepente, quod per naturam non possem, artificialiter alicuius scripti amminiculo memorie reseruarem.

79. *PJ*, 95–96; Thietmar, *Liber*, 11:

Si quis autem hoc scriptum tetigerit et mecum delectari volet, in id ipsum mihi non succenseat et huic sucum arrogantie non impingat, cum vtique ad eliminandum otium et ad recogitandum loca sancte terre et miracula illa virtute Dei facta presentis scripti seriem non pompatice, sed simpliciter viderit compilatam.

80. On the variety of florilegial forms, see Richard H. Rouse and Mary A. Rouse, *Preachers, Florilegia, and Sermons* (Toronto: Pontifical Institute, 1979).

81. Carruthers, *Book of Memory*, 197; Harry A. Wolfson, "The Instinctual Senses," *Harvard Theological Review* 28 (1955): 69–133 (at 91–93).

82. Janet Coleman, *Ancient and Medieval Memories: Studies in the Reconstruction of the Past* (Cambridge: Cambridge University Press, 1995), 93–95.

83. Augustine, *St. Augustine's Confessions*, 2 vols., ed. William Watts, W.H.D. Rouse, et al. (London: William Heinemann, 1912), vol. 2, bk. 10, chap. 11, pp. 106–7. The larger Latin passage reads: "ut denuo velut nova excogitanda sint indidem iterum—neque enim est alia regio eorum—et cogenda rursus, ut sciri possint, id est velut ex quadam dispersione colligenda, unde dictum est cogitare. Nam cogo et cogito sic est, ut ago et agito, facio et factito." See also Janet Coleman, *Ancient and Medieval Memories*, 93–95.

84. "Cicero," *Rhetorica ad Herennium*, ed. Harry Caplan (Cambridge, MA: Harvard University Press, 1999). See esp. III.xix.31–xx.33, where cogitation is three times associated with the "eye of the mind" and its capacity to invent imaginary places. For instance: "Hence, if we are not content with our ready-made supply of backgrounds, we may in our imagination (*cogitatione*) create a region for ourselves and obtain a most serviceable distribution of appropriate backgrounds (*idoneorum locorum*)" (at III.xix.32).

85. *PPTS*, 7:48–49; Fabri, *Evagatorium*, 1:61–62. I have italicized certain English phrases in order to call attention to the close association that Fabri makes between travail, composition, and the spatial orientation of the pilgrim's memory work—and also to the imprecise English terms used to translate vocabulary related to cognition and imagination.

86. The *Zardino de oration* (1454), a devotional guide written for young girls, tells its readers to construct imaginary architectural backdrops for their mental re-creations of biblical events, using elements of places they know in order to fashion this mise-en-scène: "Fix the places and people in your mind—a city, for example, which will be the city of Jerusalem, taking for this purpose a city that is known to you." Quoted in Michael Baxandall, *Painting and Experience in Fifteenth Century Italy: A Primer in the Social History of Pictorial Style* (Oxford: Oxford University Press, 1988), 45.

87. On the medieval ambivalence toward the faculty of the imagination (a concept that was by no means uniform across the writings of premodern thinkers), see Alastair Minnis, "Medieval Imagination and Memory," in *The Cambridge History of Literary Criticism*, vol. 2, *The Middle Ages*, ed. Alastair Minnis and Ian Johnson, 239–74 (Cambridge: Cambridge University Press, 2005). Recall, as well, that Albertus Magnus viewed the construction of mnemonic loci as described in the *Ad Herennium* as the occupation of the imagination, and therefore not identical with the rational process of recollection: "But physical backgrounds, at least ones of this sort, are in the image-making faculty." Cited in Carruthers, *Book of Memory*, 272.

88. Carruthers, *Book of Memory*, 197–207.

89. Geoffrey of Vinsauf, *Poetria nova*, trans. Margaret F. Nims (Toronto: Pontifical Institute, 2010), 20.

90. The English is from "A Certain Englishman (1344–45)," in *Western Pilgrims: The Itineraries of Fr. Simon Fitzsimons (1322–23), a Certain Englishman (1344–45), Thomas Brygg (1392), and Notes on Other Authors and Pilgrims*, ed. and trans. Eugene Hoade

(Jerusalem: Franciscan Printing Press, 1970), 48. The Latin is from Girolamo Golubovich, *Biblioteca bio-bibliografica della Terra Santa e dell'Oriente francescano*, vol. 4 (Rome: Collegium S. Bonaventurae, 1923), 435–60 (at 435–36), reads: "Primo de magno mari mediteraneo quod mare grecum appellatur, non sine causa tractare dignum duxi. Mare grecum in hominis effigie ymaginando depinxi. . . . In capite Apulie . . . extendit brachia sua, totam Apuliam."

91. Theoderic, *Peregrinatio*, in *Peregrinationes tres: Saewulf, John of Würzburg, Theodericus. With a Study of the Voyages of Saewulf by John H. Pryor*, ed. R.B.C. Huygens (Turnhout, Belgium: Brepols, 1994), line 44: "In qua civitas sancta Iherusalem quasi oculus in capite sita est," accessed through Library of Latin Texts, http://clt.brepolis.net /LLTA/pages/TextSearch.aspx?key=MWIRZC1392.

92. Alessandro Ariosto, *Itinerarium (1476–1479)*, ed. Fabio Uliana (Alessandria, Italy: Edizioni dell'Orso, 2007); Francesco Suriano, *Il trattato di Terra Santa e dell'oriente*, ed. Girolamo Golubovich (Milan: Tipografia editrice Artigianelli, 1900).

93. Recent research has confirmed that at least one recension of Burchard's *Description* included a graphic map of the Holy Land that corresponds to this description; later versions of the work added different kinds of maps or included wind-based mnemonic diagrams based on this passage. Some maps seem designed to help readers master the structural order of the *Description*, facilitating their recollections of toponyms and helping them recall where in the book this or that place was described. There is no definitive critical edition for this surprisingly popular work. For a comprehensive attempt to document its complex manuscript tradition and associated maps, see P.D.A. Harvey, *Medieval Maps of the Holy Land* (London: British Library, 2012), 107–44.

94. *PJ*, 242–43. As always, my adjustments to the translation—which attempt to show the remarkable overlap that exists in this passage among the domains of physical geography, the mental image, and the written page—are signaled by brackets. For the corresponding Latin, see J.C.M. Laurent, *Peregrinatores medii aevi quatuor: Burchardus de Monte Sion, Ricoldus de Monte Crucis, Odoricus de Foro Julii, Wilbrandus de Oldenborg* (Leipzig, 1864), 20–21:

> Aduertens autem, quomodo possem hec utiliter describere, ita ut possent a legentibus imaginatione facili comprehendi, cogitaui centrum aliquod in ea ponere et circa illud totam terram modo debito ordinare. Et ad hoc elegi ciuitatem achonensem, tanquam plus aliis notam. Que tamen non est in medio, sed in occidentali eius fine supra mare sita. Et ab ipsa protraxi quatuor lineas quatuor mundi partibus respondentes, et quamlibet quartram diuisi in tria, ut responderent duodecim diuisiones iste duodecim uentis celi, et in singulis diuisionibus posui ciuitates et loca in scripturis magis nota, ut singulorum locorum situs et dispositio posset de facili reperiri, ad quam partem mundi esset collocata.

95. Thomas Aquinas, *Sententia super metaphysicam*, in *Commentary on Aristotle's Metaphysics*, trans. John P. Rowan (Notre Dame, IN: Dumb Ox, 1995), I.1.17.

96. For details on these and other comparable editorial revisions, see the introduction to *Peregrinationes tres* (ed. Huygens).

97. This practice was so widespread that it has prompted Josephine Berfield, *A Guidebook for the Jerusalem Pilgrimage in the Late Middle Ages* (Amsterdam: Hilversum, 1994), to posit the existence of a now-lost common source for dozens of late medieval pil-

grimage accounts. Given the wide availability of works of travel writing and the fact that we know for certain that pilgrims read the works of others when composing and revising their accounts, this thesis is not especially convincing.

98. Translation mine. Fabri, *Evagatorium*, 1:2: "Pro certo autem dico, quod non tantum laborem habui de loco ad locum peregrinando, quantum habui de libro ad librum discurrendo, quae rendo, legendo, et scribendo, scripta corrigendo et concordando."

99. This is not to say that all medieval authors shared in this generally permissive attitude. Niccolò da Poggibonsi was so averse to the thought of his work being used without attribution that he embossed his *Libro* with an authorial acrostic. This precaution did not, however, deter a physician by the name of Gabriel Muffel from translating the *Libro* nearly word for word into German in the following century, without crediting his source. For details, see Kathryn Blair Moore, "The Disappearance of an Author and the Emergence of a Genre: Niccolò da Poggibonsi and Pilgrimage Guidebooks between Manuscript and Print," *Renaissance Quarterly* 66, no. 2 (2013): 357–411.

100. Carruthers, *Book of Memory*, 172–73, 200–204.

101. Ibid., 64–68.

102. Marco Polo, *Le divisement du monde*, 6 vols., ed. Philippe Ménard et al. (Geneva: Droz, 2001–9), 1:131:

> Et [il] comme sages et connoissans toute la maniere du Seigneur, se penoit moult de savoir et d'entendre toutes choses qu'il cuidoit qui pleussent au Grant Caan, si que a [ses retornees] li contoit tout [ordoneement], si que pour ce le Seignour l'amoit moult, et li plaisoit moult.

103. Ramusio, *Navigazione*, 3:22: "veramente è cosa meravigliosa a considerare la grandezza del viaggio. . . . E oltra di questo, come il predetto gentiluomo sapesse così ordinatamente descrivere ciò che vidde, essendo pochi uomini di quella sua età intelligenti de cotal dottrina, ed egli allevato tanto tempo appresso quella rozza nazione de'Tartari, senza alcuna accommodata maniera di scrivere."

104. Niccolò, *Libro*, 33:

> Al nome di Dio, e delle sua santissima madre Virgine Maria e del beato santo Francesco e di santa Caterina e di santa Barbara e di tutti i suoi santi e sante, che ci doni sua grazia, sì ch'io possa dire per ordine e contare le sante luogora d'Oltramare sanza fallimento come io le visitai.

105. Ibid., 42: "Poi, essendo in Gerusalem, io pigliai una misura di braccio, con uno passo, andando, e tutto per ordine, come qui udirete, sì misurava gli spazii e le lunghezze e le larghezze e recalve tutte a misura, e poi subito lo scriveva." In the previous sentence, the text specifies that these notes were taken "in su un paio di tavolelle che allato portava."

106. Ibid., 131: "dì per dì scriveva in su uno paio di tavolelle ingessate ch'io portava allato."

107. Ibid., 42: "Converrebbe molto l'uomo essere savio e discreto in providenzia ed essere bene accorto a ritenere alla sua memoria; e per non fallare io scriverò tosto delle luogora d'Oltremare."

108. Ibid., 42–43.

109. Ibid., 43:

Ma acciò che la mia fatica corporale nulla persona il detto travaglio, ch'io ho avuto per lo detto libro, a sé no·llo riputi né che dica che l'abbia fatto altro che io, frate Nicolò, e chi il mio nome vorrà trovare, e anche il nome di mio padre Corbizo, e donde io fui, e la prima lettera miniata del capitolo che da ora innanzi si comincia, lettera per lettera, tutto il troverrà per ordine.

Niccolò makes a nearly identical statement in the prologue of the work (at 33).

110. Adamnán, *Adamnán's De Locis Sanctis*, ed. Denis Meehan (Dublin: Dublin Institute for Advanced Studies, 1958), 46–47, where Adamnán refers to the exemplars provided by Saint Arculf as being made "in paginola . . . cerata." The characterizations of tablets that follow in this chapter are informed by: Richard H. Rouse and Mary A. Rouse, "The Vocabulary of Wax Tablets," *Vocabulaire du livre et de l' écriture au moyen âge: Actes de la table ronde Paris 24–26 septembre 1987*, ed. Olga Weijers (Turnhout, Belgium: Brepols, 1989); Peter Stallybrass et al., "Hamlet's Tables and the Technologies of Writing in Renaissance England," *Shakespeare Quarterly* 55, no. 4 (2004): 379–419; Michelle Brown, "The Role of the Wax Tablet in Medieval Literacy: A Reconsideration in Light of a Recent Find from York," *British Library Journal* 29, no. 1 (1994); Roger Chartier, *Inscription and Erasure: Literature and Written Culture from the Eleventh to the Eighteenth Century* (Philadelphia: University of Pennsylvania Press, 2007); Richard H. Rouse and Mary A. Rouse, "Wax Tablets," *Language and Communication* 9, nos. 2–3 (1989): 175–91.

111. On the slate tablet, see Jessie Ann Owens, *Composers at Work: The Craft of Musical Composition, 1450–1600* (Oxford: Oxford University Press, 1998), 74–99.

112. The process is described in Stallybrass et al., "Hamlet's Tables," 385–88.

113. Chartier, *Inscription and Erasure*, chap. 1; Curtius, *European Literature and the Latin Middle Ages*, 317.

114. Niccolò, *Libro*, 42–43.

115. For an overview of this pilgrimage-within-the-pilgrimage, see Nicole Chareyron, *Pilgrims to Jerusalem in the Middle Ages*, trans. W. Donald Wilson (New York: Columbia University Press, 2005), 127–46.

116. Niccolò, *Libro*, 145: "per la scurità ch'io ebbi, vedendole così grandissime, io no·lle potei misurare: ma lo compagno mio ne misurò una, la quale fu più lunga di lui uno palmo grosso; e io l'avisai secondo nostra misura, tre braccia e mezzo."

117. Cennino d'Andrea Cennini, *The Craftsman's Handbook: Il libro dell'arte*, ed. Daniel V.J. Thompson (New Haven, CT: Yale University Press, 1933), 1–4.

118. Moore, "Disappearance."

119. See ibid., 365–72, for a discussion of this and the other illustrated copies of the work.

120. At the very least, it pushes back the timeline for the widespread use of the gypsum tablet, which Stallybrass et al., "Hamlet's Tables," suggests is a fifteenth-century phenomenon.

121. *PPTS*, 7:56; Fabri, *Evagatorium*, 1:66:

Non enim praetermisi nec unum diem in itinere existens, quin aliquid scriberem, etiam in mari tempore tempestatum, in terra sancta, et per desertum saepe scripi sedens in asino, vel in camelo, vel noctibus, quando alii dormiebant, ego sedi et visa in scriptis deduxi.

122. *PPTS*, 7:408–9; Fabri, *Evagatorium*, 1:331–32.

123. For a discussion of all of the above, see Rouse and Rouse, "Wax Tablets"; and Brown, "Role of the Wax Tablet," 1–9.

124. *PPTS*, 8:528; Fabri, *Evagatorium*, 2:437:

> Ego in hoc valle rescripsi paene totum iter a Gaza usque huc; scripseram enim sedens in asino dispositiones et habitudines regionum et viarum in tabula de cera, quam cingulo portavi et ibi totum in libello rescripsi et de cera delevi, ut consequenter alia scriberem. Saepissime descendi de asino et itinera, montes et valles descripsi, quia non esset possible mente retineri singula, nisi homo quasi singulis horis laboraret.

125. My perspective on Fabri's tablets owes a debt to Bruno Latour's concept of "articulation"—which offers a remarkably nuanced way of thinking about how technology and habit participate in the creation of human subjects. See his "How to Talk about the Body? The Normative Dimension of Science Studies," *Body and Society* 10, nos. 2–3 (2004): 205–29 (at 208–14). Thanks to Jeffrey Jerome Cohen for introducing me to this piece.

126. Ogier d'Anglure, *The Holy Jerusalem Voyage of Ogier VIII, Seigneur d'Anglure*, trans. Ronald R. Brown (Gainesville: University Presses of Florida, 1975), 166.

127. Bertrandon de la Broquière [Brocquière], "The Travels of Bertrandon de la Brocquière, A.D. 1432 and 1433," in *Early Travels in Palestine: Comprising the Narratives of Arculf [and Others]*, trans. Thomas Wright, 283–382 (New York: Ktav Publishing House, 1968), 289.

128. *PPTS*, 8:528; Fabri, *Evagatorium*, 2:429.

129. By the fifteenth century, pilgrimage to the Holy Land had become a family tradition, as had travel writing. See chap. 4, p. 161.

130. For example, Nompar de Caumont, *Voyaige d'oultremer*, 1–5. The manuscript that attests to the pilgrimages of William Wey (Oxford, Bodleian Library MS Bodley 565) begins with his will.

131. See Franca Allegrezza, "La diffusione di un nuovo prodotto di bottega: Ipotesi sulla confezione dei libri di famiglia a Firenze nel quattrocento," *Scrittura e civiltà* 15 (1991): 247–65.

132. Jacopo da Verona, *Le pèlerinage du Moine Augustin Jacques De Vérone (1335)*, ed. Reinhold Röhricht (Paris, 1895).

133. See Giorgio Gucci, "Viaggio ai Luoghi Santi," in *Pellegrini scrittori: Viaggiatori Toscani del trecento in Terrasanta*, ed. Antonio Lanza and Marcellina Troncarelli, 257–312 (Florence: Ponte alle Grazie, 1990), 305–11.

134. Martoni, *Liber peregrinationis*, 578.

135. See Martha Carlin and David Crouch, eds., *Lost Letters of Medieval Life: English Society, 1200–1250* (Philadelphia: University of Pennsylvania Press, 2013), 92–98.

136. For details, see James Black, "Henry IV's Pilgrimage," *Shakespeare Quarterly* 34, no. 1 (1983): 18–26.

137. Ogier d'Anglure, *Holy Jerusalem Voyage*, 22–35.

138. On the aristocratic character of Holy Land pilgrimage in the fifteenth century, see Morris, *Sepulchre*, 306–10.

139. Luchino Dal Campo, *Viaggio del marchese Nicolò d'Este al Santo Sepolcro, 1413* (Florence: L.S. Olschki, 2011); Leo of Rozmital, *The Travels of Leo of Rozmital through Germany, Flanders, England, France, Spain, Portugal, and Italy, 1465–1467*, ed. Malcolm Letts (Cambridge: Cambridge University Press, 1957); Philippe de Voisins, *Voyage à Jérusalem de Philippe de Voisins, Seigneur de Montaut*, ed. Philippe Tamizey de Larroque (Paris: H. Champion, 1883); Henry Ellis, ed., *The Pylgrymage of Sir Richard Guylforde to the Holy Land, A.D. 1506* (London: printed for the Camden Society, 1851).

140. See Wes Williams, "'Rubbing Up against Others': Montaigne on Pilgrimage," in *Voyages and Visions: Towards a Cultural History of Travel*, ed. Jaś Elsner and Joan-Pau Rubiés, 101–23 (London: Reaktion Books, 1999).

141. Charles Henri Auguste Schefer, ed., *Le voyage de la saincte cyté de Hierusalem: Avec la description des lieux, portz, villes, citez, et aultres passaiges, fait l'an 1480, estant le siège du grand Turc à Rhodes et regnant en France loys unziesme de ce nom* (Amsterdam: Philo Press, 1970), 2. Translation mine.

142. Ibid. Translation mine.

143. Adorno, *Itinéraire*.

144. Translation mine. Felix Fabri, *Felix Fabri, Die Sionpilger*, ed. Wieland Carls, Texte des späten Mittelalters und der frühen Neuzeit 39 (Berlin: Erich Schmidt, 1999), 529: "sein bilgerfart indem aüssern raüchen wandel von ainer tagraiß zu der andern aün alle Einzüg der hochen vernüftigen speculacion."

145. Albrecht Classen, "Imaginary Experience of the Divine: Felix Fabri's *Sionpilger*—Late-Medieval Pilgrimage Literature as a Window into Religious Mentality," *Studies in Spirituality* 15 (2005): 109–28. See also the vital contribution of Kathryne Beebe, *Pilgrim & Preacher: The Audiences and Observant Spirituality of Friar Felix Fabri (1437/8–1502)* (Oxford: Oxford University Press, 2014), 178–210.

146. Randall Herz, *Die "Reise ins Gelobte Land" Hans Tuchers des Älteren (1479–1480): Untersuchungen zur Überlieferung und kritische Edition eines spätmittelalterlichen Reiseberichts* (Wiesbaden: Reichert Verlag, 2002), 624.

147. Broquière, "Travels," 283, 382.

148. Denis Possot, *Voyage de la Terre sainte, composé par Denis Possot et achevé par Charles Philippe [1532]*, ed. Charles Schefer (Paris: E. Leroux, 1890), 193.

149. Capgrave, *Solace*, 101.

150. Translation mine. Ruy González de Clavijo, *Embajada a Tamorlán*, ed. Francisco López Estrada (Madrid: Editorial Castalia, 1999), 2–3:

> Porque la dicha embaxada es ardua e a lueñes tierras, es necesario e cumplidero de poner en escripto todos los lugares e tierras por do los dichos embaxadores fueren e cosas que les ende acaescieron, por que no cayan en olvido e mejor e más verdaderamente se puedan contar e saber. Por ende, en'l nombre de Dios, en cuyo poder son las cosas, e de la Virgen Santa María, su madre, començé a escrivir desde el día que los embaxadores llegaron al Puerto de Santa María, cerca de Calíz, para entrar en una carraca en que avían de ir.

151. Ludolph von Suchem, "Ludolph Von Suchem's Description of the Holy Land, and of the Way Thither: Written in the Year A.D. 1350," trans. Aubrey Stewart, *PPTS*, 12:2.

152. Mandeville, *Livre* (ed. Deluz), 479, note *k*.

153. John Mandeville, *The Metrical Version of Mandeville's Travels: From the*

Unique Manuscript in the Coventry Corporation Record Office, ed. M.C. Seymour (London: Oxford University Press for the Early English Text Society, 1973), p. 1, lines 31–34.

154. Polo, *Description of the World,* 2:v.

155. Ramusio, *Navigazione e viaggi,* 3:21.

156. *PPTS,* 9:216; Fabri, *Evagatorium,* 3:85.

157. *PPTS,* 7:299; Fabri, *Evagatorium,* 1:322.

158. For Fabri's reflections on caverns, see *PPTS,* 8:589–90.

CHAPTER FOUR

1. See Rita George-Tvrtković, *A Christian Pilgrim in Medieval Iraq: Riccoldo da Montecroce's Encounter with Islam* (Turnhout, Belgium: Brepols, 2012); Suzanne M. Yeager, *Jerusalem in Medieval Narrative* (Cambridge: Cambridge University Press, 2008); Morris, *Sepulchre,* 260–82, 310–23; Rosamund Allen, ed., *Eastward Bound: Travel and Travellers, 1050–1550* (Manchester, UK: Manchester University Press, 2004).

2. Martin Jacobs, *Reorienting the East: Jewish Travelers to the Medieval Muslim World* (Philadelphia: University of Pennsylvania Press, 2014); Houari Touati, *Islam and Travel in the Middle Ages* (Chicago: University of Chicago Press, 2010); Roxanne Leslie Euben, *Journeys to the Other Shore: Muslim and Western Travelers in Search of Knowledge* (Princeton, NJ: Princeton University Press, 2006); Josef W. Meri, *The Cult of Saints among Muslims and Jews in Medieval Syria* (Oxford: Oxford University Press, 2002); Amikam Elad, *Medieval Jerusalem and Islamic Worship: Holy Places, Ceremonies, Pilgrimage* (Leiden, Netherlands: Brill, 1995).

3. Zur Shalev, *Sacred Words and Worlds: Geography, Religion, and Scholarship, 1550–1700* (Leiden, Netherlands: Brill, 2012); Carol Delaney, *Columbus and the Quest for Jerusalem: How Religion Drove the Voyages that Led to America* (New York: Free Press, 2011); F. Thomas Noonan, *The Road to Jerusalem: Pilgrimage and Travel in the Age of Discovery* (Philadelphia: University of Pennsylvania Press, 2007); Wes Williams, *Pilgrimage and Narrative in the French Renaissance: "The Undiscovered Country"* (Oxford: Oxford University Press, 1998).

4. Donald R. Howard, *Writers and Pilgrims: Medieval Pilgrimage Narratives and Their Posterity* (Berkeley: University of California Press, 1980); Christian K. Zacher, *Curiosity and Pilgrimage: The Literature of Discovery in Fourteenth-Century England* (Baltimore: Johns Hopkins University Press, 1976).

5. Stephen Greenblatt, *The Swerve: How the World Became Modern* (New York: Norton, 2011). A soothing balm is found in Kellie Robertson, "Medieval Materialism: A Manifesto," *Exemplaria* 22, no. 2 (2010): 99–118.

6. Hans Blumenberg, *The Legitimacy of the Modern Age* (Cambridge, MA: MIT Press, 1983).

7. On the question of whether there were "pilgrims" before Constantine, see J. Murphy O'Connor, "Pre-Constantinian Christian Jerusalem," in *The Christian Heritage in the Holy Land,* ed. Anthony O'Mahony, 13–21 (London: Scorpion Cavendish, 1995).

8. D. Golan, "Hadrian's Decision to Supplant 'Jerusalem' by 'Aelia Capitolina,'" *Historia* 35 (1986): 226–39.

9. An early source for these events is Eusebius's *Life of Constantine.* See *PPTS,* 1:1–7,

for an English translation of the story of this recovery effort. On the identification of sacred places in late antiquity, see Pierre Maraval, *Lieux saints et pèlerinages d'Orient. Histoire et géographie. Des origines à la conquête arabe* (Paris: Les Editions du Cerf, 1985); and Timothy D. Barnes, *Constantine and Eusebius* (Cambridge, MA: Harvard University Press, 1981), 108–11.

10. For an overview of sources on both imperial quests and their related controversies, see Joachim Jeremias, *Golgotha* (Leipzig: E. Pfeiffer, 1926); Jan Willem Drijvers, *Helena Augusta: The Mother of Constantine the Great and the Legend of Her Finding of the True Cross* (Leiden, Netherlands: Brill, 1992).

11. On Jerome's geographical thought, see Weingarten, *Saint's Saints*; John Wilkinson, "L'apport de saint Jérôme à la topographie de la Terre Sainte," *Revue Biblique* 81 (1974): 245–57.

12. Translated in Hunt, *Holy Land Pilgrimage*, 94.

13. Jerome, *Select Letters and Works*, letter XLIV, 189.

14. On Augustine's mostly circumspect view of devotional travel, see Bitton-Ashkelony, *Encountering the Sacred*, 106–39.

15. Edward Peters, ed., *The First Crusade: The Chronicle of Fulcher of Chartres and Other Source Materials* (Philadelphia: University of Pennsylvania Press, 1971), 88.

16. Albert of Aachen, *Historia Ierosolimitana: History of the Journey to Jerusalem*, ed. and trans. Susan B. Edgington (Oxford: Clarendon Press, 2007), 435.

17. For an overview of these changes, see Denys Pringle, *Churches, Castles and Landscape in the Frankish East* (Farnham, Surrey, UK: Ashgate Variorum, 2013).

18. John of Würzburg, *Peregrinatio*, in *Peregrinationes tres: Saewulf, John of Würzburg, Theodericus. With a Study of the Voyages of Saewulf by John H. Pryor*, ed. R.B.C. Huygens (Turnhout, Belgium: Brepols, 1994), accessed through *Library of Latin Texts*, online resource, lines 20–26: "Quam descriptionem tibi acceptam fore estimo, ideo scilicet, quia evidenter singula per eam notata tibi, quandoque divina inspiratione et tuitione huc venienti, sponte et sine inquisitionis mora et difficultate tanquam nota tuis sese ingerunt oculis."

19. Ibid., lines 27–35.

20. Ibid., line 12: "precipue in civitate sancta Iherusalem, quanto expressius et studiosius potui denotando, in eis facta et epygrammata sive prosaice sive metrice stili officio colligere laboravi."

21. Ibid., lines 1440–47:

Sicsic describendo venerabilia loca in sancta civitate Iherusalem, incipiendo ab aecclesia Sancti Sepulchri circumeundo per Portam David usque ad eandem reversi sumus, plures omittendo capellas et inferiores aecclesias, quas habent ibi diversarum nationum et linguarum homines. Sunt namque ibi Greci, Latini, Alemanni, Ungari, Scoti, Navarri, Brittanni Anglici, Rutheni, Boemi, Gorgiani, Armeni, Suriani, Iacobitae, Syri, Nestoriani, Indi, Egiptii, Cepthi, Capheturici, Maroni et alii quam plures, quos longum esset enumerare, sed in his finem huius opusculi faciemus Amen.

22. Theoderic, *Peregrinatio*, lines 27–37:

Et harum quidem urbium omnia loca vel nomina antiquitus cunctis patebant, a modernis vero utpote adventiciis, non nativa habitatione ibidem manentibus, preter paucorum nomina locorum, que postea suo loco narrabimus, ignorantur . . . Vespasianus et Tytus, Romani principes, cum exercitu Iudeam intrantes templum et civitatem solo coequaverunt, totius Iudee civitates et castella destruxerunt. . . . Idcirco omnia tam populi quam totius provincie instrumenta sive emolumenta deleta sunt, quin et si quorumlibet aliqua patent locorum vestigia, omnium tamen fere nomina sunt immutata.

23. Benjamin of Tudela, *Itinerary*, 78.

24. For background, see Amikam Elad, "Pilgrims and Pilgrimage to Hebron (al-Khalil) during the Early Muslim Period (638?–1099)," in *Pilgrims & Travelers to the Holy Land*, ed. Bryan F. Le Beau and Menachem Mor, 21–62 (Omaha: Creighton University Press, 1996).

25. Benjamin of Tudela, *Itinerary*, 76–77.

26. Ibid., 77.

27. See, for example, the arguments that Benjamin advances for the claim that the ruined town of Harama was "built by our ancestors," as well as his counterimperial account of the Jewish history of monuments in the city of Rome. Benjamin of Tudela, *Itinerary*, 39–41, 79.

28. Meri, *Cult of Saints*, 126–39.

29. Ibn Battuta, *Travels*, 1:74–75.

30. See *PJ*, 1–19; English translations of relevant sources can be found in Wilkinson, Hill, and Ryan, *Jerusalem Pilgrimage, 1099–1185*.

31. *PJ*, 87.

32. Ibid., 179.

33. Jacopo da Verona, *Le pèlerinage*, 72: "a paucis temporibus elapsis in partibus ultramarinis res sunt multum mutate et maxime in detrimentum cristianorum."

34. Catherine Delano-Smith, "The Intelligent Pilgrim: Maps and Medieval Pilgrimage to the Holy Land," in *Eastward Bound: Travel and Travellers, 1050–1550*, ed. Rosamund Allen, 107–30 (Manchester, UK: Manchester University Press, 2004).

35. See chap. 3, pp. 122–23.

36. *PJ*, 241; Burchard of Mount Sion, *Descriptio Terrae Sanctae*, in *Peregrinatores medii aevi quatuor: Buchardus de Monte Sion, Ricoldus de Monte Crucis, Odoricus de Foro Julii, Wilbrandus de Oldenborg. Quorum duos nunc primum edidit duos ad fidem librorum manuscriptorum recensuit*, ed. J.C.M. Laurent, 1–100 (Leipzig, 1864), 19.

37. *PJ*, 242; Burchard of Mount Sion, *Descriptio*, 20:

quantum potui, consideraui, et notaui diligenter, et studiose descripsi, hoc lectorem scire uolens, quod nichil in hac descriptione posui, nisi quod uel presencialiter in locis ipsis existens uidi, uel stans in montibus aliquibus uel locis aliis oportunis, ubi accessum habere non potui, a Syrianis uel a Sarracenis aut aliis terre habitatoribus diligentissime, quod querebam, interrogans annotaui.

38. *PJ*, 243; Burchard of Mount Sion, *Descriptio*, 20.

39. *PJ*, 81–82, 151–52. The topographical debate would be taken up again by early modern authors. See Shalev, *Sacred Worlds*, 157–60.

40. *PJ*, 284; Burchard of Mount Sion, *Descriptio*, 59.

41. *PJ*, 285; Burchard of Mount Sion, *Descriptio*, 60.

42. Meri, *Cult of Saints*, 200–201.

43. *PJ*, 242; Burchard of Mount Sion, *Descriptio*, 20.

44. Marino Sanudo Torsello, *The Book of the Secrets of the Faithful of the Cross*, tr.

Peter Lock (Farnham, Surrey, UK: Ashgate, 2011). For a survey of the maps that accompanied this work, see Harvey, *Medieval Maps of the Holy Land*, 107–27.

45. Lionardo Frescobaldi, "Viaggio in Terrasanta," in *Pellegrini scrittori: Viaggiatori Toscani del trecento in Terrasanta*, ed. Antonio Lanza and Marcellina Troncarelli, 167–215 (Florence: Ponte alle Grazie, 1990); Emmanuel Piloti, *Traité d'Emmanuel Piloti sur le passage en Terre Sainte, 1420*, ed. Pierre-Herman Dopp (Louvain, Belgium: Pierre-Herman Dopp, 1958).

46. These portions of Riccoldo's work were intentionally omitted from *PJ*. They were subsequently translated in George-Tvrtković, *Christian Pilgrim*.

47. George-Tvrtković, *Christian Pilgrim*, 175.

48. Ibid., 93.

49. On the ownership history and patronage context for this manuscript, see Richard H. Rouse and Mary A. Rouse, *Manuscripts and Their Makers: Commercial Book Producers in Medieval Paris, 1200–1500*, 2 vols. (Turnhout, Belgium: Harvey Miller, 2000), 1:212, 1:244–47, 1:250, 1:254.

50. On the Royal manuscript, see George F. Warner and Julius P. Gilson, *Catalogue of Western Manuscripts in the Old Royal and King's Collections*, 4 vols. (London: British Museum, 1921), 2:339–41.

51. Ursula Ganz-Blättler, *Andacht und Abenteuer: Berichte europäischer Jerusalem- und Santiago-Pilger, 1320–1520* (Tübingen: Gunter Narr Verlag, 1990), 39–43; Reinhold Röhricht, ed., *Bibliotheca geographica Palaestinae: Chronologisches Verzeichnis der auf die Geographie des Heiligen Landes bezüglichen Literatur von 333 bis 1878 und Versuch einer Cartographie* (Berlin, 1890), 45–50, counts over 150 written between 1200 and 1400. Estimates vary depending on the generic definitions adopted by the individual scholar. By any measure, late medieval Jerusalem pilgrims produced a corpus of travel accounts that is unprecedented in the western literary tradition.

52. Abu-Lughod, *Before European Hegemony*, 102–31; Epstein, *Purity Lost*, 113–20, 163–65.

53. On the little that is known about William, see Iain M. Higgins, "William of Boldensele," in *Trade, Travel, and Exploration in the Middle Ages: An Encyclopedia*, ed. John B. Friedman and Kristen M. Figg, 645–46 (New York: Garland Pub., 2000).

54. Norman P. Zacour, "Petrarch and Talleyrand," *Speculum* 31, no. 4 (1956): 683–703.

55. *PJ*, 237–41; Simon's account is collected in *Western Pilgrims: The Itineraries of Fr. Simon Fitzsimons (1322–23), a Certain Englishman (1344–45), Thomas Brygg (1392), and Notes on Other Authors and Pilgrims*, ed. and trans. Eugene Hoade (Jerusalem: Franciscan Printing Press, 1970); Jacopo da Verona, *Le pèlerinage*.

56. Gregory of Tours, *Decem libri historiarum*, in *Monumenta Germaniae Historica, Scriptores rerum Merovingicarum*, vol. 1, pt. 1, ed. Bruno Krusch and Wilhelm Levison (Hannover, 1965), bk. 1, §10.

57. William of Boldensele, "Des Edelherrn Wilhelm von Boldensele Reise nach dem Gelobten Lande," in *Zeitschrift des Historischen Vereins für Niedersachsen*, ed. C. L. Grotefend, 209–86 (Hanover, 1855), 252: "Horum versuum obscura expositio aliquantulum me tenebat. Dicunt simplices haec maxima monumenta fuisse granaria Pharaonis. . . . Verum quod monumenta sint, versus praescripti attestantur et multa alia ipsa praesentialiter intuenti."

58. Mandeville, *Book* (ed. and trans. Higgins), 32; Mandeville, *Livre* (ed. Deluz), 155–56.

59. William of Boldensele, "Reise," 253.

60. Ibid.

61. Mandeville, *Book* (ed. and trans. Higgins), 36; Mandeville, *Livre* (ed. Deluz), 164.

62. Mandeville, *Book* (ed. and trans. Higgins), 31–32; Mandeville, *Livre* (ed. Deluz), 154–55.

63. Mandeville, *Book* (ed. and trans. Higgins), 86–87; Mandeville, *Livre* (ed. Deluz), 278–80.

64. Mandeville, *Book* (ed. and trans. Higgins), 15–17; Mandeville, *Livre* (ed. Deluz), 115–17.

65. For discussions of this fascinating scene, see Shirin Khanmohamadi, "Worldly Unease in Late Medieval Travel Reports," in *Cosmopolitanism and the Middle Ages*, ed. John M. Ganim and Shayne Legassie, 105–20 (New York: Palgrave, 2013); Akbari, *Idols in the East*, 54–58; Higgins, *Writing East*, 116–22.

66. Mandeville, *Livre* (ed. Deluz), 280.

67. Richard Beauchamp, *The Pageants of Richard Beauchamp, Earl of Warwick, Reproduced in Facsimile from the Cottonian Ms. Julius E. IV, in the British Museum*, ed. British Library and Roxburghe Club (Oxford: Roxburghe Club, 1908), 37.

68. von Harff, *Pilgrimage*, 103–5, 239–40.

69. Martoni, *Liber peregrinationis*, 644–45.

70. Joos van Ghistele and Ambrosius Zeebout, *Tvoyage van Mher Joos van Ghistele*, ed. R.J.G.A.A. Gaspar (Hilversum, Netherlands: Verloren, 1998), 370:

> Item men seit dat in Lango [i.e., Rhodes] Ypocras vele schoonder saken ghedaen heeft ende daer vonden vele consten van medecinen; daer wassen ooc vele goeder cruden van medecinen. Eeneghe boucken zegghen, dat de dochtere vanden zelven Ypocras noch daer zijn zoude bij fairien inde ghedaente van eender draken, bijder nigromancien vander goddinnen Dyana.

71. Cristoforo Buondelmonti, *Librum insularum archipelagi*, ed. G.R.L. von Sinner (Leipzig: Reimer, 1824), 103. For background, see George Tolias, "Isolarii, Fifteenth to Seventeenth Century," in *HC*, 3:265–67; P.D.A. Harvey, "Local and Regional Cartography in Medieval Europe," in *HC*, 1:473–76; and Thomas Goldstein, "Geography in Fifteenth-Century Florence," in *Merchants & Scholars: Essays in the History of Exploration and Trade, Collected in Memory of James Ford Bell*, ed. John Parker, 9–32 (Minneapolis: University of Minnesota Press, 1965).

72. Ludolph von Suchem, *Ludolph von Suchem's Description of the Holy Land and of the Way Thither*, in *PPTS*, 12:2.

73. Ibid., 12:13–16.

74. Ibid., 12:23–26.

75. Ibid., 12:22.

76. Ibid., 12:18–19.

77. Pietro Casola, *Canon Pietro Casola's Pilgrimage to Jerusalem in the Year 1494*, trans. M. Margaret Newett (Manchester, UK: Manchester University Press, 1907).

78. Alessandro di Filippo Rinuccini, *Sanctissimo peregrinaggio del Sancto Sepulcro, 1474*, ed. Andrea Calamai (Pisa, Italy: Pacini, 1993), 4–5.

79. *PPTS*, 8:334.

80. Ibid.

81. Ibid., 8:335.

82. Ibid., 8:334.

83. Ibid., 9:250–58.

84. Petrarch, *Letters on Familiar Matters*, 3:279–80.

85. Christiane Deluz, "Prier à Jérusalem: Permanence et évolution d'après quelques récits de pèlerins occidentaux du Vᵉ au XVᵉ siècle," in *La prière au Moyen Age: Littérature et civilisation*, 189–210 (Aix-en-Provence, France: CUERMA, 1981).

86. As mentioned in the previous chapter, Jacopo da Verona, writing in 1335, is one of the first pilgrim travel writers to include a list of indulgences, but does so at the beginning of his book.

87. See Chareyron, *Pilgrims to Jerusalem*, 86–87.

88. William Wey, *The Itineraries of William Wey*, ed. Francis Davey (Oxford: Bodleian Library, 2010), 130–31.

89. *PPTS*, 9:340.

90. Ibid.

91. Ibid., 8:415–16.

92. Petrarch, *Itinerary*, 16.2.

93. Ibid., 16.2–3.

94. Christine de Pizan, *Chemin*, lines 1275–82. Translation mine.

95. *PJ*, 112.

96. Sebald Rieter et al., *Das Reisebuch Der Familie Rieter*, ed. Reinhold Röhricht and Heinrich Meisner (Stuttgart, 1884), 14.

97. Ludovico di Varthema, *The Travels of Ludovico di Varthema in Egypt, Syria, Arabia Deserta and Arabia Felix, in Persia, India, and Ethiopia, A.D. 1503 to 1508*, ed. George Percy Badger, trans. John Winter Jones (London, 1863).

98. Howard, *Writers and Pilgrims*, 107.

99. Shalev, *Sacred Worlds*, 83.

100. Mark Monmonier, *Rhumb Lines and Map Wars: A Social History of the Mercator Projection* (Chicago: University of Chicago Press, 2004), 2–4.

101. Michel de Montaigne, *The Complete Essays*, ed. and trans. M.A. Screech (New York: Penguin, 2003), 206.

102. Felix Fabri, *Fratris Felicis Fabri tractatus de civitate ulmensi, de eius origine, ordine, regimine, de civibus eius et statu*, ed. Gustav Veesenmeyer (Tübingen, 1889).

INTRODUCTION TO PART THREE

1. On the novelty of Gerald's geoethnographic writing, see Robert Bartlett, *Gerald of Wales: A Voice of the Middle Ages* (Stroud, Gloucestershire, UK: Tempus, 2006), 149–50; Khanmohamadi, *In Light of Another's Word*, 37–40.

2. For example: J.H. Elliott, *The Old World and the New, 1492–1650* (Cambridge: Cambridge University Press, 1970); Geoffroy Atkinson, *La littérature géographique française de la Renaissance* (Paris: Picard, 1927).

CHAPTER FIVE

1. For a documentary and philological account of the process behind Petrarch's epistolary anthology, see Giuseppe Billanovich, *Petrarca letterato*, vol. 1, *Lo scrittoio del Petrarca* (Rome: Edizioni di Storia e Letteratura, 1947), 1–55.

2. Thomas M. Greene, "Petrarch *'Viator'*: The Displacements of Heroism," *Yearbook of English Studies* 12 (1982): 35–57; Theodore J. Cachey Jr., "Petrarch, Boccaccio, and the New World Encounter," *Stanford Italian Review* 10 (1991): 45–59; Theodore J. Cachey Jr., "Petrarch's Cartographical Writing," in *Humanisms in the Intellectual World: 12th–16th Century*, ed. Bert Roest and Stephen Gersh, 73–91 (Leiden, Netherlands: Brill, 2003); Theodore J. Cachey Jr., introduction to Petrarch, *Itinerary*, 1–50.

3. Jakob Burckhardt, *The Civilization of the Renaissance in Italy*, trans. S.G.C. Middlemore (New York: Harper, 1958), 201–5.

4. Lynn Thorndike, "Renaissance or Prenaissance?" *Journal of the History of Ideas* 4, no. 1 (1943): 65–74.

5. Blumenberg, *Legitimacy of the Modern Age*, 341–42.

6. Cachey, "Petrarch's Cartographical Writing," 74–75.

7. Thomas Peterson, "Out of Babylon: The 'Figura' of Exile in Tasso and Petrarch," *Annali d'Italianistica* 20 (2002): 127–47; Greene, "Petrarch *'Viator'*"; Ernest Hatch Wilkins, "Peregrinus Ubique," *Studies in Philology* 45 (1948): 445–53.

8. For two recent readings of Petrarch's geographical writing that successfully integrate his aesthetic and political passions, see Jennifer Summit, "Topography as Historiography: Petrarch, Chaucer, and the Making of Medieval Rome," *JMEMS* 30, no. 2 (2000): 211–46; and David Wallace, *Premodern Places: Calais to Surinam, Chaucer to Aphra Behn* (Malden, MA: Blackwell, 2004), 203–38.

9. For an overview of these debates, see Robin Cohen, *Global Diasporas: An Introduction* (New York: Routledge, 2008); Rogers Brubaker, "The 'Diaspora' Diaspora," *Ethnic and Racial Studies* 28, no. 1 (2005): 1–19; Jonathan Boyarin and Daniel Boyarin, *Powers of Diaspora: Two Essays on the Relevance of Jewish Culture* (Minneapolis: University of Minnesota Press, 2002). Boyarin and Boyarin defend the usefulness of foregrounding the largely Jewish roots of the term, an argument that seems especially convincing in the case of Petrarch, who, after all, viewed the "Babylonian captivity" of the papacy in Avignon as the defining political upheaval of his life.

10. On this facet of Petrarch's career, see Christopher S. Celenza, "Petrarch, Latin, and Italian Renaissance Latinity," *JMEMS* 35, no. 3 (2005): 509–36.

11. Girolamo Tiraboschi, *La Storia della letteratura italiana*, 15 vols. (Modena, Italy, 1787–94), 5:130–33.

12. Billanovich, *Petrarca letterato*, 47–55.

13. Petrarch, *Letters on Familiar Matters*. Subsequent citations from this translation appear parenthetically in the body of the chapter. Corresponding Latin citations can be found in the notes. All Latin quotations of this work are drawn from Francis Petrarch, *Le familiari*, 4 vols., ed. Vittorio Rossi and Umberto Bosco (Florence, Italy: Sansoni, 1933–42): "diebus ac noctibus tam miserabili quam cupido fovebat amplexu" (I.4.8).

14. "sub gelida rigentique lingua repertam festinabundus avexit" (I.4.12).

15. "Aquis forte tum rex cum proceribus suis habitabat; ex eoque tempore cuntis civitatibus sedes illa prelata est" (1:4.15).

16. "illis aquis uti mira cum voluptate, illius odore veluti suavissimo delectari" (I.4.15).

17. "quandiu romani frena imperii theutonica manus aget" (I.4.16). The political significance of this anecdote is explored in lively detail in Angela Matilde Capodivacca, "'Di pensier in pensier, di monte in monte': Petrarch's 'Modern Curiosity' in the *Familiares*," *MLN* 127, no. 1 (2012): 54–63.

18. "Gallias ego nuper nullo quidem negotio, ut nosti, sed visendi tantum studio et iuvenili quodam ardore peragravi" (I.4.1).

19. See Greene, "Petrarch '*Viator*,'" 8–9; Giuseppe F. Mazzotta, "Petrarch's Epistolary Epic: Letters on Familiar Matters (Rerum familiarum libri)," in *Petrarch: A Critical Guide to the Complete Works*, ed. Victoria Kirkham and Armando Maggi, 309–20 (Chicago: University of Chicago Press, 2009).

20. "Pace tua dixerim, nimis tibi Parvus Pons parisiensis impressit nec testudinei quidem sui arcus effigiem; nimis aures tuas subterlabentis Secane murmur oblectat; postremo nimis calceo tuo gallicus pulvis insedit. Oblitus michi videris illius qui interrogatus cuias esset, mundanum se esse respondit; tu usque adeo gallus es ut Gallie fines excedere quamlibet ob causam exilium voces" (IX.13.10). The "man" in question is Socrates.

21. "Germaniam tandem Rhenique ripas attigi, contemplatus solicite mores hominum et aspectu telluris incognite delectatus, ac singula cum nostris conferens. Et licet multa utrobique magnifica viderim, me tamen italice originis non penitet; imo, ut verum fatear, quo latius peregrinor, eo maior natalis soli subit admiratio" (I.4.1).

22. "Longior fui in hac narratione quam debui; sed quoniam peregrinatio longinqua librorum solatio destituta est et in perpetuo motu facilius est multa cogitare quam grandia, iustum epystole modum implere seriis non valens, eam, ut vides, obviis quibusque confercio" (I.4.17).

23. W. Scott Blanchard, "Petrarch and the Genealogy of Asceticism," *Journal of the History of Ideas* 62, no. 3 (2001): 401–23; Gur Zak, *Petrarch's Humanism and the Care of the Self* (Cambridge: Cambridge University Press, 2010); Giles Constable, "Petrarch and Monasticism," in *Francesco Petrarca: Citizen of the World*, ed. Aldo S. Bernardo, 53–99 (Padua: Antenore, 1980); Armando Maggi, "'You Will Be My Solitude': Solitude as Prophecy," in *Petrarch: A Critical Guide to the Complete Works*, ed. Victoria Kirkham and Armando Maggi, 165–77 (Chicago: University of Chicago Press, 2009).

24. On the ideology of literary pleasure, see Glending Olson, *Literature as Recreation in the Later Middle Ages* (Ithaca, NY: Cornell University Press, 1982).

25. For Cachey's characterization of Petrarch as a long-distance specialist, see his introduction to Petrarch, *Itinerary*, 5–6; and Cachey, "Petrarch's Cartographical Writing," 75–77. See chapter 2 of this book for more on this concept.

26. "Ut de terris ad quas ibam, et de singulis que vidissem audivissemque, perinde te certiorem scripto facerem ac verbo soleo . . . Promisi me facturum; promissum crebris ex itinere literulis implesse videor" (I.5.14).

27. "Mos michi tuus olim notus; nil ignorare potes equo animo, ita generosum spiritum inexplebilis noscendi cupiditas exagitat. Gessi voluntati tue morem, quotiens

Arthon aut Occasum circuire fortuna me voluit mea; nunc michi diversum iter, mens eadem est, idem parendi propositum" (V.4.1).

28. I.4.4:

Pariseorum civitatem, regni caput, que auctorem Iulium Cesarem pretendit, introii non aliter animo affectus quam olim Thesalie civitatem Ypatham dum lustrat, Apuleius. Ita enim solicito stupore suspensus et cunta circumspiciens, videndi cupidus explorandique vera ne an ficta essent que de illa civitate audieram, non parvum in ea tempus absumpsi, et quotiens operi lux defuit, noctem superaddidi. Demum ambiendo et inhiando, magna ex parte didicisse videor quis in eadem veritati, quis fabulis locus sit; que quoniam longa narratio est neque hoc loco satis explicabilis, differenda est, donec ex me omnia coram audies.

29. Apuleius, *The Golden Ass; or, A Book of Changes*, trans. Joel C. Relihan (Indianapolis: Hackett, 2007), 23.

30. Ibid.

31. "Sed bene habet, quia quod laboriose querimus, impune nescimus. Lateat ad aquilonem Thile, lateat ad austrum Nili caput; modo non lateat in medio consistens virtus et huius vite brevis semita, per quam magna pars hominum palpitando titubandoque proficiscitur ad incertum finem ambiguo calle festinans. Ne ergo nimis magnam operam impendamus in inquisitione loci, quem forsan inventum cupide linqueremus, claudenda iam epystola et tempus curis melioribus impendendum est" (III.1.14–15).

32. From Petrarch, "On His Own Ignorance and That of Many Others," in Petrarch, *Invectives*, trans. David Marsh (Cambridge, MA: Harvard University Press, 2003), 238:

He knows that the phoenix is burned on an aromatic pyre and is reborn from its ashes; that the sea urchin can halt a vessel launched with great force. . . . In most cases, these things are false, as was revealed when such animals were brought to our part of the world. . . . What use is it, I ask, to know the nature of beasts and birds and fish and snakes and to ignore or neglect our human nature, the purpose of our birth, or whence we come and whither we are bound? I have often made these and similar objections to these scribes, who consider themselves most learned, not in the law or Moses or Christ, but in that of Aristotle.

33. William J. Kennedy, "The Economy of Invective and a Man in the Middle," in *Petrarch: A Critical Guide to the Complete Works*, ed. Victoria Kirkham and Armando Maggi, 263–76 (Chicago: University of Chicago Press, 2009).

34. Petrarch, "Invective against a Detractor of Italy," in Petrarch, *Invectives*, trans. David Marsh (Cambridge, MA: Harvard University Press, 2003), 223.

35. For discussions of this event and an English translation of the coronation oration, see Ernest H. Wilkins, "Petrarch's Coronation Oration," *PMLA* 68, no. 5 (1953): 1241–50.

36. "et Avinionem, ubi te nunc ac genus humanum Romanus Pontifex detinet" (I.5.16).

37. "Confestim, amicorum monitu—nam et ibi amicos prius michi fama pepererat quam meritum" (I.5.2).

38. I.5.5–6:

Nam et hoc inter cunta mirabere, celum illud spiritus pyerios alere. Itaque dum muratur Iuvenalis quod "Gallia causidicos docuit facunda Britannos," miretur itidem

"Docta quod argutos aluit Germania vates." At ne me auctore fallaris, scito ibi nullum Maronem esse, Nasones plurimos; ut dicas verum fuisse "presagium" quod in fine libri *Methamorphoseos*, multum vel posteritatis gratie vel ingenio suo fidens, posuit. Siquidem "qua romana potentia", seu verius qua romanum nomen, domito orbe, se porrigit plausibiliter nunc faventis "populi ore perlegitur."

39. For a discussion of Ovidian tropes in Petrarch's lyrics, see Teodolinda Barolini, "The Self in the Labyrinth of Time," in *Petrarch: A Critical Guide to the Complete Works*, ed. Victoria Kirkham and Armando Maggi, 33–62 (Chicago: University of Chicago Press, 2009).

40. "Audiebam Ovidium, cuius quo lascivior Musa eo michi severior graviorque confessio et incorruptius testimonium veri erat" (XXIV.1.6).

41. Petrarch, *The Life of Solitude*, trans. Jacob Zeitlin (Urbana: University of Illinois Press, 1924), claims that Ovid was a man of "extremely effeminate temper, who found pleasure in the company of women to such an extent that he placed in them the sum and apex of his happiness" (273). The indictment in its original Latin reads: "Ille michi quidem magni vir ingenii videtur, sed lascivi et lubrici et prorsus mulierosi animi fuisse, quem conventus feminei delectarent usque adeo, ut in illis felicitatis sue apicem summamque reponeret." From Petrarch, *De vita solitaria*, in *Prose*, ed. Guido Martellotti et al. (Milan: Ricciardi Editore, 1955), 286–593 (at 532).

42. Zak, *Petrarch's Humanism*, 122–30.

43. I.5.3–4:

Omnis enim ripa preclaro et ingenti mulierum agmine tegebatur. Obstupui: dii boni, que forma, quis habitus! amare potuisset quisquis eo non preoccupatum animum attulisset. In loco paulum altiore constiteram, unde in ea que gerebantur, intenderem. Incredibilis sine offensione concursus erat; vicissimque alacres, pars herbis odoriferis incincte reductisque post cubitum manicis, candidas in gurgite manus ac brachia lavabant, nescio quid blandum peregrino murmure colloquentes. Vix usquam clarius intellexi quod Ciceroni placet et veteri proverbio dici solet, inter linguas incognitas omnes propemodum surdos ac mutos esse.

44. For a classic rumination on love, distance, and subjectivity, see Denis de Rougemont, *Love in the Western World*, trans. Montgomery Belgion (Princeton, NJ: Princeton University Press, 1983). For specific considerations of subjectivity in Petrarchan lyric, see John Freccero, "The Fig Tree and the Laurel: Petrarch's Poetics," *Diacritics* 5 (1975): 34–40; and Giuseppe Mazzotta, "The Canzoniere and the Language of the Self," *Studies in Philology* 75 (1978): 271–96.

45. I.4.7:

His ego comitibus, ubi quid audiendum seu respondendum incidit, pro lingua et pro auribus usus sum. Unum igitur ex eo numero, admirans et ignarus rerum, percontatus virgiliano illo versiculo:

Quid vult concursus ad amnem?
Quidve petunt anime?

responsum accepi, pervetustum gentis ritum esse, vulgo persuasum, presertim femineo, omnem totius anni calamitatem imminentem fluviali illius diei ablutione purgari et deinceps letiora succedere; itaque lustrationem esse annuam inexhausto semper studio cultam colendamque.

46. "Ad hec ego subridens: 'O nimium felices' inquam, 'Rheni accole, quorum ille miserias purgat! nostras quidem nec Padus unquam valuit purgare, nec Tyberis. Vos vestra mala Britannis, Rheno vectore, transmittitis; nos nostra libenter Afris atque Illiriis mitteremus; sed nobis, ut intelligi datur, pigriora sunt flumina'. Commoto risu, serum tandem inde discessimus" (I.5.8).

47. The classic study of medieval Virgilian lore is Domenico Comparetti, *Vergil in the Middle Ages*, trans. E.F.M. Benecke (Princeton, NJ: Princeton University Press, 1997), 239–358.

48. I.5.11–12:

> Vidi Capitolium, effigiem nostri; nisi quod pro senatu illic pacis ac belli consilia agitante, hic formosi iuvenes ac puelle mixtim nocturnas laudes Deo concinunt eterna concordia; ibi rotarum et armorum strepitus ac gemitus captivorum, hic quies et gaudium et iocantium voces; denique, illuc bellicus, huc pacificus triumphator ingreditur. Vidi templum urbe media pulcerrimum quamvis inexpletum, quod haud immerito summum vocant. Magorum ibi regum corpora, ab ortu ad occasum tribus saltibus transvecta, quos ethereum quondam Regem ad presepia vagientem cum muneribus veneratos legimus, venerabundus aspexi.

49. "Proximis aliquot diebus, a mane ad vesperam civitatem eisdem ducibus circuivi; haud iniocundum exercitium, non tam ob id quod ante oculos erat, quam recordatione nostrorum maiorum, qui tam procul a patria monimenta romane virtutis tam illustria reliquissent" (I.5.9).

50. See Petrarch, *The Canzoniere; or, Rerum vulgarium fragmenta*, trans. Mark Musa (Bloomington: Indiana University Press, 1996), 28.46–60.

51. For vital perspectives on Petrarch, humanism, and the Crusades, see Nancy Bisaha, *Creating East and West: Renaissance Humanists and the Ottoman Turks* (Philadelphia: University of Pennsylvania Press, 2004), 13–42; and Nancy Bisaha, "Petrarch's Vision of the Muslim and Byzantine East," *Speculum* 76, no. 2 (2001): 284–314.

52. "Hic igitur expectare in animo est, donec et estas ipsa deferveat, quam hucusque non senseram, et me vegetiorem quies faciat, qui me fessum esse hoc ipso primum loquente perpendi. Nulla quidem fatigatio maior quam animi est. Quodsi reliqui itineris tedium subierit, Rodanus michi pro vehiculo erit" (I.5.18).

53. "In presens nichil est quod inchoare ausim, miraculo rerum tantarum et stuporis mole obrutus" (II.14.1).

54. Michel de Montaigne, *The Journal of Montaigne's Travels in Italy by Way of Switzerland and Germany in 1580 and 1581*, 3 vols., ed. and trans. W.G. Waters (London: Murray, 1903), 2:70–71.

55. Edward Gibbon, *The Autobiographies of Edward Gibbon*, ed. John Murray (London: John Murray, 1897), 266–67.

56. Ibid., 302.

57. Johann Wolfgang von Goethe, *Goethe's Travels in Italy*, trans. Charles Nisbet (London, 1885), 114.

58. Sigmund Freud, *The Complete Letters of Sigmund Freud to Wilhelm Fliess, 1887–1904*, trans. Jeffrey M. Masson (Cambridge, MA: Belknap Press of Harvard University Press, 1995), 336.

59. E.R. Curtius, *Essays on European Literature / Kritische Essays Zur Europäischen Literatur*, trans. Michael Kowal (Princeton, NJ: Princeton University Press, 1973).

60. "Rome, Idibus Martiis, in Capitolio" (II.14.3).

61. From Wilkins, "Petrarch's Coronation Oration," 1245:

I venture to relate that at one and the same time, a year or so ago, I was invited both to Rome and to Paris, rivaling each other in their invitations to receive this honor—to Rome by the Senate that was then in office and by certain noblemen of Rome, some of whom are present in this gathering, and to Paris by that excellent man and Master, Robert, Chancellor of the University of Paris, and by other well-known men of that city and that university.

62. "Nulla michi letior dies et amicorum comitatu et varietate rerum illustrium et vicinia multorum tristium dierum" (V.4.4).

63. "Etsi non sim nescius fuisse magis hoc humane voluptati quam romane severitati dignum domicilium. Ideoque et Marius, natura vir asperior, et Pompeius et Cesar, humanis moribus altiores, in montibus edificasse laudantur; unde, quod viros decuit, non immersi sed subducti effeminantibus animos munditiis, nauticum strepitum et Baianas ex alto despicerent voluptates" (V.4.8).

64. "Scipio autem Africanus, vir incomparabilis et cui in virtute omnia, nullum cum voluptate commercium, consilio relique vite simillimo, non tam ex alto despicere, quam prorsus non aspicere decrevit hunc locum suis artibus adversum. Extra prospectum igitur secessit et Literni quam Baiis habitare maluit; quam villulam hinc non abesse scio, nilque avidius spectassem, si quo duce in loca tanto habitatore nobilia penetrare potuissem" (V.4.9).

65. "Ad que tamen nunc etiam e finitimis urbibus ingens omnis sexus etatisque concursus est" (V.4.6).

66. "Siquidem, expectationis inutilis ac diuturne tedio affectus, Garganum montem Brundusiique portum atque illum omnem Superi Maris tractum lustrare decreveram, non magis illa videndi quam ista linquendi desiderio; quod tamen, regina seniore dissuadente, compescui et longioris peregrinationis impetum ad proximiora certe et mirabiliora converti" (V.4.2).

67. "Iam minus miror romana menia, romanas arces, romana palatia, quando tam procul a patria—quamvis excellentibus viris ubique sit patria—romanorum ducum similis cura protenditur, quibus ultra centesimum lapidem esse quasi suburbane fuerant hiberne delitie" (V.4.7).

68. "Precipua armorum cura est, animus ferri mortisque contemptor. Bellum cum finitimis hereditarium gerit, quo multi iam ultro citroque periere. Interdum sola, sepe paucis comitata, manum cum hoste conseruit; ubique ad hunc diem victrix. Preceps in prelium ruere, lenta discedere, animose hostem aggredi, caute insidias texere; famem sitim frigus estum somnum lassitudinem incredibili patientia perferre, sub divo pernox et sub armis agere, humi requiescere, herbosum cespitem vel substratum clipeum in delitiis habere" (V.4.10–11).

69. "Multa de illa fabulis similia narrantur; ego quod vidi referam. Convenerant e diversis mundi partibus viri fortes et armorum exercitio durati, quos, alio tendentes, illic fortuna deposuerat; auditaque mulieris fama, experiendi vires cupiditas incesserat" (V.4.13).

70. "Sola erat, et ante templi fores, nescio quid cogitans, obambulabat; adventu nostro nichil mota est. Instamus orare, ut virium suarum aliquod nobis experimentum prebeat; illa, diu excusata brachii valitudine, tandem grave saxum ac ferream trabem iussit afferri; quam cum in medium proiecisset, ut tollerent atque experirentur hortata est. Quid multa? longa ibi, inter pares, contentio, et magno res acta certamine, spectatrice quidem illa singulorum vires in silentio extimante. Postremo, facili iactu, adeo se superiorem approbvit ut reliquos stupor ingens, me etiam pudor invaderet" (V.4.13–14).

71. "Inter tam continuos labores multum brevi tempore mutata est; quantulum est enim, quod me Romam ac Neapolim ad regem Siculum iuvenilis studium glorie attraxit! profecto, quam tunc inermem videram, hodie armata et armatis septa cum ad me salutandum accessisset, miratus sum; et velut ignoto viro salutem reddidi, donec, risu eius et comitum monitu pressius intuitus, vix tandem sub casside torvam et incultam virginem recognovi" (V.4.12).

72. "Fama est Robertum, summum illum et virum et regem, his quondam litoribus magna classe prenavigantem, permotum talis femine miraculo, videndi gratia substitisse Puteolis; quod ideo apud me veri faciem non habet, quia, in tanta vicinitate terrarum, evocaturus illam fuisse videatur; sed fortassis aliam ob causam cum illuc applicuisset, rem novam spectare voluit ardens et noscendi cupidum illud ingenium. Verum huiusce rei fides, ut ceterarum quas auditui credidimus, penes narratores maneat" (V.4.15–16).

73. "Dum repente, quasi letum quiddam accidisset, plausus inenarrabilis ad celum tollitur. Circumspicio, et ecce formosissimus adolescens, rigido mucrone transfossus, ante pedes meos corruit. Obstupui, et toto corpore cohorrescens, equo calcaribus adacto" (V.6.5).

74. "Sed de his hactenus; nam et tragicum opus est et multa super his inter obstinatos cives verba iam perdidi. Minime vero mirabere amicos tuos, tanto avaritie premio proposito, in ea urbe vinctos esse, in qua hominem innoxium occidere ludus est; quam licet unam ex omnibus Virgilius 'dulcem' vocet" (V.6.6).

75. "Ut te obsecrem ne me unquam amplius vitam ventis ac fluctibus credere iubeas. Hoc enim est in quo neque tibi neque Romano Pontifici neque patri meo, si ad lucem redeat, parere velim" (V.5.19).

76. See Cachey's introduction to Petrarch, *Itinerary*, 18–27.

77. Petrarch, *Letters of Old Age*, 1:60. Original Latin: Petrarch, *Epystole seniles*, in *Opera omnia*, ed. Pasquale Stoppelli (Rome: Lexis Progetti Editoriali, 1997), II.3.1.

78. For more on this episode, see chap. 2, p. 9, in this book.

79. Petrarch, *Letters of Old Age*, I.62; Petrarch, *Epystole seniles*: "Hoc unum tacitus mecum volvens: 'heu quam cara, simulque quam vilis est vita mortalibus'!" (II.3.2).

80. See Cachey's introduction to Petrarch, *Itinerary*, 1–32.

81. Petrarch, *Itinerary*, proem, 7.

82. Ibid., 21.0–1.

83. Ibid., 1.0.

84. James Mill, *The History of British India*, 6 vols. (London, 1826), 1:xii.

CHAPTER SIX

1. Guzmán was an important literary patron and a dynastic power broker. See María Mercè López Casas, "Fernán Gómez de Guzmán: El envés histórico de la figura del comendador de *Fuenteovejuna,*" in *Las órdenes militares: Realidad e imaginario,* ed. Maria Dolores Burdeus, Elena Real, and Joan Verdegal, 469–80 (Barcelona: Univ. de Jaume I, 2000). The best exploration of what Tafur might have hoped to gain from addressing his narrative to Guzmán can be found in Lisa Merschel's dissertation "Traveling in Pursuit of Nobility: A Study of Pero Tafur's *Andanças é viajes*" (University of North Carolina, 2003).

2. On mobility in the premodern Mediterranean, see Peregrine Horden and Nicholas Purcell, *The Corrupting Sea: A Study of Mediterranean History* (Oxford: Blackwell, 2000), 342–400 (on commercial travel) and 403–60 (on religious travel).

3. Although romance often insists on a sharp, inimical distinction between Christians and Muslims, East and West, it is also a literary form that figures such polarities in more complex ways, suited to a range of secular interests. See E. Jane Burns, *Courtly Love Undressed* (Philadelphia: University of Pennsylvania Press, 2005), 181–229; and Sharon Kinoshita, *Medieval Boundaries: Rethinking Difference in Old French Literature* (Philadelphia: University of Pennsylvania Press, 2006).

4. On the influence of chivalric romance on knightly travel writing and exploration in the medieval and early modern periods, see Michael Murrin, *Trade and Romance* (Chicago: University of Chicago Press, 2014); Jennifer R. Goodman, *Chivalry and Exploration, 1298–1630* (Suffolk, UK: Boydell, 1998); Irving A. Leonard, *Books of the Brave: Being an Account of Books and of Men in the Spanish Conquest and Settlement of the Sixteenth-Century New World* (Berkeley: University of California Press, 1992); Martin de Riquer, *Caballeros andantes españoles* (Madrid: Espasa-Calpe, 1980). On Tafur's use of romance commonplaces, see Sofía M. Carrizo Rueda, *Poética del relato de viajes* (Kassel, Germany: Edition Reichenberger, 1997), 36.

5. Pero Tafur, *Andanças é viajes de Pero Tafur por diversas partes del mundo avidos,* vol. 8 of the Colección de libros españoles raros ó curiosos, ed. Marcos Jiménez de la Espada (Madrid, 1874), 1–2. Subsequent citations of Tafur will appear within the body of this chapter. Translations mine.

6. For overviews of the ideologies that justified the existence and exploitation of the peasantry, see Paul Freedman, *Images of the Medieval Peasant* (Stanford, CA: Stanford University Press, 1999).

7. John Edwards, *Christian Córdoba: A City and Its Religion in the Late Middle Ages* (Cambridge: Cambridge University Press, 1982), 131.

8. Freedman, *Images of the Medieval Peasant,* 114–18.

9. Juan Carlos Ochoa, "El viaje de Pero Tafur por Tierra Santa," in *Actas II Congreso Internacional de la Asociación Hispánica de Literatura Medieval,* vol. 2, ed. José Manuel Lucía Megías et al., 597–608 (Alcalá de Henares, Spain: Universidad de Alcalá, 1992), 601.

10. Chareyron, *Pilgrims to Jerusalem,* 70–77.

11. Casola, *Canon Pietro Casola's Pilgrimage,* 258. Bertrandon de la Broquière decides not to enter a mosque in Hebron because of the potentially fatal consequences. See Broquière, "Travels," 288–89.

12. At least two other fifteenth-century chivalric travel writers also engineered a secretive entry into a mosque. Neither of them develops his account to the extent that Tafur does. See von Harff, *Pilgrimage*, 153–54; Broquière, "Travels," 300.

13. Mandeville, *Livre* (ed. Deluz), 198.

14. Gucci, "Viaggio ai Luoghi Santi," 295.

15. Angus MacKay, *Spain in the Middle Ages: From Frontier to Empire, 1000–1500* (London: Macmillan Press, 1977), 66.

16. Edwards, *Christian Córdoba*, 179.

17. Rafael Ramírez de Arellano, "Pero Tafur," *Boletín de la Real Academia de Historia* 41, no. 4 (October 1902): 278–98 (see 287).

18. Like Jerusalem, Troy was a setting associated with the literary genre of romance. See Alan Deyermond, "The Lost Genre of Medieval Spanish Literature," *Hispanic Review* 43, no. 3 (1975): 231–59 (at 235).

19. The return of people who had been captured or who had accidentally strayed across the border was a perennial concern of the civic governments of southern Spain, as well. See Jarbel Rodríguez, *Captives and Their Saviors in the Medieval Crown of Aragon* (Washington, DC: Catholic University Press, 2007); and Angus MacKay, "Ritual and Propaganda in Fifteenth-Century Castile," in *Love, Religion and Politics in Fifteenth Century Spain*, ed. Ian Macpherson and Angus MacKay, 43–81 (Leiden, Netherlands: Brill, 1998).

20. Dwayne E. Carpenter, "Alfonso the Learned and the Problem of Islam," in *Estudios en homenaje a Enrique Ruiz-Fornells*, ed. Juan Fernández Jiménez, José J. Labrador Herraiz, and Teresa L. Valdivieso (Erie, PA: Asociación de Licenciados y Doctores Españoles en Estados Unidos, 1990).

21. Juan de Mata Carriazo, "Relaciones fronterizas entre Jaén y Granada. El año 1479," *Revista de Archivos, Bibliotecas y Museos* 61, no. 1 (1955): 24–51 (see esp. 28–33).

22. Ibid., 29. See also the documents from fourteenth-century Valencia in R.I. Burns, "Renegades, Adventurers and Sharp Business Men," *Catholic Historical Review* 58 (1972): 341–62, which also do not discuss conversion in terms of belief.

23. Gauri Viswanathan observes a similar tension between the humanist myth of a self-determining subject of conversion as exemplified by Augustine and William James and the reality of colonial politics in British India, which contributed to the legislation of identities in a way that effaced the agency of converts. See her *Outside the Fold: Conversion, Modernity, and Belief* (Princeton, NJ: Princeton University Press, 1998), 82–89.

24. Abu-Lughod, *Before European Hegemony*, 212–50.

25. Horden and Purcell, *Corrupting Sea* (at 388–91), have argued that premodern slavery in the Mediterranean was a strategy for gaining access to mobility.

26. Wallace, *Premodern Places*, 188–89. Wallace relies on Iris Origo, "'The Domestic Enemy': The Eastern Slaves in Tuscany in the Fourteenth and Fifteenth Centuries," *Speculum* 30, no. 3 (1955): 321–66.

27. Fernando Gómez Redondo observes that this argument about travel resembles the one made by the character Roboán in the fourteenth-century Castilian romance *El libro del Caballero Zifar*. Gómez, *La historia de la prosa medieval castellana: Las orígenes del humanismo, el marco cultural de Enrique III y Juan II*, vol. 3 (Madrid: Cátedra, 2002), argument at 3404.

28. See Joan Corominas with José A. Pascual, *Diccionario crítico etimológico castellano e hispánico*, 6 vols. (Madrid: Gredos, 1991–97), s.v. "ver," 6:773–74.

29. The most succinct articulation of this common claim is found in Zumthor, "Medieval Travel Narrative," 809–24; Guéret-Laferté, *Sur les routes*, distinguishes between two axes of narration in medieval travel narrative: the "axe syntagmatique," which moves the narrative forward in time and space, and the "axe paradigmatique," which digresses from the forward trajectory of the narrative (49–50, 163–83).

30. Barry Taylor, "Late Medieval Travellers in the East: Clavijo, Tafur, Encina, and Tarifa," in *Eastward Bound: Travel and Travellers, 1050–1550*, ed. Rosamund Allen, 221–34 (Manchester, UK: Manchester University Press, 2004), 227.

31. For a narratological take on Tafur, see Sofía Carrizo Rueda, "Hacia una poética de los relatos de viajes: A propósito de Pero Tafur," *Incipit* 14 (1994): 103–44.

32. Compare Tafur's in-the-know description of elephants at the court of Cairo to Franciscan Niccolò of Poggibonsi's statement about Cairo's menagerie: "I saw many things, numberless animals, the names of which I could not ask, for then I had no interpreter." In *A Voyage beyond the Seas (1346–1350)*, trans. T. Bellorini and E. Hoade (Jerusalem: Franciscan Press, 1945), 92.

33. For the historical context of Tafur's visit to the Byzantine world and his exchanges with the emperor at the Council of Ferrara, see A. Vasiliev, "Pero Tafur, a Spanish Traveler of the Fifteenth Century and His Visit to Constantinople, Trebizond, and Italy," *Byzantion: Revue Internationale des Études Byzantines* 8 (1932): 75–122.

34. Webb, *Pilgrims and Pilgrimage*, 171–72, includes two English documents that suggest that pilgrims vowed not to shave their beards until they had returned safely from their travels; cf. introduction, p. 8.

35. Francesco Balducci Pegolotti, the author of a manual for Florentine merchants traveling abroad, recommends growing a beard in order to better assimilate to eastern cultures. Pegolotti, "Notices of the Land Route to Cathay," in *CWT*, 1:143–71. Grooming advice at 1:151.

36. According to Mandeville, Greeks criticize foreign men's facial grooming, saying that the Latins "commit mortal sin in shaving our beards because it is the sign of a man" ("nous peccheons mortelment a raser noz barbes qar ceo est signe del homme"). Mandeville, *Livre* (ed. Deluz), 111–12. In defending the superiority of Italy to Byzantium, Petrarch reports to a friend that a Greek adversary has sent him a letter "longer and more unkempt than his beard and his hair" ("barba et crinibus suis horridior maiorque"). Francis Petrarch, *Res seniles*, 3 vols., ed. Silvia Rizzo with Monica Berté (Florence: Casa Editrice Le lettere, 2006–9), letter 3.6 (citation at 1:232).

37. Anonymous, *Los hechos del condestable Don Miguel Lucas de Iranzo: Crónica del siglo XV*, ed. Juan de Mata Carriazo (Madrid: Espasa-Calpe, 1940), 195.

38. Ibid., 98–100.

39. Teofilo Ruiz, "Elite and Popular Culture in Late Fifteenth-Century Castilian Festivals," in *City and Spectacle in Late Medieval Europe*, ed. Barbara A. Hanawalt and Kathryn L. Reyerson, 296–318 (Minneapolis: University of Minnesota Press, 1994).

40. Here I am drawing on Gayatri Spivak, "Can the Subaltern Speak?," in *Marxism and the Interpretation of Culture*, ed. Cary Nelson and Lawrence Grossberg, 271–313 (Urbana: University of Illinois Press, 1988), esp. 276–80.

41. Ernst H. Kantorowicz, *The King's Two Bodies: A Study in Medieval Political Theology* (1957; repr., Princeton, NJ: Princeton University Press, 1997).

42. Mary Douglas, *Purity and Danger: An Analysis of Concepts of Pollution and Taboo* (New York: Routledge Classics, 2002), 143–44.

43. See María Teresa Ferrer Mallol, *Els Sarraïns de la corona catalano-aragonesa en el segle XIV: Segregació i discriminació* (Barcelona: Anuario de estudios medievales, 1987), 42.

44. See R. Burns, "Renegades." Although much discourse about racial and religious difference was concerned with the bodies of men, women were key to the maintenance of ethnoreligious distinctions. For example, David Nirenberg has argued that prostitutes may have played a role in policing the sexual boundaries between Christians, Muslims, and Jews. David Nirenberg, *Communities of Violence: Persecution of Minorities in the Middle Ages* (Princeton, NJ: Princeton University Press, 1996), 127–65.

45. MacKay, *Spain in the Middle Ages*, 203.

46. Angus MacKay, "The Ballad and the Frontier in Late Medieval Spain," in *Love, Religion and Politics in Fifteenth Century Spain*, ed. Ian Macpherson and Angus MacKay, 1–27 (Leiden, Netherlands: Brill, 1998). See also Miguel Ángel Ladero Quesada, *Los señores de Andalucía: Investigaciones sobre nobles y señoríos en los siglos XIII a XV* (Cádiz, Spain: Universidad de Cádiz, 1998), 590–91.

47. Barbara Weissberger, "'A Tierra, Puto!': Alfonso de Palencia's Discourse of Effeminacy," in *Queer Iberia: Sexualities, Cultures, and Crossings from the Middle Ages to the Renaissance*, ed. Josiah Blackmore and Gregory Hutcheson (Durham, NC: Duke University Press, 1999), 291–324.

48. The bibliographies on the fifteenth-century Castilian nobility, *conversos*, and the Inquisition are enormous. The following is a list of works that have most informed this chapter's characterization of Iberian nobility: Martin de Riquer's *Caballeros andantes españoles*; Marie-Claude Gerbet, *Les noblesses espagnoles au Moyen Age: XIᵉ–XVᵉ siècle* (Paris: A. Colin, 1994); Jesús D. Rodríguez Velasco, *El debate sobre la caballería en el siglo XV: La tratadística caballeresca castellana en su marco europeo* (Salamanca, Spain: Junta de Castilla y León, 1996). On struggles over political power involving the *conversos* and the Inquisition, see B. Netanyahu, *Origins of the Inquisition in Fifteenth Century Spain* (New York: Random House, 1994).

49. On the long life of "neo-Gothic" discourses, see Patricia E. Grieve, *The Eve of Spain: Myths of Origins in the History of Christian, Muslim and Jewish Conflict* (Baltimore: Johns Hopkins University Press, 2009), 1–18.

50. This skepticism about the truth of social symbols is elucidated by David Nirenberg's argument that the forced conversions of Jews to Christianity in the fourteenth century caused a crisis in what he calls "the christological hermeneutic" that had framed Spanish thought. According to Nirenberg, this hermeneutic relied on the absolute conceptual distinction between Christians and Jews and was undermined by the presence of *conversos*. David Nirenberg, "Enmity and Assimilation: Jews, Christians, and Converts in Medieval Spain," *Common Knowledge* 9, no. 1 (2003): 137–55. My analysis of category slippages is also indebted to Steven F. Kruger, *The Spectral Jew: Conversion and Embodiment in Medieval Europe* (Minneapolis: University of Minnesota Press, 2005).

51. Juan del Encina, "Égloga de Mingo, Gil y Pascuala," in *Obra completa,* ed. Miguel Ángel Pérez Priego (Madrid: Biblioteca Castro, 1996), 838. Translation mine.

52. Sebastiano Gentile, *Firenze e la scoperta dell'America: Umanesimo e geografia nel '400 fiorentino* (Florence: Olschki, 1992), 173–75, 239–47.

53. Rubiés, *Travel and Ethnology,* 85–123.

54. On Tafur's location of Prester John in the Indies, rather than in Abyssinia or near Cathay, see Rubiés, *Travel and Ethnology,* 120. The best historical and philological study of Prester John's letter is the apparatus in Friedrich Zarncke's "Der Brief des Priesters Johannes an den byzantinischen Kaiser Emanuel," in *Abhandlungen der philologisch-historischen Classe der königlich sächsischen Gesellschaft der Wissenschaften* 7 (1879): 827–1030. For a consideration of Prester John's uncanny medieval and early modern afterlives, see C.E. Nowell, "The Historical Prester John," *Speculum* 28 (1953): 435–45; and Michael Uebel, "Imperial Fetishism: Prester John among the Natives," in *The Postcolonial Middle Ages,* ed. Jeffery Jerome Cohen, 261–82 (New York: Palgrave, 2000).

55. In a digest of Columbus's logbook made by Bartolomé de las Casas, the Genoese explorer positions his journey as part of an ongoing effort to forge alliances with eastern powers against Islam. After stating that he witnessed the Christian victory at Granada, Columbus adds: "And later in that same month . . . your Highnesses decided to send me, Christopher Columbus, to see these parts of India and the princes and peoples of those lands and consider the best means for their conversion." See Christopher Columbus, *The Four Voyages,* ed. and trans. J.M. Cohen (New York: Penguin, 1969), 37.

56. On the legacy of ancient ideas about *civility, civilization,* and city life, see John Gillingham, "From *Civilitas* to Civility: Codes of Manners in Medieval and Early Modern England," *Transactions of the Royal Historical Society* 12 (2002): 267–89; cf. K. Phillips, *Before Orientalism,* 148–71.

CODA

1. Cited among many other examples in Stallybrass et al., "Hamlet's Tables," 406.

2. Count Leopold Berchtold, *An Essay to Direct and Extend the Inquiries of Patriotic Travellers: With Further Observations on the Means of Preserving the Life, Health, & Property of the Unexperienced in Their Journies by Land and Sea . . .* (London, 1789).

3. Williams, "'Rubbing Up against Others,'" 101–10.

4. Martin Martin, *A description of the Western Islands of Scotland: Containing a full account of their situation, extent, soils, product, harbours, bays, tides, anchoring-places, and fisheries . . .* (London, 1703), preface. I have modernized spellings in this quotation and the one that follows it.

5. Martin Martin, *A late voyage to St. Kilda, the remotest of all the Hebrides, or the Western isles of Scotland . . .* (London, 1698), preface.

6. Jean-Jacques Rousseau, *Émile; or, On Education,* trans. Allan Bloom (New York: Basic Books, 1979), 450.

7. Ibid., 455.

8. Jane Austen, *Pride and Prejudice,* ed. Donald Gray (New York: Norton, 2001), 103.

9. Wolfgang Schivelbusch, *The Railway Journey: The Industrialization of Time and Space in the Nineteenth Century, With a New Preface* (Oakland: University of California Press, 2014).

10. William Wordsworth, *The Prose Works of William Wordsworth*, 3 vols., ed. Alexander B. Grosart (London, 1876), 2:340.

11. John Ruskin, *Modern Painters* (London, 1872), III.iv.300.

12. Ibid.